FEMINIST HISTORY IN CANADA

FEMINIST HISTORY IN CANADA
New Essays on Women, Gender, Work, and Nation

Edited by Catherine Carstairs and Nancy Janovicek

UBCPress · Vancouver · Toronto

21 20 19 18 17 16 15 14 13   5 4 3 2 1

Printed in Canada on FSC-certified ancient-forest-free paper (100% post-consumer recycled) that is processed chlorine- and acid-free.

Library and Archives Canada Cataloguing in Publication

Feminist history in Canada : new essays on women, gender, work, and nation / edited by Catherine Carstairs and Nancy Janovicek.

Includes bibliographical references and index.
Issued in print and electronic formats.
ISBN 978-0-7748-2619-8 (bound). – ISBN 978-0-7748-2620-4 (pbk.)
ISBN 978-0-7748-2621-1 (pdf). – ISBN 978-0-7748-2622-8 (epub)

   1. Women – Canada – History.   2. Women – Canada – Social conditions.
3. Women – Canada – Biography.   4. Feminism – Canada – History.   I. Carstairs, Catherine, writer of introduction, editor of compilation.   II. Janovicek, Nancy, writer of introduction, editor of compilation.

HQ1453.F42 2013   305.40971   C2013-905251-8
                                            C2013-905252-6

Canadä

UBC Press gratefully acknowledges the financial support for our publishing program of the Government of Canada (through the Canada Book Fund), the Canada Council for the Arts, and the British Columbia Arts Council.

This book has been published with the help of a grant from the Canadian Federation for the Humanities and Social Sciences, through the Awards to Scholarly Publications Program, using funds provided by the Social Sciences and Humanities Research Council of Canada.

The authors' royalties from this book will be donated to the Barbara Roberts Fund.

UBC Press
The University of British Columbia
2029 West Mall
Vancouver, BC V6T 1Z2
www.ubcpress.ca

Contents

Acknowledgments

This book emerged from the conference "Edging Forward, Acting Up: Gender and Women's History at the Cutting Edge of Scholarship and Social Action." We are grateful to the conference co-chairs, Willeen Keough and Lara Campbell, and to the program chair, Lisa Chilton, for organizing this stimulating conference. The conference was supported by a grant from the Social Sciences and Humanities Research Council of Canada. This grant also aided our work by providing funds for copy-editing this volume and for translating two of the chapters from French to English.

Thanks to all the contributors for making our job as editors much easier. You were a wonderful group to work with – enthusiastic, hard-working, and patient. It was especially fun to meet with most of the group for an extra day at the annual meeting of the Canadian Historical Association in Fredericton, New Brunswick. A University of Calgary Faculty of Arts Scholarly Activities Grant provided the funds to support this one-day workshop.

Darcy Cullen, at UBC Press, is a marvel. She attended the "Edging Forward" conference, as well as our workshop in Fredericton, and ably ushered us through every aspect of preparing the manuscript. We are grateful for her wise counsel, her enthusiastic cheerleading, and her attention to detail. Lesley Erickson did a superb job as our production editor and copy editor. We value their editorial expertise and their commitment to women's and gender history.

The College of Arts, University of Guelph, helped to support the translation of the two chapters by Catherine Charron and Hélèn Charron from French into English. Many thanks to Matthew Kayahara for undertaking the translation.

In keeping with this book's focus on feminist activism, the royalties will be donated to the Barbara Roberts Fund. Barbara was a historian, feminist, and peace activist. Her books – *Whence They Came: Deportation from Canada, 1900–1935* and *A Reconstructed World: A Feminist Biography of Gertrude Richardson* – are well known to Canadian historians, but Roberts was also an activist. In 1985, she helped set up the Peace Tent at the "United Nations Decade for Women" conference in Nairobi, and in 1995 she co-authored *Strategies for the Year 2000: A Woman's Handbook*. The Canadian Committee on Women's History/Comité canadien de l'histoire des femmes (CCWH-CCHF) fundraised to establish this prize, which currently gives $2,500 annually for research into the study of feminist perspectives on peace, social justice and human rights, workplace and unions, and women's studies education.

We believe that the feminist history project is still an important part of the women's movement. We would need to write another book to acknowledge all of the activists and scholars who have inspired our commitment to writing feminist history. But we'd like to thank a few people whose commitment to feminist scholarship and teaching sparked our excitement for women's and gender history. Catherine thanks historians Franca Iacovetta and Carolyn Strange; her mother, Sharon Carstairs; and Donna Goodman, her high school history teacher. Nancy thanks Joy Parr, Marjorie Griffin Cohen, Mary-Lynn Stewart, and Margaret Conrad.

Catherine would like to thank Greg Downs for his good ear, his generous help with computer glitches, and his enthusiasm for her work. Nancy thanks Martin L'Heureux for technical assistance, correcting French grammar in correspondence with francophone colleagues, and the day-to-day support for her work.

The wonderful thing about collaborative projects is that respected colleagues become good friends. Over the course of editing this volume and serving together on the executive of the CCWH-CCHF, we have developed a greater appreciation for each other's skills and knowledge. Working with each other has been a delight!

FEMINIST HISTORY IN CANADA

Introduction
Productive Pasts and New Directions

CATHERINE CARSTAIRS AND NANCY JANOVICEK

At the end of August 2010, feminist historians from across the country gathered in Vancouver for a conference sponsored by the Canadian Committee on Women's History/Comité canadien de l'histoire des femmes (CCHW-CCHF). "Edging Forward, Acting Up: Gender and Women's History at the Cutting Edge of Scholarship and Social Action" attracted more than a hundred participants for four lively days of papers, art, theatre, wine, and conversation. Delegates paid tribute to several of the pioneers of women's history in Canada, discussed the links between feminist history and activism, and explored new methodologies and topics in feminist history.[1] Although this was the first stand-alone conference sponsored by the CCWH-CCHF, it built on almost forty years of feminist scholarship. The CCWH-CCHF, founded in 1975 as an affiliated committee of the Canadian Historical Association, has long nurtured feminist historians through its dinner and reception at the annual meeting of the Canadian Historical Association, its sponsorship of the Hilda Neatby and Barbara Roberts Prizes, and its website, which provides a bibliography, links to syllabuses, and our newsletter.[2]

Attending the Vancouver conference and editing this associated volume, which you have here, provided us with an opportunity to reflect on how forty years of feminist scholarship has shaped women's and gender history and to assess its impact on the broader field of Canadian history. It has been almost a decade since there has been a new collection of essays in Canada devoted to gender and women's history. This is not because women's history or gender history is in decline. Quite the opposite: there have been numerous specialized collections that focus on immigrant and Aboriginal women, women and health, and on women in particular regions.[3] The Oxford University Press collection, *Rethinking Canada: The Promise of Women's History*, first published in 1986, continues to be released in new editions (the sixth edition came out in fall 2010), although recent editions reprint already-published work rather than publishing new work in the field. This volume, by contrast, provides a sampling of exciting new work. At the same time, it recognizes that the cutting-edge research of today builds on over forty years of scholarship. We were intrigued by how many of the papers delivered at the conference were on topics that the founders of the CCWH-CCHF had researched in the 1970s: paid and unpaid work, professional women, women's political action, and women's experiences of marriage and family. In the end, four themes emerged as focal points: biography, women's work, activism, and transnationalism. Informed by developments in feminist theory, the chapters included here have been enriched by recent attention to the importance of transnational travels and identities, new feminist theorizing about the body, critical race studies, and the resurgence of interest in biography as a lens for understanding culture and society.

The early scholarship on women in Canada sought to write women into the national story. Scholars focused on women's involvement in politics, including the right to vote and their involvement in turn-of-the-century reform movements. The development of women's history in Canada ran parallel to the growth of social history, prompting considerable interest in women's work experiences and the life cycle, especially the experiences of motherhood and child rearing.[4] Scholars critically examined the rhetoric that stated that woman should be in the home while also pointing out the contradictions: working-class women often worked for wages; the history of nuns showed their important role in education and health (especially in the province of Quebec); and even in the late nineteenth century, women were joining the ranks of the professions, albeit with difficulty.[5] This scholarship showed that women had made important contributions to the economic, social, and cultural life of the country. By the 1980s, the first textbooks in the field appeared: *Histoire des femmes au Quebec depuis quatre siècles* (1982) and *Canadian Women: A History* (1988).[6] Feminist history began finding its way into survey texts, most notably when Pearson hired Margaret Conrad and Alvin Finkel to produce *History of the Canadian Peoples*, first released in 1993. Veronica Strong-Boag's *The New Day*

Recalled: Lives of Girls and Women in English-Speaking Canada, 1919–1939 (1989) and Joy Parr's *The Gender of Breadwinners: Women, Men, and Change in Two Industrial Towns, 1880–1950* (1991) both won the John A. Macdonald Prize, the most prestigious book prize awarded by the Canadian Historical Association, a recognition that feminist scholarship was becoming part of the canon. By the early 1990s, most history departments taught women's studies and had hired at least one women's historian. Many of these historians were active in founding women's studies programs, thus establishing a fruitful dialogue among feminist scholars from different disciplines as well as an important network in which to advocate for equity programs on campus.[7] Historians working in other fields turned to feminist theory to deepen their analysis. Immigration historians, historians of the welfare state, and rural historians all began paying attention to the experiences of women.

Incorporating feminist scholarship and women's issues into academe did not occur without struggle: feminist historians sometimes fought lonely battles for respect and recognition within their departments. Canada's constitutional crisis of the early 1990s also led to considerable hand-wringing by a few male historians who criticized social and gender historians for focusing on "housemaid's knee in Belleville" instead of the history of nation building, which had been the traditional focus of Canadian history.[8] Feminist historians countered these criticisms by pointing to the important role women had played in establishing social services and their important behind-the-scenes role in early Canadian politics, and they urged political historians to be more cognizant of the ways in which gender ideologies shaped political practices and institutions.[9]

Indeed, by this time, Joan Wallach Scott's call to use gender as a category of historical analysis instead of focusing exclusively on women was transforming the field.[10] In Canada, several collections drew attention to the advantages of gender history: these benefits included a better understanding of the complexity of power in people's lives and identities, greater attention to issues of class and race and to divisions among women, and a deeper understanding of how political and economic structures were formed.[11] Gender history was not without controversy: gender historians' call to theorize and understand the relational constructions of masculinity and femininity caused some to worry that women's experiences would again be marginalized. Others argued that focusing on symbolic meanings of gender would cause historians to ignore the material conditions of women's lives. Some historians feared that a focus on gender would depoliticize women's history and that gender historians were misrepresenting the scholarship of an earlier generation of historians.[12]

As these debates raged, exciting new scholarship emerged, by those who embraced the new gender history and by those who did not. New attention to how leisure and culture were gendered resulted in innovative studies of women's magazines, honeymooning practices, and roller rinks, just to name a few examples.[13] Critical race theory and queer studies compelled historians to examine how changing conceptualizations of race and sexuality are integral to understandings of nation, citizenship, and economic and social change. Scholars investigated the experiences of Aboriginal, Asian, and African Canadian women to demonstrate how racialized thinking has pervaded the feminist movement in Canada as well as feminist constructions of citizenship.[14] Historians examined the construction of sexual identities and the experiences of women who lived their lives outside of or on the margins of sexual respectability.[15] Related to this was a deep interest in the moral regulation of women's lives that prompted many to scrutinize social work and criminal case files.[16] More recently, several historians have examined adoption and fostering in a way that analyzes intimate family stories within the context of international political, economic, and cultural transformations.[17] The growing breadth and diversity of the field means that, as Rebecca Edwards describes for the United States, "it is hardly possibly, today, to identify any single central conversation that is taking place among historians of women and gender."[18] Gender and women's history have become important parts of every field in Canadian history: gender historians work on environmental history, food history, agricultural history, political history, the history of the welfare state, the history of international development, and military history.

For us, one of the most striking aspects of the conference in Vancouver was the return to some of the questions that have long interested feminist historians: the lives of individual women, women's work experiences, women's activism, and women's relationship to government. Although scholars have never abandoned these topics, they have been given new life by growing interest in transnational and global history, flourishing interest in a political history that goes beyond the tales of great leaders to focus on the messy details of policy making and the influence of social movements, a renewed interest in the challenges and strategies of professional women, growing attention to workplace culture, and our greater understanding of race and sexuality. While the linguistic turn has made scholars far more attentive to the ways in which language creates meanings and shapes lives, this collection also shows that women's and gender historians in Canada have maintained an ongoing interest in an empirical scholarship grounded in the rich details of people's daily lives. It also demonstrates that Canadian feminist historians continue to be interested in how region shapes identities and lives. Many of the chapters focus on a single province or city, while others capture experiences from throughout the country to paint a fuller picture of how economic and social developments have played out across the nation. Combined with attention to border crossings and transitions, this collection provides a portrait of the diversity of Canadian women's experiences while still acknowledging that state structures, both provincial and national, have dictated and continue to dictate the contours of women's lives.[19]

This volume has a strong focus on biography, reflecting growing interest in using biography as a way to provide rich descriptions of local conditions and experiences.[20] Historians in Canada, including some of the first feminist historians, have always written biographies, including important histories of some of Canada's first female doctors, artists, and suffragists, but there has been unease about the methodology in some quarters because some historians believe that biography lacks critical perspective compared to other types of historical work.[21] The biographies included here involve a careful and reflexive examination of sources and approach biographical writing as a process that locates women "in complex and contradictory ways, even within the span of a single life."[22] Biographies written in such a way reveal much about the culture and society of particular times and places while enabling the author to present a nuanced portrait of the ways social forces shape individuals.

In Chapter 1 in this volume, Adele Perry provides a joint biography of James Douglas, the first governor of the colony of British Columbia, and his wife, Amelia. She examines how Douglas, the child of a mixed marriage and a colonial upbringing in the British Caribbean, thought about marriage and family in colonial British Columbia. Unlike his father and father-in-law, who discarded their "Native" wives when they returned to metropolitan settings, Douglas remained with his well-connected Metis wife, Amelia Connolly. Douglas defended the sanctity of their marriage when Protestant missionary Herbert Beaver attacked it, and he described Connolly affectionately. Unfortunately, we know less about Connolly's experience of their marriage and family life. Perry draws attention to the role of the colonial archive in deciding which papers and, by extension, whose stories were important. In Chapter 9, Kristina Llewellyn describes the career of Hazel Chow, a home economics teacher in postwar British Columbia, and shows how she invoked feminine respectability to carve out a place for herself in a racist environment. When she reflects on the disappointment she felt when Chow refused to discuss racism, Llewellyn realizes that she had imposed her own research goals on Chow's identity and self-conceptions. In Chapters 3 and 4, Karen Balcom and Lorna McLean investigate Canadian women who were involved in international work during the interwar period. They examine their close relationships with American colleagues and show the significance of friendship and networking to women's activism and professional careers.

Other chapters, while not focused on a single individual, likewise explore individual lives in some depth as a way to better understand collective experiences. In Chapter 6, Heidi MacDonald uses three diaries from across Canada to explain women's decision to marry or remain single during the Great Depression, while Gail Campbell, in Chapter 2, uses diaries to explore the lives of eight New Brunswickers in the mid-nineteenth century. Campbell stresses that people kept diaries for different reasons and shows that although men's and women's diaries differed in their telling of daily events, women and men still shared a great deal in their day-to-day lives. Both Campbell and MacDonald emphasize the importance of age and life stage in determining what was important to an individual diarist.

There has been an ongoing interest in women's work in Canadian feminist history. In its more recent iterations, historians combine a focus on the factory, office, or department store floor with an interest in working-class women's leisure and political activities, thus providing a broad perspective on their lives and concerns.[23] Some of the earliest members of the CCWH-CCHF examined women's labour and produced fine studies on domestic servants, cotton workers, and women's paid and unpaid work during the Second World War.[24] Knowing that much of women's work has taken place within the home, historians also paid careful attention to washing, cleaning, childrearing, and other home-based work activities such as piecework and taking in boarders.[25] From the 1980s onwards, historians examined women's position within the labour movement as both auxiliaries and unionists.[26] There has also long been interest in the lives of nuns and professional women, especially doctors, teachers, social workers, and lawyers.[27] More recently, this interest has extended to work on nurses, physiotherapists, pharmacists, and nutritionists.[28] In the 1980s and 1990s, historians, often women who were part of the community under consideration and who spoke the necessary languages, completed studies of immigrant and racialized women workers and showed how ethnicity and race had shaped women's employment patterns and opportunities.[29] Historians who studied the paid labour of Aboriginal women explained their marginalization in the labour force but also demonstrated that these women made significant contributions not only to the economic histories of indigenous peoples but also to the development of provincial and national economies.[30] More detailed studies of women's work during the Great Depression and after the Second World War explained how working outside the home became a norm for the majority of women. Recent work has also expanded definitions of labour by examining women's unpaid work as consumers and by taking seriously the work involved in jobs such as exotic dancing.[31]

Nearly every author in this collection pays some attention to women's labour. Gail Campbell's chapter on nineteenth-century New Brunswick calls into question the idea that there were separate spheres of responsibility for middle-class men and women. She shows that although men and women did perform different tasks, they were well aware of each other's work and that women often took more public roles than we might expect: Catharine Cameron Gillespie took over the management of her family's busy farm during her husband's frequent absences while Lucy Morrison ran her own commercial gardening business while also carrying out family responsibilities. In Chapter 13, Catherine Charron examines paid domestic work in Quebec since the 1960s and shows that although women are participating in the labour force in ever-greater numbers, their work is often low-paid and insecure. This is particularly true for women who have extended their traditionally defined "nurturing roles" to take on jobs outside of the home as housekeepers, nannies, and caregivers for the elderly. In Chapter 7, Donica Belisle uses the in-house newsletters of department stores to describe the workplace culture of retail workers. Women enjoyed the pleasures of display offered by the newsletters: they chose to dress attractively and to pose for seductive photos. At the same time, their presentation as sexual objects shows that they were valued more for their looks than for their brains.

This collection continues the strong tradition in Canadian women's history of examining the lives of professional women, including the women described in the aforementioned chapters by McLean, Llewellyn, and Balcom. In Chapter 5, Catherine Gidney explores the experiences of women who worked as deans of women, doctors, nurses, dietitians, and physical-training instructors at Victoria College in Toronto between 1900 and 1940. She shows that these women conveyed mixed messages about work outside the home to their female charges: they told women that motherhood was their highest calling, and yet they themselves were empowered by their professional work and responsibilities. Hélène Charron, by contrast, in

Chapter 8 looks at the gendered career trajectories of male and female social work professors in Quebec City. She demonstrates that the male professors often used their professorial positions as a stepping stone to positions of responsibility in Quebec's expanding social welfare state; female professors, by contrast, were relegated to community studies, which university officials deemed to be less prestigious. This trend occurred while the Quiet Revolution was transferring responsibility for health care and education away from nuns, who had previously played a key role in providing these services, into the hands of male bureaucrats. Although many of the professional women studied in this volume entered professions that have become female-dominated or at least equal in our own time, Ruby Heap in Chapter 11 examines the growing number of women in engineering, a field that is still male-dominated and is often regarded as hostile to women.

The authors in this collection pay careful attention to how work affected or influenced women's decisions to marry, remain single, engage in intimate relations with other women, or find other ways of building family and community. The first generation of professional women rarely married, as Lorna McLean, Catherine Gidney, and Hélène Charron demonstrate. Some of these women, such as Marion Hilliard or Charlotte Whitton, established intimacies with other women. By the latter decades of the twentieth century, as Hélène Charron, Kristina Llewellyn, and Ruby Heap reveal, some women combined a career with heterosexual marriage. Heidi MacDonald's chapter shows that her middle-class diarists often prioritized work over marriage during the Great Depression. While most scholars argue that the low marriage rate during the Great Depression reflected young men's unemployment and their inability to provide for a family, MacDonald's research suggests that the low marriage rate might have had something to do with female choice. These women were ambivalent, or at the very least cautious, about marriage; in contrast, Donica Belisle suggests that many young department store workers were eager to court and marry and hoped that their paid work would enhance their romantic opportunities. Catherine Charron's chapter shows how marriage and raising a family affected working-class women's participation in the workforce. Her oral histories of women who worked as caregivers show these women deeply enmeshed in caring for their children and husbands. Their poorly paid work was frequently an extension of their work in the home. At the same time, her chapter draws attention to the devastating economic effects of divorce on many working-class women: their need to care and provide for their children left them with few opportunities for training for or seeking better paid and more secure work.

Building on several decades of scholarship, the contributors also pay careful attention to women's activism. Early feminist history focused on women's efforts to win the vote and be recognized as full citizens, the battles of Canada's early female politicians, and women's involvement in reform at the turn of the century.[32] Some of this scholarship discussed the class and racial biases of many of these female reformers.[33] Women's involvement in the labour movement and on the left demonstrates that working-class women employed class-based feminist analysis when they engaged in debates about the woman question.[34] Studies of local struggles to develop social services such as orphanages and hospitals, gain better quality education, improve children's health, and increase the safety of local communities demonstrate how women's community-based activism was a crucial component of local governance and social policy.[35] These studies include important research on women's political action in the nineteenth century.[36] Although we do not know enough about the political work of women from marginalized communities, historians have explored the tremendous efforts of African Canadian, indigenous, and immigrant women to gain equal rights and fair treatment for themselves and their families.[37] More recently, the literature on social movements and human rights has reinvigorated the literature on women's politics and activism. We now know much more about women's activism in the years between the winning of the vote and the Royal Commission on the Status of Women and especially about the strategic utility of maternal and liberal feminism during the Cold War.[38]

Contributors to this volume focus on feminist activism in the late twentieth century. Ruby Heap's chapter about women engineers in the 1970s and 1980s points to the tenuous links between the women's movement and women engineer organizations. Although prominent feminist activists, such as Ursula Franklin, were involved in projects to remove barriers to women in science, younger women insisted that they were equal, even though they recognized the need to increase the number of women in the profession. These women also benefitted from federal government initiatives to promote technology and science, and they did not always sympathize with the women's movement, which was becoming increasingly opposed to government policies, such as free trade and the Meech Lake Accord. In Chapter 12, Anthony Hampton explains how New Brunswick's protest against the Meech Lake Accord began at the kitchen tables of feminists who drew on their political connections among elected representatives and in the women's movement, labour groups, and political parties. Feminists mobilized people in the province against the constitutional deal because it was unfair not only to women but also to Atlantic Canadians. Hampton explains that ad hoc feminist groups were effective in addressing immediate political issues. In Chapter 10, Rose Fine-Meyer examines the efforts of the Ontario Women's History Network/Le réseau d'histoire des femmes to connect university-based researchers to teachers to facilitate curriculum reform and to provide teachers with the materials they need to teach women's history.

Many of the chapters in this volume place Canadian women's lives in the context of transnational networks of politics and friendship. Inspired by the postcolonial literature on empire, historians have been thinking more critically about Canada's history of colonialism, about its status as a colony of the British Empire and, more importantly, about its status as a colonial power in its own right. This scholarship has elucidated the links between metropole and empire, compared the experiences of empire within various white settler societies, and made us all more aware of how the legacies of colonialism affect Canada today.[39] Scholars of colonialism and borderlands also argue that a narrow focus on "the national story" fails to explain the experiences of the people who moved and lived within shifting international borders.[40] Indeed, in North America, the border cut through indigenous communities' existing territorial boundaries, dispossessed them from their land, and fractured their nations. Canadian history is replete with stories of women and their families who moved back and forth across borders for better opportunities or who were forced to leave their homes. Historians of migration and diasporas demonstrate that immigrants have maintained connections to their families by sending money to them, by encouraging them to immigrate, or by following their families to places they hoped would be more welcoming.[41] Understanding these stories in the context of a transnational migration of peoples makes more sense than analyses that make them part of the Canadian "mosaic." As Elizabeth Jameson puts it, "We all have multiple identities, only some of which are rooted in where we live or the passports we carry."[42]

Many of the chapters in this book analyze the complex relationship between local circumstances and global trends. Adele Perry's chapter, which emerged out of her keynote address to "Edging Forward, Acting Up" conference, follows the movements of James Douglas, Amelia Connelly, and their kin. She argues that the multiple racial and gendered identities that shaped both their public and intimate lives were not contained within what would become provincial or national borders. Other chapters show how global feminist debates influenced Canadian feminists and how, in turn, Canadian feminists shaped debates.[43] In her chapter about Julia Grace Wales, a peace activist and Shakespearian scholar who was born in Canada and spent most of her adult life teaching in Wisconsin, Lorna McLean argues that scholars have overlooked this prominent peace activist because her transnational life does not fit into the national story. Wales used her multiple identities strategically in her political lobbying but forged a transnational identity through her educational and religious connections with other women. In her chapter, Catherine Gidney also stresses the importance of Methodist connections to the international friendships and alliances of the nonacademic professional women who worked at the University of Toronto. Karen Balcom shows how North American child welfare activists used the League of Nations to build alliances to promote what they saw as "modern" child welfare practices and to counter Catholic practices that they deemed to be backwards. Hélène Charron follows the careers of social work professors at Laval University, many of whom were trained at the University of Chicago; their transnational training and connections influenced their social work practice and differentiated them from colleagues at the Université de Montréal, who were trained at home.

There were many exciting papers delivered at "Edging Forward, Acting Up," and not all of them could be included in this collection. This volume has less material on sex and race than we would have liked. This is not because these themes were absent from the conference or because there is a slackening of interest in these topics. Some participants presented research in its earliest stages, and we look forward to hearing and reading more about their research in the future. Reflecting a broader trend in Canadian history, this collection does not have many chapters about the pre-Confederation period. As Allan Greer pointed out fifteen years ago, few historians are working in the field, especially in English-speaking Canada.[44] Moreover, scholars of early Canadian history are not well-represented within the ranks of the CCWH-CCHF. Only three of the papers presented at the conference focused on the pre-Confederation period. The vibrant interest in borderland and colonial studies has meant that many scholars of earlier time periods have found their academic homes elsewhere. Many historians find that they have more in common with their international peers than with Canadian historians, who are heavily focused on the twentieth century. The diminishing number of scholars working on the pre-Confederation period and their drift away from the Canadian Historical Association (and, by extension, the Canadian Committee on Women's History) is a significant loss to historians of the more recent past. We need to better understand women's lives and gender relations in earlier periods in order to construct more complete portraits of recent times.

More encouraging has been the increasing participation of a new generation of francophone scholars in the CCWH-CCHF. Indeed, the CCWH has always attracted members from both linguistic communities, although for the past fifteen years, at least, the meetings have been almost uniformly English. This book includes translations of chapters by two early career francophone scholars – Hélèn Charron and Catherine Charron. A third chapter, by Ruby Heap, pays careful attention to francophone engineers. Although three chapters out of thirteen is far from ideal, it is a positive trend.[45] In our view, there is much to be learned by increasing the dialogue between francophone and anglophone scholars.[46] This is partly because they draw on different historiographical traditions: francophone historians draw more on the insights of European scholarship while anglophone historians tend to reach for the literature from the United States and Britain. Francophone scholars have a much longer tradition of collaborative historical work, something which granting councils are now encouraging all of us to do. It is important to acknowledge how linguistic, cultural, and religious differences between French- and English-speaking peoples created tensions and sometimes very difference experiences. However, focusing on these differences too often occludes analysis of how Québecois experiences can shed light on trends and patterns in other parts of Canada and around the world.

Since beginning work on this collection, we have both served on the executive of the CCWH-CCHF. As we read the chapters, the importance of feminist networks in the professional and personal lives of women in the past resonated with us. The CCWH-CCHF is an organization that has been vital to our own development as historians, and we hope that it will continue to nurture future generations. We feel that the CCWH-CCHF has far to go in advocating for and helping to bring about a more diverse profession. We need to continue to foster a meaningful dialogue between anglophone and francophone historians, and we need to reach out to the broader community of people who believe in the importance of women's history, including teachers and feminist activists. To this end, the royalties from this book will be donated to the Barbara Roberts Prize, which promotes the study of feminist perspectives on peace, social justice and human rights, workplace and unions, and women's studies education.

NOTES

1 Colleagues, friends, and former students organized sessions to celebrate the contributions of Jean Barman, Andrée Lévesque, and Veronica Strong-Boag.
2 Veronica Strong-Boag, "Work to Be Done: The Canadian Committee on Women's History," pamphlet, no publisher, 1995; Deborah Gorham, "Women's History: Founding a New Field," in *Creating Historical Memory: English-Canadian Women*

and the Work of History, ed. Beverly Boutilier and Alison Prentice (Vancouver: UBC Press, 1997), 273–97.

3 Georgina Feldberg, Molly Ladd-Taylor, Alison Li, and Kathryn McPherson, eds., *Women, Health, and Nation: Canada and the United States since 1945* (Montreal/ Kingston: McGill-Queen's University Press, 2003); Cheryl Krasnick Warsh, ed., *Gender, Health, and Popular Culture: Historical Perspectives* (Waterloo: Wilfrid Laurier University Press, 2011); Mary-Ellen Kelm and Lorna Townsend, eds., *In the Days of Our Grandmothers: A Reader in Aboriginal Women's History in Canada* (Toronto: University of Toronto Press, 2003); Sarah Carter and Patricia A. McCormack, eds., *Recollecting: Lives of Aboriginal Women of the Northwest and Borderlands* (Edmonton: Athabasca University Press, 2011); Judith Fingard and Janet Guildford, eds. *Mothers of the Municipality: Women, Work, and Social Policy in Post-1945 Halifax* (Toronto: University of Toronto Press, 2005); Sarah Carter, Lesley Erickson, Patricia Roome, and Char Smith, eds., *Unsettled Pasts: Reconceiving the West through Women's History* (Calgary: University of Calgary Press, 2005); Elizabeth Jameson and Sheila McManus, eds., *One Step over the Line: Toward a History of Women in the North American Wests* (Edmonton: University of Alberta Press/Athabasca University Press, 2008); Marlene Epp, Franca Iacovetta, and Frances Swyripa, eds., *Sisters or Strangers? Immigrant, Ethic, and Racialized Women in Canadian History* (Toronto: University of Toronto Press, 2004); Myra Rutherdale, ed., *Caregiving on the Periphery: Historical Perspectives on Nursing and Midwifery* (Montreal/Kingston: McGill-Queen's University Press, 2010); Myra Rutherdale and Katie Pickles, eds., *Contact Zones: Aboriginal Women and Settler Women in Canada's Colonial Pasts* (Vancouver: UBC Press, 2005); Janet Guildford and Suzanne Morton, eds., *Making up the State: Women in 20th-Century Atlantic Canada* (Fredericton: Acadiensis Press, 2010); Bettina Bradbury and Tamara Myers, eds., *Negotiating Identities in 19th-and 20th-Century Montreal* (Vancouver: UBC Press, 2005).

4 Catherine Cleverdon, *The Woman Suffrage Movement in Canada* (Toronto: University of Toronto Press, 1950); Veronica Strong-Boag, *Parliament of Women: The National Council of Women, 1893–1929* (Ottawa: National Museum of Man, 1976), Linda Kealey, ed., *A Not Unreasonable Claim: Women and Reform in Canada, 1980s-1920s* (Toronto: Women's Press, 1979); Joy Parr, ed., *Childhood and Family in Canadian History* (Toronto: McClelland and Stewart, 1982); Susan Mann Trofimenkoff and Alison Prentice, eds., *The Neglected Majority: Essays in Canadian Women's History* (Toronto: McClelland and Stewart, 1977); Susan Mann Trofimenkoff and Alison Prentice, eds., *The Neglected Majority: Essays in Canadian Women's History,* vol. 2 (Toronto: McClelland and Stewart, 1986); Veronica Strong-Boag and Anita Clair Fellman, eds., *Rethinking Canada: The Promise of Women's History* (Toronto: Copp Clark Pitman, 1986); Veronica Strong Boag, *The New Day Recalled: Lives of Girls and Women in English Canada, 1919–1939* (Toronto: Copp Clark Pittman, 1988); Meg Luxton, *More Than a Labour of Love: Three Generations of Women's Work in the Home* (Toronto: Women's Educational Press, 1980).

5 Marta Danylewcyz, *Taking the Veil: An Alternative to Marriage, Motherhood, and Spinsterhood in Quebec, 1840–1920* (Toronto: McClelland and Stewart, 1987); Micheline Dumont and Nadia Fahmy-Eid, with Johanne Daigle, *Les couventines: L'education des filles au Quebec dans les congregations religieuses enseignantes,*

1840–1960 (Montreal: Boréal, 1986); Veronica Strong-Boag, *A Woman with a Purpose: The Diaries of Elizabeth Smith* (Toronto: University of Toronto Press, 1980).

6 Clio Collective, *Histoire des femmes au Québec* (Montreal: Les Éditions de l'Hexagone, 1982); Alison Prentice, Paula Bourne, Gail Cuthbert Brandt, Beth Light, Wendy Mitchinson, and Naomi Black, *Canadian Women: A History* (Toronto: Harcourt Brace Javonovich, 1988).

7 Wendy Robbins, Meg Luxton, Margrit Eichler, and Francine Descarries, eds., *Minds of Our Own: Inventing Feminist Scholarship and Women's Studies in Canada and Quebec, 1966–76* (Waterloo: Wilfrid Laurier University Press, 2008).

8 J.L. Granatstein, *Who Killed Canadian History?* (Toronto: Harper Collins, 1998). See also Michael Bliss, "Privatizing the Mind: The Sundering of Canadian History, the Sundering of Canada," *Journal of Canadian Studies* 26 (1991): 5–17, and for a more recent criticism of the impact of social and cultural history, see Christopher Dummitt, "After Inclusiveness: The Future of Canadian History," in Christopher Dummitt and Michael Dawson, ed., *Contesting Clio's Craft: New Directions and Debates in Canadian History* (London: Institute for the Study of the Americas, 2009).

9 Gail Cuthbert Brant, "Presidential Address: National Unity and the Politics of Political History," *Journal of the Canadian Historical Association/Revue de la Société historique du Canada* 3, 1 (1992): 10. Shirley Tillotson's examination of tax policy is an excellent example of scholarship that demonstrates how women participate in "high politics." See Shirley Tillotson, "The Family as Tax Dodge: Partnership, Individuality, and Gender in the Personal Income Tax Act, 1942–1970," *Canadian Historical Review* 90, 3 (2009): 391–426, and "Relations of Extraction: Taxation and Women's Citizenship in the Maritimes, 1914–1955," *Acadiensis* 39, 1 (2010): 27–57.

10 Joan Wallach Scott, "Gender: A Useful Category of Historical Analysis," *American Historical Review* 91, 5 (1986): 1053–75.

11 These included Franca Iacovetta and Mariana Valverde, eds., *Gender Conflicts: New Essays in Women's History* (Toronto: University of Toronto Press, 1992); Joy Parr, ed., *A Diversity of Women: Ontario, 1945–1980* (Toronto: University of Toronto Press, 1995); and Kathryn McPherson, Cecilia Morgan, and Nancy Forestell, eds., *Gendered Pasts: Historical Essays in Femininity and Masculinity in Canada* (Don Mills, ON: Oxford University Press, 1999). At roughly the same time, there were two more celebratory collections: see Elspeth Cameron and Janice Dickin, eds., *Great Dames* (Toronto: University of Toronto Press, 1997) and Sharon Cooke, Lorna McLean, and Kate O'Rourke, *Framing Our Past: Constructing Canadian Women's History in the Twentieth Century* (Montreal/Kingston: McGill-Queen's University Press, 2001).

12 Joan Sangster provided an important critique in "Beyond Dichotomies: Re-assessing Gender History and Women's History in Canada" *Left History* 3, 1 (Spring 1995): 109–21, and in the introduction to *Through Feminist Eyes: Essays on Canadian Women's History* (Edmonton: Athabasca University Press, 2011).

13 Lynne Marks, *Revivals and Roller Rinks: Religion, Leisure, and Identity in Late-Nineteenth-Century Small Town Ontario* (Toronto: University of Toronto Press, 1997); Karen Dubinsky, *The Second Greatest Disappointment: Honeymooning and Tourism at Niagara Falls* (Toronto: Between the Lines Press, 1999); Valerie Korinek, *Roughing It in the Suburbs: Reading Chatelaine in the Fifties and Sixties* (Toronto: University of Toronto Press, 2000).

14 The focus on Aboriginal women has a long history. See, for instance, Sylvia Van Kirk, *Many Tender Ties: Women in Fur Trade Society, 1670–1870* (Winnipeg: Watson and Dyer, 1980) and Jennifer Brown, *Strangers in Blood: Fur Trade Families in Indian Country* (Vancouver: UBC Press, 1980). Other books include, but are by no means limited to, Karen Anderson, *Chain Her by One Foot: The Subjugation of Women in Seventeenth-Century New France* (London: Routledge, 1991) and Sarah Carter, *Capturing Women: The Manipulation of Cultural Imagery in Canada's Prairie West* (Montreal/Kingston: McGill-Queen's University Press, 1997). There is less research on African Canadian and Asian women, but see Peggy Bristow, Dionne Brand, Linda Carty, Afua P. Cooper, Sylvia Hamilton, Adrienne Shadd, eds., *We're Rooted Here and They Can't Pull Us Up: Essays in African-Canadian Women's History* (Toronto: University of Toronto Press, 1994); Afua Cooper, *The Hanging of Angelique: The Untold Story of Canadian Slavery and the Burning of Old Montreal* (Toronto: Harper Collins, 2006); and Karen Flynn, *Moving beyond Borders: A History of Black Canadian and Caribbean Women in the Diaspora* (Toronto: University of Toronto Press, 2011). For Asian women, see Pamela Sugiman, "'A Million Hearts from Here': Japanese Canadian Mothers and Daughters and the Lessons of War," *Journal of American Ethnic History* 26, 4 (2007): 50–68, and "Memories of Internment: Narrating Japanese Canadian Women's Life Stories," *Canadian Journal of Sociology* 29, 3 (2004): 359–88; Lisa Mar, "The Tale of Lin Tee: Madness, Family Violence and Lindsay's Anti-Chinese Riot of 1919," in *Sisters or Strangers: Immigrant, Ethnic, and Racialized Women in Canadian History*, ed. Marlene Epp, Franca Iacovetta, and Francis Swyripa (Toronto: University of Toronto Press, 2004), 108–29. For more on race and citizenship, see Veronica Strong-Boag, ed., *Painting the Maple: Essays on Race, Gender, and the Construction of Canada* (Vancouver: UBC Press, 1998) and Sherene Razack, *Race, Space, and the Law: Unmapping a White Settler Society* (Toronto: Between the Lines Press, 2002).

15 Karen Dubinsky, *Improper Advances: Rape and Heterosexual Conflict in Ontario, 1880–1929* (Chicago: University of Chicago Press, 1993); Carolyn Strange, *Toronto's Girl Problem: The Perils and Pleasures of the City, 1880–1930* (Toronto: University of Toronto Press, 1995); Becki Ross, *The House That Jill Built: A Lesbian Nation in Formation* (Toronto: University of Toronto Press, 1995); Mary Louise Adams, *The Trouble with Normal: Postwar Youth and the Making of Heterosexuality* (Toronto: University of Toronto Press, 1997); Elise Chenier, *Strangers in Our Midst: Sexual Deviancy in Postwar Ontario* (Toronto: University of Toronto Press, 1998); and Cameron Duder, *Awfully Devoted Women: Lesbian Lives in Canada, 1900–65* (Vancouver: UBC Press, 2010).

16 Franca Iacovetta and Wendy Mitchinson, eds., *On the Case: Explorations in Social History* (Toronto: University of Toronto Press, 1998); Joan Sangster, *Regulating Girls and Women: Sexuality, Family, and the Law in Ontario, 1920–1960* (Don Mills, ON: Oxford University Press, 2001); and Joan Sangster, *Girl Trouble: Female Delinquency in English Canada* (Toronto: Between the Lines Press, 2002).

17 Veronica Strong-Boag, *Fostering Nation: Canada Confronts Its History of Childhood Disadvantage* (Waterloo: Wilfrid Laurier University Press, 2012); Veronica Strong-Boag, *Finding Families, Finding Ourselves: English Canada Encounters Adoption from the Nineteenth Century to the 1990s* (Don Mills, ON: Oxford University Press, 2006); Karen Dubinsky, *Babies without Borders: Adoption and Migration across the*

Americas (Toronto: University of Toronto Press, 2010); Karen Balcom, *The Traffic in Babies: Cross-Border Adoption and Baby-Selling between the United States and Canada, 1930–1972* (Toronto: University of Toronto Press, 2011).

18 Rebecca Edwards, "Women's and Gender History," in *American History Now*, ed. Eric Foner and Lisa McGirr (Philadelphia, PA: Temple University Press, 2011), 337.

19 Joan Sangster, "Archiving Feminist Histories: Women, the 'Nation,' and Metanarratives in Canadian Historical Writing," *Women's Studies International Forum* 29 (2006): 255–64.

20 Historians did not abandon biography as can be seen in Mary Kinnear, *Margaret McWillians: An Interwar Feminist* (Montreal/Kingston: McGill-Queen's University Press, 1991); Terry Crowley, *Agnes MacPhail and the Politics of Equality* (Toronto: J. Lorimer, 1990). For some recent examples, see Veronica Strong-Boag and Carole Gerson, *Paddling Her Own Canoe: The Times and Texts of E. Pauline Johnson (Tekahionwake)* (Toronto: University of Toronto Press, 2000); Andrée Lévesque, *Eva Circe-Côté: Libre penseuse* (Montreal: Les Éditions du remue-ménage, 2010); Terry Crowley, *Marriage of Minds: Isabel and Oscar Skelton* (Toronto: University of Toronto Press, 2003); Jean Barman, *Sojourning Sisters: The Letters and Lives of Jessie and Annie McQueen* (Toronto: University of Toronto Press, 2002); and Roberta Hamilton, *Setting the Agenda: Jean Royce and the Shaping of Queen's University* (Toronto: University of Toronto Press, 2002).

21 Alice Kessler-Harris, "AHR Roundtable: Why Biography?" *American Historical Review* 114, 3 (2009): 625–30; Lois Banner, "AHR Roundtable: Why Biography?" *American Historical Review* 114, 3 (2009), 579–86; Mary Quayle Innis, *Clear Spirit: Twenty Canadian Women and Their Times* (Toronto: Canadian Federation of University Women/University of Toronto Press, 1967); Carlotta Hacker, *Indomitable Lady Doctors* (Toronto: Clarke, Irwin, 1974); Byrne Hope Sanders, *Famous Women: Carr, Hind, Gullen* (Toronto: Clarke, Irwin, 1958). For earlier generations of women historians, who often took a biographical approach, see Beverly Boutilier and Alison Prentice, eds., *Creating Historical Memory: English-Canadian Women and the Work of History* (Vancouver: UBC Press, 1997) and Donald Wright, *The Professionalization of History in English Canada* (Toronto: University of Toronto Press, 2005).

22 Gillian Whitlock, *The Intimate Empire: Reading Women's Autobiography* (London: Cassel, 2000), 3.

23 Joan Sangster, *Transforming Labour: Women and Work in Postwar Canada* (Toronto: University of Toronto Press, 2013); Donica Belise, *Retail Nation: Department Stores and the Making of Modern Canada* (Vancouver: UBC Press, 2011).

24 Marilyn Barber, "The Women Ontario Welcomed: Immigrant Domestics for Ontario Homes, 1870–1930" *Ontario History* 72, 3 (1980): 148–72; Ruth Roach Pierson, *They're Still Women after All: The Second World War and Canadian Womanhood* (Toronto: McClelland and Stewart, 1986); Gail Cuthbert Brandt, "The Transformation of Women's Work in the Quebec Cotton Industry," in *The Character of Class Struggle: Essays in Canadian Working Class History*, ed. Bryan Palmer, (Toronto: University of Toronto Press, 1986), 115–37. This, of course, is just a sampling of the fine work completed by labour historians such as Joan Sangster, Linda Kealey, and Suzanne Cross. A fine example of the work of feminist labour historians in Quebec

is Marie Lavigne and Yolande Pinard, eds., *Travailleuses et féministes: Les femmes dans la sociéte québecoise* (Montreal: Boréal Express, 1983). The Clio Collective also paid important attention to women's work in *L'histoire des femmes au Québec*.

25 Some of the most important work here is as follows: Bettina Bradbury, *Working Families: Age, Gender, and Daily Survival in Industrializing Montreal* (Toronto: McClelland and Stewart, 1993); Strong-Boag, *The New Day Recalled;* Luxton, *More Than a Labour of Love;* Denise Baillageron, *Ménagères au temps de la crise* (Montreal: Éditions de Remue-Ménage, 1991); and Marjorie Griffin Cohen, *Women's Work, Markets, and Economic Development in Nineteenth-Century Ontario* (Toronto: University of Toronto Press, 1988).

26 Nadia Fahmy-Eid and Lucie Piché, *Si le travail m'était conté autrement: Les femmes dans la Confédération des syndicates nationaux depuis 1920* (Montreal: CSN, 1987); Sylvie Murray, *À la jonction du mouvement ouvrier et du mouvement des femmes: La ligue auxiliaire de l'Association international des machinists Canada 1903–1980* (Montreal: Regroupement des chercheurs-chercheures en histoire des travailleurs et travailleuses du Québec 1990); Ruth Frager, *Sweatshop Strife: Class, Ethnicity, and Gender in the Jewish Labour Movement of Toronto* (Toronto: University of Toronto Press, 1995); Pamela Sugiman, *Labour's Dilemma: The Gender Politics of Auto Workers in Canada, 1937–1979* (Toronto: University of Toronto Press, 1994); Gillian Creese, *Contracting Masculinity: Gender, Class, and Race in a White-Collar Union* (Toronto: Oxford University Press, 1999); and Nancy M. Forestell, "The Miner's Wife: Working-Class Femininity in a Masculine Context, 1920–1950," in *Gendered Pasts: Historical Essays in Femininity and Masculinity in Canada*, ed. Kathryn McPherson, Cecilia Morgan, and Nancy M. Forestell (Toronto: Oxford University Press, 1999): 139–55.

27 Hacker, *The Indomitable Lady Doctors;* Ruby Heap and Alison Prentice, eds., *Gender and Education in Ontario: A Historical Reader* (Toronto: Canadian Scholars Press, 1991); Constance Backhouse, *Petticoats and Prejudice: Women and Law in Nineteenth-Century Canada* (Toronto: Osgoode Society for Canadian Legal History, 1991); Patricia T. Rooke, *No Bleeding Heart: Charlotte Whitton, A Feminist on the Right* (Vancouver: UBC Press, 1987); Sara Z. Burke, *Seeking the Highest Good: Social Service and Gender at the University of Toronto* (Toronto: University of Toronto Press, 1996); Marta Danylewcyz *Taking the Veil: An Alternative to Marriage, Motherhood, and Spinsterhood in Quebec, 1840–1920* (Toronto: McClelland and Stewart, 1987); Heidi MacDonald, "Who Counts? Nuns, Work, and the Census of Canada" *Social History/Histoire sociale* 43, 86 (2010): 369–91; Dumont and Fahmy-Eid, with Johanne Daigle, *Les couventines*.

28 Kathryn McPherson, *Bedside Matters: The Transformation of Canadian Nursing, 1900–1990* (Toronto: Oxford University Press, 1996); Meryn Stuart and Jayne Elliott, eds., *Place and Practice in Canadian Nursing History* (Vancouver, UBC Press, 2008); Ruby Heap, "Training Women for a New 'Women's Profession': Physiotherapy Education at the University of Toronto," *History of Education Quarterly* 35, 2 (1995): 135–59; Nadia Fahmy-Eid, Aline Charles, Johanne Collin, Johanne Daigle, Pauline Fahmy, Ruby Heap, and Lucie Piché, *Femmes, santé et professions: Histoire*

des diététistes et des physiothérapeutes au Quebec et en Ontario, 1930–1980 – L'affirmation d'un status professionnel (Montreal: Fides, 1997); Elizabeth Smyth, Sandra Acker, Paula Bourne, and Alison Prentice, eds., *Challenging Professions: Historical and Contemporary Perspectives on Women's Professional Work* (Toronto: University of Toronto Press, 1999).

29 Jean Burnet, ed., *Looking into My Sister's Eyes: An Exploration in Women's History* (Toronto: Multicultural History Society of Ontario, 1986); Franca Iacovetta, *Such Hardworking People: Italian Immigrants in Postwar Toronto* (Montreal/Kingston: McGill-Queen's University Press, 1992); Dionne Brand, ed., *No Burden to Carry: Narratives of Black Working Women in Ontario 1920s to 1950s* (Toronto: Women's Press, 1991); Varpu Lindstrom-Best, *Defiant Sisters: A Social History of Finnish Immigrant Women in Canada* (Toronto: Multicultural History Society of Ontario, 1992); and Iacovetta, Swyripa, and Epp, *Sisters or Strangers*.

30 Mary Jane Logan McCallum, "Labour, Modernity and the Canadian State: A History of Aboriginal Women and Work in the Mid-Twentieth Century" (PhD diss., University of Manitoba, 2008); Joan Sangster, "Making a Fur Coat: Women, the Labouring Body, Working-Class History" *International Review of Social History* 52, 2 (2007): 241–42; Robin Jarvis Brownlie, "'Living the Same as the White People': Mohawk and Anishinabe Women's Labour in Southern Ontario, 1920–1940," *Labour/Le Travail* 61 (2008): 41–68; Paige Raibmon, "Indigenous Women at Work in the Hop Fields and Tourist Industry," *Labor: Studies in Working-Class History of the Americas* 3, 3 (2007): 23–56; and John Lutz, *Makuk: A New History of Aboriginal-White Relations* (Vancouver: UBC Press, 2008).

31 The scholarship is far too vast to include all of it. Some recent studies are Becki Ross, *Burlesque West: Showgirls, Sex, and Sin in Postwar Vancouver* (Toronto: University of Toronto Press, 2009); Belisle, *Retail Nation*; Joan Sangster, *Transforming Labour*; and Katrina Srigley, *Breadwinning Daughters: Young Working Women in a Depression-Era City, 1929–1939* (Toronto: University of Toronto Press, 2010).

32 Cleverdon, *The Women Suffrage Movement in Canada*; Kealey, *A Not Unreasonable Claim*; Linda Kealey and Joan Sangster, eds., *Beyond the Vote: Canadian Women in Politics* (Toronto: University of Toronto Press, 1989); Crowley, *Agnes MacPhail*; Linda Carty, ed., *And Still We Rise: Feminist Political Mobilizing in Contemporary Canada* (Toronto: Women's Press, 1993). See also the website *Women Suffrage and Beyond*. This site, launched by Veronica Strong-Boag, Genevieve LeBaron, and Kelly Christensen, examines the connections between past suffrage campaigns and today's democratic deficit and illustrates the ongoing importance of transnational connections among feminist activists. Available at http://womensuffrage.org/.

33 Carol Bacchi, *Liberation Deferred? The Ideas of the English-Canadian Suffragists, 1877–1918* (Toronto: University of Toronto Press, 1983).

34 Linda Kealey, *Enlisting Women for the Cause: Women, Labour, and the Left in Canada, 1890–1920* (Toronto: University of Toronto Press, 1998); Janice Newton, *The Feminist Challenge to the Canadian Left, 1900–1918* (Montreal/Kingston: McGill-Queen's University Press, 1995); Andrée Lévesque, ed., *Madeleine Parent, militante* (Montreal: Remue-ménage, 2003). On working-class women's contribution to late-twentieth-century feminist politics, see Meg Luxton, "Feminism as a

Class Act: Working-Class Feminism and the Women's Movement in Canada," *Labour/Le Travail* 48 (Fall 2001): 63–88; Julia Smith, "Organizing the Unorganized: The Service, Office, and Retail Workers' Union of Canada (SORWUC), 1972–1986" (master's thesis, Simon Fraser University, 2009).

35 Carmen Nielsen Varty, "'A Career in Christian Charity': Women's Benevolence and the Public Sphere in a Mid-Nineteenth-Century Canadian City," *Women's Review of History* 14, 2 (2005): 243–64; Mariana Valverde, "The Mixed Social Economy as a Canadian Tradition," *Studies in Political Economy* 47 (Summer 1995): 36–60; Cynthia Comacchio, *Nations Are Built of Babies: Saving Ontario's Mothers and Children* (Montreal/Kingston: McGill-Queen's University Press, 1993); Denyse Baillargeon, *Un Québec en mal d'enfants: La médicalisation de la maternité, 1910–1970* (Montreal: Remue-ménage, 2004); Aline Charles, *Travail d'ombre et de lumière: Le bénévolat féminin à l'Hôpital Ste-Justine, 1907–1960* (Quebec, IQRC, 1990); Chenier, *Strangers in Our Midst.*

36 Gail Campbell, "Disenfranchised but Not Quiescent: Women Petitioners in New Brunswick in the Mid-19th-Century," *Acadiensis* 18, 2 (1989): 22–25; Rusty Bittermann, "Women and the Escheat Movement: The Politics of Everday Life on Prince Edward Island," in *Separate Spheres: Women's Worlds in the 19th-Century Maritimes,* ed. Janet Gildford and Suzanne Morton (Fredericton: Acadiensis Press, 1994), 23–38; Bettina Bradbury, "Women at the Hustings: Gender, Citizenship, and the Montreal By-Elections of 1832," in *Rethinking Canada: The Promise of Women's History,* 5th ed., ed. Mona Gleason and Adele Perry (Toronto: Oxford University Press, 2006), 75–94; Allan Greer, *The Patriots and the People: The Rebellion of 1837 in Rural Lower Canada* (Toronto: University of Toronto Press, 1993); and Janice Potter McKinnon, *While the Women Only Wept: Loyalist Refugee Women* (Montreal/Kingston: McGill-Queen's University Press, 1993).

37 See essays by Peggy Bristow and Sylvia Hamilton in Linda Carty, ed., *And Still We Rise: Feminist Political Mobilizing in Contemporary Canada* (Toronto: Women's Press, 1993); Janet Silman, *Enough Is Enough: Aboriginal Women Speaking Out* (Toronto: Women's Press, 1987); Afua Cooper, *The Hanging of Angélique* (Toronto: Harper Collins, 2006); Bristow et al., *We're Rooted Here;* Kim Anderson and Bonita Lawrence, eds., *Strong Women Stories: Native Vision and Community Survival* (Toronto: Sumach Press, 2003).

38 Shirley Tillotson, *Contributing Citizens: Modern Charitable Fundraising and the Making of the Welfare State, 1920–66* (Vancouver: UBC Press, 2006); Tarah Brookfield, *Cold War Comforts: Canadian Women, Child Safety, and Global Insecurity, 1945–1975* (Waterloo: Wilfrid Laurier Press, 2012); Dominique Clement, *Canada's Rights Revolution: Social Movements and Social Change, 1937–82* (Vancouver: UBC Press, 2008).

39 Adele Perry, *On the Edge of Empire: Gender, Race and the Making of British Columbia, 1849–1871* (Toronto: University of Toronto Press, 2001); Pickles and Rutherdale, *Contact Zones;* Lisa Chilton, *Agents of Empire: British Female Migration to Canada and Australia, 1860s–1930s* (Toronto: University of Toronto Press, 2007).

40 C.A. Bayly, Sven Beckert, Matthew Connelly, Isabel Hofmeyr, Wendy Kozol, and Patricia Seed, "AHR Conversation: On Transnational History," *American Historical Review* 111, 5 (2006): 1441–64.

41 Frances Swyripa, *Wedded to the Cause: Ukrainian-Canadian Women and Ethnic Identity, 1891–1991* (Toronto: University of Toronto Press, 1993); Royden K. Loewen, *Family, Church, and Market: A Mennonite Community in the Old and New Worlds, 1850–1930* (Urbana/Chicago: University of Illinois Press, 1993); Franca Iacovetta, *Such Hardworking People.*

42 Elizabeth Jameson, "Connecting the Women's Wests" in *One Step over the Line: Toward a History of Women in the North American Wests,* ed. Elizabeth Jameson and Sheila McManus (Athabasca: Athabasca University Press, 2008), 22.

43 Maureen Moynagh and Nancy Forestell, "General Introduction," in *Documenting First Wave Feminisms*, vol. 1, *Transnational Collaborations and Crosscurrents,* ed. Maureen Moynagh with Nancy Forestell (Toronto: University of Toronto Press, 2012), xxii.

44 Allan Greer, "Canadian History: Ancient and Modern," *Canadian Historical Review* 77, 4 (1996): 575–90.

45 Denyse Baillargeon "Des Voies/x paralleles: L'histoire des femmes au Quebec et au Canada anglais (1970–1995)," *Sextant 4* (1995): 133–68. *Gender Conflicts* contains nothing about French Canada while *Gendered Pasts* has only one article out of eleven. *Great Dames* has one article out of fifteen. *Rethinking Canada* has always had significant content on French-speaking Canada, but most of it is written by anglophones rather than francophones.

46 Magda Fahrni, "Reflections on the Place of Quebec in Historical Writing on Canada," in *Contesting Clio's Craft: New Directions and Debates in Canadian History,* ed. Christopher Dummit and Michael Dawson (London: Institute for the Study of the Americas, 2009): 1–20.

1

James Douglas, Amelia Connolly, and the Writing of Gender and Women's History

ADELE PERRY

Studying the elite, translocal Creole/Metis family of James Douglas (1803–77) and Amelia Connolly (1812–90) sheds light on three critical points in the writing of Canadian women's and gender history. The first is that this history cannot be easily, productively, or best contained within the nation and needs to be mapped across and beyond national and imperial boundaries. Over the course of the long nineteenth century, Connolly, Douglas, and their kin lived in the Caribbean, the United Kingdom, and a range of sites in northern North America, most notably Red River, Oregon, and British Columbia. Their gendered history within these diverse spaces brushes up against and challenges a historiography implicitly or explicitly presumed to mirror the national boundaries of present-day nation-states projected backwards in time. The second point raised by the history of this colonial family is something that historians of women and gender have long argued within the Canadian context: that gender and the related categories of sexuality, family, intimacy, and the body matter to history writ large, not simply to women and the so-called private sphere. Third, this history reminds us that conventional historical methodology has genuine limits when it comes to excavating the histories of indigenous peoples and women. The history of the Douglas-Connolly family prompts us to think about terms of endearment and terms of reference in ways that confirm long-standing arguments made by historians of women and gender in Canada and push them in new directions.

At the centre of this story, or at least the one that can be narrated from the available written archives, is James Douglas. His story, or important parts of it, is reasonably well known to historians of Canada and, more particularly, of British Columbia. James Douglas's life (and, to a much lesser extent, that of his wife, Amelia Connolly) has been figured as a narrative of heroic, self-made frontier masculinity in the political biographies of the early twentieth-century, as a sign of the persistence of mixed-race fur trade intimacies in the feminist historiography of the 1970s and 1980s, and, more recently, as a revealing example of Canada's particular history.[1]

I see something different in Douglas and Connolly's story. Douglas was born in 1803 in Demerara (now postcolonial Guyana), a sugar colony that clung to South America's Atlantic coast and moved back and forth between Dutch and British possession in the early years of the nineteenth century. Douglas's father, John, was a peripatetic and seemingly unremarkable Scottish man tied to a family with sugar and shipping interests. His mother was probably a free woman of colour named Martha Ann Telfer. Telfer made only the slightest marks on the archive of nineteenth-century Demarara, but her likely mother, Rebecca Ritchie, was harder to miss. Ritchie was a "free coloured woman" who circulated throughout the British West Indies, knew her way around the colony's legal system, and owned a considerable amount of property, including slaves, in both Demerara and Barbados.[2]

The relationship between Martha Ann Telfer and John Douglas went unrecorded in the colonial archive and, presumably, unmarked by church ceremony. The absence of a clear archival trace is part of the story of this kind of imperial intimacy. As historian Durba Ghosh explains, the imperial archive exerted its considerable political authority in part by keeping "native mistresses, out-of-wedlock children, and multiple families" out of it.[3] The children born to these couples were their archive. Martha and John had three children, and the pattern of their births was determined by the transatlantic separations and reunions: two boys, Alexander and James, were born when John was in Demerara in the first years of the nineteenth century; Cecilia, a daughter, was born in 1812 after John returned from a stay in Scotland. Around this time, he returned to Scotland and married a Scottish woman with whom he had four children.[4] It was the Scottish family that was acknowledged as his official family during his life and, by his will, after his death.[5]

Given what we know about their families, locations, identities, and material resources, it is fair to assume that John Douglas and Martha Ann Telfer shared a relationship that fits within a particular genre of domestic relationships in which women of colour were long-term *housekeepers* and white men *masters* within an *establishment*. This language emphasizes the hierarchy at the core of this form of imperial intimacy (and the significance of labour to them) and situates imperial households outside of the sentimentalized discourse of domestic space, figured implicitly as the exclusive property of the metropole. Travellers to nineteenth-century Demerara sketched the basic outlines. One British observer wrote that "it was customary for the managers of estates, merchants, and other white men, to have what was called an establishment, presided over by a black or coloured woman, who looked after the servants and the comfort of her master generally."[6] These women, explained an observer in 1807, "embrace all the duties of a wife, except presiding at table."[7] These relationships existed alongside brutal and unrelentingly exploitative imperial intimacies, which were documented in the testimony of enslaved women who complained to the colonial officials of Demerara and neighbouring Berbice.[8]

The intimacies between transient white men and their so-called housekeepers in nineteenth-century Demerara offer us a vision of mixed-race intimacies that were acknowledged and regulated by known norms and that played out in a local imperial terrain that put some blacks, especially free ones, and petty bourgeois whites into conversation and contact. Class was significant, not only for conditioning the kind of intimate possibilities available to white men in the Caribbean, as Cecelia Green has recently argued, but also for how it could empower women.[9] Demerara was organized around absentee ownership, and the men who came to manage the colony's plantations or government rarely settled permanently. Until emancipation in the 1830s, the primary social cleavage was freedom and unfreedom rather than blackness and whiteness per se. In the colony's city, women of colour had the advantage of local knowledge and kin connections. If free, they could and did participate in a lively market economy that included owning other people. For women such as Telfer, relationships with men such as Douglas occurred in a context of relative female empowerment and thick local knowledge.

Intimacies such as these complicate characterizations of a geographic economy of intimacy that positioned the Caribbean as a place of sex and England as a place of family.[10] For John Douglas, both Demerara and Scotland were places of family. Yet anthropologist Raymond T. Smith's conceptualization of a West Indian "dual marriage system" fails to account for the realities of spacialization and inequality in Douglas's two families.[11] Only one family was acknowledged by law and church, recorded in the archive, and rewarded with the transmission of wealth; the other was customary, unofficial, and did not inherit. The differential positioning of the two Douglas families was predicated on a series of overlapping relationships between gender, race, space, and life stage. Unlike the families of the US South studied by Nell Irvin Painter, the two Douglas families had, most of the time, an ocean between them.[12] The spacialization of empire sustained inequality and made it deceptively workable. As Ghosh explains in her study of nineteenth-century India, "By keeping indigenous women out of European marital and familial networks, concubinage was not a departure from the normative practice of marriage, but rather a practice that sustained the racial and gendered hierarchies of colonial societies by denying interracial relationships the public or social recognition that marriage entailed."[13] This spacialized arrangement also fit with widespread patterns of work, migration, and family among European men during the age of empire. John Douglas went to Demerara as a young man, formed a family with a local woman, which he maintained for over a decade, before returning to Scotland to marry a Scottish woman in a church ceremony, have children, and live out the remainder of his life. His intimate life, like those of so many other European men involved in the colonial world, was lived in two spacialized and hierarchically ordered imperial stages, each with a family to fit its position.

The children of this imperial family did not receive their father's property, but the sons were provided with a metropolitan education, a critical ingredient that allowed Creole boys of colour throughout the eastern Caribbean to cautiously and provisionally access the privileges of whiteness. Alexander and James likely accompanied their father on his return to Scotland in 1812.[14] They were placed at the Lanark Grammar School, and it was there that James acquired the cultural capital that Scots parlayed into opportunities throughout the nineteenth-century British Empire and some raw materials from which to construct a viable national identity. In 1819, the connections that linked Scottish merchant capitalism in the Caribbean to merchant capitalism in North America were put into play, and the two Douglas boys were apprenticed to the Montreal headquartered North West Company. Douglas would work in the fur trade for more than three decades, concluding his career as the dominant Hudson's Bay Company (HBC) official on the Pacific Coast. As Britain renegotiated its authority over the northwestern part of North America, necessity prompted the Colonial Office to appoint Douglas, then the chief factor of Fort Victoria, governor of the new colony of Vancouver Island in 1851. In 1858, he assumed the governorship of the new mainland colony of British Columbia, and he held this dual position until he retired in 1863–64.[15] Douglas died in 1877 in Victoria, the home that he was by then more than reluctant to leave.

Douglas's career in the fur trade cannot be understood outside of his marriage into an elite Metis family. In 1828, Douglas married Amelia Connolly, the daughter of his direct superior at Fort St. James. The marriage was *à la façon du pays*, the customary mode of intimacy so carefully sketched by historian Sylvia Van Kirk in her 1980 book, *"Many Tender Ties."*[16] If the intimacies of Douglas's Demerara boyhood were structured by the plantation and merchant economies and the all-encompassing practice of slavery, marriage à la façon du pays was produced out of the particular economy of the fur trade and its mercantilism and dependence on indigenous economies and trade networks.

Marriage marked and cemented Douglas's ties to the Northwest and signalled his rejection of the mode of imperial manhood practised by his father – lived on two stages, with two unequal families – and went hand-in-hand with a renewed commitment to the fur trade and the geographic space of northern North America. In 1827, Douglas had given notice of retirement.[17] "Mr. James Douglas is bent on leaving the Country," explained a colleague in March 1828: "I am very sorry for it. Independent of his abilities as an Indian Trader he possesses most amiable qualities and an accomplished Young Man."[18] In his mid-twenties, and with eight years of wage labour behind him and £166,147 in savings, Douglas would have been in a good position to establish himself in a modest but relatively secure middle-class trade elsewhere. But he chose otherwise. Douglas and Connolly married in April of 1828, not long after Douglas received a substantial raise from £60 to £100 per year.[19]

Amelia was herself a child of this kind of marriage. Her mother, Miyo Nipay, was Cree, and her father, William Connolly, was a Canadian of Irish extraction, Roman Catholic faith, and French Canadian connections.[20] In 1803, in Rivière-aux-Rats, Athabasca Country, Miyo Nipay and William married according to "the usages and customs of the Cree nation to which she belonged," which emphasized mutual consent, the approval of her family, and local repute.[21] Connolly would later explain that he had married in part to access critical indigenous trade networks, but the economics and diplomacies of the trade did not explain the twenty-eight years that Miyo Nipay and William lived together or the six children they raised to adulthood together.[22]

Connolly and Douglas's relationship, like the unions that produced them both, provides a revealing window into imperial intimacies in a local imperial context. If Douglas's father-in-law used marriage to access Cree trade networks, Douglas used it to access new opportunities in the fur trade. By marrying a factor's daughter, Douglas tied himself into networks of patronage and affinity in a system that, as historian Jennifer Brown has shown, emphasized connections between senior men and their chosen juniors.[23] These ties could be established by kinship or clan or be activated by marriage. Establishing ties through heterosexual marriage was particularly critical for men such as Douglas, men who had limited kin connections within the trade. Men who could not depend on an influential father or uncle could be knit into complicated and influential relations of patronage and mentoring through marriage. When he became Amelia's husband, Douglas tied himself to Connolly, and that connection would serve him well. In 1829, a peer reported that "Mr. Douglas immediately after his return from Alexandria was married to Miss Connolly, the young Lady promised to Mr. Yale."[24] Douglas was promoted shortly after his marriage to a position for which intimate and knowledgeable observers considered him unqualified.[25] While twentieth-century biographers presented Douglas as a proverbial self-made man, his contemporaries explained his meteoric rise up the ranks of the fur trade as a result of a marriage made well. "A C.F. [chief factor] for a father-in-law to a rising clerk nowadays is good support," one opined. "James Douglas is at Vancouver & rising fast in favour."[26] Douglas was registered as "Connolly's son in law" well into the 1830s.

In 1836, the first missionary arrived at Fort Vancouver, where Douglas was by then chief trader. Like Douglas, Herbert Beaver was a mobile subject of empire whose travels spanned Britain, the Caribbean (in his case St. Lucia), and North America. At Fort Vancouver, Beaver was horrified not so much by mixed-race intimacies but by the status accorded to indigenous women and customary wives in fur trade society, particularly by the social authority exercised by Amelia Connolly and Maria Barclay, and, especially, by Marguerite Waddin McKay, Chief Factor John McLoughlin's Metis wife. Beaver was pleased when two of the company's officers, one of them Douglas, agreed to marry their customary wives according to Anglican rites.[27] But Beaver did not think this good enough. He explained to London that the fort was "a common receptacle for every mistress of an officer in the service."[28] Beaver proposed that the HBC adopt a rigid spacialized distinction between women he considered wives and those he considered concubines and a rigid economic distinction between men with customary relationships and those with churched ones.

Beaver's relationship with McLoughlin broke down in a hail of acrimony, chaos, and violence in 1838. Douglas maintained a working relationship with Beaver until he read the missionary's forty-one-page October 1838 report to HBC headquarters and things fell apart irreparably.[29] Writing to Beaver, Douglas objected to what the missionary had written "respecting the inmates of my dwelling."[30] In undated entries in his private journal, Douglas reflected seriously on questions of gender and intimacy. Putting to use Fort Vancouver's small library, his own private collection of books, which he had carefully saved for, and the newspapers and books that travelled with men in the fur trade, Douglas accessed a set of generic ideas about manliness, womanliness, and marriage then circulating throughout the nineteenth-century English-speaking world. He quoted from treatises on "Conjugal Felicity" and "Wedded Love" and clipped an undated short essay on the "Qualities Requisite to Make Marriage Happy."[31] Good husbands were wise, he thought, and also discrete, virtuous, and good-natured.[32] Women were made happy with domestic work such as needlework but proved their value through sexual morality.[33] "Chastity is the great principle which woman is taught," Douglas reiterated, and "when she had given up that principle she had given up every notion of female honour and virtue."[34]

The books and articles that Douglas could find on marriage and gender would have offered him little to explain the imperial intimacies that had defined his own life and to which Beaver took such vitriolic offence. His sources were necessarily oral and experiential. In a lengthy response sent to London, Douglas offered a complex and nuanced understanding of intimacy and respectability that worked to reconcile long-standing fur trade practice with mainstream metropolitan ideals. He adopted a measured tone, working to seize the language of genteel British manhood back from Beaver. "The intrusion of Dr. McLoughlin's private affairs into a public report ... is decidedly in bad taste," declared Douglas, "and I deeply regret that Mr. Beaver sullied those pages with unhandsome reflections upon Mrs. McLoughlin, who is deservedly respected for her numerous charities, and many excellent qualities of heart."[35] He went on to explain that rigid ideas of female morality needed to be modified to suit local circumstances. "The woman who is not sensible of violating any law, who lived chastely with the husband of her love, in a state approved by friends and sanctioned by immemorial custom, which she believes highly honourable," Douglas argued, "should not be reduced to the level of the disgraced creature who voluntarily plunges into promiscuous vice, sacrifices the great principle which, from infancy, she is taught to revere, & consider the ground work of female virtue, who lives a disgrace

to her friends, and an outcast from society."[36] With these words, Douglas
aims to recalibrate nineteenth-century discourses of female respectability to
include indigenous women and customary marriage.[37] Whether these rigid
codes could bear the weight and challenge that imperial intimacies represented is another question.

The conflicts that marked Beaver's brief time at Fort Vancouver were a
sign of wider changes occurring at mid-century. American and British mis-
sionaries, agricultural settlers, and white wives were an increasingly regular
part of fur trade life. In 1840, Douglas explained transitions in marriage and
race to a colleague. "There is a strange revolution, in the manners of the
country. Indian wives were at one time the vogue, the half breed supplanted
these, and now we have the lovely tender exotic torn from its parent bed,
to pine and languish in the desert."[38] Douglas made clear where his own
allegiances lay. His personal papers list the date of his marriage by local
custom – 27 April 1828 – and not the date of the Anglican ceremony that
followed a decade later as the day of his marriage. He clearly positioned the
local rite as a valid and originary one.[39] He was sentimental about his wife,
the thirteen children she bore, and the six children and handful of grandchildren they raised to adulthood. Writing as a middle-aged man, Douglas
explained that intimate kin were "the great charm of life; particularly amid
the solitude of this country where the cheerful solace of agreeable society
is so seldom found." The "vapid monotony of an inland trading post," he
explained, could only be "softened as it is by the many tender ties, which
find a way to the heart." By naming indigenous women, Creole marriages,
and children as the "many tender ties" of imperial life, Douglas provided
at least two historians with evocative titles and, more to the point, offered
an alternative reckoning of imperial intimacies. But it was a cautious, partial, and ultimately private reckoning, one that rested on the same tenets of
bourgeois metropolitan respectability that it challenged.

The questions that Douglas addressed in his journals and letters to London were later debated in a high-profile court case heard in Lower Canada
in 1864. The case ensured that the intimacy of Miyo Nipay and William
Connolly would be documented in the imperial archive. In 1832, William
Connolly joined a wave of prominent fur traders who married white women
when he wed Julia Woolrich, his much younger cousin, by Roman Catholic ceremony and made arrangements for the support of Miyo Nipay. John
Connolly was one of the children born to William and Miyo Nipay, and by
the 1860s he was a prominent Montreal lawyer. After Woolrich died and
passed her fortune on to her two children, John took the case to court and

gathered together an impressive legal team and a long roster of witnesses, including a judge, a number of old fur traders who had been present at his parent's marriage, and the Roman Catholic priest who had baptized his sisters.

Connolly used the details of his own family history to make a point of far-reaching legal consequence to the overlapping history of empire and intimacy. He argued that the marriage between his father and mother had been conducted according to Cree law, and since no other ceremony had been available in Rivière-aux-Rats in 1803, the law was valid and binding and William Connolly's subsequent marriage bigamous. At stake was the definition of what, exactly, constituted a marriage in Canadian law and, by extension, the legality – and perhaps morality – of imperial manhood. The defence argued that "the Indian woman was Connolly's concubine" and not his wife.[40] In rejecting their argument, Judge Samuel Monk gave special weight to the fact of Miyo Nipay's residence in Lower Canada and to Connolly's acknowledgment of her as his wife there as well as in the fur trade country.[41] The spacialization of their relationship ruptured the claim that Connolly had led an imperial manly life in two stages and in two distinct geographical spaces. By taking Miyo Nipay to Lower Canada and introducing her as wife, Connolly had, in effect, forfeited his ability to lay claim to the models of imperial manhood practised in so many different imperial contexts, including by John Douglas in Demerara.

This case forced the judge to grapple not only with the range of ways that societies regulate marriage but also with the enormously consequential issue of indigenous legal authority within territories claimed by Britain. In a lengthy and intellectually lively decision that historian Sidney Harring has called "the boldest and most creative common law decision on Indian rights in nineteenth-century Canada," Monk validated the indigenous marriage and the children produced by it.[42] The court could not, he explained, expect "Mr. Connolly to carry with him this common law of England to Rat River in his knapsack, and much less could he bring back to Lower Canada the law of repudiation in a bark canoe."[43] Connolly's considerable estate – at that time the largest ever probated in Quebec – was reallocated to his six Metis children, including Amelia Connolly.[44] Douglas and Connolly followed the case closely from Victoria and had a lot at stake in it, both in terms of financial wealth and the slippier but perhaps not less important currency of social respectability. Douglas saw Connolly's victory as a vindication: "John is a noble fellow and has bravely won his rights, alone and unsupported by his family; but to me the most pleasing part is, that he has vindicated his Mothers good name; and done justice to the high minded old Lady, now at rest in the peaceful grave – and worthy of a kinder husband than poor Connolly."[45]

Connolly vs. Woolrich reminds us of the complicated trajectories that imperial intimacies could and did take. The case successfully turned imperial legal apparatuses that most often denied legal rights and inherited wealth to indigenous families on their head and used them to proclaim the illegitimacy of the white family and the legitimacy of the indigenous one, to impoverish the former and bolster the wealth of the latter. The judgment was upheld on appeal two years later but was later settled out of court, likely in anticipation of a less favourable ruling from the Privy Council. The decision was definitively overruled in 1884, when the Privy Council ruled that the only marriage that counted was that conducted according to Christian law.[46]

Imperial intimacies that had been critical to the fur trade did not disappear: they were re-landscaped within a context of diminished rights and recognition. From 1838 onwards, Connolly was Douglas's wife according to British law, Anglican rite, and local repute. When Douglas was appointed governor of Vancouver Island in 1851 and of British Columbia in 1858, Amelia became the governor's lady, and she became Lady Douglas when James was made Knight Commander of the Order of the Bath in 1864 and was named in his will when he died in 1877. The difference of Connolly's womanhood and marriage was not marked by the blunt instrument of illegitimacy but by a series of subtle symbols of racial difference and inferiority, most of which were spacialized. Connolly took on few of the public roles performed by governor's wives elsewhere in the empire. By 1868, she rarely left the house "except for a walk in the garden."[47] Connolly had a limited circulation in Victoria's polite society and none in the imperial world beyond it. Indigenous women could be wives and even ladies, but their status was local, untranslatable, and contingent. The less circumspect among Douglas's critics might have hinted at Douglas's birth and racial identity, but after the 1830s, they rarely spoke of it. Instead, his critics made use of a more available and effective racial and gendered language by taking issue with his long residence in North America, his lack of metropolitan connections, and his indigenous wife. In the last half of the nineteenth century, relationships such as that of Connolly and Douglas were lived against the backdrop of a settler society that increasingly pathologized relationships between indigenous women and non-indigenous men. Yet, as Jennifer Brown has recently commented, and as Durba Ghosh has argued in the context of India, a straightforward narrative of decline fails to capture the variable history of imperial intimacies in this part of North America.[48]

What does the story of the Connolly-Douglas family tell us about terms of endearment and reference or, to put it in different terms, about the global, the local, and the writing of women's and gender history? It makes a clear case for the need to think beyond the borders of the nation-state. Karen Balcom's study of international organizations in this volume makes the case for the need to situate women's and gender history in a wider compass. These points also prompt us to think differently about the nineteenth century, a period when formal national boundaries had little purchase. The history of Connolly and Douglas was made in Britain, in the Caribbean, and in parts of North America later territorialized as both the United States and Canada. To take up the story once it begins in the national context best known and most studied is to misunderstand it. In her study of Julia Grace Wells in this volume, Lorna McLean points out that stories that fall outside of national narratives can too easily escape our attention. One can hardly make this claim for Douglas, who has long been a stalwart figure in regional and national histories. In this case, it is not his history per se but parts of it that come to new light when we look beyond national borders. Doing so suggests different points of connection, including, in this case, the one recently raised by Ryan Eyford – namely, that historians need to pay greater attention to connections between the history of slavery and abolition in the Caribbean and the history of the fur trade and settler colonialism in northern North America.[49] We have no way of knowing whether Douglas's history as a child from a customary mixed-race relationship in Demerara directly influenced his choices as a Metis husband and father in North America, but it is also hard not to connect these histories, just as we need to connect the history of Douglas's administration with a wider British Empire. This confirms a point made in the rich scholarship on the global and transnational connections of the imperial world.[50] It also returns to some of the rich contributions of early women's history in Canada. Sylvia Van Kirk and Jennifer Brown situated their enduring histories of the fur trade in a wide colonial field, as did contributors to Linda Kealey's 1979 collection *A Not Unreasonable Claim: Women and Reform in Canada, 1880s–1920s.*[51] The burst of recent work that includes but is not limited to Canada reminds us of the richness of viewing gender and women's history through a wide-angle lens.[52]

This story also suggests gender and women's history's enormous power to resituate even the most seemingly conventional of historical topics. For a decade in the middle of the nineteenth century, James Douglas was the highest representative of the British imperial state on North America's west coast, an authority he exercised with a curious mixture of political canniness, cultural polyvocality, and devastating violence. Douglas helped ensure that British Columbia was one of the few parts of British North America where indigenous land was not ceded by treaty and where, as a direct result, indigenous dispossession and settler possession were, and remain, profoundly contested.[53] Outside of an occasional brief nod to Douglas's intimate life – such as Margaret Ormsby's reference to him as a "devoted family man" and John Adams's fine popular study of Douglas and Connolly – studies of Douglas as a fur trader and governor run a separate track from those of him as a family member.[54] Yet circuits of family and kin – and especially ties between fathers- and brothers-in-law – run subcutaneous throughout this history, and indeed throughout the history of nineteenth-century politics, and as Gail Cuthbert Brandt showed us some time ago, there is enormous potential for re-reading nineteenth-century politics if we take on board the feminist insight that the personal and political can only be presumed separate at great cost.[55]

These histories also speak to the challenges and enormous interpretative possibilities of analyzing the past as gendered and doing so in a way that acknowledges women as full historical actors. Amelia Connolly is a major figure in this study but one that, in some ways, I know little about. She left a very modest written archive. Amelia received letters and read them with pleasure, but unlike her sister Marguerite Connolly, who wrote in a beautiful hand, she wrote none beyond short notes acknowledging gifts or turning down invitations. Douglas explained that "we cannot induce her to take pen in hand."[56] Visitors to Victoria often wrote about Amelia but rarely offered more than the most expected of racial stereotypes. The records left by Douglas, the couple's children, and some friends make clear how significant Amelia was to them and to their extended network of friends and kin in Victoria. They emphasize her affection for the children, grandchildren, and the children put under her care and her efforts to keep them close to her; how she tended the sick and the dead; and the remarkable gardens and chickens she kept. Metis visitors remember her joy at hearing what Connolly called "the old language," or conversation "in French, in Indian and in mixed English," and her fondness for country foods such as buffalo tongue and camas, an edible root.[57]

But these are snippets and the snippets of others; they do not and cannot shift the fact that the archive of the Douglas family is one in which men speak with greater force and regularity than women. This disparity reflects the uneven relationship between oral indigenous cultures and literate European or imperial ones as well as the variable access men and women had to writing and archival preservation. The discipline of history was born alongside the nation-state in the late nineteenth-century, and at its disciplinary core lay a linked set of scholarly conventions that have worked to privilege alphabetic textual records and treat the oral, the material, and the performative as less stable sources of historical knowledge.[58] This has come alongside the discipline's intentional and highly strategic coding as masculine and its tendency to exclude or invalidate indigenous scholars.[59] Instead of seeing the enormous unevenness of the Douglas family archive as an impediment, I am following Antoinette Burton's call to make the colonial archive a constituent part of the history to be analyzed.[60] Read from this perspective, the limitations as well as possibilities of the Douglas archive reveal not only much about the nineteenth-century colonial societies in which Douglas and Connolly lived but also much about the early-twentieth-century world that was critical to identifying and preserving an official archive and the late-twentieth-century world that produced historical knowledge, both scholarly and popular, about Douglas and, to a much lesser extent, his family.[61]

This is an essay about one family during the nineteenth century and what it can tell us about the writing of gender and women's history in the Canadian context. Like Kristina Llewellen's study of Hazel Chong in this volume, this chapter tracks people whose lives were forged at the juncture of multiple racial identities and currents of racial meaning. This history of James Douglas and Amelia Connolly reminds us of the power of a historical practice that reaches beyond contemporary national borders. Theirs was a history lived in the Caribbean, in the United Kingdom, and in parts of North America that were colonies, some later becoming parts of the United States and some Canada, and we need to pay attention to all of these spaces and histories to make sense of their lives. The challenges to writing feminist and postcolonial history remain. So do the possibilities. The history of Connolly, Douglas, and their family suggests how we might read the material we have often bracketed as conventional political history – governors and colonies – as gendered history. Douglas's history as a political figure is inseparable from his history as a man, a father, and a husband.

NOTES

I would like to acknowledge the support of the Canada Research Chairs program. Jarett Henderson, Laura Ishiguro, and Anne Lindsay contributed to the research here. John Adams, Charlotte Girard, and Sylvia Van Kirk all shared their knowledge with me, and conversations with Jean Barman, Bettina Bradbury, Karen Dubinsky,

Ryan Eyford, Gerry Friesen, Jean Friesen, and Mary Jane Logan McCallum have been critical to my thinking, and I am grateful for their engagement.

1 See, for instance, Walter Sage, *Sir James Douglas* (Toronto: Ryerson Press, 1930); Sylvia Van Kirk, *"Many Tender Ties": Women in Fur Trade Society in Western Canada, 1670–1870* (Winnipeg: Watson and Dwyer, 1980); John Raulston Saul, *A Fair Country: Telling Truths about Canada* (Toronto: Viking, 2008).

2 See *Royal Gazette* (Demerara and Berbice), 29 October 1825, 2. Charlotte Girard's research on Douglas deserves mention and credit. See Charlotte S.M. Girard, "Sir James Douglas' School Days," *BC Studies* 35 (Autumn 1977): 56–63; "Sir James Douglas' Mother and Grandmother," *BC Studies* 44 (Winter 1979–80): 25–31; and "Some Further Notes on the Douglas Family," *BC Studies* 72 (Winter 1986–87): 3–27. For evidence of Ritchie's slaveholding in both Demerara and Barbados, see petition of Rebecca Ritchie, 12 July 1820, in "Petitions, March 1820 to 1 October 1820–1821," Walter Rodney Archives (WRA), Georgetown, Guyana, A01/5. According to the petition, Ritchie entered Demerara with twenty-six enslaved men and women, which put her well above the average urban householder in Guyana, who owned fewer than six slaves. See Alvin O. Thompson, *Unprofitable Servants: Crown Slaves in Berbice, Guyana, 1803–1831* (Kingston: University of West Indies Press, 2002).

3 Durba Ghosh, *Sex and the Family in Colonial India: The Making of Empire* (Cambridge: Cambridge University Press, 2005), 253.

4 See Girard, "Sir James Douglas' Mother and Grandmother" and "Some Further Notes on the Douglas Family," and see W. Kaye Lamb, "Some Notes on the Douglas Family," *British Columbia Historical Quarterly* 17, 1–2 (1953): 41–51.

5 Will of John Douglas, 16 April 1841, National Archives of Scotland, SC70/1/60, 546–51. See also Girard, "Some Further Notes," 12.

6 Henry Kirke, *Twenty-Five Years in British Guiana* (London: Sampson Low, Marston and Co., 1898), 45.

7 Henry Bolingbroke, *A Voyage to the Demerary, Containing a Statistical Account of the Settlements There, and Those on the Essequebo, the Berbice, and Other Contiguous Rivers of Guyana* (Norwich: Richard Phillips, 1807), 43.

8 "Further Papers Relating to Slaves in the West Indies (Berbice)," in House of Commons (Britain), *Papers and Correspondence Relating to New South Wales Magistrates; The West Indies; Liberated Africans; Colonial and Slave Population; Slaves; The Slave Trade; &c.,"* Session 2 February to 31 May 1826, vol. 16, 12.

9 Cecilia A. Green, "Hierarchies of Whiteness in the Geographies of Empire: Thomas Thistlewood and the Barretts of Jamaica," *New West Indian Guide/Nieuwe West-Indishce Gids* 80, 1–2 (2006): 4–53. See also her "'A Civil Inconvenience'? The Vexed Question of Slave Marriage in the British West Indies," *Law and History Review* 25, 1 (2007): 1–59.

10 Catherine Hall, *Civilizing Subjects: Metropole and Colony in the English Imagination, 1830–1867* (Chicago: University of Chicago Press, 2002), 9.

11 Raymond T. Smith, "Hierarchy and the Dual Marriage System in West Indian Society," in *Gender and Kinship: Essays toward a Unified Analysis*, ed. Jane Fishburne Collier and Sylvia Junko Yanagisako (Palo Alto, CA: Stanford University Press, 1987). See also his *The Negro Family in British Guiana: Family, Structure, and Social Status*

in Two Villages (London: Routledge and Kegan Paul, 1956); *Kinship and Class in the West Indies: A Genealogical Study of Jamaica and Guyana* (Cambridge: Cambridge University Press, 1988); and Raymond T. Smith, *The Matrifocal Family: Power, Pluralism, and Politics* (New York: Routledge, 1996).

12 Nell Irvin Painter, "Women and Freud: A Non-Exceptionalist Approach to Race, Class, and Gender in the Slave South," in *Feminists Revision History*, ed. Ann-Louise Shapiro (New Brunswick, NJ: Rutgers University Press, 1994).

13 Ghosh, *Sex and Family*, 9.

14 See Girard, "Sir James Douglas' School Days," 57.

15 See, for a summary, Margaret Ormsby, "Douglas, Sir James," *Dictionary of Canadian Biography*, http://www.biographi.ca.

16 Sylvia Van Kirk, *"Many Tender Ties."* For a more recent reflection, see Sylvia Van Kirk, "From 'Marrying-In' to 'Marrying-Out': Changing Patterns of Aboriginal/Non-Aboriginal Marriage in Colonial Canada," *Frontiers: A Journal of Women Studies* 23, 3 (2002): 1–11. Recent work on fur trade marriage includes Heather Devine, *The People Who Own Themselves: Aboriginal Ethnogenesis in a Canadian Family, 1660–1900* (Calgary: University of Calgary Press, 2005); Susan Sleeper-Smith *Indian Women and French Men: Rethinking Cultural Encounter in the Western Great Lakes* (Amherst: University of Massachusetts Press, 2001); Carolyn Podruchny, *Making the Voyageur World: Travelers and Traders in the North American Fur Trade* (Toronto: University of Toronto Press, 2006); and Brenda Macdougall, *One of the Family: Metis Culture in Nineteenth-Century Saskatchewan* (Vancouver: UBC Press, 2009).

17 "Servants Characters and Staff Records," Hudson's Bay Company Archives (HBCA), A 34/1, 82.

18 George McDougall to John McLeod, 8 March 1828, journals and correspondence of John McLeod, British Columbia Archives (BCA), AB 40 M22K, transcript, 107.

19 James Douglas, "Private Account," BCA, Add Mss B/90/1, entry for 1 June 1827.

20 See, on them, Bruce Peel, "Connolly, William," *Dictionary of Canadian Biography*, vol. 7, and Bruce Peel, "Connolly, Suzanne," *Dictionary of Canadian Biography*, vol. 9, both accessed at biography.ca.

21 Justice Samuel Monk, *Connolly vs. Woolrich and Johnson et al., Lower Canada Jurist: Collection de decisions du Bas Canada*, vol. 11 (Montreal: John Lovell, 1867), 197. Hereafter *Connolly vs. Woolrich.*

22 Ibid., 234.

23 Jennifer S.H. Brown, *Strangers in Blood: Fur Trade Families in Indian Country* (Vancouver: UBC Press, 1980), Chap. 3.

24 Francis Ermatinger to Edward Ermatinger, 5 March 1829, in *Fur Trade Letters of Francis Ermatinger: Written to His Brother Edward during His Service with the Hudson's Bay Company, 1818–1853*, ed. Lois Halliday McDonald (Glendale, CA: Arthur H. Clarke Company, 1980), 92.

25 Francis Ermatinger to Edward Ermatinger, 4 March 1830, in McDonald, ed., *Fur Trade Letters of Francis Ermatinger*, 132.

26 Archibald McDonald to Edward Ermatinger, 20 February 1831, in Jean Murray Cole, *This Blessed Wilderness: Archibald McDonald's Letters from the Columbia, 1822–44* (Vancouver: UBC Press, 2001), 91.

27 Herbert Beaver to Benjamin Harrison, 10 March 1837, in Jesset, ed., *Reports and Letters of Herbert Beaver*, 35.
28 Herbert Beaver to Governor and Committee, in Jesset, ed., *Reports and Letters of Herbert Beaver*, 2 October 1838, 120.
29 W. Kaye Lamb, "The James Douglas Report on the 'Beaver Affair,'" *Oregon Historical Quarterly* 18 (March 1946): 19–28.
30 James Douglas to Herbert Beaver, 2 October 1838, in Jesset, ed., *Reports and Letters of Herbert Beaver*, 144.
31 Undated note, James Douglas, "Notebook and Clipping Book," "Journals, Notebooks and Clipping Books, etc., 1835–1873," BCA, MS 0678, microfilm A00792 (hereafter "Notebook and Clipping Book").
32 Douglas, "Qualities Requisite to Make Marriage Happy," in "Notebook and Clipping Book," n.p.
33 Douglas, "Mrs. Sigourney, On Domestic Employments," in "Notebook and Clipping Book," n.p.
34 Douglas, "Notebook and Clipping Book," n.p.
35 James Douglas to Governor, Deputy Governor, and Committee of Hon. Hudson's Bay Co., 5 October 1838, in Jesset, ed., *Reports and Letters of Herbert Beaver*, 141.
36 "The Educated Female," in "Notebook and Clipping Book," n.p.
37 James Douglas to James Hargrave, 24 March 1842, in G.P. De T. Glazebrook, ed., *The Hargrave Correspondence, 1821–1843* (Toronto: Champlain Society, 1938), 381.
38 James Douglas to James Hargrave, 26 February 1840, in Glazebrook, ed., *Hargrave Correspondence*, 311.
39 "Notes," n.d., in James Douglas, "Private Account," BCA, Add Mss B/90/1, n.p.
40 *Connolly vs. Woolrich*, 236.
41 Ibid., 199.
42 Sidney L. Harring, *White Man's Law: Native People in Nineteenth-Century Canadian Jurisprudence* (Toronto: University of Toronto Press, 1998), 169. See also Constance Backhouse, *Petticoats and Prejudice: Women and Law in Nineteenth-Century Canada* (Toronto: Osgood Society for Canadian Legal History/Women's Press, 1991), 11–13, and Sarah Carter, *The Importance of Being Monogamous: Marriage and Nation-Building in Western Canada until 1915* (Alberta: University of Alberta Press, 2008), Chap. 4.
43 *Connolly vs. Woolrich*, 214.
44 Harring, *White Man's Law*, 170.
45 James Douglas to Mr. Armstrong, 23 September 1867, in private letter book of Sir James Douglas, correspondence outward, 22 March 1867–11 October 1870, transcript, BCA, Add Mss B/40/2 (hereafter "Private Letter Book").
46 Harring, *White Man's Law*, 172, 173.
47 James Douglas to Jane Douglas, 13 July 1868, "Private Letter Book." On the Douglas family in nineteenth-century Victoria, see Sylvia Van Kirk, "Tracing the Fortunes of Five Founding Families of Victoria," *BC Studies* 115–16 (Autumn-Winter 1997–98): 148–79; Sylvia Van Kirk, "Colonised Lives: The Native Wives and Daughters of Five Founding Families of Victoria," *Pacific Empire: Essays in Honour of Glyndwr Williams*, ed. Alan Frost and Jane Samson (Melbourne: Melbourne University Press, 1997), 215–36; Sylvia Van Kirk, "A Transnational Family in the

Pacific North West: Reflecting on Race and Gender in Women's History," in Elizabeth Jameson and Shelia McManus, eds., *One Step over the Line: Toward a History of Women in the North American Wests* (Edmonton: University of Alberta Press, 2008).

48 Carter, *The Importance of Being Monogamous,* and Jennifer S.H. Brown, "A Partial Truth: A Closer Look at Fur Trade Marriage," in *From Rupert's Land to Canada: Essays in Honour of John E. Foster,* ed. Ted Binnema, Gerhard Ens, and R.C. McLeod (Edmonton: University of Alberta Press, 2002), 59–80.

49 Ryan Eyford, "Slave Owner, Missionary, and Colonization Agent: The Transnational Life of John Taylor, 1835–1884," in *Within and Without the Nation: Transnational and Canadian History,* ed. Adele Perry, Karen Dubinsky, and Henry Yu, (Toronto: University of Toronto Press, in press).

50 See, for instance, Hall, *Civilizing Subjects;* Ann Laura Stoler, ed., *Haunted by Empire: Geographies of Intimacy in North American History* (Durham, NC: Duke University Press, 2006); Antoinette Burton, "Who Needs the Nation? Interrogating 'British History,'" *Journal of Historical Sociology* 10, 3 (1997): 227–48; David Lambert and Alan Lester, eds., *Colonial Lives across the British Empire* (Cambridge: Cambridge University Press, 2006); Tony Ballantyne, *Orientalism and Race: Arayanism and the British Empire* (London: Palgrave, 2001); and Ann Curthoys and Marilyn Lake, eds., *Connected Worlds: History in Transnational Perspective* (Canberra: ANU E Press, 2005).

51 Van Kirk, *"Many Tender Ties";* Brown, *Strangers in Blood;* and Linda Kealey, ed., *A Not Unreasonable Claim: Women and Reform in Canada, 1880s–1920s* (Toronto: Canadian Women's Educational Press, 1979).

52 See, for instance, Karen Dubinsky, *Babies without Borders: Adoption and Migration across the Americas* (Toronto/New York: University of Toronto Press/New York University Press, 2010); Cecilia Morgan, *A Happy Holiday: English Canadians and Transatlantic Tourism, 1870–1930* (Toronto: University of Toronto Press, 2008); and Jameson and McManus, *One Step over the Line.*

53 See, for instance, Cole Harris, *Making Native Space: Colonialism, Resistance, and Reserves in British Columbia* (Vancouver, UBC Press, 2003), and Paul Tennant, *Aboriginal Peoples and Politics: The Indian Land Question in British Columbia, 1849–1989* (Vancouver: UBC Press, 1990).

54 Ormsby, "Douglas"; John Adams, *Old Square Toes and His Lady: The Life of James and Amelia Douglas* (Victoria: Horsdal and Schubert, 2001).

55 Gail Cuthbert Brandt, "National Unity and the Politics of Political History," *Journal of the Canadian Historical Association* 3 (1992): 3–11.

56 James Douglas to Martha Douglas, 4 November 1873, "Letters to Martha Douglas, 30 October 1871 to 27 May 1874," Transcript, BCA B/40/4A.

57 Christina McDonald McKenzie Williams, "The Daughter of Angus McDonald," *Washington Historical Quarterly* 13 (1922): 116; F.W. Howay, William S. Lewis, and Jacob A. Meyers, "Angus McDonald: A Few Items of the West," *Washington Historical Quarterly* 8, 3 (1917): 225.

58 See Jorge Cañizares-Esguerra, *How to Write the History of the New World: Histories, Epistemologies, and Identities in the Eighteenth-Century Atlantic World* (Palo Alto, CA: Stanford University Press, 2001).

59 See Donald A. Wright, *The Professionalization of History in English Canada* (Toronto: University of Toronto Press, 2005), Chap. 5, and Mary Jane Logan McCallum, "Indigenous Labor and Indigenous History," *American Indian Quarterly* 33, 4 (2009): 523–44. On the wider context, see Bonnie G. Smith, *The Gender of History: Men, Women, and Historical Practice* (Cambridge, MA: Harvard University Press, 1999).

60 Antoinette Burton, *Dwelling in the Archive: Women Writing House, Home, and History in Late Colonial India* (London: Oxford, 2003); Antoinette Burton, ed., *Archive Stories: Facts, Fictions, and the Writing of History* (Chapel Hill, NC: Duke University Press, 2006).

61 See Chad Reimer, *Writing British Columbia History, 1784–1958* (Vancouver: UBC Press, 2009).

2

Using Diaries to Explore the Shared Worlds of Family and Community in Nineteenth-Century New Brunswick

GAIL G. CAMPBELL

Diaries offer insights into the dynamics of family and community life in past times. Historians seeking such insights must consider the personalities of the diarists, the nature of the lives they led, and the private purpose of the individual diary. The diarist's particular perspective, then, is the first category of analysis. That perspective is shaped by intersections of gender, age, class, culture, time, and place. Using gender as a category of analysis, this chapter draws on men's and women's diaries to provide intersecting perspectives on the nature of the insights diaries can offer into the dynamics of family and community in nineteenth-century New Brunswick. Gender may appear to be the primary determinant, yet age – or one's stage in the life course – is at least as significant, as Heidi Macdonald's chapter in this collection also shows. Although diaries of people of all ages offer insights into the nature of family life, for the historian interested in broader community patterns, the often mundane daily entries of the middle-aged are more intrinsically interesting than the livelier entries of the young. I have, therefore, chosen to focus on late-middle-aged, married diarists, a cohort central to family and community life. As Adele Perry notes in her chapter, archives generally collected more material about men's lives, and men's diaries were more likely to be retained and published than were women's diaries. Juxtaposing women's and men's diaries demonstrates not only that we cannot understand the worlds of household and community if we view them through a single lens but also that women's angle of vision provides a richer and more comprehensive perspective on community as well as on family life than can be gained from men's diaries alone. By examining women's diaries alongside those of men, we may readily appreciate that men's constructions of their world have coloured our perceptions of the gendered nature of private and public life in past times.

In nineteenth-century New Brunswick, as elsewhere, diary keeping was largely confined to the middle classes and was most common among Protestants.[1] The eight diarists examined here fit this description. Thus, although Acadians constituted almost 20 percent and Roman Catholics over 30 percent of the province's population between 1851 and 1881, neither of these groups is represented among these diarists. Five – Thomas Miles (b. 1789), James Brown (b. 1790), Janet MacDonald (b. 1795), David Wetmore (b. 1836), and Ann Eliza Moore (b. 1837) – lived in rural communities. Three – Lucy Morrison (b. 1823), John Robinson (b. 1824), and Sophy Carman (b. 1828) – lived in the province's capital.[2] All but James Brown, who arrived in the province in 1810, were New Brunswick-born.

At mid-century, in New Brunswick, as elsewhere in British North America, the majority of families were farm families. The experiences of three diarists – Thomas Miles of Sunbury County on the St. John River just east of Fredericton, James Brown of Charlotte County in the southwest corner of the province, and Janet MacDonald of Queen's County on the lower St. John River – might be considered representative of the most successful of such families, their success depending, in part, on their ability to supplement their farm earnings with other income. As well as managing productive farms, both Miles and Brown represented their counties in New Brunswick's legislative assembly and served in other capacities, most notably as superintendents of roads, at both local and provincial levels. Janet MacDonald's husband and sons ran a sawmill, which supplemented the farm income. All three diaries provide insight into the day-to-day operation of an established family farm.

Although the two men were rooted in their families, the work of the farm as presented in their diaries was largely a male preserve. Miles's entry for a warm Saturday in May 1849 was typical: "Wm spread manure, I sow seven bushels black oats ... near the back of the meadow. Wood harrows them in & ploughs afternoon. Alex has two bushels of the Duffy oats ... to sow in front of the road near the fence. Sally, Woody & children come."[3] Similarly, in May 1858, James Brown "[s]owed oats and grass seed where we had potatoes last year, harrowed and bushed the ground, and put up the fences. Had a large party at the house in the evening. Cold."[4] Contrast this with Janet MacDonald's portrayal of farm work on a windy day in May 1861: "They are sawing. It rained today. Mr. Harris is here. We are picking wool. Beckah is helping." And the following day, she wrote: "Finished picking wool today. It is clear and warm. They are sawing. George ploughing."[5] Here, we see the family economic unit at work.

Women are not absent from the pages of men's diaries: Thomas Miles's wife, Ann Carmen, "my companion who is only eight months younger than myself," figures largely in his diary.[6] As matriarch and family caregiver, she was called upon whenever their beloved Sally, the eldest of their three children and their only daughter, fell ill. Thus, on a February evening in 1850, after entertaining six guests at dinner, five of whom stayed to tea, "Mrs. Miles goes up with Woody to see Sally who is sick." She stayed for nine days, her husband anxiously monitoring Sally's progress and visiting occasionally.[7] But Miles's diary provides no sense of his wife's daily routine. Only once, and this in preparation for a snowstorm, when he reported that he got the young bull in from the woods, while the hired hand sawed wood, did he note that "Mrs Miles" was making candles.[8] And unlike Janet MacDonald, Ann is not found picking or washing wool. Nonetheless, "Mrs Miles" was undoubtedly responsible for the twenty-six pounds of wool salvaged "from 7 sheep-skins," the sheep having been "killed by Miss Harding's dog on the 13th January last."[9] Miles had no reason to record who had undertaken this unanticipated job any more than who had churned the butter or sowed the oats or other products regularly delivered to family and friends as well as to market. Rather, the inclusive language in his records of business transactions – reports of people sowing seeds, delivering goods to market, repairing chairs "for us" – recognizes the contributions of all members of the household to the family economy.

James Brown's household included his second wife, Catherine Cameron Gillespie, and young family. Catherine was often left to manage the household on her own as her husband's responsibilities as a member of the legislative assembly, inspector of schools, and superintendent of roads took him away from the family for weeks and months at a time. Brown depended on his adult sons from his first marriage to help maintain the farm when he was at home and to ensure its smooth operation when he was away.[10] But with his sons now married and heading their own households, these arrangements increasingly involved negotiation, and in 1857 they broke down altogether. During Brown's absence, his eldest son, James Jr., seeking to cover a debt he had incurred, gave up a deed for a farm his father had acquired. Nor had James paid his brothers for their work on the home farm.[11] Faced with the necessity of making good his son's debts, Brown demonstrated his

confidence in his wife's competence by assigning her the management of
the farm during his absences.[12] Yet, although Catharine became the pivot
around which Brown's household revolved, taking responsibility for provi-
sioning the family and paying her stepsons for tasks undertaken while their
father was away, we learn little more than this from her husband's diary.

The omission in the men's diaries of any mention of their wives' or
daughters' routine contributions to the work of the farm reflects the physical separation of women's and men's work, especially on well-established
farms. In the cadences of Janet MacDonald's diary, bespeaking the daily
and seasonal rhythms of farm life, this physical separation of work emerges
as a companionable division of labour. "They are sawing, we are quilting.
George and B. and Jemima has gone over the lake. Father gathering apples.
Malcolm's birthday, he is twenty-one." Here, the family farm emerges as a
panorama of activities, of coming and going, of hard work relieved by more
leisurely tasks, with time for contemplation: "N.E. wind, clear and fine. They
are digging. G. finished this forenoon, then helped James. D. in the shop to
work. This is washing day. I picked a bowl of blackberries this afternoon.
The comet looks beautiful; I go and look at it every evening." In that solitary
pleasure, at the end of a late September day in 1858, Janet MacDonald un-
selfconsciously situates herself within a wider frame: like people the world
over, she was watching the progress of Donati's Comet.[13]

Work and leisure intersect naturally in MacDonald's record of farm life
as she takes her grandchildren berry picking or as a son and daughter-in-
law combine business and pleasure when they go "over the lake" on a warm
summer's day. In contrast, in the Miles and Brown diaries, which provide
more detailed snapshots of particular aspects of farm work – with male
family members, farm hands, and sometimes neighbours all busy at specific
tasks – there is a clear, if unstated, distinction between the physical work of
the farm and other business or leisure activities. In MacDonald's diary, work
and visiting blend seamlessly, possibly because visitors often necessitated
food preparation on the part of the women, possibly because visits often
had work-related purposes. Although the work of the farm portrayed in the
men's diaries may seem unrelenting, MacDonald's record mediates this picture. "They are sawing and ploughing. We are washing today," she reported
one day in early May 1859. "I took their dinners down today. Fred went with
me."[14] And though we cannot be sure, we may imagine the men, pausing in
their work when they see grandmother and grandson crossing the fields,
setting aside their tools for a brief respite from their labour, perhaps taking
pleasure in congenial conversation along with their dinner.

Readers require no imagination to discern that all three diarists were firmly embedded within a strong network of extended kin. Unlike James Brown, a Scot who had arrived in New Brunswick at the age of twenty, MacDonald and Miles had siblings as well as children living close by. Betsy Miles, sister to Ann and the widow of Thomas's brother George, managed her own farm, and Miles regularly transacted business with her. In May 1841, he noted that his son "Odber got a load of hay from Betsy with his horse and cart ... and one with my oxen & cart ... Exchanged an old horse called 'Dick the Thresher' with Betsy Miles for a colt she had from Mc Connacher ... Got Cate shod by McEwin & paid 2/6 – borrowed 1/10½ from Betsy."[15] Janet MacDonald had siblings living nearby. And three of her six sons and their wives were involved in the family's farming and milling operations. For MacDonald, this meant that she could depend on the help of daughters-in-law in the production of wool, among other tasks.

Moving beyond the bonds of family, farm work, by its nature, encouraged patterns of mutuality that cemented ties of neighbourhood and community. These ties promoted and facilitated the kind of sociability described in all three diaries. That business and pleasure could be combined in a variety of ways is suggested by an entry in Janet MacDonald's diary involving her husband ("Father"); four of her adult children (Susan, James, Donald, and William); her daughter-in-law Sally; and her five-year-old grandson Fred:

> N.W. wind, clear and fine. James went to Webster's mill. Fred went with him. They cleaned the grain this morning ... Father went over in the afternoon to wait for the grist. Donald and William is over to Susan's. They have a barn raised this afternoon. Annabell Cameron and Adaline McDonald was over today. Mary and Elinor went down to James Hendry's after the brass kettle and saw a bear along the road. This forenoon I was twisting thread and yarn. Mary is ironing. Sally and Elinor is cleaning the chamber and cellar.[16]

As Donica Belisle's chapter in this volume demonstrates for a much later period, both men and women combined work and heterosexual sociability. Work bees, such as Susan's barn raising, brought friends and family together in a spirit of mutuality and sociability. A measure of reciprocal work exchange, work bees can sometimes be used to determine the boundaries of neighbourhoods.[17]

Similarly, visiting patterns can be used to map neighbourhood and community networks.[18] Nineteenth-century New Brunswick farms were far from isolated, and all three diarists offer a picture of farm life as an endless round of visiting among family and friends, no matter what the weather. On a rainy day in August, Thomas and Ann Miles took the opportunity to entertain: "Young Clowes Carman with us all day & Charles Harrison & Elizabeth & Elijah Miles & Charles & Nancy to tea."[19] But visiting did not require a rainy day. On a Friday in mid-July, following the departure of an overnight guest, Janet MacDonald "[w]alked down to James Hendry's ... In the evening Alexander came after me with the wagon. It is still and beautiful this evening, it lightens some."[20] And on a fine day at the height of haying season, James Brown "[h]ad the Messrs Scott and their families to see us, and a large party of relatives and friends. Spent the day in rambling about the fields & visiting the haunts of auld lang syne. Splendid day."[21] Although all three diarists offer insight into the shared worlds of family and community, because Janet MacDonald recorded the visiting patterns of other members of the family as well as her own, the parameters of family and community emerge most clearly in her diary.

Ann Eliza Moore of Hopewell Hill, a rural community in Albert County, provides a different, but equally valuable, lens on family and community life. Widowed with three small children in 1866, Ann Eliza Rogers Gallacher married Lemuel Moore – a carpenter, farmer, and sometime storekeeper – three years later. By 1888, she was fifty-one years old and the mother of eight. The Moores, like the MacDonald and Miles families, were embedded in a web of extended kin, many of whom lived nearby. On 27 April, Ann Eliza and her eighteen-year-old daughter, Ellie, "went up to see Aunt Susan Clarke"; on 29 May, her two youngest sons, eleven-year-old Donald and eight-year-old Dodge, "went up to their Uncle George's to visit Willie Patchell, this is his 11th birthday"; and on 3 June, "Lemuel and I went up to his father's for tea." But Moore's diary, which rarely focuses on the routine work of the household, further reveals that community networks extended well beyond the bounds of family and neighbourhood, that young people, including adolescent girls, ranged widely throughout the countryside. In mid-July, on a day when their older sister Achsah had gone to Hillsborough to visit friends, Moore's younger daughters, Ellie and sixteen-year-old Jennie, went on a picnic at the Cape.[22] On 25 August, "Achsah & Ellie went to Albert in the [horse] cars, will walk back. Will call at Mr Embre's. Ellie wants a recommendation to take to Normal school."[23]

Moreover, Ann Eliza Moore's diary situates her community of Hopewell Hill within an even broader frame. From its earliest days, Hopewell, bordering on the Bay of Fundy, had been a community in motion. As an adolescent,

Ann Eliza had observed the comings and goings of members of her community, and during her first marriage, she had, herself, been among the comers and goers. In the nineteenth century, ships built in Albert County plied the oceans of the world, creating a cosmopolitan society with networks of family and friends extending southward to the "Boston States" and eastward across the Atlantic to Liverpool. Regular shipping routes meant that regular visits rarely proved difficult. However, although migration of individuals and families had long been common, a greater movement was now in train. The economic downturn of the late 1880s led to significant outmigration from many areas of New Brunswick. The nature of this outmigration, and the continuing role of chain migration in the movement, is captured effectively in Ann Eliza Moore's 1888 diary entries. On 12 April, she reported that "Charles Cutter & wife (Annie Bacon) & children came from Calafornia to visit her people. They have been gone 7 years." A month later, on 14 May, she commented: "Dan Lynds was here to tea last evening. He with several others are going to Calafornia in a few weeks." By 23 May, the party was on its way, and Moore recorded, "Charley Cutter, wife & children have gone back to Calafornia. Others went with them." She names ten men and three women and refers to yet more who accompanied the Cutters. In further noting that "[t]hey are going via Montreal. They will see Frank" (her son, then living in LaConner, Washington) "& Mary" (her sister, whose family had settled in New Westminster, BC), Moore suggests how the recently completed Canadian Pacific Railway facilitated community networks that spanned the continent. On 11 June comes "word from out West. Got there all right." Few diarists observed demographic patterns as systematically or with as much informed commentary as Ann Eliza Moore. Her diary documents the changing nature of community during one woman's lifetime. Moore's purpose in keeping her diary was as important as her particular personality, and perhaps more important than her gender, in determining her construction of her world.

Men and women who kept diaries as a record of their business dealings constructed their world differently from those who kept a more personal record. In early May 1878, David Wetmore, a market gardener and farmer on the Kingston Peninsula, near Saint John, reported:

A dull day. The weather has not been very good for farming for the last week. Finished taking the brush off strawberries today. I think it would have been as well if the strawberries had been left covered till about this time but raspberries should be up earlier. Set about 1/3 of an acre of raspberries today ... Commenced to set some strawberries in the same field & got about 1000 set. Pulled & took 6 lbs rhubarb to the city yesterday.

By 24 May, he had sent 1,039 pounds of rhubarb to market.[24]

The diary of Lucy Morrison, a commercial gardener in Fredericton, parallels Wetmore's in tone and approach. In early July 1881, Morrison "was out 4 a.m. making boquets for Miss Howies wedding. Lawrence has 5 long trenches dug for celery & 9 half length ones. I was picking strawberries & gooseberries most of today. Have picked 6½ large pails of gooseberries. Potted a large number of verbena & Heliotrope cuttings. Cinnerara seed up in saucer." By 8 July, she had sent away 1,281 celery plants and had orders for 350 more.[25]

Differences between the two diaries reflect gendered thinking and expectations. As a married, middle-class woman, Lucy Morrison had family and social responsibilities that went beyond superintending the work of the household. Nor could her highly competent housekeeper, Agnes McNabb, relieve her of the dual roles played by women in nurturing the bonds of extended family and cultivating the bonds of community. In July 1881 – busy as she was supplying flowers, berries, and celery to customers as far away as Saint John – Lucy Morrison recorded receiving callers on eight separate days. These visitors included a business associate of her husband, who stayed overnight. Morrison herself made an equal number of calls, some accompanied by relatives who visited between 21 and 28 July. She had little time to visit her daughter-in-law, Kate, who gave birth to a baby on 5 July. Business concerns remained the focus of her diary, however, and on 26 July, she noted curtly, "Company keeping all my work back."[26]

That David Wetmore recorded no such interruptions in the document he referred to as his "farm diary" should not lead us to conclude that his life was fully taken up with his commercial enterprise.[27] Certainly, his wife Minta Flewelling's 1873–74 diary indicates that the couple regularly received a significant number of callers.[28] Other documents reveal that in addition to serving as a school trustee and an Anglican church warden, Wetmore was active in the local Agricultural Society, the temperance movement, the Masonic Lodge, and the Kings County militia.[29] Although these activities were occasionally hinted at in earlier diaries, by 1878, when his market-gardening enterprise was at its height, Wetmore had streamlined his entries to focus exclusively on his business.

The parallels between the Morrison and Wetmore diaries demonstrate that an author's particular purpose in keeping a diary may be more important than gender in determining the nature of the information recorded.

At the same time, a comparison of the two diaries affords insight into the gendered nature of the diarists' shared worlds of family and community. Lucy Morrison's earlier diaries hint that her decision to turn her hobby into a commercial enterprise had a good deal to do with the precariousness of her husband's sawmill operations. As she made the transition, she, too, streamlined her diary entries to focus on her business. Yet, even as she established a thriving business, which made a significant contribution to the family economy, she also recorded the progress of John's mill and continued to maintain her position as a respectable middle-class matron.[30] Her diary, like Janet MacDonald's, provides a more comprehensive portrait of family and community by widening the lens.

John Robinson and Sophy Carman were, like Lucy Morrison, residents of Fredericton during the 1870s. Juxtaposing their diaries provides a window on urban life. While Morrison's business and social life intersected in her diary, Robinson, unlike the other male diarists examined, recorded little about his work. Instead, his diary entries parallel those of Sophy Carman, as he situated himself and his wife, Mary Hyde Roberts, whom he calls P[olly], within a broad social network of family and friends.

In town, as in the country, the world of family and community intersected in a wide variety of private and public settings. On a Thursday in early February 1873, Sophy Carman "went to Prayers & to see Mrs G. Thompson (she has broken her arm) & Sarah Straton ... Had a little walk with dear Mrs Medley, she had been to see Mother." As her mother was "not very well," Carman "Made some Irish moss mixture & took it after tea." On 18 February, "Mrs Wilmot called & took me for a drive." On 21 April, Carman "went to invite the Stratons & Hanningtons to tea" and the next day was "[b]usy all the morning preparing for my tea-party," which "went off better than I expected."[31] Two years later, in 1875, Lucy Morrison found time to canvas on behalf of the British and Foreign Bible Society.[32] With her greenhouse in operation for the first winter, she reported that, on 10 March, she "[w]ent to party at Steadmans. Took splendid boquet." Like Carman, Morrison both visited and entertained friends. The first of April found her "out making calls," while the following day she had "The Mrs Hunt, Bedel & Inches here to tea." In June, Morrison organized "a croquet & evening party" for her sons and their friends: "11 girls & 8 young men. Passed off nicely." Croquet was a popular summer pastime for all ages, and on 8 July, the day she got the "1st celery set," Lucy and her husband, John, "Went to Judge Steadmans Croquet Party."[33] John Robinson also reported an active social life. On a January day in 1877, he took a "short walk with father. P & I to Mr Streets in evening." The following evening, "P & I with a party of 23 went to the Oromocto at 6 p.m in Richey & Bros large sleigh to a tea & fancy sale at the Temperance Hall, the proceeds for Church purposes, returned home arriving at 12:30."[34] In spring and summer, Robinson enjoyed fishing and hunting trips with his brothers and friends.[35] In winter, despite cold and often snowy weather, he reported long daily walks; on 26 January, his brother "Phil and I took my walk up Nashwaaksis to Gibson and home in 1¾ hours." In early February, "P. & I took my walk as far as St Marys then down town and home. After dinner we snowshoed across the river, first time for me on these for 10 or fifteen years. Ketchums snowshoes." This was practice for the main event, which occurred the following day: "Snowshoeing party at Govt House. P & I there."[36]

Although few enough Frederictonians received invitations to snowshoeing parties at Government House, the fact that the city was the seat of government shaped the community in myriad ways. Carman's barrister husband, William, depended for his livelihood on his government appointment as both clerk of pleas in the Supreme Court and clerk in equity, while Lucy Morrison did a brisk business in the sale of buttonholes when the legislature was in session. As the provincial capital, Fredericton, though small, was an intellectual and cultural centre that had a full range of educational institutions, from primary schools through to the collegiate school, the normal school, and the university. From John Robinson, we learn that Fredericton boasted a Boston Philharmonic Club, and from Sophy Carman, a voracious reader, we learn that Hall's Bookstore carried a wide selection of both fiction and nonfiction. Fundamental to that selection and to intellectual life in any nineteenth-century community were treatises on religion and religious belief. Unlike rural communities, where people might be dependent on itinerant ministers or on travelling some distance to attend church, the people of Fredericton could readily attend the church of their choice. Indeed, as members of the Church of England, the Carmans and Robinsons could choose between Christ Church Cathedral or the Parish Church of St Anne's.

Whether diarists lived in urban or rural communities, whether they walked to church or travelled some distance, the centrality of religion to family and community life emerges clearly in their diaries. On Sundays, regardless of the purpose of their diaries or the nature of their diary keeping, men and women described pausing for a day of rest, worship, and visiting. David Wetmore, an active member of the Anglican Church, rarely wrote in his diary on Sundays, but when he did pick up his pen, it was usually to record attending service at the Kingston Church. Sophy Carman, an equally active Anglican and a loyal friend and supporter of Bishop Medley and his wife, regularly attended services at the cathedral in Fredericton. On New Year's Day 1873, accompanied by her sister Jean, her son, Bliss, and her daughter, Murray, she "went to service at 11 a.m. Jean & I received the Holy Communion." She and Jean had also been "to mid-night service last night ... The Bp gave a beautiful sermon ... I wish I could remember every word, & live up to it." John Robinson and his family divided their loyalties between the cathedral and St. Anne's Parish Church, normally attending both of a Sunday. Thomas and Ann Miles also regularly attended the Anglican church, but although he was an Anglican church officer in his local parish, Miles did not approve of the changes that Bishop Medley had instituted. After attending a Good Friday service in Fredericton in1849, he confided to his diary, "sermon by the Bishop on the sufferings of the Savior – too much chanting for me."[37]

Perhaps as a result of this disaffection, or perhaps because his stepmother was a Baptist and his youngest son, George, had become a Baptist minister, Miles took more than a passing interest in Baptist meetings. When the Baptist Association Meeting was held in their community in July 1850, Thomas and Ann Miles went to the meeting house and "witnessed the baptism of young Day ... After prayer we repaired to the river side where Mr. Bill and the young man went down into the water and ... Mr. Bill baptized him by immersing him wholly in the water and saying 'on profession of thy faith I Baptize thee in the name of the Father and of the Son and of the Holy Ghost, Amen' ... Mr. Bill made ... strong persuasions to prevail upon Mrs. Miles & myself to be baptized on the morrow morning but without success. We came home in much the same state of mind as when we left." That Sunday, after stopping by the river to watch their son George baptize two converts, Thomas and Ann went on to the Anglican church, where they were pleased to find "a pretty large congregation."[38]

Thomas Miles was not unique, for in the nineteenth century people did move from one church to another.[39] Raised a Presbyterian, James Brown was eclectic in his choice of churches. On Sundays spent in Fredericton, he regularly attended the Presbyterian Kirk in the morning and the Methodist Church or the Baptist Chapel in the evening.[40] At home in St. David in May 1858, he reported: "Went to our own meeting house. Service by Dr George, the first Universalist discourse I have heard for a long time."[41] Ann Eliza Moore had attended the Presbyterian Church with her first husband, John Gallacher, but had returned to the Methodist fold. On 2 July 1889, she noted in her diary: "Dominion Day as yesterday was Sunday ... Methodist Sunday

School are having a concert this evening. Our children are singing and re-
citing." Like James Brown, Janet MacDonald had been raised a Presbyterian. Married to a Baptist, she converted to her husband's faith at the age
of forty-four. Having become a leading member of her local congregation,
MacDonald was particularly pleased with the results of a revival that swept
through her community in December 1858. She reported on 20 December:
"There is meeting at the meeting house at 10 A.M. ... a large congregation.
Mr Duval preached. His text ... 'and he went on his way rejoicing.' Then
we all repaired to the lake shore and there the Rev. Joseph C. Skinner baptized twelve willing converts," including "Emaline MacDonald, my grand-
daughter and my own dear William L. MacDonald," her son. Lucy Morrison
and her husband, John, remained staunch supporters and active members
of St. Paul's Presbyterian Church in Fredericton, and although no conver-
sion was involved, her brief diary entry, written on a Sunday in March 1875,
reflects the same kind of parental pleasure and satisfaction as that of Janet
MacDonald: "Sunday. Our communion. Willie the 1st time."[42] Family and
community, private and public life intersected in churches and here, too, the
diarists intersect in their various approaches to diary keeping.

Like the private world of the family, the public world of the community
was a shared world.[43] Women established, nurtured, and maintained neighbourhood networks, not only through regular visiting but also through caring for the sick and the reciprocal exchange of skills and goods. As well
as hosting quilting bees and carpet-making parties, women were central to
barn raisings and other men's bees and frolics, all of which involved food
and socializing, fundamental components of any such reciprocal exchange
of work. Indeed, women helped to define the parameters of neighbourhood
and community and to create the various public communities of interest or
of faith. Through sewing circles, box and pie socials, or tea and fancy sales,
such as the one the Robinsons attended, women not only raised money for
their churches, they also created public and often activist communities of
women. And many women teachers, including two of Ann Eliza Moore's
daughters, became part of a broader community of interest when they attended the government sponsored annual Teachers Institutes.

Nowhere is the shared world of community more clearly illustrated than
in men's and women's participation in the temperance movement, the most
popular voluntary movement of the nineteenth century, and one that, on
many levels, defined the parameters of middle-class respectability. While
men were generally the speakers at mixed-member temperance meetings,
women ensured the success of fundraising and other events. Thomas Miles

provides a rare description of the preparations for one such occasion. Things began modestly enough with "Mrs. Miles making a cake for a tea meeting." Four days later, "Betsy & Hannah Miles [were] at our house all day making cakes for tea meeting. Susan helps." The following day, "the cake makers are busy. Betsy & Susan goes home evening." The meeting itself was a gala affair that featured the leading temperance advocates in the province as speakers. Miles reported on the event:

> [A]ll hands all day preparing for the Tea Meeting – left home about two – met several at the Courthouse. There were 14 tables set, bountifully provided and most of them elegantly ornamented – the party consisting of about 300 persons arrived a little after six when the first set sat down to tea – after them a second and third set – which occupied the time until after nine.

No less than eight speeches, both serious and amusing, followed, until "[t]he last and least person, but not address – was delivered by Punch – Mr Needham who entertained the meeting for about an hour – during which time there was roars of laughter and merriment closed the scene about one o'clock."[44]

A generation younger than Miles, Ann Eliza Moore had been raised as a strong advocate of temperance, her father having opened a temperance inn in 1852, when she was not yet sixteen. She was a long-time member of the temperance lodge and had written for the "Division newspaper." Yet she was not intolerant; she viewed addiction as an affliction as much as a failing. Noting, in January 1874, that "Allen A. Peck was found dead in Noris's tavern yesterday morning at Hillsborough," she commented: "He has been drinking very bad lately." However, when "his people" refused to "bring him home and bury him," she judged it "a shame & disgrace to them to have him laid in a pauper's grave all because the poor fellow was a drunkard. Because he was not as strong minded as they. Every person is disgusted with their actions. Ah Foolish ones Who maketh them to differ."[45]

John Robinson, a man who depended on the liquor trade for his livelihood, could scarcely be expected to wholeheartedly support the temperance cause. He did not accompany his wife when she attended a "C of E. Temperance Meeting in evening. I to whist & came home with her."[46] Nonetheless, he did share her Victorian notions of respectability and did not approve when his brother and business partner occasionally succumbed to the temptations of alcohol. He noted cryptically on 29 September: "Fine day. Phil absented himself yesterday morning. First spree he has been on in 1877."[47] In the temperance movement, men and women engaged in a public discourse that defined and redefined notions of respectability.[48]

The evidence presented here suggests that women diarists' constructions of their world were more comprehensive than those of their male counterparts. Yet scholars have tended to look to men's diaries for insights into public life and to women's diaries for insights into private life. In recent years, historians have revised our understanding of men's roles as fathers of families by drawing extensively on their diaries and correspondence to discuss their relationships with their wives and children, particularly their sons.[49] While men are now at home in the private world of the family, women remain uneasily situated in the public sphere, where their activities are frequently portrayed as negotiated or subversive. Although it is tempting to conclude, on the basis of those sections of men's diaries that focus on their own work, that the authors perceived the public world of work as a world without women, a closer reading of such diaries allows us to locate women in that world. Women were prominent among the list of berry pickers David Wetmore employed in the 1870s. James Brown's school inspections included female as well as male teachers. Widows such as Ann Miles's sister Betsy managed farms, raised crops, and bought and sold livestock. When the provincial legislature was sitting, members of the House of Assembly took lodging in boarding houses managed by women. Women's diaries add depth and breadth to the picture. Lucy Morrison's gardening business left no public record, but her diary and those of others confirm the scope of her commercial enterprise. Sophy Carman regularly purchased her garden plants, flowers for vases, and strawberries, gooseberries, and currants from Lucy Morrison.[50] Similarly, John Robinson reported: "We ... went to Mrs. Morrison and P purchased a few flowers in pots."[51] In affording glimpses of all these activities, diaries provide evidence, seldom available in other sources, that women functioned comfortably within the public sphere.[52]

Just as diarists constructed themselves and their world in their diaries, readers reconstruct diarists and their world in their reading. Analyses of individual diaries have led and continue to lead to new insights concerning the nature and parameters of family and community life.[53] Comparative analyses that draw on a number of diaries to develop and extend these insights are less common.[54] By examining diaries within a comparative frame, by juxtaposing gender and genre, we may, perhaps, reconstruct a world our diarists themselves would recognize. This preliminary foray into the field of comparative analysis indicates that by using gender as the key category of analysis, a focus on middle-aged, married diarists can lead to the construction of a composite and suggestive portrait of family and community life in nineteenth-century New Brunswick. Particular approaches to diary keeping are not gender specific. The diaries of middle-aged women have more in common with those of their male contemporaries than with those of their daughters, granddaughters, or even of their younger selves. At the same time, the genre is not gender-neutral. The diaries of late-middle-aged women provide a broader picture of both family and community life than do those of their male counterparts, making it possible to situate women alongside men in their communities as well as in their families.

NOTES

1 Of course, class and culture also shaped family life as well as family values. Furthermore, the nature of community life depends on when and where one lives. Not all these determinants can readily be addressed through an analysis of diaries.

2 Thomas O. Miles Diary, transcript in possession of the author. Celia Munro kindly provided me with a transcription of her great-great-great-grandfather's diaries. See also Thomas O. Miles fonds, MC451, Provincial Archives of New Brunswick (PANB); James Brown Diaries, MC295, PANB; Janet Hendry MacDonald Diaries, MG H 108, University of New Brunswick Archives (UNBA); Ann Eliza Rogers [Gallacher Moore] Diaries, MC260, PANB; Lucy Everett Morrison Diaries, MC1958, PANB; John Robinson Diaries, MC2668, PANB; Sophia Bliss Carman Diaries, William F. Ganong Papers, F218–4, F516-S225, New Brunswick Museum Archives (NBMA); and David Picket Wetmore Diaries in Judith Baxter, ed., *Clifton Royal: The Wetmores and Village Life in Nineteenth-Century New Brunswick* (Gatineau, PQ: Museum of Civilization, 2004), 6–45. I have retained the diarists' original spelling.

3 Miles Diary, 19 May 1849.

4 Brown Diary, 19 May 1858.

5 MacDonald Diary, 7–8 May 1861.

6 Miles Diary, 20 April 1849. Aside from this reference on his sixtieth birthday, Miles refers to his wife interchangeably as "Ann" or "Mrs. Miles."

7 Miles Diary, 14–28 February 1850. On another occasion, when Sally was ill and her mother had gone to care for her, Miles noted that her husband "Woody has gone a gunning. I think he had better staid home": 9–15 September 1851, quote from 12 September.

8 Miles Diary, 21 November 1850.

9 Miles Diary, 13 January 1851, and Addendum, 12 February, at the end of the 1851 diary.

10 Brown Diary, 25 July, 21 September, and 6 November 1857. James Brown and his first wife, Sarah Sherman, had ten children, of whom seven survived. Sarah died in 1839. Three years later, Brown married Catherine (Cameron) Gillespie, a young widow who had an infant son. They had eight children, of whom seven survived. See James Brown fonds, MC295, PANB.

11 Brown Diary, 30 January and 12 April 1858.
12 Brown Diary, 2 February, 15 April, and 22 May 1858.
13 MacDonald Diary, 15 October 1857 and 28 September 1858. Discovered by Giovanni Donati in June 1858, Donati's Comet, among the brightest and most visible comets of the nineteenth century, was at its brightest magnitude in late September and came closest to Earth on 9 October.
14 MacDonald Diary, 5 May 1859.
15 Miles Diary, 3 May 1841.
16 MacDonald Diary, 2 July 1858.
17 See Catharine Anne Wilson, "Reciprocal Work Bees and the Meaning of Neighbourhood," *Canadian Historical Review* 82, 3 (2001): 431–64.
18 Cameron Lynne Macdonald and Karen V. Hansen, "Sociability and Gendered Spheres: Visiting Patterns in Nineteenth-Century New England," *Social Science History* 25, 4 (2001): 535–61.
19 Miles Diary, 5 August 1851.
20 MacDonald Diary, 17 July 1857.
21 Brown Diary, 9 August 1858.
22 Moore Diary, 16 July 1888.
23 Hopewell Cape, Hillsborough, and Albert are communities in two different parishes (townships) in Albert County.
24 Wetmore Diary, 4, 24, 25, and 28 May 1878, 41–43.
25 Morrison Diary, 6 and 8 July 1881.
26 Ibid., 1–31 July 1881.
27 Wetmore Diary, 21 April 1876, 27. This entry also includes a very rare reference to his wife, Rebecca Araminta Flewelling: "Minta planted seeds in hot bed yesterday ... Minta is just now planting some sweet peas on the upper side of the garden."
28 Rebecca Araminta Wetmore Diary, 1873–74, in Baxter, *Clifton Royal*, 85–92. Araminta Wetmore, not included in this analysis as she was not yet forty during the period covered by her diary, like other women diarists, reported her husband's as well as her own daily activities.
29 Baxter, *Clifton Royal*, 5; see also Wetmore Diary, 30 May 1871, 11.
30 For an exploration of the financial contributions of middle-class matrons to the family economy, see Janet Guildford, "'Whate'er the Duty of the Hour Demands': The Work of Middle-Class Women in Halifax, 1840–1880," *Histoire sociale/Social History* 30, 59 (1997): 1–20.
31 Carman Diary, 6 and 18 February and 21 and 22 April 1873.
32 Morrison Diary, 1 February 1875.
33 Morrison Diary, 1 and 2 April, 14 June, and 8 July 1875.
34 Robinson Diary, 23 and 24 January 1877.
35 Robinson Diary, 30 April, 18 June, and 21–24 August 1877.
36 Robinson Diary, 26 January and 9 and 10 February 1877.
37 Miles Diary, 6 April 1849. Bishop John Medley was appointed in 1845.
38 Miles Diary, 18 and 22 July 1850.
39 For an analysis of this phenomenon in the New Brunswick context, see Hannah M. Lane, "Tribalism, Proselytism, and Pluralism: Protestants, Family, and

Denominational Identity in Mid-Nineteenth-Century St. Stephen, New Brunswick," in *Households of Faith: Family, Gender, and Community in Canada, 1760–1969*, ed. Nancy Christie (Montreal/Kingston: McGill-Queen's University Press, 2002).

40 See, for example, Brown Diary, 3 January and 7 February 1858.

41 Brown Diary, 16 May 1858.

42 Morrison Diary, 7 March 1875.

43 For a similar argument, see Catherine E. Kelly, *In the New England Fashion: Reshaping Women's Lives in the Nineteenth Century* (New York: Cornell University Press, 1999), and Julia Roberts, *In Mixed Company: Taverns and Public Life in Upper Canada* (Vancouver: UBC Press, 2009).

44 Miles Diary, 6, 10, 11, and 14 March 1851.

45 Rogers Diary, 16 and 18 January 1874.

46 Robinson Diary, 30 January 1877.

47 Robinson Diary, 29 September 1877. For tavern keepers' attitudes towards drunkenness, see Roberts, *In Mixed Company,* 91–94.

48 Here, the concept of the public sphere as defined by contemporary philosopher Jürgen Habermas in "The Public Sphere: An Encyclopedia Article (1964)," *New German Critique* 3 (Autumn 1974) could be applied.

49 See John Tosh, *A Man's Place: Masculinity and the Middle-Class Home in Victorian England* (New Haven: Yale University Press, 1999), and J.I. Little, "The Fireside Kingdom: A Mid-Nineteenth-Century Anglican Perspective on Marriage and Parenthood," in Christie, *Households of Faith*, 86–92.

50 See Sophia Carman receipt files from the early 1880s (24 May through 7 July [5.75]; 3 June through 29 July [$5.32]; 14 June [$4.75]) "Paid to Lucy A. Morrison," Ganong Collection, F512, NBMA.

51 Robinson Diary, 15 June 1877.

52 Here, I am referring to the public sphere of the market, which nineteenth-century commentators often contrasted with the private sphere of the home.

53 See, for example, Laura Thatcher Ulrich, *A Midwife's Tale: The Life of Martha Ballard, Based on Her Diary, 1785–1812* (New York: Vintage Books, 1991); Katherine Carter, "An Economy of Words: Emma Chadwick Stretch's Account Book Diary, 1859–1860," *Acadiensis* 29, 1 (1999): 43–56; Nancy Christie, "'On the Threshold of Manhood': Working-Class Religion and Domesticity in Victorian Britain and Canada," *Histoire sociale/Social History* 36, 71 (2003): 145–74; Julia Roberts, "Women, Men, and Taverns in Tavern-Keeper Ely Playter's Journal," *Histoire sociale/Social History* 36, 72 (2003): 371–405; and B. Anne Wood, *Evangelical Balance Sheet: Character, Family, and Business in Mid-Victorian Nova Scotia* (Waterloo: Wilfrid Laurier University Press, 2006).

54 See Nancy G. Osterud, *Bonds of Community: The Lives of Farm Women in Nineteenth-Century New York* (Ithaca, NY: Cornell University Press, 1991), and Françoise Noël, *Family Life and Sociability in Upper and Lower Canada, 1780–1870: A View from Diaries and Family Correspondence* (Montreal/Kingston: McGill-Queen's University Press, 2003).

"A Little Offensive and Defensive Alliance"
Friendship, Professional Networks, and International Child Welfare Policy

KAREN BALCOM

In 1938, Charlotte Whitton, executive director of the Canadian Welfare Council (CWC), submitted the final version of an ambitious report titled *The Placing of Children in Families* to the Child Welfare Committee of the Advisory Committee on Social Questions of the League of Nations.[1] *The Placing of Children* was widely recognized as a major achievement for the advisory committee, and delegates to the Fifth Committee of the League Assembly singled out Whitton for praise.[2] Despite this personal recognition, *The Placing of Children* is best seen as the product of sustained collaboration between Whitton and her close friend and professional ally Katharine Lenroot, chief of the US Children's Bureau (USCB). This document laid out general principles and specific practices for the care of children outside of their original homes; in so doing, it reflected the priorities animating child welfare reform in North America. These priorities included a strong preference for foster-home care as opposed to institutional care and an insistence on professional training for social workers. Both of these approaches became core elements in the New World philosophy of child welfare championed by North Americans at the League. Whitton and Lenroot viewed the report as a victory for the self-styled "North American alliance," which had struggled since the early 1920s to promote its version of New World, progressive child welfare, as opposed to what they saw as Old World or Latin commitments to voluntarism, institutional care, and a religious ethos in social welfare.[3] As work on the report drew to a close, Lenroot noted with satisfaction that "I do think that we have accomplished some-thing significant."[4]

Lenroot's *we* referenced her personal ties to Whitton and also the wider connection between the CWC and the USCB at the League. As early as 1926, former USCB chief Julia Lathrop captured this relationship when she suggested that in League child welfare work, "perhaps it is strategically well that Canada and the United States should form for the present a little of-fensive and defensive alliance on the basis of a mutual admiration society."[5] This chapter focuses on that alliance as it was established and enacted in the transnational space of the Child Welfare Committee at the League of Nations. I begin and end with *The Placing of Children in Families* because the report was an important product of the alliance, one that clarified the perceived New World–Old World division in child welfare. My focus, how-ever, is on process and strategy. I ask questions about how the Canadian and US social workers drew on their personal relationships, shared profes-sional commitments, and broader political resources in their League work. As Beryl Metzger argues, "while the League was made up of sovereign states implementing its policies, its work was heavily substantiated and moved by complex transnational networks."[6] Here, I explore the USCB-CWC relation-ship as one example of such a network.

The most important scholarship on the Child Welfare Committee comes from Dominique Marshall, who explores the Child Welfare Committee as part of a larger study of the emergence of children's rights discourse and prac-tices in the twentieth century.[7] She puts Canadian child welfare in conversa-tion with transnational developments by exploring Canada's influence on the transnational and the implications of transnational work for development in *les espaces locaux.*[8] Marshall's conception captures both the intentions and the effect of USCB-CWC collaboration at the League. More broadly, Mar-shall's framework also suggests connections to Adele Perry's chapter in this volume, for both authors look at the transnational roots of domestic histories and, conversely, at the transnational implications of local histories.

Marshall's work contributes to scholarship on the struggle to establish the child as an object of international relations – in other words, as a subject that belonged in the rarified space of the new League.[9] Indeed, Lathrop first named the "offensive and defensive alliance" after Sir Austen Chamberlain, the British foreign secretary, challenged the legitimacy of the committee on the grounds that it trespassed on purely domestic policy areas.[10] As Carol Miller argues, the contested entry of child welfare and other humanitarian concerns into international relations opened new, though constrained, spaces for women as policy actors.[11] This observation can be applied to women who worked in the League Secretariat (the majority worked in the Social Questions Section) or to those who represented their governments, voluntary groups in social welfare, or international women's organizations in Geneva.

Connections can also be drawn between women's emerging role in the international space of child welfare on the one hand and the well-documented role of women in the creation and administration of domestic welfare states in Europe and white settler colonies on the other hand. The US literature on women and the welfare state emphasizes the myriad personal and professional connections that wove leading reformers together into a white women's welfare network that operated separately from that of black women.[12] The English Canadian equivalent of the white women's network is sometimes referred to as the "Whitton connection," although Suzanne Morton's forthcoming study of social worker Jane Wisdom reveals networks that went beyond Whitton, and Hélène Charron's work in this volume examines a separate network of professional women in social welfare in French Catholic Quebec.[13] Extensive women's networks are also important in the stories told by Catherine Gidney, Rose Fine-Meyer, and Anthony Hampton in this volume. Many of the child welfare workers in my study also participated in the transnational pacifist women's networks examined by Lorna McLean in Chapter 4. In all of these examples, self-conscious women's networks provided personal and professional support to their members. These networks were based on friendships, and they were potent vehicles for advancing both personal careers and the larger agenda of reform. Studying the evolving relationship between the US Children's Bureau and the Canadian Welfare Council – in particular the pairing of Whitton and Lenroot – offers a unique opportunity to trace the development and deployment of personalized welfare networks into the transnational space of child welfare.

Founded in 1912, the USCB was the branch of the US federal government responsible for promoting and protecting the health and welfare of children and, by extension, that of their mothers.[14] Canadian social reformers hoped to establish an equivalent of the US Children's Bureau inside the Canadian federal government, but when their plans fell through, a national child welfare conference in 1920 led to what would become the Canadian Welfare Council. Charlotte Whitton became the founding executive director of a small organization that sought to become a national research and advocacy body in child welfare, one that would mirror the work of the USCB and eventually expand into other arenas of social welfare activity.[15] As it grew, the USCB developed an international reputation in child welfare research and expertise.[16] In the international arena, the bureau's closest partner was the CWC, a connection that is hardly surprising. There were important, pre-existing links between Canadian and US social welfare leaders, who connected with one another in professional associations and conferences, in universities and training institutes, and in US-based job placements. Such placements were a frequent part of a Canadian career in social work.[17] Travelling back and forth across the border facilitated professional exchanges and helped build important personal connections between key figures at the USCB and the CWC and in Canadian child welfare more broadly. Although it is tempting to assume that the much larger USCB dominated the relationship, in the period before 1950, the two national bodies worked in respectful and personalized collaboration.[18] The give and take of the relationship appears most clearly in the joint work of the CWC and the USCB at the League of Nations in the interwar period.

Article 23(c) of the Covenant of the League of Nations committed the League to "the general supervision of agreements with respect to the traffic in women and children."[19] A 1921 conference led to a permanent Advisory Commission on the Traffic in Women and Children, which was supported by the Social Questions Section of the League Secretariat.[20] The new advisory commission asked the United States and Germany, non-League countries, to join its work. President Harding subsequently selected Grace Abbott, chief of the USCB, to serve the commission in an "unofficial and consultative capacity."[21] In 1924, the League Assembly directed the advisory commission to develop a program in child welfare, and Abbott was asked to suggest a structure and basic agenda for the new work.[22] Abbott recommended a program of scientific study that would not only pay attention to children in crisis but also promote the development of "normal" children, an approach that reflected USCB and CWC priorities in child welfare work.[23] Abbott also insisted on dividing the advisory commission into two committees – one on the traffic in women and children, one on Child Welfare. The committees would have common national delegates but separate sets of nonvoting assessors who would represent voluntary expertise in each field.

Abbott was unhappy, however, with the Eurocentric focus of the original commission. She pushed to have new assessors from North and South America as well as Asia and Australia on the new Child Welfare Committee. It seemed, at first, that only one new assessor would be appointed from the Americas and that that assessor would be from South America, not North America.[24] Because the United States was not a member of the League, US officials could not press the issue of representation for the Americas through formal diplomatic channels.[25] In a pattern that would be repeated, Abbott, Whitton, and the Canadian legation at Geneva worked to create more space for North Americans on the Child Welfare Committee and to increase the chances that Whitton would be appointed from Canada.[26] Whitton argued that the CWC should be represented in Geneva because the council represented child welfare interests in both English and French Canada and thus spoke for two traditions in welfare provision.[27] In the end, the North Americans got two of the new assessors. Charlotte Whitton and Julia Lathrop, as the representative of the US National Conference on Social Work, went to Geneva.[28] Whitton represented Canada until the outbreak of the Second World War. Julia Lathrop served until 1931. Grace Abbott attended few meetings in person but contributed to the work regularly, and when she retired in 1934, the new USCB chief, Katherine Lenroot, took over. Lenroot sent Elsa Castendyck, the USCB's director of delinquency, to Geneva in 1938 and 1939. These women – Abbott, Lathrop, Lenroot, Castendyck, and Whitton – were the core of the "North American Alliance" in child welfare. They shared the belief that if the committee could set appropriate international standards and provide models of scientific child welfare, it could improve the lives of children around the world and contribute to the larger cause of securing world peace.[29]

The North Americans were often frustrated and even embarrassed by the committee's lack of focus and by the poor quality of its studies and publications.[30] Lathrop eventually resigned from her position in protest, and the others considered this option at different points. They were particularly upset by a study of neglected children funded by the American Social Hygiene Association. The study had been entrusted in 1928 to Leonie de Chaptal, a pioneer in the French tradition of the visiting nurse and past president of the International Association of Nurses. She attended committee meetings as a technical expert assisting the French delegate. Whitton, Abbott, and Lathrop felt Chaptal lacked the technical skills required in child welfare. They were appalled that the study framed neglected children as "children in moral danger," and they were upset by what they viewed as the haphazard nature of Chaptal's hasty field research in Canada and the United States.[31] As Dominique Marshall points out, the conflict over Chaptal and her study reflected diplomatic rivalries, competing visions of professionalism and training for welfare workers, and deep divisions between delegates from predominantly Protestant and Catholic nations. Despite Whitton's pretense that her council represented both English and French social welfare traditions in Canada, this controversy revealed her strong bias against the French Catholic model.[32] Indeed, Whitton was horrified when the final report praised the institutional child care institutions of the Catholic Church in Quebec, which she viewed as the most backward and embarrassing in Canada. She was upset that a League report had publicized what she deemed to be an obvious weakness in the Canadian system just as she and her American allies were presenting themselves as the representatives of a New World philosophy of progressive and scientific child welfare.[33]

The North Americans traced problems in the committee to the delegates, the assessors, and the staff of the Social Questions Section. They complained, with justification, that the Social Questions Section was vastly underfunded and that staff members lacked professional training and practical experience in social welfare.[34] As for the delegates, both Abbott and Whitton expressed frustration that many countries either sent diplomats (instead of experienced social workers) or experts in prostitution to the child welfare meetings.[35] The North Americans saw themselves, alongside the Scandinavians and (usually) the British, as the representatives of what they called a "New World," or progressive, approach to child welfare. This model emphasized constructive or positive child welfare, criticized institutional child care, embraced a significant role for the state in social welfare, and insisted on professional training for social workers. The New World stood in contrast to "Old World" or "Latin" approaches to welfare work, which were associated with voluntarism, opposition to expanding state structures, and the dominance of the Catholic Church.[36]

The distinctions these women made between *New World* and *Old World* and between *Latin* and *progressive* reflected a slippery and sometimes contradictory conflation of geography and religion, mixed in with healthy doses of colonialism and an underlying racism. The Canadian deployment of *New World–Old World* and *Latin-Progressive* was complicated further by the way these contrasts interacted with French-English, Protestant-Catholic distinctions within the country.[37] Most importantly, the terms were a shorthand for the common frustrations experienced by North Americans on the Child Welfare Committee, capturing their sense of themselves as people situated on the worldwide, progressive edge of child welfare research and reform. In other words, these terms were a way of marking a unity of purpose and interest between the CWC and the USCB in an international forum. Of course, the North Americans were but a tiny minority on a committee that grew, by 1936, to include fifteen national delegates and eighteen assessors. As the work of the Committee progressed, they found important like-minded collaborators in the Old World and even among the so-called Latins.[38]

The New World alliance was useful to the US representatives. It helped them make the most of their personal and political influence in Geneva. As chiefs and former chiefs of the US Children's Bureau, Grace Abbott, Katharine Lenroot, and Julia Lathrop all had well-deserved international reputations in child welfare. Abbott and then Lenroot were relatively free to decide when and whether they should consult the State Department on a particular issue, but the two women were always conscious of how the State Deparment might react to the various positions they considered.[39] In general, State Department officials maintained an attitude of "friendly cooperation" towards the bureau's presence at the League and sometimes engaged in important "behind-the-scenes" manoeuvring in support of the bureau's objectives.[40]

Still, the United States was not a member nation of the League. In 1935, Cordell Hull, the secretary of state, told US diplomats in Geneva to transmit a formal message to the secretary general of the League that the US government had designated Katharine Lenroot to succeed Grace Abbott. At the end of the message, Hull appended an additional instruction: US officials should "tell Avenol [the secretary general] *informally* that we regard Miss Lenroot's membership and its attributes as identical with those of any other member of the Committee."[41] In reality, Lenroot's position could not be "identical" to that of other government delegates: the United States did not have a voting presence in the League Assembly and support from the US State Department had to be communicated to the League informally or through representatives of other countries. Lenroot and Abbott could not afford to lose sight of the political complications that could arise from their activity at the League. In the early 1930s, the "friendly cooperation" of the State Department was matched by an overt "political hostility" towards the League inside the Department of Labor.[42]

In this context, Canada's institutional voice at the League proved valuable to the Americans. Canada was not only a voting member of the League; from 1927 to 1930, it also held a seat on the League Council. Canada's permanent representative in Geneva, W.A. Riddell, was a strong supporter of Whitton, as was O.D. Skelton, Canada's under-secretary of state for foreign affairs. As a result, Whitton frequently convinced the Canadian delegation to promote the Canadian-American perspective or to lodge formal complaints about actions in the Child Welfare Committee.[43] When Whitton engaged with Riddell or Skelton, she spoke for herself and for the Americans.[44] This access had obvious benefits for the Americans, but there were also important advantages for Whitton and the Canadian diplomats. Abbott and then Lenroot, despite their "consultative status," were voting members of the committee. Whitton, as an assessor, could not vote. Furthermore, Whitton, when she first went to the League, was not a well-known figure outside of Canada; she was considerably younger and far less experienced than most of the women serving as delegates or assessors at the League. Her association with Abbott and Lathrop enhanced her position, and hence that of Canada, in the committee. Taking a broader view, what was good for the cause of Whitton was also good for Canada as an emerging diplomatic force at the League. Canada's work at the League was critical to the Dominion's fight in the 1920s and 1930s to establish a foreign policy and an international presence separate from that of Great Britain. Charlotte Whitton's rising profile in the League's social welfare work, which was supported by her American allies, contributed to this larger cause.[45] On the Child Welfare Committee, the United States and Canada needed each other.

Whitton and the Americans did not always agree, however. Until the late 1930s, the Americans were extremely reluctant to launch formal protests or to ask the State Department to do so on their behalf.[46] Whitton was frustrated when Abbott refused, in 1933, to back up Canada's protest that Whitton had been unjustly passed over when several other nations were invited to become permanent, and thus voting, members of the Advisory Commission.[47] Yet, despite conflicts over timing and political strategy, the overall project of securing delegate status for Canada (and with it another vote for the North Americans in the Child Welfare Committee and Traffic in Women Committees) was important to the Americans as well as the Canadians. In 1935, Canada's prime minister, R.B. Bennett, backed by the continuing efforts of Riddell in Geneva, finally secured delegate status for Whitton on the Advisory Commission.[48] In return, the United States surrendered its assessorships on the Child Welfare and Traffic in Women Committees.[49]

Political resources melded with deep personal connections in child welfare work. Lathrop and Whitton had met when Lathrop attended a conference in Toronto in 1920. At that time, Lathrop was already chief of the USCB, and Whitton was a young college graduate in her first job. Lathrop became an important mentor for Whitton, as she was for so many others in white women's social welfare and progressive networks in the United States.[50] The Child Welfare Committee meetings in Geneva in 1926 brought Lathrop and Whitton closer together. The two shared long workdays, lodged at the same hotel, and spent much of their free time together. This ongoing relationship between Lathrop and Whitton – intensified by the experience of going to Geneva – not only held deep personal importance for the two women, but it also helped to cement the alliance between the CWC and the USCB.[51]

The relationship between Whitton and Abbott also grew stronger through their work for the League, although the two never became intimates. Whitton and Abbott, perhaps tellingly, never attended the Geneva meetings at the same time. But League work took place in many other venues. Most of the strategizing, the drafting of reports, and the working out of common priorities occurred through correspondence or at face-to-face meetings in North America.[52] Personalized exchanges were in some ways particularly valuable for the Americans because they had to be careful about the written expression of "official" views.[53] Over time, Abbott and Whitton became if not close friends then at least friendly allies who frequently traded frank assessments of League business and cutting criticisms of League personnel while taking care to identify their exchanges as confidential or personal.[54]

Lenroot and Whitton had worked together on League matters and consulted on common projects in North America, but they did not spend a significant amount of time together until they both attended League meetings in Paris and Geneva in the spring of 1936. Their experience at the European meetings was in some ways reminiscent of that shared by Whitton and Lathrop a decade earlier: long days of often frustrating meetings followed by late-night strategy sessions that pulled the women together as colleagues and as friends. Indeed, the European meetings proved to be the defining experience in the relationship between Whitton and Lenroot. They returned home with a deep affection, abiding respect, and intense loyalty to each other that would last to the end of their long lives.

Whitton clearly expressed her fond remembrances of this time, and her sense of the personal relationship as a political resource, in a letter to Lenroot from Geneva in 1937. Lenroot was unable to return to Geneva for meetings that year.

> Dear, Dear *Étas-Unis,*
>
> Why! O Why! have you deserted me? I knew that last year I would find future sessions even more desolate and discouraging than all the past – that all the tomorrows were as yesterday and you were ... here, and that would be in grave part in sustaining my role. It is even worse than I had envisioned ... I have been given your room of last year, even the twin beds, and I have found no one whom I would wish to bring in to declaim from one of them at two or three in the morning ... The North American alliance has been working splendidly ... But you can send half the union and it goes nowhere in occupying the void your own absence creates. Please do not do it again, for I now know I accomplish so little without you, in fact do positive harm

by my irascibility. And how I *do* miss you personally: the lovelier the day, the lonelier I feel ...

Affectionately, Charlotte[55]

Lenroot and Whitton had complementary personalities. Lenroot's composure and cautious conservatism countered Whitton's irascibility, and there were many similarities in their life choices and experiences. Both chose a life of dedicated public service as unmarried career women. Professionally, they worked in organizations dominated by women, but they moved in a larger mixed-sex environment that brought them into contact with male and female reformers and government officials. On both a personal and a professional level, they drew strength from interconnected female social networks similar to those first established by their mentors earlier in the century. And, like many of their mentors, both women established long-term relationships with single professional women. Lenroot shared her life with Emma Lundberg for thirty-nine years, and Whitton lived with Margaret Grier for twenty-five years until Grier's devastating death at a young age.[56]

Whitton and Lenroot were also close in age. Lathrop was forty years older than Whitton, and Abbott was twenty years the Canadian's senior. Whitton (b. 1896) and Lenroot (b. 1891) were contemporaries, and by the time the two women travelled to Geneva, they were both prominent and experienced leaders in social welfare. The issue was not only closeness in age but also transition between generations. Historian Linda Gordon argues that by the 1930s older patterns and styles of female reform had lost much of their influence. By the end of that decade, public criticism of single women's same-sex relationships had come to the fore; more married, middle-class women had moved into the workforce; advancement within bureaucratic structures had become the most important model of career development for female professionals; and female leadership in social welfare had been challenged by a new generation of male technocrats.[57] Katharine Lenroot and Charlotte Whitton were transitional figures linked to the values, priorities, and people of an earlier generation of reformers, but they also operated within this new environment.

Whitton and Lenroot also proved to be potent allies, especially at the 1936 meetings, where Whitton used her new status as a voting national delegate. The proper scope of the Child Welfare Committee was a matter of long-standing debate, and by the mid-1930s, North Americans were not alone in their argument that the committee needed revamping.[58] At a special reorganization meeting in Paris, Whitton and Lenroot worked with allies from Great Britain and (Latin) Chile to produce a plan for an amalgamated Advisory Committee on Social Questions. The plan dropped permanent assessors from voluntary organizations, added a cadre of technical experts who would work on specific issues, and adopted terms of reference that reflected the North American view of progressive social work. Whitton and Lenroot were then appointed to a subcommittee working on a major study of foster placements as an alternative to institutional care. This study took up a critical issue for the CWC and the USCB. The transition from institutional child care to home-like foster care is often cited as a key distinction between nineteenth-century child saving and twentieth-century child welfare in North America, and the divide between foster and institutional care was at the core of the New World–Latin division, as well as Whitton's ongoing concerns about child welfare in Quebec.[59]

Whitton and Lenroot had to defend the reorganization plan against opposition from international women's organizations. Their members saw the proposal to replace permanent assessors with temporary technical advisers as a major setback for internationalist women at Geneva.[60] Although Whitton and Lenroot consistently championed opportunities for *professional* women in domestic and transnational spaces, neither assumed that volunteer women were automatic allies in their campaign to professionalize League work on child welfare. Whitton and Lenroot always privileged professionalization over allegiances to traditional women's reform organizations, a choice that says much about their priorities in international work and about the generational shift in women's social reform work inside North America.[61] Thus, Whitton pressured the Canadian legation to stand firm in support of the reorganization.[62] Lenroot asked international women's organizations in the United States not to support the protests and suggested to the US Consul in Geneva that although "the United States is not in a position to take any action in this matter ... a word or two to American friends in Geneva connected with women's organizations might help."[63] The protest ultimately failed, and the international women's organizations that lost their assessorships considered it an important defeat not only for themselves but also for the role of nongovernmental organizations at the League.[64] For Whitton and Lenroot, this sacrifice was necessary for the larger goal of advancing child welfare work.

Lenroot and Whitton spent the next two years working on the child placement study. The 1938 final report, *The Placing of Children in Families,* was the most important material product of the cooperation between the Canadians and the Americans at the League. During the first year, the work remained nominally under the control of a Hungarian assessor, but when assessors were removed from the committee, Whitton, at Lenroot's suggestion, was appointed rapporteur.[65] Work on the report kept Whitton and Lenroot in constant contact. They exchanged several letters per week on this and other League business.[66] They considered the main themes and topics of the report, and they exchanged background information and draft sections. At the same time, the two also traded tales of frustration related to the League and developed strategies to ensure that the Advisory Committee would approve the report.[67]

This correspondence deepens our view of the relationship between the two women. Almost every letter combined a discussion of professional concerns with inquiries into the other's health and general happiness. Both women looked forward to formal meetings in North America set up to advance work on the report on child placing. In October 1937, Whitton scribbled a note confirming an upcoming meeting in Toronto: "Am I happy," she wrote, "at the prospect of actually seeing you, again, and being able to relate much that remained unwritten about Geneva, *et al.*"[68] Anticipating a week in Washington in January 1937, Lenroot predicted "it will be glorious to have you here."[69]

The report solidified a bond not only among the leadership of the CWC and the USCB but also among members at their base. Lenroot and Whitton directed the project and did considerable writing and editing, but the largest portion of the work fell to their associates. They considered this work a "gift of staff services worth thousands of dollars" to League work.[70] At the USCB, Elsa Castendyck, director of the delinquency division, and Anna Kalet Smith, foreign language specialist, were most involved. In Canada, Robert E. Mills, executive director of the Toronto Children's Aid Society, drafted the material for the first volume. Work on the report also led to a friendship between Castendyck and Whitton that would flower when Elsa and Charlotte were in England and Geneva together in 1938.[71]

The content of the report was as significant as the production process. As early as 1936, the Child Welfare Committee had agreed to three broad principles when it came to placing children outside their homes. The first was that placing children in foster homes was a valuable means of securing "the normal experience of home and community life" for children "whose parents are unable to care for them." Children should never, however, be removed from parents solely because of poverty. The second principle was that "all child-placing agencies should make provision for the complete study of the child they are placing ... as well as the home into which he is to be placed." Third, the committee agreed that "supervision by competent workers should be provided for the child in the foster home."[72] *The Placing of Children in Families* affirmed the priorities of progressive North American child welfare. It emphasized professionalization; underlined the responsibility of the state in protecting the child in foster care; stressed the importance of public education to support improved standards in child welfare; insisted on a careful match between the child and the foster family; and pointed out the need to connect child-placing services with "other services for family assistance, public health and child welfare."[73]

This report's principles and recommendations represented ideals towards which the USCB and the CWC were still working *inside* North America. This point is critical. It illustrates that, notwithstanding their pose as international advocates of the highest standards, the North Americans recognized weaknesses in their own child welfare systems, and it demonstrates their determination to use the report as part of their reform work at home.[74] Whitton, for example, explicitly used the report to give the League of Nations imprimatur her long-standing critique of institutional care for children in Quebec.[75] On the issue of permanent child adoption, the report also made recommendations on the critical role of state oversight in the adoptive process, the importance of a probationary period before finalizing an adoption, and the need for communities to recognize adoption as a "social as well as a legal process."[76] These recommendations mirrored the adoption reform agenda emerging in the United States and Canada in the 1930s. Thus, the report served as an external model of best practices in adoption for CWC and USCB reformers at home. Transnational reform would therefore move in two directions: the report was a New World example placed before other nations, and it was a standard against which domestic reform in Canada and the United States could be measured. Setting external standards as a goal was a critical way for USCB and CWC leaders to use their personal ties and shared professional goals and diplomatic resources at the League to shape both domestic and transnational reform agendas.[77] To return to Dominique Marshall's insights, here we have a concrete example of the interplay between the transnational and the local.

The Canadians and Americans now saw some potential to do good work at the League, and their alliance was stronger than ever. Whitton and Lenroot were explicit about their common cause in their communications with each other, with the League, and with their governments.[78] Canadian-American collaboration advanced to the point where Lenroot met with Canadian diplomats in Washington to discuss League business.[79] Still, the North Americans remained frustrated by the slow pace of change. The reorganization was not accompanied by any improvement in either the budget or the staff of the Social Questions Section. The Advisory Committee remained divided between diplomats and social workers, between advocates of professionalism and advocates of voluntarism, and between Old World (or Latin) and New World approaches to social welfare – even as the balance tipped in favour of the North Americans.[80] Whitton missed Lenroot terribly at the 1937 meetings. She complained of the "petty intrigue and discouraging lack of objective interest that have prostituted this Committee itself from the beginning."[81]

As the 1938 meetings loomed, Whitton remained committed to her work on the report on child placing, which was approved by the committee that year, but she felt despondent about the deteriorating world situation as well as the immediate work of the Advisory Committee. In the context of increasing international tensions in the late 1930s, Whitton thought it was perhaps futile to attempt to "get nations to sit about a common board for the preservation of child life" while "international highwaymen" played with the "life of nations and people generally."[82] Lenroot concurred, but added, "I presume that we have to keep going ... on the assumption that carrying on with some of these humanitarian undertakings even to the last minute is worthwhile."[83]

Hitler's attacks on the Western Front made the 1940 meeting of the Advisory Committee impossible.[84] The intensification of the war brought an effective end to US-Canadian collaboration at the League of Nations, though the ties created there continued after the war. There are also direct links – some running through the person of Katharine Lenroot – between the Child Welfare Committee and the humanitarian and social work of the United Nations in the postwar period. And the war itself brought new challenges and produced further collaboration between the CWC and the USCB. For example, Whitton and Castendyck worked closely together to arrange for the care and housing of British children shipped to North America (mostly to Canada) for the duration of the war.[85]

The leaders of the CWC and the USCB were frustrated by their experience at the League of Nations because there was so much more they felt they could have done had the Advisory Commission been run efficiently and professionally or, to restate the issue, had it been run according to their New World philosophy. Inside North America, this sense of a shared project in professional child welfare survived as one of the most important products of the League's work in child welfare. This is not to argue that Whitton and her US colleagues came to think of Canada and the United States as having identical goals in child welfare. They believed that child welfare policy and practice must take different forms in countries with separate histories, religious mixes, racial politics, and legal and constitutional systems. They agreed, however, on the basic goals and approaches to child welfare. The political strength of Canada at the League helped to ensure that the relationship evolved as a relatively equal partnership, even though the CWC was a vastly smaller organization than the USCB.

The League experience also personalized the connection between the CWC and the USCB, creating and strengthening bonds between Whitton on the one hand and Lathrop, Abbott, Castendyck, and Lenroot on the other. At the League of Nations, these friendships and professional collaborations advanced a shared North American agenda, reflected most strongly in *The Placing of Children in Families*. Beyond the League, these women used their networks to improve child welfare standards inside North America. One important example of this ongoing work came in joint efforts to establish better standards in adoptive placements in both countries and to combat a fast and loose "traffic in babies" across the Canada-US border.[86] Thus, the CWC-USCB alliance continued to influence politics in domestic and transnational spaces, although its personalized aspects eventually faded as an earlier generation of female reformers retired and as welfare and professional structures became more impersonal and bureaucratic. In 1944, Nora Lea, acting executive director of the CWC, expressed her sense of the relationship near its peak. "Indeed," noted Lea, "so warm is the relationship, and so much have we depended upon your very generous sharing of information and advice that we have come to regard the staff and publications of the ·Children's Bureau almost as our other selves."[87]

NOTES

1 Advisory Committee on Social Questions, *The Placing of Children in Families*, Geneva, 1938, League of Nations document C.260.M.155.1938.iv. Funding for this research was generously provided by the Social Sciences and Humanities Research Council of Canada. I am grateful to Megan Armstrong, Eileen Boris, and Leila Rupp for comments on earlier versions of this essay.

2 Canada, *Report of the Canadian Delegation to the League of Nations* (Ottawa: King's Printer, 1939), 17.

3 Whitton to Lenroot, 18 April 1937, Columbia Oral History Library (COL), Katharine Lenroot fonds, 16/Advisory Committee.

4 Lenroot to Whitton, 16 March 1938, Library and Archives Canada (LAC), Canadian Council on Social Development/Canadian Welfare Council fonds (CWC), 130/2359 (1936–38).

5 Lathrop to Whitton, 3 July 1926, LAC, CWC, 2/15 (1926).
6 Beryl Metzger, "Towards an International Human Rights Regime during the Inter-war Years: The League of Nations' Combat of Traffic in Women and Children," in *Beyond Sovereignty: Britain, Empire and Transnationalism, c. 1880–1950,* eds. Kevin Grant, Phillippa Levine, and Frank Trentmann (Palgrave: London, 2007), 54.
7 Dominique Marshall, "The Construction of Children as an Object of International Relations," *International Journal of Children's Rights* 7 (1999): 103–47; "Tensions nationales, ethniques et religieuses autour des enfants: La participation canadienne au Comité de protection de l'enfance de la Société des Nations," *Liens Social et Politiques* RIAC, 44 (Fall 2000): 101–23; "Dimensions transnationales et locales de l'histoire des droits des enfants: La Société des Nations et les cultures politiques canadiennes, 1920–1960," *Genèses* 71 (June 2008): 47–63; "Conflicting Ideas about Families and Social Policies between the Wars: The Committee on Child Welfare of the League of Nations, from a Canadian Perspective" (paper presented at the "Carleton Conference on the History of the Family," Carleton University, Ottawa, May 1997).
8 Marshall, "Dimensions transnationales," 48.
9 Marshall, "The Construction of Children"; Carol Miller, "The Social Section and the Advisory Committee on Social Questions of the League of Nations," in *International Health Organisations and Movements, 1914–1939,* ed. Paul Weindling (Cambridge: Cambridge University Press, 1995), 161–65; Patricia Rooke and R.L. Schnell, "Internationalizing a Discourse: 'Children at Risk' and the Child Welfare Committee at the League of Nations, 1922–1938," *New Education* 14, 2 (1992): 67–78.
10 "Memorandum from the Canadian Assessor: Organization and Scope of the Committee," 30 April 1927, LAC, CWC 1/15 (1927); Miller, "Social Section and Advisory Committee," 163–64, 171nn31–34.
11 Carol Miller, "Women in International Relations? The Debate in Inter-War Britain," in *Gender and International Relations,* ed. Rebecca Grant and Kathleen Newland (Bloomington: Indiana University Press, 1991), 64–82; Carol Miller, "Geneva – The Key to Equality: Interwar Feminists and the League of Nations," *Women's History Review* 3, 2 (1994): 219–45.
12 This is a voluminous literature. For the United States, see Linda Gordon, *Pitied but Not Entitled: Single Mothers and the History of Welfare, 1890–1935* (New York: Free Press, 1994) and Robyn Muncy, *Creating a Female Dominion in American Reform* (New York: Oxford University Press, 1991). International examples include Seth Koven and Sonya Michel, *Mothers of a New World: Maternalist Politics and the Origins of Welfare States* (New York: Routledge, 1993); Ulla Wikander, Alice Kessler-Harris, and Jane Lewis, *Protecting Women: Labour Legislation in Europe, the United States, and Australia, 1880–1920* (Urbana: University of Illinois Press, 1995).
13 Patricia Rooke and R.L. Schnell, *No Bleeding Heart: Charlotte Whitton – A Feminist on the Right* (Vancouver: UBC Press, 1987), 38, 204; James Struthers, *No Fault of Their Own: Unemployment and the Canadian Welfare State, 1914–1941* (Toronto: University of Toronto Press, 1983), 75; Suzanne Morton, "Wisdom, Justice, and Charity: Jane Wisdom and Canadian Social Welfare, 1884–1975," forthcoming book.

14 Kriste Lindemeyer, *A Right to Childhood: The US Children's Bureau and Child Welfare, 1912–46* (Urbana: University of Illinois Press, 1997).

15 R.L. Schnell, "'A Children's Bureau for Canada': The Origins of the Canadian Council on Child Welfare," in *The Benevolent State: The Growth of Welfare in Canada,* ed. Allan Muscovitch and Jim Albert (Toronto: Garamond Press, 1987), 95–110.

16 Letter of 7 January 1974 concerning the international activities of the US Children's Bureau, up to and including the fiscal year 1951, COL, 11/International Activities.

17 Tamara Hareven, "An Ambiguous Alliance: Some Aspects of American Influences on Canadian Social Welfare," *Histoire sociale/Social History* (April 1969): 82–98.

18 Karen Balcom, *The Traffic in Babies: Cross-Border Adoption and Baby-Selling between the United States and Canada, 1930–1972* (Toronto: University of Toronto Press, 2011), Chaps. 1–3.

19 Quoted in Miller, "Women in International Relations," 157.

20 This story is told in detail in Marshall, "The Construction of Children."

21 Harding, quoted in Lela Costin, *Two Sisters for Social Justice: A Biography of Grace and Edith Abbott* (Chicago: University of Chicago Press, 1983), 91–92.

22 Patricia Rooke and R.L. Schnell, "'Uncramping Child Life': International Children's Organisations, 1914–1939," in *International Health Organisations and Movements, 1914–1939,* ed. Paul Weindling (Cambridge: Cambridge University Press, 1995), 190–91.

23 On the USCB's vision of child welfare for the "normal child," see Lindemeyer, *A Right to Childhood.*

24 Letter of 7 January 1974, COL, 11/International Activities, 13.

25 Miller, "Social Section and Advisory Committee," 159–60.

26 Whitton to Abbott, 5 October 1925, LAC, CWC, 2/15 (1925); Charlotte Whitton, "Grace Abbott's Work with the League of Nations," *The Child* 4, 2 (1939): 55.

27 Marshall, "Tensions nationales," 102–3.

28 Letter of 7 January 1974, COL, 11/International Activities, 13.

29 Whitton, "Grace Abbott's Work," 54–55; Whitton to Dame Katharine Furse, 5 November 1926, and Lathrop to Whitton, 3 July 1926, LAC, CWC, 2/15 (1926).

30 Lathrop to Whitton, 13 January 1929, CWC, 2/15 (1929).

31 Whitton to W.A. Riddell, 21 December 1928, and Abbott to Whitton, 26 December 1928, LAC, CWC, 2/15 (1928).

32 Marshall, "Tensions nationales," 107–15.

33 Marshall, "Conflicting Ideas," 8, 19; Rooke and Schnell, *No Bleeding Heart,* 77–78.

34 Whitton to Lathrop, 28 December 1928, LAC, CWC, 2/15 (1928); Whitton to W.A. Riddell, 30 June 1933, LAC, CWC, 2/15 (1933).

35 "Preliminary Conference of Government Representatives on Organization of the Commission, 1936," Part 4, 1, 3, United States Children's Bureau fonds (USCB), 1933–36, 465/0.1.0.7.1 (1), October 1936.

36 Whitton to Riddell, 30 June 1933, and Riddell to Whitton, 25 August 1933, CWC 2/15 (1933).

37 Marshall, "Tensions nationales."

38 The best descriptions of the shifting New World–Old World–Latin divisions and alliances are found in Charlotte Whitton's reports to Lenroot from Geneva in 1937, collected in COL, 16/Advisory Committee.

39 "List of Dispatches Prepared by the American Consulate, Geneva, Switzerland on the Social Work of the League of Nations, 1933," USCB, 1933–36, 465/0.1.0.7.1 (1).

40 Arthur Sweetser to Abbott, 10 February 1933, USCB, 1933–36, 464/0.1.0.7.1 (1).

41 Telegram Sent – AM Legation Bern (Switzerland), 3 April 1935, USCB, 1933–36, 464/0.1.0.7.1 (1) (emphasis added).

42 Arthur Sweetser to Abbott, 10 February 1933, USCB, 1933–36, 464/0.1.0.7.1 (1).

43 Canada, *Report of the Canadian Delegation to the League of Nations* (Ottawa: King's Printer, 1933), 14; Canada, *Report of the Canadian Delegation to the League of Nations* (Ottawa: King's Printer, 1937), 17.

44 Whitton to Riddell, 21 December 1928, LAC, CWC, 2/15 (1928).

45 Marshall, "Conflicting Ideas," 18.

46 Abbott to Whitton, 26 December 1928, LAC, CWC, 2/15 (1928).

47 Abbott to Whitton, 16 October 1933, LAC, CWC, 2/15 (1933).

48 This negotiation can be traced in LAC, Department of External Affairs fonds, 32/25-3-2, Part 2, and in USCB, 1933–36, 465/0.1.0.7.1 (1).

49 Canadian Welfare Council, *Social Work at the League of Nations* (Canada: Canadian Welfare Council, 1936), 13.

50 Rooke and Schnell, *No Bleeding Heart,* 41–42.

51 On international congresses and women's transnational ties, see Leila Rupp, *Worlds of Women: The Making of an International Women's Movement* (Princeton: Princeton University Press, 1997), 10, 180–204.

52 Whitton to Abbott, 29 May 1933, LAC, CWC, 1933–36, 465/0.1.0.7.1.

53 Abbott to Whitton, 22 October 1928, LAC, CWC, 2/15 (1928).

54 Whitton to Abbott, 26 July 1933, USCB, 1933–36, 465/0.1.0.7.1; Abbott to Whitton, 22 October 1928, LAC, CWC, 2/15 (1928).

55 Whitton to Lenroot, 18 April 1937, COL/16/League of Nations Advisory Committee.

56 Gordon, *Pitied but Not Entitled,* 79–80; Patricia Rooke and R.L. Schnell, "Chastity as Power: Charlotte Whitton and the Ascetic Ideal," *American Review of Canadian Studies* 15, 4 (1985): 389–403.

57 Gordon, *Pitied but Not Entitled.*

58 S.W. Harris to Abbott, 1 May 1934, USCB, 1933–36, 465/0.1.0.7.1.

59 "Preliminary Conference of Government Representatives on Organization of the Commission, 1936," Part 4, 1–4, USCB, 1933–36, 465/0.1.0.7.1, Canadian Welfare Council, *Social Work at the League of Nations,* 71–72.

60 Alison Neilans to Members of the Equal Moral Standard Committee of the International Alliance of Women for Suffrage and Equal Citizenship, 29 July 1936, USCB, 1933–36, 465/0.1.0.7.1.

61 "Preliminary Conference of Government Representatives on Organization of the Commission, 1936," Part 4, 2, USCB, 1933–36, 465/0.1.0.7.1.

62 Whitton to Harris, 2 July 1936, USCB, 1933–36, 465/0.1.0.7.1.

63 Lenroot to Prentiss Gilbert, 13 July 1936, USCB, 1933–36, 465/0.1.0.7.1.

64 Miller, "The Social Section," 166; Rupp, *Worlds of Women,* 216.

65 Maria de Stellar to Lenroot, 13 March 1937, USCB 1937–40, 665/0.1.0.7.1.

66 Communications received from Miss Lenroot, November 1936, LAC, CWC, 129/2345 (1936–41).

67 Lenroot to Whitton, 28 February 1938, LAC, CWC, 129/2359; Whitton to Lenroot, 10 September 1937, USCB, 1937–40, 820/7.3.3.2.

68 Whitton to Lenroot, 1 October 1937, USCB, 1937–40, 820/7.3.3.2.

69 Lenroot to Whitton, 8 September 1936, USCB, 1937–40, 820/7.3.3.2.

70 "Report of the Delegate of Canada to the Advisory Committee on Social Questions, May 1938," 14, LAC, CWC, 129/2343.

71 Castendyck to Whitton, 30 March 1938, USCB, 1937–40, 820/7.3.3.2; Whitton to Castendyck, 28 March 1940, USCB, 1937–40, 665/0.1.0.7.1.

72 League of Nations, Advisory Commission for the Protection and Welfare of Children and Young People, *Report on the Work of the Commission in 1936* (Geneva: League of Nations, 1936), 17.

73 "Some General Conclusions to Be Derived from the Study of Placing Children in Families," Appendix 2 in League of Nations, Advisory Committee on Social Questions, *Report on the Work of the Committee in 1938* (Geneva: League of Nations, 1938), 21–24.

74 Marshall, "Conflicting Ideas," 14–15.

75 Ibid.

76 Robert Mills, "The Placing of Children in Families, Part III: Considerations in the Organization of Child Placing Measures," *Canadian Welfare Summary* 14, 3 (1938): 28.

77 Whitton to Lenroot, 3 May 1937, USCB, 1937–40, 820/7.3.3.2. On the general approach, see Wikander, "Some 'Kept the Flag Waving': Debates at International Congresses on Protecting Women Workers," in *Protecting Women: Labour Legislation in Europe, the United States, and Australia, 1880–1920* (Urbana: University of Illinois Press, 1995), 29–62.

78 Lenroot to E.E. Ekstrand, 6 February 1937, USCB, 1937–40, 665/0.1.0.7.1; "Report of the Delegate of Canada to the Advisory Committee on Social Questions," May 1938, LAC, CWC, 129/2343.

79 Lenroot to Norman Robertson, 18 April 1938, LAC, CWC, 129/2359 (1936–38).

80 Canada, *Report of the Canadian Delegation* (1937), 17; Miller, "Social Section and the Advisory Committee," 169–70; Rooke and Schnell, "Uncramping Child Life," 197.

81 Whitton to Lenroot, 18 April 1937, COL, 16/Advisory Committee.

82 Whitton to Lenroot, 15 March 1938, USCB, 1937–40, 665/0.1.0.7.1 (1).

83 Lenroot to Whitton, 19 March 1938, USCB, 1937–40, 665/0.1.0.7.1 (1).

84 Meeting of the Advisory Committee on Social Questions of the League of Nations, 6 April 1940, USCB, 1937–40, 665/0.1.0.7.1.

85 Elsa Castendyck, Conference on Refugee Children, Ottawa, 3 and 4 June 1940 and 8 June 1940, COL, 17/War Refugee Problems.

86 Balcom, *The Traffic in Babies*, Chaps. 1–4.

87 Quoted in Hareven, "An Ambiguous Alliance," 94.

"The Necessity of Going"
Julia Grace Wales's Transnational Life as a Peace Activist and a Scholar

LORNA R. MCLEAN

On Thursday, 24 November 1915, Julia Grace Wales received the following telegram: "Will you come as my guest aboard the ship, the Oscar second of the Scandinavian-American line sailing from New York December fourth for Christiana Stockholm and Copenhagen ... Jane Addams and Thomas A Edison ... have accepted today ... Please wire reply, Biltmore Hotel. Henry Ford."[1] After receiving support from the president of the University of Wisconsin, who arranged for her leave of absence from the English Department, Wales set sail on an international adventure that would last for more than a year.[2] By meeting with European government officials and peace activists, Wales and her shipmates hoped to establish an international conference dedicated to negotiating an end to the war.

It is perhaps not surprising that Ford invited the Canadian-born Wales to set sail on the peace expedition. One year earlier, in December 1914, after witnessing the devastating effect of the war on her family, friends, and students, Wales had conceived a plan to bring an end to the war. Originally titled "Continuous Mediation without Armistice," her plan urged the US government to call a conference and invite delegates from neutral nations to advance proposals to end the war. The Wisconsin Peace Society and the Wisconsin legislature adopted Wales's plan, and following acclamation by the National Peace Conference, it was forwarded to the president, Woodrow Wilson. Several months later, Wales teamed up with forty-one American women as delegates to the International Congress of Women at The

Hague, where her plan was endorsed by Congress. She spent the following year touring northern Europe and meeting with diplomats and heads of
state. Upon returning to her position as instructor of English at the University of Wisconsin, she received the telegram from Henry Ford inviting her to
embark on a second European expedition.

Given her significant role as the sole author of the peace plan (and in
light of its significance for international organizations and for opening dialogue among European heads of state), one might expect the Canadian-
born Wales to have received recognition in national and international peace
histories. Yet, to date, few studies in Canada or elsewhere have documented
her peace work.[3] Only recently have two former teachers – one in Canada
and the other in the United States – written book-length publications about
her peace endeavours from 1914 to 1918.[4] In other words, Wales's experiences, and the importance of her achievements, have been obscured by a
historiographical tradition dominated by nationally bounded subjects and
by the accomplishments of women whose political profiles were marked
by public office, organizational leadership,[5] feminist reforms, or "popular"
causes.

In this chapter, I argue that Wales's transnational life experiences influenced her achievements and commemoration as a peace activist to later be
omitted from nationally dominated histories.[6] Wales's life – and ultimately
her legacy – was forged by her religious beliefs, professional career, multinational educational training as a Shakespearean scholar, and encounters with
national and international organizations. Her life history demonstrates that
a transnational framework can illuminate interconnections among states.
Equally important, it illustrates the connections and movements that have
transcended or surpassed national boundaries and, in so doing, illuminates
how these relationships shaped one woman's life in positive and negative
ways.[7]

Wales's transnationalism, mobility, and identification with the peace
movement also shed new light on women's international peace activism.
As Veronica Strong-Boag asserts, although "Canadian women have rarely been the agents of official diplomacy ... [t]hey have, nonetheless, made
their own contribution to the Dominion's external relations. Inasmuch as
Canadians have been world-minded and ultimately peace-minded, they
owe much to the efforts of organized women."[8] Wales may not have been
successful in mediating an end to the war, but her recommendations for a
"world thinking organ" did find their way into Woodrow Wilson's Fourteen
Points, the League of Nations and, later, the United Nations.[9] In this chapter,

I extend notions of rhetoric, activism, and political literacy beyond national boundaries by applying insights from the international literature on social movements to the following transnational structures in Wales's life: intercontinental religious influences and membership in the global Woman's Christian Temperance Union (WCTU), formal education at international universities, and involvement with the Women's International League for Peace and Freedom. All of these influences and structures facilitated Wales's movement across boundaries. Although her travels and engagements with peace organizations slowed down in the late 1920s – when she began her tenure as an assistant professor of English at the University of Wisconsin – Wales maintained her activism through letter-writing campaigns with church, university, and government leaders. Her final publication, *Education for Democracy*, a lengthy primer intended for adult learners and secondary students, was issued in 1942 – five years before her retirement from the university.

Wales was born in the town of Bury, in the eastern townships of Quebec, in 1881. She spent her retirement years living with her sisters in eastern Quebec and died in 1957 at the age of seventy-six. As the eldest of four children, she grew up in a prominent, socially conscious, privileged household in which her father practised as a physician and surgeon. Given her mother's ill health, she often assumed responsibility for running the household and did not attend school until age eleven. Her early formal education resembled that of other white, middle-class, Protestant girls in Quebec – she attended a local girls' academy and, later, McGill University in Montreal.[10]

Four significant influences shaped Wales's life course during her formative years: her close family ties, her strong attachment to the church, her early involvement in women's transnational activist organizations, and her international educational experiences. Her personal papers contain thick files of communication with her family. A steady flow of letters back and forth between Canada, the United States, and numerous European countries helped her stay in close contact as she travelled throughout Canada and across national boundaries. In her prose, she recounted her peace plans and travel adventures, the personal details of day-to-day life, and the events of her social and church-centred engagements. These letters reveal much about her intimate connection with her family and her deep religiosity, which emboldened her wherever she resided. As an adolescent in Canada, Wales attended church services regularly and led Sunday School classes. When she moved to the United States, she attended lectures by religious leaders, spoke at church meetings and youth groups, and taught a course

on the Bible at the University of Wisconsin.[11] Although her transnational
experiences were at times frightening and the "uncertainties of adventure"
caused her concern, Wales inevitably turned to religion for guidance and
revelations. She later mused: "The Christian religion is to me all that makes
life livable, all that makes one's own or other people's troubles bearable. It
must prevail in the end."[12]

At McGill, Wales's religious beliefs and membership with the WCTU
connected her faith with broader international ambitions. Like the women
who became involved in advocacy and policy initiatives for child welfare at
the League of Nations (discussed by Karen Balcom in Chapter 3), Wales became linked with a cadre of women who participated in global social justice
organizations (some religious, others secular) such as the United Church of
Canada and the League of Nations Society to denounce war and organize
and lobby for peace.[13] At age eighteen, after attending her first WCTU convention, Wales wrote a lengthy article about her impressions for the *Montreal Daily Witness*. From her early days in the WCTU, Wales was impressed
with the profound knowledge and organizing capability of the women. "To
any [one] unfamiliar with the work of the Woman's Christian Temperance
Union these [meetings] must have been in many respects a revelation. The
scope of effort shown in the report of departments, the ability, the conscien-
tious thinking and the strength of purpose revealed in all the proceedings
must indeed have been little short of astonishing."[14] Wales continued her
active membership in the WCTU throughout her four years at McGill University, and this experience marked the beginning of a lifetime engagement
with international women's organizations, in which she learned the value of
female-centred political action.[15]

As a university student at McGill, Wales established scholarly networks
and enhanced her rhetorical skills. She arrived just fifteen years after the
university had permitted women to enter the college under the generous endowment of Donald Smith.[16] Writing to her family on a Sunday evening after a week of classes, she declared that she was "feeling homesick" and "not
altogether lik[ing] the atmosphere up at the college."[17] Over time, however,
she connected with the cohort of female students known as the "Donaldas"
and took part in a variety of college activities. As a Donalda, Wales took her
first- and second-year classes with a hundred other female students at Royal
Victoria College, and she attended senior and laboratory classes on the Mc-
Gill campus.[18] At the college, she signed on for the Delta Sigma, McGill
Women's Literacy Society debates, and served as a member of the editorial
board for McGill's annual publication. Since most courses at McGill were

taught by men,[19] the single-sex environment of extracurricular activities allowed for the formation of female identity within the larger college.[20] Debating societies and editorial boards also helped Wales develop her rhetorical skills as a writer and public speaker.

As was the case at other colleges in Canada, the United States, and Britain, Wales attended McGill during a time of polarized and acrimonious debate about women's ability to cope with higher education and the gendered structure of the colleges that women should attend – co-education versus women-only colleges.[21] Without doubt, Wales was an excellent scholar: she graduated from McGill with first-rank honours in English literature, delivered the Class Prophecy Speech, received the Shakespeare Gold Medal, and was awarded the Edward Austin Scholarship to complete her master's degree at Radcliffe College, Harvard University. Of the four recipients who received the $200 scholarship in 1903, Wales was the sole Canadian.[22]

Scholarships made it possible for Wales to pursue her transcontinental studies, first at Radcliffe and five years later in London. Award funds not only facilitated her travels, they also extended her international connections and exposed her to academic expertise.[23] Moving to the United States and obtaining a master's degree from a prestigious American university also expanded her career options. That Canada had few universities – and none with all-female graduate programs – perhaps prompted her to pursue studies beyond the border. As Donald Wright asserts in his study of the professionalization of history in English Canada, Canadian women historians were often encouraged to pursue graduate programs in the United States or England to enlarge their academic career opportunities.[24] Wales's educational path resembled that of a cohort of women from former British colonies who travelled transnationally in New Zealand, Australia, the United States, and Europe in the early twentieth century in search of scholarly expertise.[25]

Women who entered Radcliffe in the first three decades of the twentieth century received mixed messages. Perhaps the most contradictory message was that they should strive for equality in educational – but not career – opportunities.[26] Like many of the seven women with whom she graduated from Radcliffe, Wales became a teacher, first at a girls' school in Montreal between 1904 and 1908 and four years later as an assistant instructor at the University of Wisconsin.[27] With her experience as a teacher in a girls' school and as a graduate of McGill and Radcliffe College, she was more than qualified to prepare "pre-freshmen" students for academic studies in English literature. Her students, children of immigrants and the first generation to attend the University of Wisconsin, enhanced Wales's enthusiasm for transnational studies in England and her membership in the International Club at the university.[28]

By studying at a US university, Wales at once advanced her professional networks and opportunities for crossborder employment. In Canada, academic positions for women were practically nonexistent. As historian Judith Fingard reports, Dalhousie University had barely begun to hire women in the 1920s. Likewise, McGill and the Universities of Manitoba, Toronto, and British Columbia employed few female professors, although, in 1910, the same year that Wales was hired at the University of Wisconsin, the University of Toronto employed fourteen female instructors.[29] Historian Alison Prentice has observed that Canada lacked the educational opportunities for nineteenth-century women because "neither the patterns that worked in the United States or in Great Britain were fully viable."[30] The early-twentieth-century academy remained the world of white, privileged men.[31] However, the expansion of land-granting universities and women's colleges in the United States increased women's chances of obtaining academic positions, bearing in mind that what was possible for women in academe "was framed by their identity as women."[32]

The University of Wisconsin particularly suited Wales as a woman academic, and it served her interests as a social reformer and political activist. Founded in 1849, the university had a history of linking academic courses with practical pursuits. Throughout the nineteenth and twentieth centuries, the university offered summer institutes for school teachers and mechanics, an education program for state farmers, an extension program in public health, and radio broadcasts (the first in the country). Wales contributed to these community-based programs by teaching English courses for new immigrants and mature students.[33] Unlike extension programs at other universities, those of the University of Wisconsin focused on the educational needs of its adult citizens. Instead of traditional lectures, instructors based their classes on a variety of innovative pedagogical methods organized by an autonomous office with its own mission and funding.[34] This approach, which inspired other programs throughout the twentieth century, became known as "the Wisconsin Idea." Based on a commitment to progressive reforms in education, the program survived numerous challenges, including the Depression and two world wars.[35] By branding the approach "the Wisconsin Idea," the University of Wisconsin imbued itself with a sense of mission, and Wales was among the faculty who demonstrated the university's ethical civic responsibility and lent an air of authenticity to its purpose.

With the exception of her involvement in the Professional Women's Club in Madison, Wisconsin (of which she was a founding member), and the University of Wisconsin International and Century Clubs, Wales's social life consisted mostly of church attendance and meetings with the WCTU and peace groups, the Thursday Club, the Wisconsin Peace Society, and the Women's Peace Party, which later became the US branch of the Women's International League for Peace and Freedom.[36] A letter to her family confirms this observation: the "thing that has made me so happy in Madison has been very largely my satisfactory church connection and the feeling of having human contact."[37] Such friendships, much like those described by Karen Balcom and Catherine Gidney in their chapters in this book, were part of a critical network of (mostly) women who were sustained by their relationships in professional groups and associations.[38] There is "no doubt," Wales wrote, "that friendship touches its highest levels in those times when people are pulling together and lending each other support in a cause that arouses the highest enthusiasm. It is in the atmosphere of active concentrated work that the strongest human relationships are developed."[39] As feminist studies of internationalism remind us, religion and related social reform work provided the basis for crosscultural women's networks such as the WCTU and peace groups.[40]

In December 1914, during the Christmas recess, Wales conceived her plan for "mediation without armistice" and presented it to the Wisconsin Peace Society. Over the next few months, a series of critical decisions had major implications for Wales's identity as the author of the peace plan. The "rebranding" of her nationality evolved in surprising ways as her plan progressed through various American and international peace organizations. From the beginning, Wales worried that her colonial status as "British" might negatively affect her plan's outcome because the United States had remained neutral while Britain was a belligerent in the war. Moreover, several authors have suggested that Wales doubted that a document prepared by a woman would be taken seriously by government officials.[41] Regardless of the rationale, when the National Peace Conference and the Wisconsin legislature adopted the published version of her plan, the Wisconsin Peace Society was listed as author.[42] The plan's Canadian author – Julia Grace Wales – was relegated to the sidelines.

By the time the Wisconsin Plan made its way through the national peace organization, Wales's Canadian nationality had been superseded by her newly fashioned identity as an American. In preparation for the American delegation's presentation at the International Congress of Women in The Hague, the American delegates, headed by Jane Addams and Emily Balch, reissued the Wisconsin Plan. In this international version, Julia Grace Wales's name, along with her national identity, now appeared as follows: "International Plan for Continuous Mediation without Armistice by Julia Grace Wales, delegate from the University of Wisconsin to the International Congress of Women at the Hague."[43] As one reporter so aptly stated: "The World War now dishonoring Europe is not barren. It has produced its great woman, produced her in the quiet academic town of Madison. She is Julia Grace Wales."[44] Wales's reputation as an American activist with international influence had been forged.

The question of Wales's national identity surfaced again when she attended the International Women's Congress at The Hague. When Wales expressed concern about joining the Women's Peace Party's expedition, Addams invited her to travel with the American delegation. Addams denied that Wales's colonial citizenship was a problem, given that "formerly liv[ing] in Canada wouldn't make the least difference in the world." In acknowledging Wales's colonial past, Addams reassured her that "six well known English women have signed the call." In the end, Wales seized the opportunity "to push forward" her plan at the peace conference.[45] In the spring of 1915, Wales joined with hundreds of women from different countries to express their international friendship. This historic event led to the founding of the Women's International League for Peace and Freedom.[46]

Wales's transnational trips and travels in Europe had a major impact on her life. While residing in Europe, she met with members of the International Peace and Freedom League, spoke at gatherings, and arranged meetings with heads of state. Wales's experiences travelling to Europe with leaders such as Addams, whom some viewed as the most respected woman in the United States,[47] and conversing with diplomats, government officials, and other reformers gave her opportunities to learn critical lessons on advocacy and negotiation. They may also have taught her that the international margins could be a place of power and strategic control. Although the margins are often seen as sites of disempowerment and limitation, they can also, as Julie Des Jardins observes in her study of academic women in the United States in the early twentieth century, be "spaces of opportunity, experimentation, and perspective."[48]

Wales's congenial relationship with Addams undoubtedly helped her hone key tactical methods to further her political ambitions. In her communications with family, Wales expressed great appreciation for Addams's erudition and leadership, qualities that she had observed while travelling with Addams in the United States and Europe, first as a member of the Women's International League and then during the Ford expedition. During the first trip, Wales anticipated Addams's unique contribution in The Hague, where "she will be the most needed, because there the hard intellectual struggle will begin."[49] Wales found her association with Addams "a most inspiring experience," and she celebrated Addams's vision of mediation, which offered "peace at every step."[50]

While on these international peace missions, Wales gained self-assurance as she lobbyied alongside her American and British counterparts. When she later recounted her experience as part of the American delegation, she stressed that "[t]he forty women, who were delegates from many American organizations, were going to the conference not as individuals, but as representatives of the enthusiasm of thousands of people. It was this sense of a strong sentiment behind us that gave us confidence."[51] As a sojourner on two European expeditions, Wales gained political capital nationally and internationally; in subsequent years, she would repeatedly draw on her transnational experiences, which had been launched and located within national frameworks and structures, to legitimate her peace campaigns.

Upon returning from Europe, and following a period of rest at her family home in Quebec, Wales resumed her teaching duties at the University of Wisconsin in 1919 and contemplated pursuing a PhD. In 1920, she won a scholarship, the first ever awarded to a female academic from North America to study in London, to continue her research on Shakespeare.[52] No doubt, her prior transatlantic experiences affected this decision. During her lengthy travels with delegates to and throughout northern Europe, Wales encountered a group of well-educated, professional women who mentored her by modelling careers that combined social justice and activism with academia. She enjoyed friendships and had a great admiration for such "remarkable women" as Sophoniba Breckenridge, assistant professor of social economy and dean of the University of Chicago School of Civics and Philanthropy, and Grace Abbott, lecturer on immigration, also at the University of Chicago.[53] Within six years of completing her dissertation at the University of London on a selection of Shakespeare's plays, Wales graduated with a PhD from the University of Wisconsin and immediately accepted an offer to be an assistant professor in the same faculty in which she had taught English as an instructor.

Wales's formative experience working within reform organizations (in particular the international WCTU and the Women's International League for Peace and Freedom, combined with her formal training as a Shakespeare scholar, helped her master the tactics of civic engagement – the strategies of dissemination, rhetoric, and effective literacy. Literacy, according to Catherine Hobbs, "in its broadest sense denotes not only the technical skills of reading and writing, but the tactical – or rhetorical – knowledge of how to employ those skills in the context of one or more communities."[54] Political literacy can be defined as methods of analyzing, assessing, arguing, and changing the political system.[55] As we shall see, while teaching at the University of Wisconsin and later during her retirement years, Wales used the tactics of civic engagement to wage a campaign with religious, academic, and government leaders as she drew upon her transnational connections and identity as a peace activist to sharpen her rhetorical strategies.

Wales's identity as a Shakespearean scholar is critical to understanding how she marshalled her rhetorical skills to generate a form of political literacy. Given her formal training – gained in Canada, the United States, and England – Wales would have been familiar with Shakespeare's rhetorical structures. Moreover, as Richard Foulkes asserts, between 1832 and 1916, Shakespeare's cultural pre-eminence, nationally and internationally, reflected the fact that the performance of his plays was an important part of empire – a kind of travelling text. Thus, there is an interesting conjuncture between Wales's interest in global connections and her choice of an author with international meaning and cachet.[56]

By the 1920s, Wales had begun to distance herself from national peace organizations but not from peace initiatives. The divide between Wales and these organizations might have been based upon differing views on tactics, leadership, and philosophical approaches to peace. It might also have been strategic. By not aligning herself with particular organizations, Wales could freely position her public message to suit the religious or political orientation of her audience. As well, given her transnational status as a Canadian and an American, she could assume either identity to find favour with each nationality in her language and rhetoric. When she wrote to the prime minister of Canada, for example, she identified herself as a Canadian citizen, and she frequently used her Quebec address in her communications with the minister's office when she visited her family home over the summer. Likewise, when corresponding with religious leaders in the United States, she used her home address in Madison, Wisconsin. However, her most frequent identity in both Canada and the United States was as a member of the international peace conference (the Women's International League for Peace and Freedom) and the Ford Peace Expedition, both of which legitimized her authority as a peace activist. To quote from one example, the biographical note to her 1940 article "Religious Leadership in Time of War," published in the Quaker journal *Friends Intelligencer*, states: "Julia Grace Wales is a teacher in Madison, Wisconsin. As author of the pamphlet 'Mediation Without Armistice,' she went with Jane Addams' group to the Women's International Conference in the Hague in 1915 and later spent a year and a half in Stockholm as a member of Henry Ford's peace expedition."[57]

For government officials and university administrators, Wales's letters and peace plans helped establish her identity and position because they showcased her rhetorical tactics, which drew upon scientific and rational forms of argumentation.[58] By paying careful attention to the nuances of rhetoric, Wales demonstrated that she understood that successful discourse in any community builds upon the style and types of conversations common to that community.[59] As a case in point, in the 1940s, she forwarded a draft of her new peace plan titled "A Suggestion for a Permanent Inter-Universities Committee on International Problems" to the president of the United States, the prime minister of Canada, and various university presidents, calling upon them to "perform an unofficial auxiliary to that of the official organs of the United Nations," which would be "set up for the specific task of dealing scientifically with points of conflict."[60]

Her letters to religious leaders combined universal humanity with sympathetic benevolence. When writing to James Franklin, chairman of the Department of International Justice and Goodwill of the Federal Council of Churches, Wales's dramatic rhetoric proclaimed that "the religious forces of the world are of tremendous and incalculable power, but like the tides of the sea are unharnessed. To concentrate that power, bring it to bear at the right spot and moment, we need a mechanism." To achieve these goals, she called upon the chivalric impulses of religious leaders to take up her plan for an "International Commission for Continuous Mediation ... to focus the thinking of mankind on the conditions of a just and permanent peace." This letter foreshadowed further flourishes of communication directed at international religious leaders.[61]

Wales routinely circulated her publications among leaders. Years of membership in the WCTU had schooled Wales in the practical details of lobbying.[62] By way of illustration, in 1940, she purchased two hundred copies of her article "Religious Leadership in Time of War: An Open Letter to the Churches" and mailed transcripts to religious and political organizations in the United States and Canada.[63] With her sister Evelyn, she also mailed copies of her book, *Democracy Needs Education,* to the ministries of education in Canada and the United States. Wales had written the textbook for use in schools and adult-education centres to promote international civic engagement; mostly, it received endorsements from the Ontario Teachers' Federation and the League of Nations Society in Canada, where it was published.[64]

The question remains as to Wales's success at negotiating her international connections to promote peace. As with most social justice initiatives, it is difficult to measure Wales's influence. Return letters reveal how some of her correspondence was received. Prime Minister King's private secretary, H.R. Henry, for example, informed her that, at "Mr. King's direction, copies of her Continuous Mediation document would be sent to the Canadian delegates of the San Francisco Conference and would be brought to the attention of the Secretary to the Canadian delegation at the Conference."[65] Others, such as Howard Wilson of Harvard University, expressed approval of and keen interest in the general objectives of her Inter-University Committee and requested additional information on the development of her plan.[66] Similarly, in 1939, Dr. Buttrick of the New York City Presbyterian Church wrote to Wales to inform her that her program for an unofficial "International Commission for Continuous Mediation" had been forwarded to the headquarters of the Federal Council of the Churches of Christ in America, along with his personal endorsement.[67] Although one of the central features of her plan – an independent body of scholars associated with the United Nations – came to fruition, it is unclear whether it was her idea or her lobbying that was the genesis for this enterprise.

Wales's optimism about the power of education and moral suasion derived from her religious beliefs, transnational academic training, and experiences as an activist. She felt a deep responsibility to act as a good Christian should by promoting global peace and social justice – a characteristic she shared with others in the peace movement.[68] Wales articulated the certainty of her convictions and her humanitarian and benevolent desire to end suffering in a brief article penned in 1949, two years after she had retired from the University of Wisconsin. In this essay, titled "The Condensed Statement of My Experience with the Ford Conference," she recalled her intense timidity at the onset of the Ford Mission: "I set out from Madison in Dec. 1915, with a feeling of dread, which proved to be not unjustified. Nevertheless, I am more profoundly thankful that I went on the Ford Expedition and if I could have known what was before me, though I should have dreaded it more, I would have felt doubly the necessity of going."[69]

Wales must have been emboldened by the candor shown in response to her correspondence with public officials and the enthusiastic endorsement of her plans for peace. But nothing in life matched the ebullience she experienced during the First World War, when her peace plan was promoted at the International Women's Peace Conference in The Hague and on the Ford Peace Expedition. It is perhaps not surprising that when Wales commenced writing her memoir at the age of seventy, she began her life narrative by quoting the telegram from Henry Ford that appears at the beginning of this chapter.[70]

*****

The historical narrative of the twentieth century includes poverty, genocide, catastrophic wars, and the displacement of populations. Like other peace reformers, Wales witnessed the horror and devastation of war and tried to imagine a better world.[71] She sustained her commitment and energy over a lifetime, sometimes with the assistance of local, national, and international organizations but more often with the support of friends and family. That she was able to maintain her steely dedication to peace without becoming overwhelmed by tragedy or embittered by disappointment says much about how her spiritual beliefs shaped her life.

As a transnational scholar, Wales succeeded in completing her graduate studies in a number of countries and was hired at a university in the United States when few female academics in Canada obtained similar positions. Moreover, when she travelled to European countries with peace expeditions, Wales experienced adventures that would not have been possible had she remained in Canada. Her journeys facilitated her academic career and peace campaigns in substantial ways; in particular, they offered her professional experience and the opportunity to network with other scholars and like-minded reformers and to establish international credentials. But she also encountered difficulties when she travelled beyond Canada; living in the United States posed challenges for her work within a transnational peace organization. Perhaps, ironically, moving across the border, coupled with her desire to participate in global concerns, led to a suppression of the multiple possibilities and multiple identities that we often associate with mobility.[72]

Wales's transnational identity as a peace activist might also have contributed to the erasure of her national and international legacy as a peace activist. As Ann Taylor Allen, Anne Cova, and June Purvis make clear, having an international or transnational perspective does not necessarily downplay the importance of national identity – in fact, it often brings it into sharp relief.[73] When Wales positioned her international commitment to peace above her own individual heroic journey, she minimized her achievements as recorded in nationally based written records. Furthermore, as some historians have observed, women's accomplishments, especially if the women were involved in unpopular causes, were often overlooked or forgotten. Dianne Dodd underscores this point in an article on Canadian heroines and historic sites. According to Dodd, women such as Agnes Macphail did not have the same appeal for commemoration at the federal level as other prominent women such as Nellie McClung. She speculates that Macphail's neglect stemmed, in part, from the fact that she was not a "colourful 'character' in her community," nor did she promote popular reform causes.[74] I argue that Wales's accomplishments have also been neglected. Despite writing a peace plan that was adopted by the Wisconsin Peace Society, the Wisconsin legislature, the National Peace Conference, and the International Congress of Women at The Hague, Wales is rarely mentioned in historical accounts of peace activism, unlike the two American leaders of the Women's International League for Peace and Freedom and the Ford Expedition – Jane Addams and Emily Greene Balch – women who received Nobel Peace Prizes in 1931 and 1946, respectively.[75]

There has been no public commemoration of Julia Grace Wales or her peace plan in Canada. In the United States, several years after her death, the University of Wisconsin marked the building of the Sellery Hall Residence by naming one of its floors after Wales. Beside her portrait in the main foyer, the plaque modestly proclaims her dual accomplishments as a transnational academic and a social activist: "Julia Grace Wales dedicated her life to international friendship and understanding and teaching of literature."

NOTES

I greatly appreciate the commentary and insights provided by Sharon Cook, Cecilia Morgan, Nancy Janovicek, Catherine Carstairs and the two anonymous peer reviewers. In addition, I thank the Women Who Write group – created by Rhonda Pyper, Telfer School of Management, and organized by Françoise Moreau-Johnson, coordinator, Centre for Academic Leadership, University of Ottawa – for its support.

1 Julia Grace Wales, letter "home" on 27 November 1915, Library and Archives Canada (LAC), Julia Grace Wales fonds, MG 30, Series C-238, Vol. 1, No. 55.
2 Draft letter to *Maclean's*, 21 December 1954, LAC, MG 30, C-238, Vol. 1, No. 52.
3 In the American historiography, there is no mention of Wales in Linda K. Schott's book *Reconstructing Women's Thoughts: The Women's International League for Peace and Freedom before World War II* (Palo Alto, CA: Stanford University Press, 1997); Anne Firor Scott's book *Natural Allies: Women's Associations in American History* (Chicago: University of Illinois Press, 1991); or Leila J. Rupp's *Worlds of Women: The*

Making of an International Women's Movement (Princeton, NJ: Princeton University Press, 1997). David Patterson's four-hundred-page book on women and peace, *The Search for Negotiated Peace: Women's Activism and Citizen Diplomacy in World War 1*, briefly mentions Wales. In Canada, there are several articles that reference Wales's peace plan. See, Veronica Strong-Boag, "Peace-Making Women: Canada, 1919–1939," in *Women and Peace: Theoretical, Historical and Practical Perspectives*, ed. Ruth Roach Pierson (Kent: Croom Helm, 1987), 170–91; Barbara Roberts, "*Why Do Women Do Nothing to End the War?" Canadian Feminist-Pacifists and the Great War* (Ottawa: Canadian Research Interests for the Advancement of Women, 1985); and Barbara Roberts, "Women against War, 1914–1918: Francis Beynon and Laura Hughes," in *Up and Doing: Canadian Women and Peace*, ed. Janice Williamson and Deborah Gorham (Toronto: Women's Press, 1989), 48–65. For full-length articles on Wales, see Carol Lawrence, "Julia Grace Wales: The Canadian Girl Who Has Won World-Wide Fame," *Women's Century*, magazine of the National Council of Women in Canada, July 1916, in LAC, MG30, Series C-238, Vol. 1; and Walter Trattner, "Julia Grace Wales and the Wisconsin Plan for Peace," *Wisconsin Magazine of History* 44, 3 (1961): 203–13. More recently, an American literacy scholar has interpreted Wales's peace plan in the First World War in light of her rhetorical strategies. See Wendy Sharer, *Vote and Voice: Women's Organizations and Political Literacy, 1915–1930* (Carbondale: Southern Illinois University Press, 2004).
4 Mary Jean Woodard Bean, *Julia Grace Wales: Canada's Hidden Heroine and the Quest for Peace, 1914–1918* (Ottawa: Borealis Press, 2005) and Donna Fortin, *A Wild Flight of Imagination* (Eau Claire, WI: Bread and Peace Publishing, 2008).
5 Cecilia Morgan makes a similar point regarding the theatrical career of Margaret Anglin in "'That Will Allow Me to Be My Own Woman': Margaret Anglin, Modernity and Transnational Stages, 1890s–1940s," in *Transnational Lives: Biographies of Global Modernity, 1700-Present*, ed. Desley Deacon, Penny Russell, and Angela Woollacott (Basingstoke: Palgrave Macmillan, 2010), 144. In Canada, I am thinking of Nellie McClung and Cairine Wilson, and in the United States, Jane Addams and Emily Balch. Archival collections are also framed by national boundaries. Library and Archives Canada is the central repository for Wales's fonds. Her University of Wisconsin papers are held at the University of Wisconsin Archives. Copies of some of Wales's documents from LAC, personal papers, and her peace society activities are found in the Wisconsin State Historical Archives. Strathmore College also has papers related to her activities with peace organizations.
6 Desley Deacon, Penny Russell, and Angela Woollacott, eds., introduction to *Transnational Lives: Biographies of Global Modernity, 1700-Present* (Basingstoke: Palgrave Macmillan, 2010); Francesca Miller, "Feminisms and Transnationalism," *Gender and History* 10, 3 (1998): 569–80; "International Feminisms," ed. Ann Taylor Allen, Anne Cova, and Jane Purvis, special issue, *Women's History Review* 19, 4 (2010).
7 Deacon, Russell, Woollacott, introduction to *Transnational Lives*, 3.
8 Strong-Boag. "Peace-Making Women," 170. See also Roberts. "*Why Do Women Do Nothing to End the War?"* For a comprehensive analysis of women's efforts to protect children's health and safety amid the global insecurity of the Cold War, see Tarah Brookfield, *Cold War Comforts: Canadian Women, Child Safety, and Global Insecurity, 1945–1975* (Waterloo: Wilfrid Laurier Press, 2012).

9   Woodward Bean, *Julia Grace Wales*, x.

10   Ibid., 3–23.

11   Julia Grace Wales, letters to family from University of Wisconsin, December 1913–June 1914, LAC, MG 30, Series C-238, Vol. 2, No. 23.

12   Ibid.

13   See Strong-Boag, "Peace-Making Women," and Deborah Gorham, "Vera Brittain, Flora Macdonald Denison and the Great War: The Failure of Non-Violence," in *Women and Peace: Theoretical, Historical and Practical Perspectives*, ed. Ruth Roach Pierson (Kent: Croom Helm, 1987), 137–48. See also Karen Balcom, "A Little Offensive and Defensive Alliance," Chap. 3 in this volume.

14   Julia Grace Wales, "Report on W.C.T.U. Convention," LAC, MG 30, Series C-238, Vol. 3, No. 8.

15   Woodward Bean, *Julia Grace Wales*, 35. On the history of the WCTU as an international movement, see Ian Tyrell, *Woman's World/Woman's Empire: The Woman's Christian Temperance Union in International Perspective, 1880–1930* (Chapel Hill: University of North Carolina Press, 1991).

16   By the time Wales arrived on campus, the old Donaldas Building had been closed, but the name remained. See Margaret Gillet, *We Walked Very Warily: A History of Women at McGill* (Montreal: Eden Press Women's Publications, 1981), 168.

17   Sunday, 24 September 1899, letter cited in Woodward Bean, *Julia Grace Wales*, 34.

18   Royal Victoria College opened in 1900. See Gillet, *We Walked Very Wearily*, 168, 174. Wales is listed in the book under "Notes on Some Notables" as a "scholar and peace activist" (434).

19   Wales had few female professors as role models: Gillet, *We Walked Very Warily*, 419.

20   Gloria Bruce, "Radcliffe Women at Play," in *Yards and Gates: Gender in Harvard and Radcliffe History*, ed. Laurel Thatcher Ulrich (New York: Palgrave Macmillan, 2004), 139.

21   The list is extensive. For a recent review essay on women's higher education internationally, see Sara Burke, "Equal Citizenship of the Mind: Recent Studies in the History of Women's Education," *Historical Studies in Education* 2 (May 2011): 81–86.

22   The Edward Austin Scholarship was awarded to "needy, meritorious students and teachers to assist them in payment of their studies." Radcliffe College Annual Reports of the President and Treasurer of Radcliffe College, 79, 87. http://pds.lib.harvard.edu/pds/viewtext/2573658?n=657&s=4&printThumbnails=no. To put this payment in perspective, Carrie Derick was hired as an assistant professor at McGill University in 1904 and received an annual salary of $1,250. See Katie Pickles, "Colonial Counterparts: The First Academic Women in Anglo-Canada, New Zealand and Australia," *Women's History Review* 10, 2 (2001): 277.

23   On crossborder connections among women graduates at the University of New Zealand, see Jenny Collins, "In Search of Scholarly Expertise: Transnational Connections and Women Graduates at the University of New Zealand, 1911–1961," *History of Education Review* 39, 2 (2010): 52–66.

24   Donald Wright, *The Professionalization of History in English Canada* (Toronto: University of Toronto Press, 2005).

25 Collins, "In Search of Scholarly Expertise."

26 Jo Anne Preston, "Negotiating Work and Family: Aspirations of Early Radcliffe Graduates," in *Yards and Gates: Gender in Harvard and Radcliffe History,* ed. Laurel Thatcher Ulrich (New York: Palgrave Macmillian, 2004), 174.

27 Radcliffe College, annual reports of the president and treasurer, http://pds.lib. harvard.edu/pds/viewtext/2573658?n=657&s=4&printThumbnails=no. In the Radcliffe graduating class of 1900, forty-nine women, or 78 percent of the students, became teachers. See Preston, "Negotiating Work and Family," 176. As with McGill University, the Trafalgar School for Girls was partially funded by Donald Smith.

28 Woodward Bean, *Julia Grace Wales,* 37.

29 Alison Prentice, "Bluestockings, Feminists or Women Workers? A Preliminary Look at Women's Early Employment at the University of Toronto," *Journal of the Canadian Historical Association* 2, 1 (1991): 240, Table 1. The first woman was hired at the University of Manitoba in 1914; by 1921, there were fourteen women, mostly in home economics; three worked in the Arts Department. See Mary Kinnear, *In Subordination: Professional Women, 1870–1970* (Montreal/Kingston: McGill-Queen's University Press, 1995), 32–33. See also Judith Fingard, "Gender and Inequality at Dalhousie: Faculty before 1950," *Dalhousie Review* 59, 4 (1984–85): 687–703; Gillett, *We Walked Very Warily;* Lee Stewart, *"It's Up to You": Women at UBC in the Early Years* (Vancouver: UBC Press/Academic Women's Association, 1990); and Catherine Gidney's, "Feminist Ideals and Everyday Life," Chapter 5 in this volume.

30 Alison Prentice, "Scholarly Passion: Two Persons Who Caught It," in *Women Who Taught: Perspectives on the History of Women and Teaching,"* ed. Alison Prentice and Marjorie Theobald (Toronto: University of Toronto Press, 1991), 259, 264. According to Patricia Palmieri, the most radical feature of Wellesley Women's College was its dedication to the principle of education of women by women scholars. See Patricia Palmieri, "Here Was Fellowship: A Social Portrait of Academic Women at Wellesley College, 1895–1920" in Prentice and Theobald, *Women Who Taught,* 235.

31 Dianne Hallman and Anna Lathrop, "Sustaining the Fire of 'Scholarly Passion': Mary G. Hamilton (1883–1972) and Irene Poelzer (1926-n.d.)," in *Women Teaching, Women Learning: Historical Perspectives,* ed. Elizabeth Smyth and Paula Bourne (Toronto: Inanna Publications and Education, 2006), 47, and Alyson King, "The Experience of Women Students at Four Universities, 1895–1939," in *Framing Our Past: Canadian Women's History in the Twentieth Century,* ed. Sharon Cook, Lorna McLean, and Kate O'Rourke (Montreal/Kingston: McGill-Queen's University Press, 2002), 160–65; Wright, *The Professionalization of History in Canada.*

32 Hallman and Lathrop "Sustaining the Fire of 'Scholarly Passion,'" 47.

33 Charles McCarthy, *The* Wisconsin *Idea* (Madison: University of Wisconsin-Madison, 1912), Wisconsin Electronic Reader, http://www.library.wisc.edu/etext/WIReader/.

34 In her study of coeducational land-granting universities in the American Midwest, Andrea Radke-Moss argues that these colleges were inherently progressive for women. See *Bright Epoch: Women and Coeducation in the American West* (Lincoln: University of Nebraska Press, 2008).

35 Daniel Schugurensky, "Selected Moments of the Twentieth Century: The 'Wisconsin Idea' Brings the University to the Community," http://fcis.oise.utoronto.ca/~daniel_schug/assignment1/1907wisconsin.html.

36 Wales kept a diary from 1922 to 1936 in which she recounted lectures and sermons she had attended and the biblical readings she had studied: LAC, MG 30, Series, C-238, Vol. 5, No. 53.

37 Wales, letters to the family from University of Wisconsin, December 1913–June 1914, LAC, MG 30, Series C-238, Vol. 2. JGW

38 Gidney, "Feminist Ideals and Everyday Life," Chap. 5, this volume, and Karen Balcom "A Little Offensive and Defensive Alliance," Chap. 3, this volume.

39 Wales, "Dear People," 5 April 1914, LAC, MG 30, Series C-238, Vol. 2.

40 Mrinaline Sinha, Donna Guy, and Angela Woollacott, "Introduction: Why Feminisms and Internationalism?" *Gender and History* 10, 3 (1998): 345–57.

41 It is not clear from Wales's papers how widespread these concerns were among other members of the Peace Society, nor do the documents confirm who actually made the changes discussed here.

42 Wisconsin Peace Society, Madison, Wisconsin, "Mediation without Armistice, the Wisconsin Plan," LAC, MG 30, Series C-238.

43 Julia Grace Wales, "International Plan for Continuous Mediation without Armistice," LAC, MG 30, Series C-238, Vol. 1, No. 28.

44 This quote is taken from a speech given by pacifist Hamilton Holt, which he repeated throughout his lecture tours throughout the United States. See Woodward Bean, *Julia Grace Wales*, 58.

45 Fortin, *A Wild Flight of Imagination*, 161.

46 Sinha, Guy, and Woollacott, "Introduction," 348.

47 Anne Wiltsher, *Most Dangerous Women: Feminist Peace Campaigners of the Great War* (Boston, MA: Pandora, 1986), 156.

48 Julie Des Jardins, *Women and the Historical Enterprise in America* (Chapel Hill: University of North Carolina Press, 2003), 93.

49 Wales, letter to family, 4 December 1915, LAC, MG 30, Series C-238, Vol. 1, Nos. 3 and 9.

50 Wales, letter to Mrs. Randall, 14 September 1950, LAC, MG 30, Series C-238, Vol. 1, No. 15.

51 Julia Grace Wales fonds, LAC, MG 30, Series C-238, Vol. 4, No. 31.

52 Newspaper clipping (not identified), obituary, 1957, LAC, MG 30, Series C-238, Vol. 3, JGW.

53 Woodward Bean, *Julia Grace Wales*, 66.

54 C. Hobbs, quoted in Sharer, *Voice and Vote*, 21.

55 Sharer, *Voice and Vote*, 9.

56 Richard Foulkes, *Performing Shakespeare in the Age of Empire* (Cambridge: Cambridge University Press, 2002), and Cecilia Morgan, "'That Will Allow Me to Be My Own Woman.'"

57 "Religious Leadership in Time of War: An Open Letter to the Churches," *Friends Intelligencer* 97, 4 (1940): 51–52, in LAC, MG 30, Series C-238, Vol. 5.

58 For this discussion on transnational analysis and rhetoric, I am drawing on Penny Russell's study of Jane Franklin. See "'Citizens of the World?' Jane Franklin's Transnational Fantasies," in *Transnational Lives: Biographies of Global Modernity, 1700-Present*, ed. Desley Deacon, Penny Russell, and Angela Woollacott (Basingstoke: Palgrave Macmillan, 2010), 195–208.

59 Christian Weisser, *Moving beyond Academic Discourse: Composition Studies and the Public Sphere* (Carbondale: Southern Illinois University Press, 2002), xii.

60 Julia Grace Wales fonds, "A Suggestion for a Permanent Inter-Universities Committee on International Problems," 1–6, LAC, MG 30, Series, C-238, Vol. 1, No. 50.

61 Julia Grace Wales fonds, "Correspondence with Churches and Others on War and Peace, 1939–1941," LAC, MG 30, Series C-238, Vol. 4, No. 34.

62 Sharon A. Cook, *"Through Sunshine and Shadow": The Woman's Christian Temperance Union, Evangelicalism, and Reform in Ontario, 1874–1930* (Montreal/Kingston: McGill-Queen's University Press, 1997), 7, 116, 153.

63 Julia Grace Wales fonds, LAC, MG 30, Series C-238, Vol. 5, No. 26.

64 Ontario Secondary School Teachers' Federation, *The Bulletin* 22, 5 (1942): 387; League of Nations Society in Canada, *News Bulletin* 1, 7 (1943): 6; "Books to Buy," in LAC, MG 30, Series C-238, Vol. 2, No. 11.

65 Letter to Miss A. Wales [Julia's sister] from H. Henry, Private Secretary, Office of the Prime Minister, Canada, 5 April 1945, LAC, MG 30, Series C-238, Vol. 4, No. 38.

66 Letter to Julia Grace Wales from Howard E. Wilson, 15 June 1945, LAC, MG 30, Series C-238, Vol. 4, No. 33.

67 Letter to Julia Grace Wales from J. Stephens on behalf of Dr. Buttrick, 2 January 1939, LAC, MG 30, Series C-238, Vol. 4, No. 34.

68 See, for example, Roberts, "Why Do Women Do Nothing to End the War?"; Rupp, *Worlds of Women*; and Strong-Boag, "Peace-Making Women."

69 Julia Grace Wales fonds, "The Condensed Statement of My Experience with the Ford Conference," 1949, LAC, MG 30, Series C-238, Vol. 4, No. 28.

70 Julia Grace Wales fonds, "Memoirs," LAC, MG 30, Series C-238, Vol. 1, No. 55.

71 For a reconsideration of people who could "imagine" a radically better world during a time of catastrophe, see Jay Winter, *Dreams of Peace and Freedom: Utopian Moments in the 20th Century* (New Haven: Yale University Press, 2006), 1–2.

72 I'm grateful to Cecilia Morgan for providing me with this perspective on Wales's transnational experience.

73 Ann Taylor Allen, Anne Cova, and June Purvis, "Introduction: International Feminisms," *Women's History Review* 19, 4 (2010): 497.

74 Dianne Dodd, "Canadian Historic Sites and Plaques: Heroines, Trailblazers, the Famous Five," *Canadian Historic Sites and Plaques* 6, 2 (2009): 50.

75 Rupp, *Worlds of Women*, 193, and Leila Rupp, "Constructing Internationalism: The Case of Transnational Women's Organizations, 1881–1945," in *Globalizing Feminisms, 1789–1945*, ed. Karen Offen (New York: Routledge, 2010), 148.

Feminist Ideals and Everyday Life
Professional Women's Feminism at Victoria College, University of Toronto, 1900–40

CATHERINE GIDNEY

In 1931, Marion Hilliard, the medical adviser to female students at Victoria College, spoke to students at the University of Toronto about being a doctor. She enthusiastically recommended the field of medicine to women, stating that female doctors were no longer pioneers but had demonstrably secured access to the field of medicine. Discrimination still existed, she admitted: "to be a first-class doctor, a woman must have twice the ability of a man in the same position." Moreover, she continued, "there are some people who would not have a woman doctor, even if they were on their death-bed, and they could not get a man." Yet Hilliard thought that opportunities in the field were "as large as the world," particularly in areas where "only a woman doctor can get in." Despite her generally positive view of women's opportunities in medicine, Hilliard offered a more mixed message about women's social roles. Repeating the dominant views of the time, Hilliard told students that "[a] first-class homemaker is better than a first-class doctor, but a woman doctor must give up any idea of getting married."[1]

Hilliard was one of an increasing number of women who took up new occupations on university campuses in the first decades of the twentieth century. Historians have documented the employment of academic women.[2] But there was another group of emerging professionals on campus – members of the nonacademic staff such as deans of women, doctors, nurses, dietitians, and physical-training instructors.[3] By the turn of the century, educators in English Canadian universities, following their US and British counterparts, had begun to express significant anxiety about the health of male and female students, particularly their sedentary lifestyle, which conflicted with their belief that students required a robust physique to fulfill their role as citizens. Such concern fit within larger Anglo-American eugenic fears regarding both the ability of citizens to produce strong stock for national regeneration and defence and women's changing roles within society. In reaction, North American colleges began to institute a variety of health measures, including compulsory physical training and medical examinations, the creation of infirmaries, and the provision of health talks.[4] As part of this process, university administrators created new occupational positions, particularly for women, to oversee the morals and health of students.

In the first half of the twentieth century, women such as Hilliard who undertook health work among students formed a small but significant presence on the university campus. Little is known about their professional lives, their interactions with one another, or their work among students. In this chapter, I focus on the women hired to fill the positions of dean, physician, and physical instructor at Victoria College, University of Toronto, in the first three decades of the century to illuminate how their professional and feminist activities intersected.[5]

In the 1970s, historians of first-wave feminism largely condemned maternal feminism and the professional women who advocated it. They argued that by adopting maternal feminism rather than a platform of equal rights, and by turning inward to their own occupational interests, these women helped arrest, or constrain, feminism after 1920.[6] Although more recent work suggests women's political activism continued after the vote, the period from 1920 to 1960 remains understudied, as does the role of professional women in this period.[7] In addition, although historians of professionalization have extended our knowledge of the nature of professional women's work, they have generally focused on professional identity, with less explicit discussion of the feminist nature of their activities.[8]

Examining the lives of the women hired at Victoria College thus opens a window not only on the feminist ideals of professional women on campus in the interwar years but also on the space they created for themselves and other women. Through their positions and their personal friendships, I argue, professional women supported female students, created female networks, and participated in women's clubs and societies. In doing so, they drew on both the language of maternal feminism and that of expertise, combining them into a form of professional women's feminism that melded their belief in women's special natures; their sense of authority, which derived from their training and professional positions; and their strong sense of social responsibility, which included a commitment to women's education and care for the moral and physical health of female citizens. Ultimately, their beliefs and actions were limited by their acceptance of the social and cultural constraints on their own and other women's lives: a continuing adherence to the rhetoric of motherhood, the need to embody Christian ideals, and their often secondary status or location on the margins of academe. These contradictions highlight a transitional period in feminism, for these women continued to adhere to elements of the maternal feminism in which they had been raised while embracing their right to a vibrant professional life, a key element of liberal rights that would be enunciated by second-wave feminists. This examination of their professional lives and the networks they created reveals the ways in which professional women's feminism abetted that transition.

The Institutional Context

First established in 1836 as a Methodist preparatory seminary in Cobourg, Ontario, Victoria College began offering university-level courses after 1841. It federated with the University of Toronto in 1887 and opened its doors in Toronto in 1892. After the union of Methodists, Presbyterians, and Congregationalists in 1925, it became affiliated with the United Church of Canada.[9]

Motivated by a belief in the importance of nurturing and disciplining the individual conscience, as well as women's familial role in raising young children, Methodists supported and facilitated women's education, though not in the same way that they did that of men. During its first six years, women attended the female department of the institution, where they received instruction in classes separate from male students and followed a modified curriculum. When Victoria College began offering university-level work, it closed its doors to female students. Women's education continued in female academies and ladies' colleges. By the 1880s, however, a combination of poor institutional finances, changing visions of womanhood, and general pressure for co-education had resulted in the re-admittance of small numbers of female students.[10]

Victoria College's move from Cobourg to Toronto offered proponents of women's education a ready means of increasing women's access to higher education and improving their experience within such institutions. In the mid- to late nineteenth century, a greater theological emphasis on moral and social improvement offered new opportunities for the growing number of educated women who answered the call to service in such forms as missionary, settlement house, and temperance, work. Some of the first alumnae of Victoria College, along with prominent female members of the Methodist community, put their energy into the creation of a women's residence, which they believed could contribute to the proper intellectual, moral, and spiritual growth of Victoria's female students if it had a female administrator. Annesley Hall opened in 1903 under the direction of a female committee of management that had charge of student regulations, finances, and staff appointments.[11]

Women's Networks

Employment at Victoria College allowed female administrators and health experts to carve out a space for themselves and other women on campus. These women did so by participating in, and creating, women's networks on a number of different levels: through their employment, in the residence, on campus, and through national and international organizations. From the 1900s to the 1940s, Victoria College hired a number of women to fill key positions within the women's residence, Annesley Hall, and its various annexes. The following women served as deans: Margaret Addison, 1902–30, with Marjory Curlette serving as acting dean from 1917 to 1918; Dr. Norma Ford, 1931–34; and Dr. Jessie Macpherson, 1934–63.[12] The university hired four doctors during this period: Leila Davis, 1902–10; Helen MacMurchy, 1910–13; Edna Guest, 1920–32; and Marion Hilliard, 1932–early 1940s. The women who filled the position of physical instructor changed fairly regularly. However, several were quite prominent, including, prior to the war, Emma Scott Raff and Mary G. Hamilton and, in the mid-1930s, Dorothy Jackson.

These women generally had significant credentials. All of the deans had bachelor degrees. Several had teaching experience: Addison at Ontario Ladies' College and several collegiate institutes and Curlette as principal of Westbourne School in Toronto.[13] Two would become faculty members at the University of Toronto: Ford in the Department of Biology and Macpherson in the Department of Philosophy.[14] All of the physicians graduated from the University of Toronto, had local family practices, and held a variety of other posts at local Toronto hospitals.[15] Emma Scott Raff founded the Margaret Eaton School, one of the first physical-training schools in Canada. The other physical instructors graduated from the Sargent School, a leading New England institution, and worked at the Margaret Eaton School.[16]

Work became available to these women in the early twentieth century when university authorities saw the need to staff newly built residences and ensure the morality and health of students. Women obtained positions at Victoria College in a variety of ways. Most had some personal connection either to Victoria College itself or to the Methodist (or, after 1925, United) Church. Addison and Scott Raff were friends of, and supported by, Nathaniel Burwash, president of Victoria College from 1887 to 1913.[17] Physicians tended to be recommended by their predecessors, but they also had some personal ties to the college. Helen MacMurchy had Leila Davis's endorsement and was a friend of Margaret Addison.[18] Marion Hilliard had lived in residence as a student from 1920 to 1924. She not only had the support of Edna Guest, the previous medical attendant, but was also friends with Jessie Macpherson, the dean at the time of her appointment. Macpherson and Hilliard had attended the University of Toronto at the same time and had both been active in campus athletics as well as the student Christian movement.[19]

The women hired usually had strong ties to the Methodist network connected to Victoria College. Personal relationships thus facilitated these women's access to employment, which in turn provided them with the opportunity to fulfill professional goals and ambitions. Once established, professional women drew on their connections to fill new positions. By hiring others, professional women and their supporters provided opportunities for other women and contributed to the building of campus networks.[20] These personal and professional ties highlight the existence, and creation, of an Anglo, Christian, urban, middle-class elite.

The women's residence provided a base from which to nurture these women's endeavours. Deans oversaw the continuing development of female students – their moral and spiritual growth, their habits and behaviour, their physical and mental health, and their intellectual progress. Yet the residence also provided a space through which they encountered other like-minded women. At Victoria College, the dean was responsible to a female committee of management, which brought her into contact with the Methodist elite of Toronto. She also worked in close association with the physicians and instructors in Physical Education and thus regularly met and interacted with other prominent professionals living in the area.

Through residence work, and an interest in women's issues, professionals employed at Victoria College became acquainted with their counterparts at other colleges on campus. Deans of women met to compare notes on their institutions and suggest solutions to campus problems. They, along with physicians and physical instructors at the University of Toronto, fought incessantly to improve women's athletic facilities, which lagged significantly behind those provided for men.[21] These women also helped create, and participated in, alumnae associations. While building and working through separate women's organizations, as was common at the time, they fought any notion that women should receive a separate, and possibly inferior, education to that of men. Thus, in 1909, when the University of Toronto Senate established a committee to investigate the possibility of creating a separate women's college, Toronto women banded together to create the United Alumnae Association to fight the proposal.[22]

Deans and physicians also forged other university networks. They participated in the activities of the University Women's Club, founded in 1903. The members of the club organized social events, lectures, and reform activities. For example, they investigated the local conditions and wages of women workers and discussed housing and employment possibilities as well as the need to improve women's educational opportunities.[23] Margaret Addison and Helen MacMurchy both attended club meetings. Indeed, in the early decades of the century, the group often met in the women's residence at Victoria College.[24] Through membership, Addison and MacMurchy socialized with campus women such as Clara Benson, a member of the Faculty of Household Science; Edith Gordon, the medical adviser to women at the University of Toronto; and Mabel Cartwright, a graduate of Lady Margaret Hall, Oxford, and dean of women at Trinity College from 1903 to 1936. Membership also brought them into contact with prominent graduates such as Edith Elwood, an 1896 graduate of Trinity College, a founding member of the club and, from 1905 to 1914, head worker at Evangelia House, one of the local settlement houses.[25]

In addition to their campus activities, many of the nonacademic staff and their acquaintances also created, and participated in, off-campus professional organizations and associations. In 1922, Margaret Addison travelled to Chicago with Mary Bollert, dean of women at UBC, to attend the meeting of the National Association of Women Deans, an American professional society established in 1916.[26] In 1924, Helen MacMurchy and Maude Abbott, a leading medical researcher in Montreal, founded the Canadian Federation of Medical Women.[27] Hilliard became president of the federation as well as both vice-president and president of the Medical Women's International Association.[28]

The women employed at Victoria College also provided leadership and inspiration through their United Church–related youth activities. At different times, Addison, Guest, and Hilliard all attended the United Church's annual student conferences held in Muskoka.[29] Hilliard also brought her influence to bear at other campuses. In 1940–41, she attended a student

Christian mission in Winnipeg. Doris Saunders, the dean of junior women
at the University of Manitoba, reported, "I was particularly impressed by
the delight experienced in the talks of Dr. Marion Hilliard to the women
students on the Broadway campus. The desire they expressed for more
knowledge of a medical and ethical kind suggests that these talks might,
with advantage, be followed by others given by Winnipeg women doctors."[30]

The creation of, and participation in, women's campus organizations
such as the Women's Athletic Association, the Building Committee, the
University Women's Club, and alumnae associations, as well as other off-
campus professional and religious organizations, forms part of a broader
North American pattern dating at least to the early nineteenth century. In
the late nineteenth century, women's and religious groups, infused by Christian idealism, began to develop international networks to bridge national di-
vides and support one another in common aims.[31] As the chapters by Karen
Balcolm and Lorna McLean in this volume indicate, many Canadian women
lived transnational lives and drew inspiration from their involvement in
international organizations. The professional women under consideration
likewise joined a variety of international associations and gatherings, in the
process forging connections with women at other campuses. In 1912, Addison attended the meetings of the World's YWCA in Swanwick, England, and
represented the United Alumnae of the University of Toronto at the Congress of the Universities of the Empire.[32] One of the sessions at that congress
was on "the position of women in universities." Addison addressed attendees at that session at the urging of Ethel Hurlbatt, warden at Royal Victoria
College, who spoke earlier in the program.[33] In 1922, Addison attended the
World's YWCA in St. Wolfgang, Austria. She was a voting delegate along
with both Nellie and Mary Rowell. Nellie Rowell, the wife of Newton Wes-
ley Rowell, a Toronto lawyer and politician, was a member of the residence
committee of management, while Mary Rowell was a faculty member in
the Department of French at Victoria College. Addison also attended the
meetings of the International Federation of University Women in Paris.[34] As
Leila Rupp notes, involvement in one group often brought women into contact with the work of other groups. For example, in 1925 the International
Council of Women created the Joint Standing Committee of the Women's
International Organizations to bring together a number of groups, such as
the World YWCA and the International Federation of University Women,
to advocate for a female appointee to the League of Nations.[35] Thus, by
participating in one organization, women often became aware of the larger
international women's movement.

Educated women not only forged professional networks but also developed supportive personal relationships. Addison and Bollert travelled together. Scott Raff and Hamilton became close friends and drew into their circle Dora Mavor, a graduate of the Margaret Eaton School. Mavor not only helped create an outdoor theatre at Hamilton's girls' camp in Algonquin Park but also assisted with theatrical productions during summers from the 1930s to the 1950s. Through her camp work, Hamilton formed friendships with other female camp operators such as Mary S. Edgar and Ferna Halliday.[36] Jessie Macpherson and Kathleen Coburn bought a small island in Georgian Bay, where they built a cottage and summered together.[37] Others developed life-long partnerships. For example, Marion Hilliard lived with Opal Boynton, a social worker. Dorothy Forward, a don at Victoria College in the mid-1920s, later shared living accommodations with Elizabeth Allin. Both were members of the Department of Physics at the University of Toronto from the 1930s to the 1960s. Some of these relationships were platonic and others romantic, but all provided these women with both financial and emotional support.[38]

Supporting Female Students

Female students often benefitted directly from the formation of women's campus networks. Within residence, professional women acted as mentors for, and supervisors of, the young women under their care. The residence hall was much more than a place to sleep and eat. Administrators believed residence life could contribute to the moral and intellectual formation of residents.[39] Addison, for example, aided women's intellectual development by bringing in speakers of local, national, and international prominence.[40] In addition, she, along with the college physicians, organized a variety of lectures for students. In doing so, she encouraged in students an awareness of public events, local social conditions, current intellectual trends, and their future economic and professional opportunities.

Professional women also supported students in other ways. At the turn of the century, popular attitudes towards women's athletics remained divided; some feared its masculinizing effects, and others encouraged modified forms for their benefits to women's mental and physical health. Addison, Scott Raff, and Guest became female patrons of women's athletic associations, which fostered a competitive spirit by providing athletic trophies for winning teams in a variety of sports.[41] Picking up on the beliefs of experts of the time regarding the relationship between healthy minds and bodies, these women helped institute and sustain compulsory physical training and medical examinations within residence and worked to extend these provisions to off-campus students. A number of the professional women became staunch supporters of improved campus athletic facilities for women. Believing that a student's physical and mental success depended on financial security, several also created scholarships for female students in need.[42]

Many staff members fought to preserve gains made by women on campus, to protect their interests, to extend facilities for students, and to expose them to the work of leading professional women in a variety of fields. In addition to these individual activities, professional women could act as role models and offer support. Historian Karine Hébert has shown that although female students gained entrance to McGill and the University of Montreal in 1884 and 1908, respectively, their full integration into campus life as students rather than as "co-eds" remained incomplete as late as the 1960s.[43] Many of the professional women employed by Victoria College and other institutions had themselves attended university, knew first-hand the difficulties female students faced, and aimed to support their educational endeavours.

Visions of Womanhood

If the women considered here created networks with one another to pursue political aims, enhance job opportunities, and encourage female students in their studies, they did so within specific bounds. As I argue elsewhere, Victoria College, like many other Canadian universities during this period, and indeed well beyond, was animated by a vision of a moral community informed by liberal Protestantism. This moral vision was open to new ideas but not at the expense of faith. It emphasized the traditional evangelical tenets of Christian nurture and evangelism but would become increasingly uncomfortable with the idea of imposing that faith on others; it emphasized social action but not at the sacrifice of individual responsibility; and it accepted a poetic or figurative understanding of Scripture in order to understand the magnificence of God's grace, which both transcended individuals and worked through them.[44] The Methodists' openness to new theological and cultural directions would help legitimize women's educational and occupational ambitions.

The activities of the women under consideration (much like those of Julia Grace Wales, examined by Lorna McLean in this volume) were significantly influenced by their religious beliefs and upbringing. Neil Semple argues that the Christian idealism of Methodists was reinforced by their "commitment to remain active in the world."[45] The belief that "service was an outward sign of a transformed spiritual nature" not only spurred an interest in improving social conditions but also led many professional women to work towards women's advancement.[46] In doing so, professional women intended to affirm, not displace, women's central role as nurturers of Christian faith and life. This vision of womanhood found institutional form within Victoria College.

British and North American administrators hired physicians, deans, and physical educators for the conservative roles of monitoring and protecting the health and morals of female students and shaping womanhood. They perceived the university as the last chance to correct and catch problems unseen by a school system that failed to inspect and train students physically or educate them regarding health matters. They also saw the university as the final place where they could mould young women who they believed were not yet fully formed – mentally, physically, or spiritually.

In considering student formation, administrators and health experts were influenced by nineteenth-century ideas regarding human development and social improvement. Physical growth became a marker of health as well as a sign of mental development and improvement, moral fortitude, and, for women, reproductive capability.[47] Physicians tended to blame the individual rather than the environment for deficiencies. Many social and moral reformers, educators, and health professionals came to believe in the institutionalization of the feeble-minded, and some, such as Helen Mac-Murchy, advocated sterilization. They linked poverty, crime, perceived sexual immorality, and even class position to mental defects rather than to the economic structure of society.[48] As supporters of liberal individualism, however, they also believed that most individuals could pull themselves up physically, thus demonstrating strength of will and character.

Shaping womanhood, then, was never simply a conservative endeavour. The women hired envisaged students as playing a role in individual and social improvement and regeneration and perceived it as their responsibility to ensure that students would be able to take on the duties of citizenship. Progressive ideals counterposed conservative realities. For example, on the one hand, Addison boldly introduced a form of self-government into residence life in 1906. On the other hand, she was responsible for her charges and felt the weight of that responsibility. In 1905, she, along with the deans at Trinity and University Colleges, felt there was too much campus socialization and thus petitioned the university to limit campus social functions.[49] Similarly, professional women supported women's athletics and physical culture but did so within existing norms that reinforced notions of female difference; they advocated physical exercise conducive to the development of essentialist ideas of femininity. For example, Edith Gordon, medical adviser to women at Toronto, emphasized the importance of competitive sport for developing a sense of fair play, cooperation, self-control, and responsibility. But she also argued that an overemphasis on competition or participation in strenuous games without supervision could result in "physical and nervous strain in the formative years."[50]

In the 1920s and 1930s, professional women also saw women's primary responsibilities as being those of mother and volunteer. They continued to emphasize late-nineteenth-century notions about female difference and women's nurturing instinct.[51] As historians have found, the importance of health and education was often stressed in relation to motherhood and citizenship. In 1923, Gordon gave a talk to teachers on "physical training for girls." She argued that physical education was more important for girls than boys because girls were the "future mothers of Canada."[52] Most of the administrators and health experts also emphasized female difference. Historian Wendy Mitchinson notes of Marion Hilliard that she worked within the "medical world she inhabited" and "the limits provided by that perspective." Hilliard, like many other men and women of the time, understood women as being defined by their bodies, saw marriage as a natural goal, and accepted the patriarchal household.[53] Similar perspectives also informed representations of saleswomen in Canadian department store magazines (see Donica Belisle's chapter in this volume).

Yet professional women's ideas about marriage and motherhood in these decades also underwent change. In the 1930s, organizations such as the Canadian Federation of University Women and the Canadian Federation of Business and Professional Women opposed discrimination on the basis of marital status.[54] Some professional women also began to write of the financial and emotional importance of work outside the home.[55] Moreover, even if professional women perceived motherhood as an important role for women, it was not the only option they presented to students. Not surprisingly, given their own situations, professional women at Victoria College opened students' eyes to the range of occupations available to them. They not only acted as role models; through speakers' series, they also introduced students to various professions opening up to women. When Addison spoke in 1912 at the Congress of the Universities of the Empire, she focused on Toronto's course in household science, which trained women to be dieticians and food analysts, two fields she felt were in their infancy but would result in opportunities for women in hospitals, laboratory work, and government.[56]

When they developed health programs at Victoria, professional women sought to help students take full advantage of these new opportunities. Although historians have stressed that experts linked overall female health to reproduction, professional women also equated female health with career success. This emphasis on health formed part of a broader North American trend of inspecting, evaluating, and instructing a wide swath of the population – including children, soldiers, and workers – to enhance their performance and, ideally, create better citizens.[57] Female doctors thus recommended to younger women the need for "a strong mental and physical constitution" to sustain career performance.[58] In other words, a robust womanhood would see women through their life's work.

Mixed Messages

Why did professional women exude the mixed messages illuminated so well in Hilliard's 1931 talk? The answer lies in the reality of their own professional lives and work, which were marked by both independence and social constraint. Indeed, much like the women discussed by Donica Belisle, Heidi MacDonald, and Lorna McLean in this volume, professional women possessed a degree of agency that allowed them to forge successful careers even as they were limited by the resources available to them and the situations in which they found themselves. Although many opportunities in higher education and the professions opened up to women, historians have shown that female students and faculty continued to face discrimination – from unequal access to social and athletic facilities at university to lower pay and limited advancement once they entered the workforce.[59] Nonacademic women on campus faced similar difficulties as well as their own particular set of advantages and constraints. Their positions offered them a significant and relatively secure income as well as a degree of control over workplace conditions.[60] Yet, as staff, they had a secondary status within the university hierarchy, and their continued employment was always contingent on their perceived usefulness to the aims of university administrators. Moreover, their decent income and the lack of alternative opportunities likely ensured their compliance to existing social and cultural norms. They were also expected to provide moral leadership. At Victoria College, for example, professional women often obtained employment through their Methodist connections, helped in running a residence designed around the idea of the Christian family home, and were expected to be role models. So, their employment depended on adhering to the moral codes, both written and unwritten, of the university. Moreover, for those living in residence, employment brought freedom from family obligations and from dependence on family members, but at a cost – limited privacy and time off.

The mixed messages also reflected the structure of employment. The women under consideration obtained their positions because of general beliefs within the university that female students needed special care and protection – work appropriate for women. In her research on the education and careers of American female scientists, Margaret Rossiter refers to this as a territorially based form of sex segregation.[61] The women hired were not only to model forms of middle-class respectability, they were also responsible for ensuring that their charges adhered to societal norms and expectations. Patricia Palmieri has argued of faculty in American women's colleges in the early twentieth century that, on the one hand, "they hoped to challenge the larger culture and to change women's role in society" and, on the other, that "they wished to maintain the image of women's colleges as reputable and respectable institutions."[62] Similarly, women at Victoria College needed to walk a fine line between exposing students to new ideas and reinforcing societal boundaries. Their employment thus depended upon their own and their students' adherence to contemporary notions of female respectability. Yet they were also able to use those notions of respectability, bolstered by their claims to expertise, to carve out professional careers.

Conclusion

The nonacademic professional women at Victoria College presented mixed messages not only to the student body but also to themselves and their cohort. They emphasized the importance of education and the need for a healthy body, and they encouraged women to consider professional careers. However, they accepted that career opportunities were greatest in fields ostensibly related to women; they reinforced the idea of the single career woman; they expressed nineteenth-century beliefs regarding the need to protect female development and reproduction; and they emphasized the superior calling of the homemaker. These mixed messages reflected the realities of their own lives and those of the women around them. And yet, in the end, these women carved out a space for themselves on campus – in the process creating female networks for themselves that extended from the local to the international level – and provided support to female students.

Historians of women and higher education in Canada have demonstrated that in the first half of the twentieth century women occupied a marginal position within universities. Indeed, historical work has focused on women's limited impact and isolation within universities.[63] Yet it seems that the women who worked in the new professions created to take care of female students had more opportunity to forge rich networks than did academic women on campus. Indeed, both in their personal and professional lives, the women of Victoria College developed friendship networks that offered an alternative to traditional family life and validated their ambitions and dedication to their work, networks that might have helped counter the ghettoization of women on campus.[64] It is also possible that their position as women on campus but outside the academy provided them with the space to forge their own careers and lives.

The creation of women's space on campus by these professional women should lead us to re-examine and re-evaluate middle-class feminism in the interwar years. In the past several decades, historians have begun to revise traditional interpretations that emphasized a significant decline in women's political activism after the vote; however, the nature and forms of women's activism after 1920 have yet to be fully explored. The nonacademic women at Victoria College drew from, and combined, the intellectual, social, and cultural currents of the day: a liberal feminism that emphasized women's progress and access to educational and professional opportunities based on individual rights; a maternal feminism that emphasized women's duty to extend their nurturing qualities into the public realm on the basis of their superior nature; a Social Darwinism that emphasized their superiority as members of the Anglo-Saxon race; a sense of social responsibility linked to late-nineteenth-century Christian idealism and internationalism; and a growing belief in the importance of professional expertise.[65] Together, these ideas shaped women's expectations and opportunities in important but contradictory ways.

The contradictions in professional women's beliefs and lived experience illuminate the transitional nature of a period in which the rhetoric of motherhood remained strong even as middle-class women had increasing opportunities to embark on careers. Despite Hilliard's statement in 1931 that a female doctor was no longer a pioneer, moving into universities and new professions remained a radical and daring act for women, one that provided them with intellectual, financial, and emotional control over their own lives. The experiences of Hilliard and her colleagues therefore show us that women's historians need to return to, and greatly expand upon, the study of professional and middle-class women's activism. The painstaking work of re-creating women's professional lives remains in its infancy. Networks between women and women's organizations remain largely hidden. This chapter goes some way in trying to elucidate those connections. Further investigation, however, would increase our knowledge of continuing forms of activism after 1920, the complicated and gradual shift from maternal to liberal feminism, and the links between first- and second-wave feminism. Historians have also begun to reveal the importance of women's clubs and organizations to the creation of nineteenth-century national and international women's movements.[66] Further study of these clubs and organizations may help us understand women's activism in Canada after the vote. By creating and participating in a variety of associations, nonacademic and professional women played a significant role in extending the venues in which women could secure an active public life.

Understanding the activism of professional women within the context of the history of feminism remains elusive. The limited, and mainly biographical, work that exists on professional women in the interwar years categorizes these women in a variety of ways: as ambiguous feminists, transitional figures, interwar feminists, or women involved in activities with "feminist outcomes."[67] Clearly, historians are struggling to understand how to place professional women of the interwar years who fit within neither the ideological fold of maternal feminism nor the middle-class liberal feminism of the second wave. Indeed, historian Franca Iacovetta notes that in light of the defeat of more radical forms of feminism, a "loosely structured liberal-reformist maternal feminism" was the option most likely to gain footing within Canadian politics.[68] Professional women embodied a particular form of feminism – a professional women's feminism – that included a variety of shades but was marked by their middle-class and Christian position, a belief in their authority as derived from their role as experts, and a strong sense of their social responsibility to shape women (and men) into educated Christian citizens. Through their commitment to these ideals, they helped sustain the desire for an expanded place for women on campus and, ultimately, within society.

Professional women's vision of women's place was always constricted – shaped by contemporary ideas about respectability and limited by existing concerns, among women and men alike, about women's role in society. Nonacademic women accepted many of the constraints on their own and other women's lives and, indeed, played a part in creating and perpetuating some of those constraints. Yet they also believed strongly in their responsibility to shape women into educated citizens who would be ready to fulfill their role as mothers, perhaps as professionals, and certainly as community leaders within organizations on the national and international stage. The connections and contacts that women made through their positions at Victoria College allowed them to create a variety of women's networks. Indeed, in the first three decades of the twentieth century, Victoria College and its environs provided an enclave where a female space flourished. There is no doubt, however, that if their everyday lives were shaped and sustained by feminist ideals, those ideals in turn were shaped and limited by their everyday lives.

NOTES

The research for this article was funded by Associated Medical Services, Inc., (Hannah Institute) and the Social Sciences and Humanities Research Council of Canada. I would like to thank Lara Campbell, Mike Dawson, Ruby Heap, the late Cathy James, Marguerite Van Die, and the anonymous reviewers and the editors of this collection for their helpful comments on earlier versions of this chapter.

1 "Women Doctors Cast Off Halo," *Toronto Globe*, 22 January 1931, University of Toronto Archives (UTA), Department of Graduate Records, A73–0026, Box 121/91.

2 See, for example, Mary Kinnear, *In Subordination: Professional Women, 1870–1970* (Montreal/Kingston: McGill-Queen's University Press, 1995); Alison Prentice, "Bluestockings, Feminists, or Women Workers? A Preliminary Look at Women's Early Employment at the University of Toronto," *Journal of the Canadian Historical Association* (1991): 231–61; Judith Fingard, "Gender and Inequality at Dalhousie: Faculty Women before 1950," *Dalhousie Review* 64, 4 (1984–85): 687–703; and Elizabeth Smyth, Sandra Acker, Paula Bourne, and Alison Prentice, eds., *Challenging Professions: Historical and Contemporary Perspectives on Women's Professional Work* (Toronto: University of Toronto Press, 1999).

3 There are brief references to these groups in Prentice, "Bluestockings," 242–43; Anne Rochon Ford, *A Path Not Strewn with Roses: One Hundred Years of Women at the University of Toronto, 1884–1984* (Toronto: University of Toronto Press, 1985), 61–64; and Margaret Gillett, *We Walked Very Warily: A History of Women at McGill* (Montreal: Eden Press Women's Publications, 1981), 428–31.

4 Catherine Gidney, "Institutional Responses to Communicable Diseases at Victoria College, University of Toronto, 1900–1940," *Canadian Bulletin of Medical History* 24, 2 (2007): 268–69, and "The Athletics–Physical Education Dichotomy Revisited: The Case of the University of Toronto, 1900–1940," *Sport History Review* 37 (2006): 132–33. For the United States, see Heather Munro Prescott, *Student Bodies: The Influence of Student Health Services in American Society and Medicine* (Ann Arbor: University of Michigan Press, 2007).

5 Victoria provides a useful case because of its rich sources on women's residential life and, in particular, on student health, especially for the period 1903 to 1940.

6 The strongest statement of the failings of maternal feminism is articulated by Carol Lee Bacchi in *Liberation Deferred? The Ideas of the English-Canadian Suffragists, 1877–1918* (Toronto: University of Toronto Press, 1983). See also Linda Kealey, "Introduction," 14; Wayne Roberts, "'Rocking the Cradle of the World': The New Woman and Maternal Feminism, Toronto, 1877–1914," 31; and Veronica

Strong-Boag, "Canada's Women Doctors: Feminism Constrained," 129, all in Linda Kealey, ed., *A Not Unreasonable Claim: Women and Reform in Canada, 1880s–1920s* (Toronto: Women's Press, 1972).

7 For post-1920s feminist activity in general, see Linda Kealey and Joan Sangster, eds., *Beyond the Vote: Canadian Women and Politics* (Toronto: University of Toronto Press, 1989). See also Gail G. Campbell, "'Are We Going to Do the Most Important Thing?' Senator Muriel McQueen Fergusson, Feminist Identities, and the Royal Commission on the Status of Women," *Acadiensis* 38, 2 (2009): 52–77; Elise Chenier, *Strangers in Our Midst: Sexual Deviancy in Postwar Ontario* (Toronto: University of Toronto Press, 2008), Chap. 2; Jennifer A. Stephen, *Pick One Intelligent Girl: Employability, Domesticity, and the Gendering of Canada's Welfare State, 1939–1947* (Toronto: University of Toronto Press, 2007), 105–6; Magda Fahrni, *Household Politics: Montreal Families and Postwar Reconstruction* (Toronto: University of Toronto Press, 2005), Chap. 5; Judith Fingard and Janet Guildford, eds., *Mothers of the Municipality: Women, Work, and Social Policy in Post-1945 Halifax* (Toronto: University of Toronto Press, 2005); and Veronica Strong-Boag, *The New Day Recalled: Lives of Girls and Women in English Canada, 1919–1939* (Toronto: Copp Clark Pitman, 1988). In the international context, see, for example, Caroline Daley and Melanie Nolan, eds., *Suffrage and Beyond: International Feminist Perspectives* (Auckland, NZ: Auckland University Press, 1994), and Brian Harrison, *Prudent Revolutionaries: Portraits of British Feminists between the Wars* (Oxford: Oxford University Press, 1987). The literature on professional women in Canada remains primarily biographical. See, for example, Mary Kinnear, *Margaret McWilliams: An Interwar Feminist* (Montreal/Kingston: McGill-Queen's University Press, 1991); Elspeth Cameron and Janice Dickin, eds., *Great Dames* (Toronto: University of Toronto Press, 1997); Jean O'Grady, *Margaret Addison: A Biography* (Montreal/Kingston: McGill-Queen's University Press, 2001); Roberta Hamilton, *Setting the Agenda: Jean Royce and the Shaping of Queen's University* (Toronto: University of Toronto Press, 2002); and Smyth et al., *Challenging Professions*. For exceptions, see, for example, Kinnear, *In Subordination*, and the essays in Ruby Heap, Wyn Millar, and Elizabeth Smyth, eds. *Learning to Practise: Professional Education in Historical and Contemporary Perspective* (Ottawa: University of Ottawa Press, 2005).

8 Kinnear, *In Subordination*; Smyth et al., *Challenging Professions*; Heap, Millar, and Smyth, *Learning to Practise*; Prentice, "Bluestockings," 231–61; and Fingard, "Gender and Inequality at Dalhousie," 687–703.

9 C.B. Sissons, *A History of Victoria University* (Toronto: University of Toronto Press, 1952), v-vi.

10 In 1892, for example, there were only 14 women in a student body of 226. See Johanna M. Selles, *Methodists and Women's Education in Ontario, 1836–1925* (Montreal/Kingston: McGill-Queen's University Press, 1996), 38, 159–68.

11 Selles, *Methodists and Women's Education*, 171–78.

12 Margaret Addison was dean of residence from 1903 until 1920, when she became dean of women and took on responsibility for both residents and commuters. O'Grady, *Margaret Addison*, 3. To avoid confusion, I refer to her throughout as dean of women.

13 O'Grady, *Margaret Addison*, 34–55, 158.

14 Ford, *A Path Not Strewn with Roses*, 48, 58.

15 Leila Davis graduated from the University of Toronto in 1889, Helen MacMurchy in 1900, Edna Guest in 1910, and Marion Hilliard in 1927. See Carlotta Hacker, *The Indomitable Lady Doctors* (Toronto: Clark, Irwin and Co., 1974), 141, 188–89, 224, 232; Martin Kendrick and Krista Slade, *Spirit of Life: The Story of Women's College Hospital* (Toronto: Women's College Hospital, 1993), 84–85, 97–98; and Angus Mc-Laren, *Our Own Master Race: Eugenics in Canada, 1885–1945* (Toronto: McClelland and Stewart, 1990), 30–31.

16 Anna H. Lathrop, "Elegance and Expression, Sweat and Strength: Body Training, Physical Culture and Female Embodiment in Women's Education at the Margaret Eaton Schools, 1901–1941" (PhD diss., University of Toronto, 1997) and John Byl, "The Margaret Eaton School, 1901–1942: Women's Education in Elocution, Drama and Physical Education" (PhD diss., State University of New York at Buffalo, 1992).

17 Lathrop, "Elegance and Expression," 37, 58–59, 64; O'Grady, *Margaret Addison*, 61, 81–82.

18 O'Grady, *Margaret Addison*, 124.

19 Marion O. Robinson, *Give My Heart: The Dr. Marion Hilliard Story* (New York: Doubleday, 1964), 281.

20 For the work of members of the Faculty of Household Science in creating career opportunities for other women on and off campus, see Ruby Heap, "From the Science of Housekeeping to the Science of Nutrition: Pioneers in Canadian Nutrition and Dietetics at the University of Toronto's Faculty of Household Science, 1900–1950," in Smyth et al., *Challenging Professions*, 161.

21 Male students gained up-to-date social and athletic facilities in 1919 with the opening of Hart House, which remained closed to women until 1972. Women did not have a modern facility until 1959. A similar situation occurred at the University of British Columbia. See Ford, *A Path Not Strewn with Roses*, 62, 72–74; Helen Gurney, *A Century to Remember, 1893–1993: Women's Sports at the University of Toronto* (Toronto: University of Toronto Women's T-Holders' Association, 1993), 18–19, 26–27, 33; and Patricia Vertinsky, "'Power Geometries': Disciplining the Gendered Body in the Spaces of the War Memorial Gymnasium," in *Disciplining Bodies in the Gymnasium: Memory, Monument, Modernism*, ed. Patricia Vertinsky and Sherry McKay, 48–73 (London: Routledge, 2004).

22 Members from Victoria included Addison, Curlette, and MacMurchy. See O'Grady, *Margaret Addison*, 116. For the circumstances surrounding this issue, see Sara Z. Burke, "'Being Unlike Man': Challenges to Co-education at the University of Toronto, 1884–95," *Ontario History* 93, 1 (2001): 11–31.

23 Cathy James, "A Passion for Service: Edith Elwood and the Social Character of Reform," in *Women Teaching, Women Learning: Historical Perspectives*, ed. Elizabeth M. Smyth and Paula Bourne (Toronto: Inanna, 2006), 111.

24 O'Grady, *Margaret Addison*, 113. See also Ford, *A Path Not Strewn with Roses*, 33.

25 James, "A Passion for Service," 111, 113, 116.

26 O'Grady, *Margaret Addison*, 180. On the National Association of Women Deans, see Carolyn Terry Bashaw, "'Reassessment and Redefinition': The NAWDC and Higher Education for Women," in *Women Administrators in Higher Education: Historical and Contemporary Perspectives*, ed. Jana Nidiffer and Carolyn Terry Bashaw (Albany: State University of New York Press, 2001), 163.

27 Margaret Gillett, "The Heart of the Matter: Maude Abbott, M.D., 1869–1940," in *Despite the Odds: Essays on Canadian Women and Science,* ed. Marianne Gosztonyi Ainley (Montreal: Véhicule Press, 1990), 191.

28 Wendy Mitchinson, "Marion Hilliard: 'Raring to Go All the Time,'" in Cameron and Dickin, *Great Dames,* 231.

29 United Church of Canada/Victoria University Archives, 90.064v, Box 3–20, Report by Guest, n.d.

30 "Report of the Dean of Junior Women," in University of Manitoba, *President's Report,* 1940–41.

31 Anne Firor Scott, *Natural Allies: Women's Associations in American History* (Urbana and Chicago: University of Illinois Press, 1993); Leila J. Rupp, *Worlds of Women: The Making of an International Women's Movement* (Princeton, NJ: Princeton University Press, 1997); N.E.S. Griffiths, *The Splendid Vision: Centennial History of the National Council of Women of Canada, 1893–1993* (Ottawa: Carleton University Press, 1993), 20.

32 O'Grady, *Margaret Addison,* 137.

33 "The Position of Women in Universities," in Congress of the Universities of the Empire, 1912, *Report of Proceedings,* 346, 352–53.

34 O'Grady, *Margaret Addison,* 181. This was common of women at other institutions. For example, as president of the Canadian Federation of University Women from 1926 to 1928, Bollert attended the meetings of the International Federation of University Women held in 1924 in Paris, in 1929 in Geneva, and in 1932 in Edinburgh. Susan Cameron Vaughan, who became warden of Royal Victoria College in the 1930s, had been president from 1923 to 1926. Allie Vibert Douglas, dean of women at Queen's, was also active in the International Federation of University Women. See Katie Pickles, "Colonial Counterparts: The First Academic Women in Anglo-Canada, New Zealand and Australia," *Women's History Review* 10, 2 (2001): 280–88, 296n83, and Alison Prentice, "Three Women in Physics," in Smyth et al., *Challenging Professions,* 131.

35 Rupp, *Worlds of Women,* 37–40.

36 Dianne M. Hallman and Anna H. Lathrop, "Sustaining the Fire of 'Scholarly Passion': Mary G. Hamilton (1883–1972) and Irene Poelzer (1926–)," in Smyth and Bourne, *Women Teaching, Women Learning,* 50–51.

37 Kathleen Coburn, *In Pursuit of Coleridge* (London: Bodley Head, 1977), 64–65.

38 Cameron Duder has documented the explicit romantic relationship between Frieda Fraser, a faculty member in the School of Hygiene at the University of Toronto, and her long-term companion, Bud Williams. Similarly, Annie Laird travelled regularly to Europe and the United States in the company of her sister, Elizabeth Laird, a physicist at Mount Holyoke in the 1920s and 1930s, to attend conferences and keep apprised of work in nutritional sciences. See Prentice, "Three Women in Physics," 128; Mitchinson, "Marion Hilliard," 229; Cameron Duder, "'Two Middle-Aged and Very Good-Looking Females That Spend All Their Week-Ends Together': Female Professors and Same-Sex Relationships in Canada, 1910–1950," in *Historical Identities: The Professoriate in Canada,* ed. Paul Stortz and E. Lisa Panayotidis (Toronto: University of Toronto Press, 2006), 344–45; and Heap, "From the Science of Housekeeping to the Science of Nutrition," 150.

39 Catherine Gidney, *A Long Eclipse: The Liberal Protestant Establishment and the Canadian University, 1920–1970* (Montreal/Kingston: McGill-Queen's University Press, 2004), Chap. 2.
40 Over the course of her career, Margaret Addison invited a host of speakers to Annesley Hall, including travelling secretaries of the YWCA, the World Student Christian Federation, and various women's missionary societies. In 1910–11, Dr. Marie Stopes spoke to students, as did J.S. Woodsworth in 1912, Emmeline Pankhurst in 1909 and 1916, and Dr. Margaret Patterson in 1924. She also invited speakers to talk about new careers opening up for women. See O'Grady, *Margaret Addison*, 123–24, 183.
41 Mrs. Ramsay-Wright offered a trophy in 1905 for women's intercollege tennis championships, Addison in 1908 for hockey, and Scott Raff in 1912 for interyear basketball. See A.E. Marie Parkes, *The Development of Women's Athletics at the University of Toronto* (Toronto: Women's Athletic Association, University of Toronto, 1961), 6, and *Acta Victoriana*, January 1912, 192.
42 "Dr. E.H. Gordon Dies Suddenly," *Globe and Mail*, 18 December 1939, in UTA, Department of Graduate Records, A73–0026, Box 121/91.
43 Karine Hébert, "Carabines, poutchinettes co-eds ou freschettes sont-elles des étudiantes? Les filles à l'Université McGill et à l'Université de Montréal (1900–1960)," *Revue d'Histoire de l'Amérique Française* 57, 4 (2004): 593–625.
44 Gidney, *A Long Eclipse*, xxiv–xxv.
45 Neil Semple, *The Lord's Dominion: The History of Canadian Methodism* (Montreal/Kingston: McGill-Queen's University Press, 1996), 275.
46 Quote from Semple, *The Lord's Dominion*, 349.
47 Jan Todd, *Physical Culture and the Body Beautiful: Purposive Exercise in the Lives of American Women, 1800–1870* (Macon, GA: Mercer University Press, 1998), 176–82; Margaret A. Lowe, *Looking Good: College Women and Body Image, 1875–1930* (Baltimore: Johns Hopkins University Press, 2003), 29; Roberta J. Park, "Muscles, Symmetry and Action: 'Do You Measure Up?' Defining Masculinity in Britain and America from the 1860s to the early 1900s," *International Journal of the History of Sport* 22, 3 (2005): 365–95.
48 McLaren, *Our Own Master Race*, 31, 37; Joan Sangster, *Regulating Girls and Women: Sexuality, Family, and the Law in Ontario, 1920–1960* (Don Mills, ON: Oxford University Press, 2001), 88, 135.
49 O'Grady, *Margaret Addison*, 7, 100–2.
50 "Sports for Girls Develop Citizenship," *Mail* (Toronto), 6 September 1928, UTA, Department of Graduate Records, A73–0026, Box 121/91.
51 Strong-Boag, "Canada's Women Doctors: Feminism Constrained," 124, and O'Grady, *Margaret Addison*, 5–8.
52 "Character Moulded by Capable Teacher," *Globe* (Toronto), 20 October 1923, UTA, Department of Graduate Records, A73–0026, Box 121/91.
53 Mitchinson, "Marion Hilliard," 228.
54 Kinnear, *In Subordination*, 157.
55 Alison Prentice, "Scholarly Passion: Two Persons Who Caught It," in *Women Who Taught: Perspectives on the History of Women and Teaching*, ed. Alison Prentice and Marjorie R. Theobald (Toronto: University of Toronto Press, 1991), 271–72; Mitchinson, "Marion Hilliard," 237; and Kinnear, *Margaret McWilliams*, 16.

56 Miss Addison, speaking at session, "The Position of Women in Universities," Congress of the Universities of the Empire, 1912, *Report of Proceedings*, 352–53.
57 See, for example, Susan L. Forbes, "Gendering Corporate Welfare Practices: Female Sports and Recreation at Eaton's during the Depression," *Rethinking History* 5, 1 (2001): 59–74, and Daniel E. Bender, "Inspecting Workers: Medical Examination, Labor Organizing, and the Evidence of Sexual Difference," *Radical History Review* 80 (2001): 51–75.
58 "Woman Doctors Cast Off Halo," *Globe* (Toronto), 22 January 1931, UTA, Department of Graduate Records, A73–0026, Box 151/33. The quote is by Hilliard, but other doctors made similar comments. See Helen MacMurchy, "The Woman in the Medical Profession," *Acta Victoriana* 47, 5 (1923): 28.
59 Fingard, "Gender and Inequality at Dalhousie"; Prentice, "Bluestockings"; Kinnear, *In Subordination;* and Pickles, "Colonial Counterparts."
60 Their salaries placed them within the top 20 percent of female wage earners and the top 40 percent of male wage earners. For more information on salaries, see Catherine Gidney, "Tending the Student Body: Youth, Health, and the Modern University" (Toronto: University of Toronto Press, under review), 165.
61 Margaret Rossiter, *Women Scientists in America: Struggles and Strategies to 1940* (Baltimore: Johns Hopkins University Press, 1982), 314.
62 Patricia A. Palmieri, "From Republican Motherhood to Race Suicide: Arguments on the Higher Education of Women in the United States, 1820–1920," in *Educating Men and Women Together: Coeducation in a Changing World*, ed. Carol Lasser (Urbana/Chicago: University of Illinois Press/Oberlin College, 1987), 58.
63 Ford, *A Path Not Strewn with Roses;* Gillett, *We Walked Very Warily;* Paula J.S. LaPierre, "The First Generation: The Experience of Women University Students in Central Canada" (PhD diss., University of Toronto, 1993), 20; Kinnear, *In Subordination,* 47; and Prentice, "Three Women in Physics," 128.
64 On the important role that friendship networks played in women's lives, see, for example, Kathryn Kish Sklar, "Hull House in the 1890s: A Community of Women Reformers," *Signs* 10, 4 (1985): 658–77; Deborah Gorham, "'The Friendship of Women': Friendship, Feminism and Achievement in Vera Brittain's Life and Work in the Interwar Decades," *Journal of Women's History* 3, 3 (1992): 44–69; and Patricia Palmieri, "Here Was Fellowship: A Social Portrait of Academic Women at Wellesley College, 1895–1920," in *Women Who Taught: Perspectives on the History of Women and Teaching,* ed. Alison Prentice and Marjorie Theobald (Toronto: University of Toronto Press, 1991), 233–57. See also the chapter by Karen Balcolm in this collection.
65 For the integration of individual rights and evolutionary discourse, see Sara Z. Burke, "Women of Newfangle: Co-Education, Racial Discourse and Women's Rights in Victorian Ontario," *Historical Studies in Education* 19, 1 (2007): 111–33. For this type of combination of ideas, see also Kinnear, *Margaret McWilliams,* 163.
66 Rupp, *Worlds of Women.* See also Scott, *Natural Allies,* and Alison Mackinnon, *Love and Freedom: Professional Women and the Reshaping of Personal Life* (Cambridge: Cambridge University Press, 1997), 213–18.
67 See P.T. Rooke and R.L. Schnell, *No Bleeding Heart: Charlotte Whitton: A Feminist on the Right* (Vancouver: UBC Press, 1987), 189; Janice Dickin, "'By Title and by

Virtue': Lady Frederick and Dr. Henrietta Ball Banting," in Cameron and Dickin, *Great Dames,* 246; Kinnear, *Maragaret McWilliams;* Katie Pickles, *Female Imperialism and National Identity: Imperial Order Daughters of the Empire* (Manchester: Manchester University Press, 2002), 177.

68 Franca Iacovetta, "'A Respectable Feminist': The Political Career of Senator Cairine Wilson, 1921–1962," in Kealey and Sangster, *Beyond the Vote,* 64–65.

Singleness and Choice
The Impact of Age, Time, and Class on Three Female Youth Diarists in 1930s Canada

HEIDI MACDONALD

In the first three years of the Great Depression, the marriage rate fell by one-quarter, from 7.7 per 1,000 population in 1929 to 5.9 per 1,000 population in 1932.[1] High rates of unemployment meant fewer male youth had the breadwinning capacity for marriage, while female youth, as historian Katrina Srigley has shown, often delayed or forwent marriage to contribute essential wages to their families, particularly when male relatives were shut out of the workforce.[2] Although these two explanations are crucial to understanding the fall in the marriage rate during the Depression, they obscure a third explanation: some women preferred single life to married life. This chapter considers the degree to which being single was a choice as revealed in the 1930s diaries of three single female youth of marriageable age. Bertha Marsh (1907–94), Edna Newton (1904–97), and Gladys Willison (1904–91) were aged twenty-two, twenty-four, and twenty-five, respectively, when the Depression began. Marsh was a rural New Brunswick teacher who supported her brother and father throughout the Depression; Newton, an office worker in Toronto's financial district; and Willison, a Calgary teacher and moral reformer. I reveal how these diarists' age, gender, and class influenced their experience of the Depression, their decision to avoid or delay marriage, and how they expressed their preference for being single or being married.

There is an assumption that men, as the main breadwinners, have historically had a stronger influence on the marriage rate and, therefore, the decision to marry.[3] From the period of industrialization until at least the Second

World War, stable employment was the preferred prerequisite for a man to contemplate marriage. Nonetheless, early- to mid-twentieth-century Canadian government statisticians might have exaggerated men's influence by emphatically correlating the decline in marriage during the 1930s with male unemployment, arguing that "the crude marriage rate has reacted to general economic conditions with barometric sensitivity" and "[s]ince the economic responsibility in marriage remains largely with the males, the proportion in which they marry will depend upon occupational opportunities as well as upon the supply of females."[4] Instead of accepting the traditional assumption that the main factor influencing the marriage rate was male employment, I employ a feminist perspective that considers women's agency in remaining single. The three subjects of this chapter underscore historian Amy Froide's assertion that not marrying was the result of a woman's "series of decisions and non-decisions."[5] I focus specifically on the 1930s because the view that men controlled marriage rates during times of economic crisis intensified during this decade.

A lack of sources makes studying individuals' marriage deliberations difficult. While journalists, social workers, and government officials of the 1930s left records that outline their efforts to tell youth they should get married, descriptions of the decision-making process among youths are much rarer.[6] Two important books on unmarried women, Marta Danylewycz's *Taking the Veil* (1987) and Katrina Srigley's *Breadwinning Daughters* (2010), rely largely on sources that reveal the perspective of mature individuals looking back on their youth and their decision to marry or not marry. Danylewycz's study of Quebec women who chose the convent over marriage and motherhood is based largely on nuns' obituaries, written by convent authorities. Because the obituaries give an overview of the nun's life, including the kind of family into which she was born and her accomplishments and experiences as a nun, Danylewycz argues that entering a convent allowed young women to change the trajectory of their lives away from the drudgeries of working-class life to convent life, which offered them greater opportunities for postsecondary education, leadership roles, and living among other women. In her study of young working women in Toronto in the 1930s, based primarily on more than one hundred oral interviews collected between 1997 and 2005, Katrina Srigley argues that daughters' wages were often crucial to their families' survival during the Depression.[7] She explains that many breadwinning daughters were so dutiful that they postponed or cancelled marriages, knowing that they could not keep their jobs if they married and that their parents badly needed their contributions to the family economy.

Whereas Danylewycz builds an argument based on obituaries written to honour and preserve the memory of nuns' lives and Srigley reaches conclusions based on interviews with people near the end of their lives, I examine documentation produced by female subjects in their twenties and thirties. Diaries, which Philippe Lejeune argues "show an identity in progress, even as they are part of the process itself of creating identity day after day," are potential spaces for young women to explain, implicitly or explicitly, why they remain single.[8] Although levels of disclosure vary widely among diarists and must be interpreted cautiously, even the "seemingly minor details" of a diary are, in Kathryn Carter's words, "dense, rich fruit" for historians.[9]

Harvey Graff, an American historian of childhood and youth, recommends using diaries to study growing up, the process of moving from dependency to autonomy, because diaries describe the individual pathways along which children progress to adulthood. Graff explains, "neither single factors nor unitary routes characterize the means and the ways that young persons follow in growing up. Some variables can make an enormous difference."[10] While life-course scholars argue that youth traditionally transitioned into adulthood by completing a predictable series of occupational events (finishing school and getting their first job) and demographic events (marriage, leaving the parental home, and the birth of the first child), Graff's study of diaries reveals that achieving adulthood is rarely a predictable or linear process. Following Graff's principle of reconstructing individual pathways to adulthood through diaries, I emphasize singleness, rather than marriage, as the culmination of adulthood.

Diaries, like any other source, present methodological issues. On the positive side, Helen Buss explains that historians can perform "a kind of archeological map making, marking out a territory for excavation, recording the location of each find, contextualizing it in terms of the total site, and thus [unearthing] the neglected, lost areas of human life, untouched by history."[11] On the other hand, diaries contain a multitude of biases related to "representativeness, egocentrism, voice and vision, articulation, and memory."[12] A diary is by no means an authentic voice and usually follows only a couple of the many threads of the writer's life.[13] Lejeune responds to criticism of the genre by explaining that diaries should not be examined as texts: "the diary is only secondarily a text or a literary genre ... the diary is first and foremost an activity. Keeping a diary is a way of living before it is a way of writing."[14] Graff and Lejeune both argue that we must not allow criticism of diaries to prevent us from studying diaries.[15] The "richness" of diaries, Graff writes, "includes the presence and relationships among these lives, their historical contexts, the forces of change and development, and comparisons across them."[16] I use diaries in the spirit of Buss, Lejeune, and Graff, recognizing that diaries present certain methodological issues even as they, more than other historical documents, allow us to construct the pathways of individual lives – in this case, the contemplation of singleness. In my analysis, I consider diary writing as an activity while foregrounding the historical context of the Great Depression; the class background of each diarist; the threads that each diarist chooses to follow; and each diarist's self-representations, activities, and relationships.

I originally collected the diaries of Bertha Marsh, Edna Newton, and Gladys Willison for a related project on the transition of youth into adulthood during the Great Depression. I consulted sixteen provincial, city, and university archives for Depression-era diaries written by people born between 1901 and 1921 and found twenty-six diaries suitable for the project. The diaries of Bertha Marsh and Gladys Willison, collected from the Provincial Archives of New Brunswick and the Glenbow Museum and Archives, respectively, were the only ones written by female subjects born in the first decade of the century who never married. Edna Newton's diaries are privately owned and were lent to me by her daughter, who attended a lecture I gave called "Coming of Age during the Great Depression" at the Galt Museum and Archives in Lethbridge in April 2010.

When the Depression began, Bertha Marsh was a twenty-one-year-old single teacher who lived at home with her parents and younger brother in the village of Nashwaaksis, New Brunswick, across the river from Fredericton. A romantic relationship that had lasted a couple of years ended just as the Depression began. Bertha had taught in other small communities, where she boarded with families, but in 1929 she moved back home to teach at the local school. Bertha's father was a mill worker who struggled to find steady employment during the 1930s because of both his health and the shortage of employment. Thus, Bertha's teaching income was crucial to sustaining the family during the Depression; indeed, she was the only income earner for most of the second half of the decade.

Bertha kept a diary for most of her life, though she did not necessarily make daily entries.[17] Her entries in the 1930s are sporadic – totalling about one-third to one-half of the days in most years – and are kept in mismatched, undated notebooks of various sizes. There is no diary for 1929 in the collection at the Provincial Archives of New Brunswick and just one entry for 1933. Bertha used her diaries to some extent as household account books; a significant number of entries refer to her financial support of her brother at graduate school in the United States. Despite spending much of her life teaching school, Bertha usually just wrote "School" on teaching days, suggesting that she viewed her work as self-explanatory and static, but she did include longer entries about her family, social, and community life.

In the late 1920s and early 1930s, Bertha's diary entries are enthusiastic, filled with references to her family, social life, shopping, and church attendance and to her own grooming and community activities. She provides short descriptions of the summer vacations she took with her younger brother Don, who also lived at home while studying economics at the University of New Brunswick between 1931 and 1935. She records that weeknights and weekends were filled with visiting friends. The following spring 1930 entries are typical:

> *March 11* Went to station and on up to store. Then we all sat out on the bench in the moonlight and ate sour apples. Ed [friend] presented me with a chocolate bar. Peace offering.
>
> *Mar 13* We went to station. Had big snow ball fight.
>
> *Mar 14* Played couple of games of cards.
>
> *Apr 19* Went to town had my teeth filled.
>
> *Sat Apr 26* Mabel and I went to town in evening. Got a little black felt hat.[18]

The mood of Bertha's entries changes in the second half of the 1930s, years that corresponded with her mother's illness, her brother's moving out of the house, and her increased domestic responsibilities. Although she never recorded her emotions, her diaries become less lively than they had been in 1928 and in the early 1930s. She represents herself as less social and more serious; references to reading, embroidery, and listening to the radio replace notes on going out in the evenings. Most notably, in 1932, she stops mentioning Hal, with whom she had a blossoming relationship in the late 1920s and early Depression years.[19]

The first difficult Depression-era situation that Bertha records is the departure of her younger brother to Louisiana to attend graduate school in September 1935. Many entries in the summer of 1935 refer to buying clothes for Don and helping him pack his trunk. One infers that Bertha is proud of Don and her role in his success. Although she does not directly express missing him, he had clearly been a link to social connections that she no longer mentions after he moved.

A few days after Don leaves, Bertha reports in her diary: "Dr to see Mama." Within a month, her mother died of liver cancer. Bertha reports briefly (just one sentence on each event) the diagnosis of the fatal illness, the doctor's home visits, the time of death, and the funeral.[20] She does not reflect on the loss of her mother but explains in her diary that the workload around the house has increased and that she has arranged to get a woman in to help with the washing.

With her mother's death and her brother's absence, Bertha's life narrowed. It is not that she reflects on these losses – she is not that kind of diarist – but there is a marked decrease in the mention of social activities. Moreover, as the decade continued, it seems that her brother made little effort to stay in contact with Bertha. Because she referred to him so often before 1935, her abrupt silence on his activities is stark. Don returned home briefly from graduate school at the University of Chicago in 1937, and Bertha again records buying his clothes and making many of his meals, just as she had in the early 1930s. Then there is a silence that lasts several months in regard to him in 1937–38. In 1939, it is surprising to read Bertha's entry for Tuesday, 6 June: "Letter from Don ... Don told us he was married last Feb 4th to Kathleen Moore. They are coming home for a while later on."[21] Another curt comment followed three weeks later: "July 1 [1939] Don and Kathleen arrived ... Kathleen is quite dark."[22] One infers Bertha's hurt in these comments, hurt from being excluded from her brother's life after all she had done for him both financially and emotionally.

Bertha's diary requires reading between the lines to consider why she remained single throughout her life. She met and began dating Hal in 1928, at the age of twenty-one, while teaching and boarding in Mouth of Keswick. She moved back home in 1929, a year for which no diary has survived; Hal is rarely mentioned in her 1931 and 1932 diaries; and then she mentions him for the final time in 1932. Around the same time, Bertha's father experienced unemployment and Bertha's income was crucial to the family economy, particularly because her brother (aged twenty-one in 1932) was enrolled in university. Bertha accepted significantly more parental-style responsibility in 1935, the year when her mother died, her father became permanently unemployed, and her brother remained in university. Bertha cared for her father from 1935 until his death at age seventy in 1943. When he died, she was thirty-six years of age and at the end of her "marriageable" years. When her relationship with Hal ended, she had been approximately twenty-two and never entered into another relationship. Rather than viewing it as a conscious choice, Bertha's single status is better explained as a product of the

Depression and increased family responsibilities that restricted her time for social activities and decreased her opportunities for marriage.

When the Depression began, Gladys Willison was a twenty-five-year-old single teacher who lived in Calgary with her mother and older sister Hilda, who also taught at Riverside School. Gladys was the youngest of six daughters, four of whom became teachers and the other two, nurses. Gladys's parents were Swedish immigrants who had met and married in Ontario and then moved to a homestead northeast of Calgary in 1900. In 1913, the family moved to Calgary, where Gladys's father worked for a few years for a sewing-machine company. Around 1922, he moved back to the farm while the rest of the family continued to live on 2nd Ave. North East.[23] Although her parents were working-class, in her diaries Gladys never expresses financial concerns and seems to have had enough money to buy clothes, eat out, and get her hair done.

From 1930 to 1933, Gladys wrote in small (approximately five centimetre by twelve centimetre) date books, but after 1933 her diaries are larger, more elaborate and, in a few cases, had locks. Gladys wrote neatly and, usually, daily. Most of her 1930 entries consist of two or three sentences that record social activities in Calgary. She represents herself as engaged with her career and community and interested more broadly in Depression-era national politics and moral reform. It is notable that Gladys's entries are occasionally girlish and playful, as if she were addressing, entertaining, and tantalizing her diary as she might a friend.

The vast majority of Gladys's diaries in the early 1930s chronicle her social activities, including shopping, going to lunch, visiting with male and female friends, attending movies, playing tennis, having her fortune told, and getting her hair done. She also mentions her teaching and her Alberta Teacher Association meetings. In 1932, she expresses anger at being expected to sign a contract agreeing to a voluntary 9 percent cut in her salary for the following year, when, in fact, she had not agreed: "Adding insult to injury! My cheque is $121.50 now."[24] She believed that male and female teachers should be paid the same but did not think it was realistic to expect this equity during the Depression.[25] Gladys's interest in politics and advocacy is also evident when she refers to obtaining the Co-operative Commonwealth Federation's manifesto in early 1935 and to attending a peace rally in 1936.

In 1934, Gladys reports that she has formed – along with her friend Emily Cragg and her minister, Mr Todd – a youth unit of the Moral Rearmament Movement in Calgary.[26] A pamphlet she saved explains that moral rearmament is the Battle for Peace, which "begins when an individual listens to God's directions instead of the voice of hate, greed, selfishness and fear."

One of the movement's slogans was "Strive for Absolute Honesty. Purity. Unselfishness. Love. Not 'Who's Right.' But 'What's Right.'"[27] Diary entries about this group mainly refer to Gladys's efforts to reform individual men. In 1935 and 1936, she frequently describes helping two particular men, Bill and Stanley, give up alcohol and cigarettes and find direction in their lives. She seems pleased to be involved:

> *Dec. 23 [1935]* – Met Bill just as we came out [of Guy's office]. He drew Duck aside and said, "You won't tell Gladys I've had a drink. Do you think she'll know I've had one?" She replied "Aren't you going to tell her." So he called me and said, trying to look nonchalant, "Could you tell by looking at me that I'd been drinking?" Then pleadingly, "You won't let this make any difference, will you?"[28]

While Gladys's entries show that she enjoys having these men depend on her, she did not seem attached to them romantically, perhaps because she saw them as below her class.

She does, however, express interest in romantic relationships, both in general and in particular. Several times a year for most of the 1930s she has her fortune told. When describing the results of the fortune telling, she always mentions the likelihood of marriage, although her only record of potential marriage comes in 1936, when she was thirty-two. She records an intense exchange with Harry, who, she mentions, had asked her to marry him five years previously, in 1931, although she does not mention him in her diary at that time. She writes that she is finally sure that she loves him but that she is too late:

> *Oct. 27 [1936]* – "Harry came up about 9.30 ... Now that Harry knows I care for him he doesn't want to be married. He's too old – if he died in 10 yrs. – where would I be! He hasn't forgotten all he went through in those 5 yrs. after I would not marry. We talked till 2, then said good-bye for good. He says life isn't worth living. He'd go to war if he could.
>
> *Oct. 28 [1936]* – Felt sort of numb and let down all day.[29]

Gladys's activities during the 1930s were fairly consistent. She lived at home, taught school, socialized with a wide group of friends, and volunteered for the moral reform movement. In 1936, she revisited a 1931 marriage proposal, expressed regret, but moved on quickly. Gladys remained single all her life, living with her sisters Hilda and Mary in the family home in Calgary and later moving to Edmonton, where she lived with her sister Evelyn.

Edna Newton was twenty-four when the Depression began. She had graduated from Grade 10 in 1920 and had been working in Toronto's financial district as an office clerk at the Canadian Life Insurance Officers Association ever since. When the Depression began, she had been dating Balfour for at least four years. She lived on Roxton Road with her parents and older sister, Lillian, who was also an office clerk and with whom she shared a car. The family was financially comfortable; Edna's father was a detective sergeant in the Toronto Police Force until his retirement in 1932, and both Lillian and Edna held full-time employment.[30]

Edna had three kinds of diaries in the 1930s. In 1931 and 1932, she used "page a day, book a month" boxed sets of diaries, which were three centimetres by six centimetres; for six weeks in 1935, she kept a travel diary that documented her trip with her older sister, Lillian, to the United Kingdom and Europe; and from 1936 to 1940, she kept a single-volume, five-year diary, which was fourteen centimetres by ten centimetres.[31] Edna tended to write fifty- to one hundred-word descriptions of the day's events, along with reflections on her job, family, friends, and boyfriend.

During 1931 and 1932, Edna's diary entries revolve around her work, social life, and family activities. Edna expresses a great sense of duty towards her job at Canadian Life Insurance Officers Association.[32] Hired as a stenographer in 1920, Edna was later promoted to supervise the other female staff. In the early 1930s, she reports working hard at her job, usually arriving by streetcar at the Bay Street office before 9 a.m. and regularly working past 5p.m., especially when preparing for regular executive meetings or the association's annual meeting in April.[33] She demarcates her work life from her family and leisure life by consistently recording the times of her arrival and departure from work.

Edna's diary entries show her confidence in being a valued and loyal employee. Despite the economic crisis, she never expresses fear about losing her job, even when she was sick and off work for six weeks in 1931. She seems satisfied with her wage and regularly refers to saving money, buying bonds, or making other purchases. Judging by her spending and saving habits, she never wanted for money. In January 1931, she records her goal to have $300 in the bank by the end of the year, and in October of that year she records buying a Dominion of Canada bond worth $500.[34] When she and Lillian decide to sell their car in 1932 and buy a new one, Balfour helps the sisters look, but Edna and Lillian take charge of the final negotiations:

March 29th (1932): Worked hard but left at 5.10 p.m. Balf called for me and told me about all the places he'd been to – best price [for selling old car]

$260. Went to National Motors and told Mr. Brown about better offer. He met it. Lillian and I went over at night and closed the deal $970 for new car, $260 for Chrysler–cash payment $717 (including licence) Balf for all his work $20 – making total $737.[35]

Although Balfour helped Edna buy the car, their relationship was not secure, and Edna's early-1930s references to him express dissatisfaction with his unemployment and his moodiness. Yet, just when she seems completely frustrated with him over having "the same old argument" about trying harder to get a job and get along with Lillian, she would write that he was "lovely" and "such a dear." They saw each other almost every day, even if only for a few minutes, and they regularly went to church together. On 4 August 1931, she writes: "Balf came down about 4 and stayed for supper ... I was not so tired as last night and he was awfully nice to me – kissed me as though he meant it so I am happy again."[36] Edna was nevertheless cautious about getting too involved with Balfour, and she never expresses an eagerness for marriage. On 24 February 1931, she writes that she had enjoyed a dinner party that evening, "but for some reason or other [I was] very glad that I was the unmarried one."[37] On 3 October 1931, she writes that she and Balfour should stop dating, at least for a while, "so that people get it out of their heads that we intend to marry. Why should we?"[38]

Edna and Balfour continued their relationship into the mid-1930s, but Edna's lack of intention to marry is suggested again in her 1935 travel diary when she describes meeting and spending time with a fellow passenger, Alex Smith, on the return voyage from Belfast to Montreal. Alex, a Hudson's Bay Company chief factor, was returning to the Arctic after a furlough in Scotland. On 25 June, Edna and Alex spent time together during the day, and of their evening together, she writes: "Rest of evening with A – delightful but not for publication."[39] Her next few entries include indecipherable shorthand, which she surely intended to keep private but must have employed to help herself remember those few pleasant days.[40] Over the next few years, Edna and Alex corresponded, although mail was received and sent only once or twice a year from Alex's Arctic posts.

In the second half of the 1930s, Edna continued to work at Canadian Life Insurance Officers Association. She still lived at home with her sister and parents, and she remained in her relationship with Balfour, although it was increasingly fraught. The announcement of Edna's promotion to treasurer and assistant secretary of Canadian Life Insurance Officers in the Toronto *Globe* and in the *Mail and Empire* in January 1936 not only demonstrates the prestige of the position; it also suggests that the association anticipated employing Edna for some time and, therefore, did not expect her to marry in the near future.[41] Although she had been dating Balfour for at least twelve years at the time of the appointment, the couple were not engaged, and, at thirty-two, she had passed her most marriageable years.[42] Edna records her increasing work responsibilities in her diaries and more frequently notes that she had worked to 10 or 11 p.m. to prepare for "big meeting[s]." She indicates her commitment to the success of the organization through expressions of relief that meetings had run "smoothly."

The main topic of Edna's diary entries in the second half of the 1930s, however, is her increasingly difficult relationship with Balfour. She blamed much of Balfour's unhappiness on his inability to find employment after losing his job at the Canadian National Railway around 1930. When he found employment but continued to be unhappy, Edna rationalized that he was not in the right job. On 1 July 1938, she writes: "After same old attempt to get things straight – asked him to stay away to find out whether he really wants me but he can't see that." At the end of that year she writes: "Home [from movie] and sat outside going over all the old arguments until 1:30."[43] Edna last mentions Balfour on 4 October 1940. Ten days later, she records that she and Lillian had driven to Montreal to pick up Alex Smith, the Hudson's Bay Company post manager.

It is not clear from the diary whether Edna had much warning that Alex was coming to Toronto, but once he arrived, they were caught up in a whirlwind romance that produced a proposal of marriage, which she accepted on 2 November 1940, just two weeks after meeting Alex in Montreal. Her diary's lack of references to Alex misrepresents their relationship. Between November 1935 and July 1940, he had sent her 226 single-spaced typed pages, and she had responded with 347 double-spaced typed pages. The two had even discussed the possibility of marriage in 1935, but Edna fails to record the conversation in the diary.[44] Their engagement in 1940 was not as brash as a reading of Edna's diaries alone would suggest. Alex, five years Edna's junior, intended to enlist, but he first got a job with Direct Winters Transport so that he would have a job to return to after the war. They married on 27 September 1941, and Alex enlisted in 1943. Edna demonstrated her commitment to Canadian Life Insurance Officers Association by working for the association right up to the day she gave birth, on 27 May 1946. She was forty-one.[45]

Although analysts and historians linked declining marriage rates during the Depression to a rise in male unemployment – thereby suggesting that

men more so than women influenced marriage patterns during the decade –
historian Katrina Srigley argues that young women delayed or cancelled
marriages in order to contribute essential wages to their families. This analysis of three women's diaries extends Srigley's argument by revealing other
reasons that women deliberately chose not to marry. Bertha Marsh and
Gladys Willison were lifelong single women, and Edna Newton married at
the age of thirty-six, thirteen years later than the average.[46] These women's
diaries do not suggest that male unemployment led directly to their single
status, and only one of them may have avoided marriage to continue contributing to the family income. While none of their diaries records a specific
moment of choosing single status over marriage, they do demonstrate these
women's agency and support Amy Froide's argument that not marrying was
usually the result of a "series of decisions and non-decisions."[47]

Bertha Marsh, the youngest subject and most sparse diarist, records having a boyfriend in 1928, but the relationship either ended or cooled considerably by 1930; her final mention of Hal is in March 1932. One gets the
impression that Bertha was interested in marriage but never got another
opportunity, partly because she accepted financial responsibility for both
her father and brother. Fulfilling this responsibility until her brother's marriage in 1939 and her father's death in 1943 contributed to her remaining
single. Bertha represents herself in her diaries as dutiful, dependable, and
without emotion. The lack of reflection characteristic of Bertha Marsh's often terse entries makes conclusions difficult, but she comes closest to being
the "dutiful daughter" described by Srigley. In her pathway to singleness,
her mother's unexpected death and her father's loss of employment can be
viewed as passive nondecisions regarding marriage.

Compared to Bertha Marsh's diaries, Gladys Willison's are more personal
and self-conscious.[48] Gladys's diaries are so neatly written and cared for, and
she explains some things in so much detail, that one has to wonder if she
hoped her diaries might be read by others. Even taking her motives into
consideration, Gladys was much more socially and politically engaged than
Bertha. Although most of her leisure time was spent with other women, her
moral reform work put her in direct contact with several men, and she refers
to marriage at least annually when she reports on having her fortune told.
Judging from her diaries, marriage was on Gladys's radar, and she seems to
have accepted the importance of marriage in a woman's life, despite having
four older sisters who were also lifelong single women. On the one hand, she
had role models and the practical support necessary to live comfortably as
a single woman. On the other hand, she goes to considerable effort in her

diary to construct herself as marriageable when she describes – five years after the fact – refusing a marriage proposal. The refusal, she makes clear, ruined the man's life and made him long to enlist in the Spanish Civil War. Gladys's pathway towards lifelong single status was composed of a reportedly dramatic decision to refuse marriage in 1931, a series of indecisions related to maintaining the comfortable home life and support system that she and her four single sisters provided for one another, and regret, expressed in 1936, that she had not accepted the 1931 proposal.

Without reading Edna Newton's diaries carefully, one could easily assume that she was a victim of the Depression, forced to delay marriage because her boyfriend did not have a steady job. But her diaries show a far more complex situation, one in which her fifteen-year courtship with Balfour never came close to producing a marriage proposal. Had Balfour proposed, it is highly doubtful Edna would have accepted. Not only does she express a wish to continue her career, dozens of her diary entries also express her doubt that Balfour's bitter personality will improve. When she weighed her options, she never factored Balfour in as marriage material. Although her swift engagement to Alex was in sharp contrast to her fifteen-year courtship with Balfour, she was an active participant in both processes. In fact, her almost complete failure to mention her five-year correspondence with Alex in her diary suggests a measured strategy. Moreover, although Edna lived at home with her parents and her sister in Toronto, her personal-spending and long-term-saving habits indicate there was ample money in the household and that she was not avoiding marriage for the reasons outlined by Srigley in *Breadwinning Daughters*. Edna, more so than Bertha or Gladys, used her diary as place where she could confide and organize her thoughts. She is in some ways quite uncensored, recording her complaints of menstrual cramps (usually marked by "first day under the weather"), joy at receiving gifts, and frustration with her boyfriend. In contrast, her silence on her 1935 marriage proposal from Alex shows a high level of censorship.

In Canada and elsewhere, single women continue to be understudied even though between the early modern era and 1931 single women constituted between one-third and one-half of all women over fifteen years of age.[49] Part of this lapse stems from the tendency to identify marriage as the most significant marker of adulthood. Until the rise of common-law unions lessened the importance of marriage in the late twentieth century, approximately 95 percent of North Americans and Europeans married at least once.[50] Associating adulthood with married life has led historians to overlook the unmarried. This chapter sheds light on women's deliberate singleness by combining the approaches of Graff and Froide. It uses Graff's model of studying individual pathways to adulthood and Froide's argument that singleness results from a series of decisions and nondecisions. These two models can also be applied to chapters in this collection by Karen Balcolm, Hélèn Charron, and Catherine Gidney, who discuss single women who could not have maintained their professional lives had they chosen to marry. Their singleness was surely also the result of a series of decisions and nondecisions made along their pathways to adulthood. The agency of these well-educated, middle-class, professional women may be more obvious than that of their working-class counterparts, yet, as this chapter shows, working-class women such as Bertha Marsh, Gladys Willison, and Edna Newton also demonstrated agency in remaining single.

Although the three women diarists studied here are not representative of lifelong or life-cycle single women, they do reveal circumstances common to many single women of their era. They were employed in occupations – teaching and clerical – in which unmarried women predominated because married women were not welcome.[51] They all lived at home with their parents, partly because it was affordable but more so because living alone was not respectable for single women.[52] Two of the three successfully relied on sibling support as an alternative to marriage. Nevertheless, to use Graff's model, key variables affected their choice to be single. For example, none of the three women suffered poverty by Depression standards, but there is no doubt that Bertha Marsh had fewer resources and thus fewer choices than Edna Newton. Edna's parents did not need her financial support or her help at home, which allowed Edna to save a significant amount of money for her future, buy a one-thousand dollar car (with her sister), work somewhat erratic hours as required by her employer, and spend most evenings socializing. Bertha, on the other hand, was tied to caring both financially and emotionally for her father and, to a lesser extent, her brother. Bertha's pathway to singleness held fewer choices and more obligations than did Edna's pathway to delayed marriage. These women's pathways to lifelong singleness or delayed marriage were no more linear than those that led to marriage. In fact, they may be more complex because it is less clear when, exactly, these women entered adulthood. It could be argued that these women's pathways were stalled after they left school and found employment but failed to leave their parental homes. Conversely, we can use their diaries to understand their progression towards the autonomy and maturity that life-course scholars historically associate with marriage.

NOTES

1   Canada, *Census of Canada, 1941,* vol. 1 (Ottawa: King's Printer, 1946), 141. See also
    John Modell, *Into One's Own: From Youth to Adulthood in the United States, 1920–
    1975* (Berkeley: University of California Press, 1989), 132–34, and Enid Charles, *The
    Changing Size of the Family in Canada,* Census Monograph No. 1 (Ottawa: Domin-
    ion Bureau of Statistics, 1948), 17.
2   Katrina Srigley, *Breadwinning Daughters: Young Working Women in a Depression-Era
    City, 1929–1939* (Toronto: University of Toronto Press, 2010).
3   Lara Campbell, *Respectable Citizens: Gender, Family, and Unemployment in On-
    tario's Great Depression* (Toronto: University of Toronto Press, 2010), 100.
4   *Census of Canada, 1941,* 1:141, 149.
5   Amy Froide, *Never Married: Singlewomen in Early Modern England* (Oxford: Oxford
    University Press, 2005), 183.
6   See, for example, "Marrying on a Small Income," Central Finance Corporation, 1936,
    1–2, Library and Archives Canada (LAC), RG 27, vol. 3350, file 18, and "Youth's Eye
    View," *Saturday Night* (11 July 1936): 11.
7   Srigley, *Breadwinning Daughters,* 4.
8   Julie Rak, "Dialogue with the Future: Philippe Lejeune's Method and Theory of
    Diary," in *On Diary,* ed. Jeremy D. Popkin and Julie Rak (Honolulu: University of
    Hawai'i Press, 2009), 24.
9   Kathryn Carter, "Introduction," in *The Small Details of Life: 20 Diaries by Women in
    Canada, 1830–1996,* ed. Kathryn Carter (Toronto: University of Toronto Press,
    2002), 20. See also Helen Buss, *Mapping Our Selves: Canadian Women's Autobio-
    graphy in English* (Montreal/Kingston: McGill-Queen's University Press, 1993), 20.
10 Harvey Graff, *Conflicting Paths: Growing Up in America* (Cambridge, MA: Harvard
    University Press, 1995), 18.
11 Buss, *Mapping Our Selves,* 10.
12 Harvey Graff, "Using First-Person Sources in Social and Cultural History," *Historical
    Methods* 27, 2 (1994): 87.
13 Philippe Lejeune, "The Practice of the Private Journal: Chronicle of an Investigation
    (1986–1998)," in Popkin and Rak, *On Diary,* 31.
14 Ibid., 153.
15 Graff, *Conflicting Paths,* 165.
16 Graff, "Using First-Person Sources," 87.
17 Public Archives of New Brunswick (PANB), MC 1764, "Bertha Marsh," (hereafter
    Marsh Diaries). This collection consists of Marsh's diaries from 1928 to 1954, exclud-
    ing the years 1929 and 1947.
18 Ibid., 11, 13, and 14 March and 19 and 26 April 1930.
19 In 1928, she wrote: "chat (serious) with Hal." Ibid., March 1928.
20 Ibid., 22 September and 1 and 15 October 1935.
21 Ibid., 6 June 1939.
22 Ibid., 1 July, 1939.
23 The youngest of six daughters, Gladys wrote diary entries that refer frequently to her
    sisters, all of whom lived in Alberta except Ida, who was also the only married sister,
    even though they were all of marriageable age (between twenty-three and forty) in

1929. See "Willison Family Fonds Finding Aid," Glenbow Archives (GA), M8770 (hereafter Willison Diary).

24 Willison Diary, 1 November 1933, GA, M8770–205.

25 Ibid., 30 March 1933.

26 Ibid., 27 October and 11 November 1934.

27 "Moral Re-armament Day," 1 August 1939, and untitled, n.d., GA, M8870, file 168.

28 Willison Diary, 23 December 1935.

29 After two weeks of not writing in her diary, Willison rationalized that a marriage to Harry would not have worked out anyway: "He seems to absorb my personality and I always have the fear that I would just be moulded into his idea of what he wants, not my own personality" (10 November 1936).

30 William Newton is ranked in the top 10 percent of the Toronto Police Force in the department's 1928 annual report, indicating a decent salary and middle-class status for his family. *Annual Report of the Chief Constable of the City of Toronto*, 1928, 45. He also received a pension after retirement. Beverly Shimazaki, email correspondence with the author, 18 April and 13 May 2011.

31 I am extremely grateful to Beverly Shimazaki, Edna Newton's daughter, for sharing these diaries with me and gathering additional information for this project.

32 The association was founded in 1894 as an umbrella group to which forty-six Canadian, American, and British companies belonged. See "The Canadian Life Insurance Officers Association," *Life Underwriters News*, June 1937, 9–11.

33 For example, in April 1932 she recorded working until 7:30 or 8:00 p.m. four nights in a row to finish bulletins, and then, on 14 April, she went home at 5:30 p.m., "Too tired to work longer." Edna Newton Diary, 10–14 April 1932, private collection of Beverly Shimazaki (hereafter Newton Diary).

34 Newton Diary, 8 January and 2 October 1931.

35 Ibid., 29 March 1932.

36 Ibid., 4 August 1931.

37 Ibid., 24 February 1931.

38 Ibid., 3 October 1931.

39 Ibid., travel diary, 25 June 1935.

40 Newton occasionally used shorthand symbols in her diary entries but never for more than one line. I have tried to get her Pitman shorthand translated but have been told that she had a personal style, as did many stenographers. The style was not decipherable to the four people I asked, one of whom commented that Newton must have wanted the text to remain private.

41 "Life Insurance Officers Named," *Globe* (Toronto), 11 January 1936, 14, and "The Canadian Life Insurance Officers Association," *Life Underwriters News*, June 1937, 9.

42 Veronica Strong-Boag, *The New Day Recalled: Lives of Girls and Women in English Canada, 1919–1939* (Toronto: Copp, Clark Pittman, 1988), 85.

43 Newton Diary, 1 July and 31 December 1938.

44 Beverly Shimazaki, email with author, 13 May 2011. Shimazaki has the correspondence in her possession.

45 "Interesting Insurance Marriage," *Canadian Insurance,* 30 September 1941, 3. Alex served with the Royal Canadian Army from 1943 to 1946. Beverly Shimazaki, interview with author, Lethbridge, 19 April 2011.

46 The average age of marriage for women was twenty-four in 1921, twenty-five in 1931, and twenty-three in 1941. Charles, *The Changing Size,* 5, 207–8.

47 Froide, *Never Married,* 183.

48 Phillipe Lejeune, "Spiritual Journals in France from the Sixteenth to the Eighteenth Centuries," in Popkin and Rak, *On Diary,* 71.

49 Martha Vicinus, "The Single Woman: Social Problem or Social Solution?" *Journal of Women's History* 22, 2 (2010): 192; Froide, *Never Married,* 2–3; and Katherine Holden, *The Shadow of Marriage: Singleness in England, 1914–60* (Manchester: Manchester University Press, 2007), 25, 44.

50 John Modell, Frank F. Furstenberg Jr., and Douglas Strong, "The Timing of Marriage in the Transition to Adulthood: Continuity and Change," in *Turning Points: Historical and Sociological Essays on the Family,* ed. John Demos and Sarane Boocock (Chicago: University of Chicago Press, 1978), 123.

51 Campbell, *Respectable Citizens,* 101.

52 Elaine S. Abelson, "The Times That Tried Only Men's Souls: Women, Work, and Public Policy in the Great Depression," in *Women on Their Own: Interdisciplinary Perspectives on Being Single,* ed. Rudolph M. Bell and Virginia Yans (New Brunswick, NJ: Rutgers University Press, 2008), 223, 233.

7

Sexual Spectacles
Saleswomen in Canadian Department Store Magazines between 1920 and 1950

DONICA BELISLE

In "Feminism and Femininity: Or How We Learned to Stop Worrying and Love the Thong" (2004), Jennifer Baumgardner and Amy Richards argue that so-called second-wave feminists created a feminist mystique. This mystique "made [young feminists] feel guilty for embellishing ourselves with girlie things," such as "having boyfriends, shaving, Brazilian bikini waxes, getting married, wanting to have a body like Gwyneth Paltrow, [and] being into fashion." According to the authors, it is time to move beyond debates about the implications of girls' and women's interests in, variously, clothes, heterosexual romance, the pursuit of mainstream beauty, and sex toys. Whereas feminists of the 1960s and 1970s were raised in an environment that defined all feminine interests as weak, feminists of the early twenty-first century grew up in a world that was more accepting of consumerism as well as of women's right to be powerful, not only in the workforce but also in the bedroom and the state. For this reason, they advocate a new kind of feminism, one that recognizes that it is possible to be both feminine, in the heterosexual sense, and feminist.[1]

Baumgardner and Richards's article highlights a growing trend within contemporary feminist writing: a dissatisfaction with the assumption that sexual objectification – or the practice of judging women according to their abilities to please the heterosexual, male gaze – is exploitative, oppressive, and alienating.[2] This dissatisfaction stems partly from the reasons that Baumgardner and Richards identify, including a decreased interest in

Marxist theories of commodification, internal conflicts among feminists over the appropriateness of heterosexuality, the wishes of many young women for beautiful bodies, and the shame young feminists have experienced for "wear[ing] high heels."[3] It also arises from the influence of Judith Butler's notion of gendered performativity. In *Gender Trouble* (1990), Butler offers "a theory of subject formation" in which "the subject becomes culturally intelligible through the assumption of a sexed body." Only by performing that sexed body does it become possible for the subject to craft an identity that will be intelligible to both the self and to others.[4] This performance, many scholars have since argued, is not inherently alienating. As Liz Conor states, rather than denoting a "loss of self-determination," it represents a means by which subjects construct visual cues that convey their individuality, confidence, and social success.[5]

This chapter calls for an alternative feminist perspective, one that is cognizant of both the exploitative elements that can be inherent within sexual objectification as well as the yearnings for transformation and empowerment that can exist among those who participate in it. It employs a case study approach, inquiring into the presentation of female employees' bodies in Canadian retailers' magazines between 1920 and 1950. During this period, all of Canada's biggest shops – Eaton's, Simpson's, the Hudson's Bay Company, and other department stores – published internal periodicals. Carrying news of employees' personal lives, photographs of staff and stores, reminders of company policies, and announcements of promotions and events, these periodicals were designed to increase loyalty and efficiency. What makes these magazines especially relevant to feminist analyses of sexualization is that they often printed overtly sexual comments about female employees' bodies. They also printed photographs of women workers posing in provocative manners.

Asking not only why department stores offered sexualized commentary regarding female employees' appearances but also why female employees posed for photographs designed to please the heterosexual, male gaze, this chapter suggests that scholarly understandings of the sexual aestheticization of women are best attained by combining critical perspectives on objectification with those provided by research into performativity. So doing, it demonstrates the continuing relevance of so-called second-wave approaches to Canadian feminist historical inquiry. It also contributes to a central theme of this volume: exploring departures and linkages among different generations of Canadian feminist historical research. Although earlier approaches to women's objectification emphasize the ways in which sexualization serves capitalism and patriarchy while more recent ones play up women's agency in the construction of alluring appearances, both generations of research ultimately ask the same questions. How has sexualization influenced women's quests for dignity, fulfillment, and respect? Does the sexual objectification of women enable or, by contrast, hinder the achievement of gender equality? And, in what ways does the creation of sexualized female spectacles influence women's quests for empowerment?

Department Stores in Twentieth-Century Canada

Department stores arose in Canada during the latter half of the nineteenth century.[6] Their emergence was part of an international transformation in retailing. By departmentalizing their stock, buying in bulk, and undergoing constant expansion, department stores in Canada, the United States, and western Europe outpaced their competitors and became world merchandising leaders.[7] During the early twentieth century, Eaton's and Simpson's in Toronto distinguished themselves among North American department stores by pursuing an aggressive branch-store strategy, and by 1930, each of them was operating stores in Halifax, Montreal, and Regina. Simpson's also had a store in London, Ontario, and Eaton's had branches in Hamilton, Port Arthur, Winnipeg, Saskatoon, Red Deer, Edmonton, Calgary, and Lethbridge. Such activity, combined with the stores' mail order departments, enabled the two companies to become Canada's most powerful retailers. They did, however, have competition. Morgan's in Montreal was a strong regional force, as was another Montreal store, the Dupuis Frères. Holman's on Prince Edward Island was significant, and on the West Coast, Woodward's of Vancouver and Spencer's of Victoria cornered the markets. Western Canada's largest store, however, was the Hudson's Bay Company (HBC). Formed in 1670 as a fur-trading enterprise, it moved into retail in 1913, when it opened a department store in Winnipeg. By the Second World War, it was the country's third largest retailer and had stores in Saskatoon, Calgary, Edmonton, Vancouver, and Victoria.

Into the 1950s, Eaton's, Simpson's, and the HBC dominated Canada's retailing scene. Their shares of the national consumer dollar, however, declined steadily. After the Second World War, the increased popularity of the automobile transformed consumers' spending patterns. During the 1920s, Canadians' per capita expenditure shifted from food, clothing, and furnishings to buying cars.[8] Chain stores, too, gained strength. By 1925, they were earning the same share of the retail market as department stores, and in 1930 they surpassed them. The arrival of the shopping mall in the 1950s was further detrimental. Opening in the suburbs and catering to affluent consumers, their low-priced chain stores, increased goods assortments, and ample parking spaces shifted shopping away from downtowns and away from department stores. Thus, although some department stores anchored within shopping malls, during the 1950s, the department stores' share of the Canadian retail market dropped to an all-time low.[9]

Notwithstanding such challenges, department stores remained Canada's largest retailers well into the 1950s. Bigger than such major US department stores as Marshall Field's and Macy's, Eaton's in particular was Canada's largest retailer and was, according to some estimates, the eighth largest in the world.[10] In addition to being Canada's most powerful retailers, department stores were among the nation's largest employers. In fact, at mid-century, Eaton's massive operations employed the nation's third largest workforce. Only the federal government and the railways employed more staff. With over forty locations across the country, Eaton's had 4,962 men and 5,981 women working in its flagship Toronto store alone; this location also had 355 male and 1,200 female employees who worked on Saturdays only.[11]

Women made up the majority of Canadian department store workforces. Managers assumed that saleswomen could relate better than salesmen to female customers; they also perceived women to be more courteous, quiescent, and affordable.[12] In 1893, Eaton's had 200 female buyers, 308 salesmen, and 463 saleswomen.[13] On the eve of the Great War, 2,432 women laboured for Eaton's, the HBC, Robinson's, and Carsley's in Winnipeg.[14] Into the postwar years, the female labour-force numbers remained steady. According to one survey of thirty-eight Canadian department stores conducted in 1971, "50 per cent of all full-time employees and 79 per cent of part-timers were women," and the "number of women on the selling floor" was even "higher," with "women making up 67 per cent of full-time and 87 per cent of part-time regular employees."[15]

Department stores might have viewed female employees as friendly, docile, and inexpensive, but women had their own reasons for working in retail. Unlike domestic, factory, and restaurant work, most department store positions enabled staff to keep their clothes and hands clean. With the exception of the vast armies of women hired as extras at Christmastime, many women also considered department stores secure employers. Some of them, such as Eaton's and Simpson's in Toronto, also closed earlier than most shops and thus allowed employees to keep their evenings free. Unlike most other workplaces, department stores also offered some, albeit slim, opportunities for advancement. In 1925, Miss Verona Hibberd obtained a job in the gloves and hosiery department office at Eaton's in Toronto, and by 1935 she had become head of the Stock Control Office.[16] Nevertheless, and despite the giant stores' willingness to promote a handful of women to management, most women who worked for Canada's largest retailers between 1920 and 1960 remained in low-level jobs.[17] According to a chart called "Supervisors, Group Managers, Heads of Departments and Assistants," produced by Eaton's in 1929, for example, out of Eaton's approximately 240 supervisory positions in Winnipeg, Regina, Saskatoon, Calgary, and Edmonton, only one was held by a woman.[18]

In addition to being characterized by limited opportunities for women's advancement, department store work was also distinguished by a highly visual work environment. As displayers and sellers of goods, department stores were key institutions in the rise of what Guy Debord calls the "society of the spectacle," or a modern, vision-centred culture.[19] Using the strategies of "color, glass, and light," they "moved" shopping, as Lorraine O'Donnell writes, from pre-existing "personalized" relationships between sellers and customers to a new and impersonal "realm of signs and appearances and looking." When customers stepped into these shopping environments, their sight was stimulated by electric lights, large galleries, floor-length mirrors, glass display cases, and spacious show windows.[20] Within this visual selling scene, salespeople's bodies took on heightened significance. Prior to the 1960s, department stores kept much of their stock in storage rooms. Customers lined up at counters, and clerks retrieved merchandise, answered queries, tallied up sales totals, arranged deliveries, and attempted to sell more articles.[21] So important were salespeople to the selling process that when shoppers were pleased with their interactions with clerks, they sometimes sent thank-you letters to the stores.[22] Salespeople were also key to selling and shopping in the sense that customers tended to interpret clerks' bodies and habits as indicators of the style and quality of merchandise offered for sale. For this reason, all of Canada's large retailers encouraged employees to develop mannerisms, patterns of speech, postures, grooming habits, hairstyles, and fashion choices that would promote their stores and products to their full advantage.[23] As an article called "Look Neat, Be Lovely," which appeared in Simpson's *Staff News* in 1947, stated, "For more customers" and "more sales ... appearance is essential!"[24]

Sexualizing Female Employees

Just as department stores sought to increase sales by making their employees' bodies as pleasing as possible in a general sense, so did they attempt to extract value from female employees' sexual allure. That is, department store managers and trainers encouraged female employees to develop an appearance both respectable and mildly titillating. In these ways, they attempted to construct female sales staff whose appearance would suggest not only that the stores were reputable but also that they were exciting, pleasurable, and accommodating. By exploring the giant retailers' training literature, particularly magazines, it is possible to gain in-depth insights into how this form of sexualization operated, as well as into why managers and trainers pursued this approach to female employee management.

The first staff periodical produced by a Canadian department store was *The Beaver*, introduced by the HBC in 1920. Until 1934, when it ceased publishing employee news, *The Beaver* contained information designed to appeal to employees, shareholders, and the general public alike. Other major magazines of the 1920s included *Le Duprex*, published by the Dupuis Frères; *Store Topics*, published by Spencer's in Vancouver; and *Staff News*, published by Simpson's in Toronto. During the 1930s, Eaton's began putting out staff bulletins, including *Flash* (Toronto), *Chinook Winds* (Calgary), and *Contacts* (Winnipeg), and the HBC began printing one magazine per location. Its many offerings included *Bay Builder* (Vancouver), *Bay Window* (Victoria), *Beaver Tales* (Calgary), *Bay Breeze* (Edmonton), and *Bayonet* (Winnipeg).[25]

Canada's largest department store magazines were edited by both male and female staff. Most articles were anonymous, though it is probable that the editors were also the magazines' chief contributors. Despite the presence of female editors, however, most of the magazines' content pertaining to women's bodies suggested their chief function was pleasing the male, heterosexual gaze. Several magazine articles complimented female workers, for example, on their cultivation of physical attributes pleasing to men. They did not, however, make comments about male employees' bodies. They also did not compliment men for physical attributes that may have been pleasing to heterosexual women, and despite the possible presence of gays and lesbians within department stores' vast workforces, the magazines never complimented men or women for being attractive to a homosexual gaze.[26]

Early instances of women's sexualization occurred in *The Beaver* and *Store Topics*. Reflecting the former's primarily male perspective, the publication frequently suggested that it featured female staff in the magazine, and by corollary in the workplace, for ornamental purposes. A report on a staff sports' day in Edmonton in 1923, for example, included a photograph of female employees holding up a large ball. The women in the photograph might have been enjoying both camaraderie and physical exertion, but the caption – "A Bevy of H.B.C. Girls at the Sports" – indicates that the editors chose not to focus on women's well-being but rather on their physical attractiveness.[27]

Spencer's *Store Topics* also conceived of female staff in primarily ornamental terms. In an article about the different types of fruit available in the Vancouver store, the magazine included one photograph of four women from the Produce Department. The women stand in a line holding up various fruits, including watermelon and pineapple. The caption reads: "Some Peaches from Department 64" (Figure 1). Given that the employees are not, in fact, holding peaches and that the term *peaches*, when applied to women, calls attention to their physical attractiveness, there is no mistaking the caption's intent. It aims to both amuse and encourage the reader to imagine all young working women at Spencer's, including those who work in the Produce Department, in terms both visual and sexual.[28]

Sexual aestheticization continued during the 1930s. In her examination of the Dupuis Frères' treatment of its staff during this period, Joan Sangster rightly points out that "allusions to sexuality were almost non-existent" in training materials. Nevertheless, *Le Duprex* did occasionally comment on its female employees' appearances. A 1931 article about an in-store hairstyle show titled "Jolis mannequins à notre Exposition de Coiffures" includes both a description of the show as well as a photograph of nine female models,

Some Peaches from Department 64.

Figure 1 "A Trip through Fruitland," *Store Topics*, June 1927, 11. City of Vancouver Archives, Spencer's fonds. *Courtesy of Sears Canada Inc.*

two of whom worked for Dupuis Frères.[29] Although this title is certainly more innocuous than remarks made in the anglophone magazines of western Canadian stores in the 1920s, it does invite readers to interpret female employees' bodies in visual, aesthetic, and subtly sexual terms. Another reference to female employees' agreeability occurred in *Le Duprex* six years later, in an article about the francophone store's female tennis players titled "Nos gentilles midinettes," which included a photograph of fifteen smiling women. The word *gentilles* does not impart a sexual connotation, but the title's use of the pronoun *nos*, together with the inclusion of the photograph, invites readers to interpret the women in the snapshot in a way that is both proprietary and appreciative.[30]

When the number of department store magazines expanded in Canada during the 1930s, examples of visual aestheticization increased apace. In Easter 1938, Vancouver's HBC magazine included a photograph of a woman who worked at the transfer desk. The caption read: "This attractive young lady is Bernice Potts ... We are indebted to Bernice for the tricky crossword puzzle in this issue." Rather than thanking Potts solely for her contribution, the piece also congratulated her for her beauty. By doing so, it downplayed Potts's intelligence and transformed her into an object of sexual aestheticization.[31] The 1930s also witnessed the sexualization of female elevator workers. To ensure the smooth operation of their elevators, department stores employed operators; to ensure that customers could easily distinguish the operators from shoppers, they made them wear uniforms. In many cases, managers inspected these women's uniforms at the beginning of each shift. This practice gave rise to a unique form of spectacularization, namely, photographing lined-up elevator employees and then printing their photographs in staff magazines. Between 1936 and 1948, internal HBC publications included at least eight instances of spectacularization. The text accompanying the pictures described female elevator employees as lovely, charming (this adjective appeared three times), neat, neat looking, fascinating, beautiful, and belles.[32]

In the 1940s, this spectacularization accelerated, partly because of the expansion of publications throughout the decade. In a bid to promote employee loyalty during the war and postwar era, Eaton's *Flash*, Simpson's *Staff News*, and the HBC's various publications became longer and more frequent, and all of them began featuring lengthier descriptions of employee events. They also began presenting more detailed biographies of individual workers. It is therefore perhaps unsurprising that references to the attractiveness of their female employees became more frequent. However, it is also possible that anxieties caused by the shipment of significant numbers of male wage earners overseas, as well as by postwar attempts to reintegrate men back into the Canadian labour force, encouraged the magazines' staff to intensify the sexualization and objectification of female workers. As Helen Smith and Pamela Wakewich point out in their study of representations of female munitions workers in Can Car's staff magazine, the sexual objectification of female staff promoted a view of working women's roles as decorative. Portrayals of women as sex objects distracted male readers from women's workplace skills and confirmed the belief that, despite women's wartime incursions into the workplace, wage earning was still masculine.[33]

Assuaging latent male fears about women's secondary workplace status was certainly the intent behind one of the most provocative pictures to appear in any internal department store magazine. In August 1948, the magazine cover for Eaton's Toronto store featured a young woman looking coyly over her shoulder while feeding a calf. The caption invited the reader to "Come and Get It" (Figure 2). This statement perhaps referred to the phrase that farmers used when they wanted to alert their cattle to the availability of new food. More likely, however, the statement was a double entendre, suggesting not only that the calf should come and get its nourishment but also that readers should come and get their sexual stimulation by perusing the publication.

In addition to soothing gender anxieties, the sexualization of women in department store literature promoted an image of female beauty pleasing to both male workers and male customers. Research on department stores between the late nineteenth and mid-twentieth centuries commonly portrays retail as designed primarily for women's pleasure, but it is also true that saleswomen served as models of consumerist female beauty, which department stores defined as heterosexual: women were to appear not only elegant but also attractive to men. Although women were the big stores' largest consumer group, men, too, visited them. Retailers thus encouraged saleswomen to present themselves both as paragons of feminine elegance and as pleasing to the male gaze.[34] The April 1943 issue of the HBC magazine for Edmonton blatantly betrayed this desire to please male customers. An article about US servicemen who had visited the store, titled "American Pilots Like Fort Garry Coffee," began by asserting: "They also like Edmonton girls – especially 'Bay' girls." Noting that the "birdmen" had stopped in at the workers' lunchroom, where they had coffee with three young ladies, the article concluded that the pilots were "particularly impressed with the friendliness of The Bay" (Figure 3).[35] When considered alongside the photograph that accompanied this article, which depicts the servicemen and employees

Figure 2 *Flash* front cover, 16 August 1948. *Courtesy of Sears Canada Inc.*

Figure 3 Front cover of the *Bayonet*, June 1946. Photo by Paul Hunter. *Courtesy of Hudson's Bay Company Archives, Archives of Manitoba.*

having coffee, the line "They also like Edmonton girls" invites the reader to see the female employees as attractive objects and to assume that the pilots also regarded the employees in these terms. By pointing out that the men were "impressed with the friendliness of The Bay," the article implies that female employees should appear both attractive and acquiescent so as to please not only the male reader but also the male customer.

Magazines also sought to compliment female staff by drawing attention to their attractiveness. This flattery served two purposes: it created employee loyalty, and it made female employees aware of their bodies' ornamentality. The cover of Winnipeg's HBC magazine for June 1945, for example, featured a collage of women workers' smiling faces. Regarding "Our Front Picture," the article on page two declared:

> You'd travel a long way before finding a more attractive group of young people than we have working in this store. To prove our point we are showing a few of their smiling faces on the cover ... girls picked here and there from the various departments. Typical Bay employees, well-groomed, alert and ambitious they go about their work with poise and confidence. Off duty they bowl and "bike," golf and ride horseback, play tennis and baseball, swim and paddle ... *to build up healthy bodies.*[36]

Drawing attention to the beauty of specific women workers, together with their amiability, the *Bayonet* compliments specific members of the HBC's staff for fulfilling their bodily labour requirements. In addition, by congratulating these women on their physical pursuits, the magazine makes a subtle connection between attractiveness and job success. Healthy bodies, the article implies, serve the women well, not only in their spare time but also on the job.

A final indication of the purposeful sexualization of female staff is the fact that although female employees often posed for photographs in contexts that had little to do with sexual objectification, the photographs that appeared within the magazine presented their bodies in almost exclusively aestheticized terms. Female members of Simpson's Swimming Club, for example, posed in their bathing suits on a diving board after receiving their life saving certificates. The photograph appeared above the caption "They Can Swim Too!" and the article declared, "Girls from the Toronto Simpson Swimming Club are known for their attractiveness as well as their prowess in the swim tank."[37] The biographies of staff newcomers also drew attention to women's bodies, even when the photographs that accompanied them did not explicitly draw attention to their attractiveness or sexuality. In 1947, the HBC's Edmonton magazine described new staff member Jean Huffman as "five feet, 4 inches. Irish ... and shouldn't we add – very easy on the eyes," and in 1948 the same publication called new employee Jacquie Scott a luscious blonde and a gorgeous creature. Each article included photographs of the employees.[38] This inclusion, combined with the presentation of text that called attention to the featured workers' bodies, encouraged both the reader and the women themselves to imagine women's beings in strictly visual and aestheticized terms.

Employees' Self-Spectacularization

Between 1920 and 1950, then, department stores spectacularized their staff within employee magazines for a number of reasons: to spur female workers to cultivate appearances that would stimulate sales, to encourage employees to view women as secondary members of the labour force, and to uphold male authority and privilege in the workplace. It is also important to consider why many female workers participated in their own spectacularization. By exploring specific instances when women struck sexualized poses, it is possible to pinpoint the particular yearnings for success and liberation that underlay their performances.

Beginning in the 1930s, store magazines began printing vacation snapshots sent in by employees. Some of these photographs were innocuous

Figure 4 "People and Places," *Bay Builder,* 15 June 1937, 2. *Courtesy of Hudson's Bay Company Archives, Archives of Manitoba.*

and depicted urban and outdoor scenery as well as employees engaged in specific activities, such as cycling, hiking, or fishing. Others, though, featured female employees striking alluring poses. A collage of pictures from the HBC's Vancouver magazine in 1936 includes images with the following captions: "Some of the girls from the Elevator Staff" (4), "A happy party from the Grocery Section" (5), and "Guess who?" (8) (Figure 4). In each of these pictures, the women strike relaxed, passive poses, smiling happily and wearing much less attire than was expected of them at work. During the following decade, these types of photographs became more common. One pictures three smiling women standing in a lake, while another shows a woman leaning against a tree. Both images appeared in the Winnipeg HBC's summer issue of 1945.[39] Women also sent in photographs of themselves striking relaxed, glamourous poses in urban locales, as the image of Olga Laruska in Edmonton in 1947 demonstrates (Figure 5). A particularly striking vacation photograph appeared in 1941, when Victoria's HBC store printed a snapshot of an employee's posterior (Figure 6).

To determine the motives that compelled female workers to send photographs of themselves to their employers' magazines, it is important to understand the culture of heterosexuality that existed within Canadian department stores. These retailers had mixed-gender labour forces that

Figure 5 "Candidly Speaking," *Bay Breeze*, August 1947, 13. *Courtesy of Hudson's Bay Company Archives, Archives of Manitoba.*

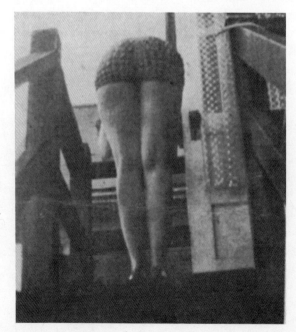

Figure 6 *Bay Breeze*, October 1941, 4. *Courtesy of Hudson's Bay Company Archives, Archives of Manitoba.*

numbered in the thousands; they offered single women and men the opportunity to meet, mingle, and develop relationships.[40] Many employees met their future spouses at work, and their marriages were often announced in staff magazines.[41] Recognizing the prevalence of flirting and courtship among staff, department stores held dances, picnics, and other events that would attract the attendance of those seeking not only diversion and sociability but also heterosexual mingling. In this way, Canada's retailers incorporated heterosexual interaction into their broader attempts to secure staff loyalty and cohesion.[42]

When female employees sent photographs of themselves striking flirtatious poses to corporate magazines, they did so within a workplace culture of heterosexual banter. In these photographs, women portrayed themselves as fun and appealing, as potentially attractive romantic partners. But the photographs operated on another level as well. As Lisa Sanders argues, "Shop assistants, like factory hands, worked in an environment defined by repetition and routine, performing the same tasks on a daily basis and expected to reproduce an attitude of deference and readiness upon each encounter with a new customer."[43] More than this, their immersion in the sales environment made female department store employees experts in fashion, self-presentation, and beauty. Their job, however, required them to dress in dark, subdued, and business-like clothing; to maintain an erect posture; and to behave with decorum and docility.[44] Small wonder, then, that when female employees went on holidays, they revelled in dressing up, having fun with friends, and behaving flirtatiously. Sending photographs of themselves to store magazines enabled these women to communicate their "off-work" personas to their co-workers.

Participating in beauty contests was another way for women to demonstrate stylishness, poise, and attractiveness. In 1922, four "salesladies" at HBC Edmonton entered a citywide beauty contest sponsored by the local newspaper. In its coverage of the event, *The Beaver* included a picture of the women, noting that they were "easy to look at and pretty hard to beat" (Figure 7). In 1946, Simpson's *Store News* boasted that Marion Saver of the Hamilton toilet goods department had been chosen by local judges to represent Hamilton at the Miss Canada contest. In 1943, noted the article, the "lovely young lady" had been Miss Toronto.[45] Other photographs of beauty contestants appeared in a 1948 issue of Calgary's HBC magazine. The company held beauty pageants at its annual summer picnic, and the women who participated posed for photographs. So impressed were store reporters with the beauty of the winners that they featured close-ups of the women on

Figure 7 "Beauty Contest," *The Beaver* (now *Canada's History*), February 1922, 25. *Courtesy of* Canada's History.

Figure 8 "Beaver Club Picnic," *Beaver Tales,* March 1949, 10-11. *Courtesy of Hudson's Bay Company Archives, Archives of Manitoba.*

the covers of subsequent issues (Figure 8).[46] By drawing attention to female workers' bodies, these articles and photographs objectified and spectaclized female employees. Yet, unlike instances discussed in the previous section, they did so within a context sanctioned by the female employees themselves.

By featuring photographs of beauty contestants in store magazines, and especially on their covers, as did *Beaver Tales*, both Simpson's and the HBC suggested that it was appropriate for female employees to parade their bodies and compete for beauty titles. Through their magazines, they implied that women's beauty could be measured and objectified, and they encouraged their female staff to cultivate a slim, poised, and agreeable appearance. In the case of swimsuit competitions, they also suggested to staff that beauty standards included smooth and unblemished skin, the ability to walk in heels, and toned muscles. More than this, they encouraged readers to gaze upon contestants' bodies and to judge them on their attractiveness.[47]

Beauty contests did, however, have other meanings. As historian Joan Sangster notes of beauty pageants in the postwar labour movement, young working-class women participated in these contests because "femininity, style, and appearance" were a form of cultural capital to which young women had access.[48] In other words, beauty contests enabled women to showcase their achievement of heterosexual attractiveness. Doing so was especially important for women who spent much of their time performing routinized, low-status paid labour and who wanted to declare their inherent worth and femininity. Moreover, the HBC pictures demonstrate that beauty contests were fun. The contestants smiled for the camera not only because the action enhanced their prettiness, but also because they were likely enjoying the feeling of sun on their bodies, the camaraderie of friends, and the esteem of their co-workers, who were no doubt in the audience.

Pin-up photographs, a final type of sexualized image, also appeared in department store magazines. Pin-ups, posters that depict women in attractive poses, became popular during the Second World War; their purpose was to boost "men's morale on both the home and battle fronts."[49] As did Can Car's *Aircrafter* magazine, Simpson's and the HBC's magazines introduced pin-ups of female staff during the 1940s. In January 1945, Simpson's *Staff News* ran a pin-up of Jean Latta, who worked in the coffee shop. According to the caption, the servicemen in convalescence at the Chorley Park Hospital had chosen her as their official pin-up girl, and she visited the men often at the wards, where her "picture is posted up ... as their most popular visitor." In comparison to the photographs of beauty contestants smiling and wearing bathing suits that appeared in HBC Calgary's magazine in 1947 and 1948, Latta presents herself as sultry and glamourous. The caption states that she looks "for all the world like a movie starlet." In keeping with the pin-up tradition, the caption also includes Latta's age (nineteen), height (five feet, seven inches), weight (120 pounds), and hair and eye colour (dark

Figure 9 Jean Latta, in Simpson's
Staff News, 19 January 1945, 8.
*Courtesy of Hudson's Bay Company
Archives, Archives of Manitoba.*

brown and blue). Latta's body conformed well to the mainstream beauty norms of the time, which favoured slim, relatively tall women (Figure 9).

In the spring of the same year, *Staff News* again printed pin-ups, this time for the benefit of returning Simpson's veterans. The first pin-up, which appeared in the Easter issue, featured "lovely, blonde Dorothy Groves of the store lingerie." Groves's image, the caption stated, would be the "first in a new series of pin-up girls for Simpson's lads in service." Having worked part-time as a model, Groves was twenty-four years old, 5 feet 4 inches tall, 110 pounds, and had "dancing hazel eyes": "She's not married and says her ideal man doesn't have to have curly hair!" (Figure 10). The second pin-up featured Mabel Findlay, a "piquant blonde" who was seventeen years old and 5 feet 2½ inches tall and who worked as an "apprentice in the advertising art department": "She has no special boy friend, but the navy lads hold a definite interest for her" (Figure 11).

The heterosexual aspect of their workplace culture; the monotonous, deferential nature of retail employment; the familiarity of retail workers with the latest fashions; the equation of attractiveness with accomplishment, both in the department store and in broader mainstream culture; and the visual scopic environment in which these women worked combined to create a context in which the successful display of one's own body – in an

Figure 10 Dorothy Groves, in "Happy Easter to You, Too!" Simpson's *Staff News*, 30 March 1945, 8. *Courtesy of Hudson's Bay Company Archives, Archives of Manitoba.*

Figure 11 Mabel Findlay, "The Second Pin-Up," Simpson's *Staff News*, 27 April 1945, 8. *Courtesy of Hudson's Bay Company Archives, Archives of Manitoba.*

appropriately sexualized, stylish, and alluring manner – became a method of proclaiming social success and distinction. In other words, women who displayed themselves as modern spectacles had learned that one path to success was the cultivation of a coy, alluring, slim, and fashionable appearance. This appearance, they knew, would win approval from male managers as well as from prospective suiters; it would serve them well in both the workplace and courtship.

Conclusion

During the first half of the twentieth century, Canada's largest department store magazines presented female employees' bodies as sexualized spectacles. Articles complimented employees on their attractive appearances and depicted their bodies as objects of male sexual attraction and appreciation. Through flattery, department stores tried to create feelings of loyalty among employees, and they encouraged female employees to continue presenting themselves in ways pleasing to both female and male customers. This sexual spectacularization at once amused male readers and reminded female employees that their primary function in the workplace was to be decorative.

Exploitation and oppression, however, are not the only categories through which women's sexual spectacularization in department store magazines can be understood. Female employees themselves sent in photographs that displayed their bodies in sexualized terms. They also took part in beauty contests, posed for provocative pictures, and agreed to serve as company pin-ups. These actions indicate that many women enjoyed performing beautiful and attractive personas, and they demonstrate that many women believed that the cultivation of beautiful bodies helped them achieve workplace success. They illustrate that many women viewed retail not only as a place where they could earn money and, possibly, advance their careers but also as a site where they could engage in heterosexual, romantic relationships. They imply that a certain longing existed among women for their co-workers to view them not as low-status drudges but as exciting, glamourous, flirtatious, and distinguished. Their participation in sexual spectacularization articulated a latent desire for liberation from hardship and toil.

When developing feminist perspectives on sexual objectification, it is crucial to recognize both the potential for exploitation and alienation that exists within women's ornamentalization and women's own motivations for self-spectacularization. Female department store employees who chose to dress fashionably, use cosmetics, present themselves as glamorous, and please the male gaze were not necessarily submissive and conservative. Therefore, the recent feminist argument that feminists must be more accepting of girls and women who strive to meet prevailing capitalist and heterosexual beauty standards is significant. Rather than disparaging women's self-spectacularization, feminists should recognize the motivations behind women's pursuit of conventional femininity. But feminist scholars must also continue to explore how heterosexual beauty standards contribute to girls' and women's exploitation, oppression, and alienation. As this chapter reveals, spectacularization in the Canadian department store between 1920 and 1950 facilitated capitalist accumulation and male privilege; it also reinforced the hierarchies of class and gender that marginalized wage-earning women. Since department stores promoted versions of female sexuality that privileged youthfulness; slimness; toned muscles; smooth, white skin; a fashionable appearance; and the male, heterosexual gaze, women who did not meet such specifications would have had difficulty achieving workplace success. Finally, the pursuit of heterosexual attractiveness might have created a sense of competition among co-workers, most overtly when female employees participated in beauty contests but also within everyday workplace situations such as seeking promotions, securing desired work schedules, and obtaining raises. This competition, in turn, might have prevented solidarity from forming among female co-workers. Therefore, despite the empowering possibilities that may exist within women's spectacularization, it must be concluded that when it occurs within patriarchal and capitalist contexts – such as those that existed in Canadian department stores between 1920 and 1950 – it becomes a narrow and ultimately untenable path towards liberation.

NOTES

1 Jennifer Baumgardner and Amy Richards, "Feminism and Femininity: Or How We Learned to Stop Worrying and Love the Thong," *All about the Girl: Power, Culture, and Identity*, ed. Anita Harris (New York: Routledge, 2004), 59–67, quote on 66.

2 See, for example, Linda Scott, *Fresh Lipstick: Redressing Fashion and Feminism* (New York: Palgrave, 2005).

3 Baumgardner and Richards, "Feminism and Femininity," 66.

4 Liz Conor, *The Spectacular Modern Woman: Feminine Visibility in the 1920s* (Bloomington and Indianapolis: Indiana University Press, 2004), 4.

5 Ibid., 3. Excellent examples in which theories of performativity have been deployed include Nan Enstad, *Ladies of Labor, Girls of Adventure: Working Women, Popular Culture, and Labor Politics at the Turn of the Twentieth Century* (New York: Columbia University Press, 1999) and Kathy Peiss, *Hope in a Jar: The Making of America's Beauty Culture* (New York: Henry Holt, 1999).

6 Donica Belisle, *Retail Nation: Department Stores and the Making of Modern Canada* (Vancouver: UBC Press, 2011).

7 H. Pasdermadjian, *The Department Store: Its Origins, Evolution, and Economics* (New York: Arno Press, 1976 [1954]); Michael Miller, *The Bon Marché: Bourgeois Culture and the Department Store, 1869–1920* (Princeton, NJ: Princeton University Press, 1981); Susan Porter Benson, *Counter Cultures: Saleswomen, Managers, and Customers in American Department Stores, 1890–1940* (Urbana: University of Illinois Press, 1988), 14–15.

8 David Monod, *Store Wars: Shopkeepers and the Culture of Mass Marketing, 1890–1939* (Toronto: University of Toronto Press, 1996), 111–12, 211–13; Bureau of Statistics, *Seventh Census of Canada, 1931*, Vol. 10, *Merchandising and Service Establishments, Part I* (Ottawa: J. O. Patenaude, 1931), xix-xx, lxxxiii.

9 Monod, *Store Wars*, 124–27, 358; *Department Stores in Canada/Les grands magasins au Canada, 1923–1976* (Ottawa: Statistics Canada, 1979), 16; Bill Lancaster, *The Department Store: A Social History* (London: Leicester University Press, 1995), 85–86.

10 Monod, *Store Wars*, 123; H.H. Stevens, *Report of the Royal Commission on Price Spreads* (Ottawa: J.O. Patenaude, 1937), 202; Bureau of Statistics, *Seventh Census of Canada, 1931*, Vol. 10, Part 1, 10, xxiv-xxv; Ralph Hower, *History of Macy's of New York, 1858–1919* (Cambridge: Harvard University Press, 1943), 399.

11 Eileen Sufrin, *The Eaton Drive: The Campaign to Organize Canada's Largest Department Store, 1948–1952* (Toronto: Fitzhenry and Whiteside, 1982), 14; Count of Toronto Staff, Statistics Notebook, 1939, Archives of Ontario (AO), F 229, Series 181, Box 1.

12 Theresa McBride, "A Woman's World: Department Stores and the Evolution of Women's Employment, 1870–1920," *French Historical Studies* 10 (Autumn 1978): 668–69.

13 Joy Santink, *Timothy Eaton and the Rise of His Department Store* (Toronto: University of Toronto Press, 1991), 83, 114, 191.

14 University Women's Club Civic Committee, *The Work of Women and Girls in the Department Stores of Winnipeg* (Winnipeg: University Women's Club of Winnipeg, 1914), 8.

15 Joan Sangster, *Transforming Labour: Women and Work in Post-War Canada* (Toronto: University of Toronto Press, 2010), 110–11.

16 "Welcome to the Quarter-Century Club," *Flash*, 17 April 1950, 11. All issues of *Flash* cited here are available at the Archives of Ontario (AO), F 229, Series 141.

17 See, for example, "Thirty-Five Years with Eaton's," *Flash*, 5 May 1950, 11.

18 "Supervisors, Group Managers, Heads of Departments and Assistants," June 1929, AO, F 229, Series 162, File 764.

19 Guy Debord, *The Society of the Spectacle* (London: Rebel Press, 2005 [1967]).

20 Theresa McBride, "A Woman's World," 665; Lisa Sanders, *Consuming Fantasies: Labor, Leisure, and the London Shopgirl, 1880–1920* (Athens: Ohio University Press, 2006), 55; Lorraine O'Donnell, "Visualizing the History of Women at Eaton's, 1869 to 1976" (PhD diss., McGill University, 2002), 301; and William Leach, *Land of Desire: Merchants, Power, and the Rise of a New American Culture* (New York: Pantheon Books, 1993), 9.

21 In "Selling Your Personality," for example, customers line up at Eaton's hat counters, behind which saleswomen retrieve and discuss hats: "Selling Your Personality," 1948, AO, T. Eaton Papers, Sound and Moving Images Collection (SMI), Series 403.

22 See, for example, "Appreciative Customers," *Flash*, 3 September 1935, 4.

23 Donica Belisle, "A Labour Force for the Consumer Century: Commodification at Canada's Largest Department Stores, 1890 to 1940," *Labour/Le Travail* 58 (Fall 2006): 125–38.

24 *Staff News*, 12 September 1947, 7. All issues of *Staff News* cited are available at the Hudson's Bay Company Archives (HBCA), Library Division.

25 All issues of *The Beaver* cited are available at Library and Archives Canada. *Le Duprex* is at the archives of HEC Montréal, and *Store Topics* is at the City of Vancouver Library, Spencer's fonds. Issues of *Bay Builder; Bay Window; Beaver Tales; Bay Breeze;* and *Bayonet* can be found at the Hudson's Bay Company Archives, Library Division.

26 Evidence of gays and lesbians within the workforces of Canadian department stores has not been found. Anecdotes related to the author by former employees and customers, however, indicate that gay men in particular found employment in the big stores, especially in such fashion-related areas as window dressing.

27 "Hudson's Bay Company Field Day," *The Beaver*, June 1921, 356.

28 "A Trip through Fruitland," *Store Topics*, June 1927, 11.

29 Sangster, *Transforming Labour*, 122; "Jolis manneqins à notre Exposition de Coiffures," *Le Duprex*, January 1931, 55, Archives of HEC Montréal.

30 "Nos gentilles midinettes," *Le Duprex*, July 1937, 51.

31 *Bay Builder*, Easter 1938, unpaginated.

32 "'Chosen for Their Courtesy," *Bay Builder*, June 1936, unpaginated; *Bay Builder*, February 1938, unpaginated; *Bay Builder*, Easter 1938, unpaginated; "Up and Down with a Christmas Smile," *Beaver Tales*, December 1940, unpaginated; "'The Up and Down Brigade,'" *The Bayonet*, February 1940, unpaginated; "The Elevator Girls in Their Neat Summer Uniforms," *The Bayonet*, March 1943, 18; and "Going Up?" *Beaver Tales*, Christmas 1948, 5.

33 Helen Smith and Pamela Wakewich, "'Beauty and the Helldivers': Representing Women's Work and Identities in a Warplant Newspaper," *Labour/Le Travail* 44 (1999): 90.

34 Sanders, *Consuming Fantasies*, 55.

35 "American Pilots Like Fort Garry Coffee," *Bay Breeze*, April 1943, 3.

36 "Our Front Picture," *Bayonet*, June 1945, 2, emphasis added.

37 "They Can Swim Too!" *Staff News*, 26 October 1945, 59.

38 "We Welcome to the Bay," *Bay Breeze*, December 1947, 8, and "Interviewing Jacquie Scott," *Bay Breeze*, June 1948), 15.

39 *Bayonet*, Summer 1945, unpaginated.

40 Suzanne Morton, *Ideal Surroundings: Domestic Life in a Working-Class Suburb in the 1920s* (Toronto: University of Toronto Press, 1995), 147.

41 "Here and There with Eatonians," *Flash*, July 1937, 3, and "Eaton Marriages," *Flash*, July 1955, 18.

42 "Spring Frolic," *Store Topics*, April 1927; "A Good Time Was Had by All," *Bay Breeze*, April 1944, 5; "Cruising Down the River," *Bay Breeze*, September 1949, 12.

43 Sanders, *Consuming Fantasies*, 98.

44 For example, "Are You Easy on the Eyes," *Beaver Tales*, March 1948, 14; "Smile Contest Winners," *Bay Window*, January 1949, 4; "Summer Dress Regulations," *Staff News*, 20 June 1947, 2.

45 "Miss Canada," *Staff News*, 12 July 1946, unpaginated.

46 *Beaver Tales*, March 1948, back cover, and *Beaver Tales*, March 1948, front cover.

47 Elizabeth Anne McCauley, as quoted in O'Donnell, "Visualizing the History of Women," 322.

48 Joan Sangster, "'Queen of the Picket Line': Beauty Contests in the Post-World War II Canadian Labor Movement, 1945–1970," *Labor* 5, 4 (2008): 102.

49 Smith and Wakewich, "'Beauty and the Helldivers,'" 86.

Gender and the Career Paths of Professors in the École de service social at Laval University, 1943–72

HÉLÈNE CHARRON

The consequences of the Quiet Revolution were paradoxical for women in Quebec. On one hand, the social changes that took place in the 1960s promoted women's access to higher education and to the political sphere. They also hastened the professionalization of salaried women and led to recognition of the principle of equality of the sexes. On the other hand, they also meant that a large number of women in a position of social power and organizational and administrative responsibility, namely, nuns, were excluded from their traditional spaces of authority or from management of the social, education, and health care sectors.[1] Rather than falling to laywomen already involved in these institutions, the highest administrative positions in these sectors fell to laymen, especially young graduates of the new francophone social science faculties in Montreal and Quebec City.

The gender dimension of this historical process remains rather poorly documented for Quebec City.[2] Also, most of the work on the gendering of social work in Canada focuses on the period before the Second World War.[3] Amélie Bourbeau's thesis describes how management of the major financial agencies in Montreal's social services sector passed from the hands of male religious figures to laymen while laywomen replaced nuns in their practice "in the field." Like Lionel-Henri Groulx, Bourbeau identifies disciplinary "preferences" that appear to lead men to administrative responsibilities and women to work in family, childhood, and community care. These differences emerge and are consolidated in the academic and university framework, where the boundary between profession and discipline in particular is defined.[4] They raise the fundamental question of the social conditions under which different professional knowledges are produced and the socio-historical process by which they are structured hierarchically. The differences observed in career progressions also concern the fundamental issues of the theoretical status granted to individual choices and preferences and the problems that result from a liberal, naturalistic outlook that makes them the expression of a freely deployed pre-social subjectivity. Professional identities are not fixed and are constantly constructed and reconstructed based on norms, experiences, and perceptions of possibilities, impossibilities, and social expectations.[5] They can be understood not only from the vantage point of various positions in institutional structures but also from biographical accounts that make it possible, from another angle, to analyze the social logics (intellectual, emotional, and so on) underlying individual movements and transfers.[6] Although the ideal may be to articulate these two dimensions of the identity-construction process, this chapter mainly addresses the diverse institutional positions and transfers of professors in the École de service social at Laval University, and indicates, in conclusion, the conditions for overcoming the limits of this approach.

The Faculté des sciences sociales at Laval University, founded and directed by father Georges-Henri Lévesque, has often been identified as an incubator for the Quiet Revolution.[7] Established in 1943, it originally comprised four departments: Sociologie (et morale sociale), Service social, Économique, and Relations industrielles.[8] Social work and, to a lesser extent, sociology, were the two most mixed disciplines in the faculty. Consequently, exploring these departments can reveal what was taking place in social relationships based on sex during the Quiet Revolution and in the years leading up to it, in a university environment at a time when the social sciences were gaining legitimacy.

I draw on student records, archives, and calendars of the École de service social to show how social relationships based on sex were organized in this new academic and professional space. More specifically, after first establishing the precise breakdown of men and women in the student body and confirming that the discipline was mixed from the very beginning, I analyze the career paths of all the professors of both sexes hired between 1943 and 1972 (when the Quiet Revolution came to an end and Quebec social work was shaken by the Castonguay-Nepveu Report) to better grasp what led men to administrative responsibilities and women to functions that were much less visible and prestigious.

Ratio of Men to Women in the Student Body

Contrary to what historians have argued – and unlike France, where the profession has been almost exclusively female and nonacademic since it started – social work in Quebec was defined almost from the beginning as mixed.[9] Its mixed nature can be explained largely by the fact that the first form of university sociology in Quebec – inspired by the Leplaysian approach, Catholic social doctrine, and the monographic approach of the Chicago School – closely linked science and social action in a type of scientific dualism.[10] Sociology and social work were thus two facets of the same need to intervene and to know, which, in order to be met, involved common training followed by one or two years of disciplinary specialization.[11] Both men and women were encouraged to study social work at Laval University, and the profession's mixed nature in the province is astonishing, even compared to the United States, where it quickly became part of the university structure but a privileged career path for women, in some cases as a form of compensation for their exclusion from sociology departments.[12] In Toronto, as in Chicago, the birth of university social work was accompanied by tensions and struggles that reflected opposition between the theoretical and applied social sciences. Initially defined as male, university-level social work in Toronto became more female after 1914, when women involved in volunteer social settlement work besieged the university in search of professional recognition for their practice.[13] At Montreal's McGill University, the ties between social work and sociology, strongly marked by the Chicago School, loosened quickly in the 1920s as sociologists jettisoned the reformist dimension of their work and built up the scientific legitimacy of their discipline by contrasting it with the dominant approaches and perspectives of social work, which they deemed insufficiently "objective."[14]

In francophone Quebec, the introduction of social work, much like the social sciences in general, into university institutions took place later. The masculinization of social work began in the latter half of the 1950s and continued until the 1970s, when the trend reversed and a large number of state-run social services were implemented. At the University of Montreal, the student body at the École de service social was up to 40 percent men in the early 1960s.[15] At Laval University, the proportion of men was even more surprising: between 1945 and 1955, men almost consistently made up between 30 percent and 40 percent of the student body (undergraduate and graduate studies combined), statistics that clearly invalidate the idea that men were absent from the first generation of social work graduates in Quebec.[16] Indeed, according to the Council on Social Work Education,

Laval's École de service social had the largest contingent of men in North America in the 1950s.[17] From 1955 to 1960, they ranged from 45 percent to 50 percent of graduates. In 1961, men reached nearly 62 percent of all students, and they held steady at between 45 percent and 55 percent for the remainder of the decade. From the start of the 1970s, the proportion of men dropped to around 32 percent, while the total number of students of both sexes more than doubled.[18]

Encouraging men to study social work was, initially, part of the new ethos of Catholic action movements; however, social services continued to be provided largely by nuns, who were practitioners par excellence.[19] The young men called to the new social sciences were above all oriented towards sociology, economics, or industrial relations, all of which were marked by theoretical ambitions, as the intellectual itineraries of Jean-Charles Falardeau, Guy Rocher, and Fernand Dumont show.[20] Male involvement in the Catholic action movement encouraged men to become invested in the social sciences generally, rather than in local social services. In 1945, the Département de service social became a school. It continued to fall under the Faculté des sciences sociales, but it enjoyed greater autonomy than the other departments. This change seems to have been encouraged by faculty authorities, who feared that the professional nature of social work would undermine the academic status of the other social sciences.[21] Thus, from the beginning, an intellectual hierarchy was constructed with social work, associated with professional practice, falling below the other social sciences, which were associated with the humanities and human sciences.

A Cohort of Pioneering Men and Women, 1943–50

When the Département de service social was established in 1943, no professors specializing in the field of welfare were available to oversee it. This task was first assigned to Gonzalve Poulin, a Franciscan graduate of the Catholic University of Paris, a known figure of the family movement in Quebec and Georges-Henri Lévesque's right hand.[22] His position was in general sociology rather than social work, and he was responsible for the most general courses in the École, namely, those in sociology and family ethics, as well as the philosophy and history of social work.[23] He was closely associated with the founding of multiple local charitable organizations, but more as director of the École than as a director of services or even a stakeholder. As director of the faculty's social research laboratory, he was also closely involved in research projects on housing in Quebec City, conducted in cooperation with the other departments in the faculty, especially sociology.[24] Poulin remained head of the school until 1957, when he returned to his ministry as a priest in a number of parishes.[25]

Two other professors completed this first cohort. Roger Marier, a law school graduate from Laval's École de sciences sociales, économiques et politiques who also held a master's of social work from the Catholic University of America, was the assistant director of the École de service social from 1943, even though he did not become a regular professor until 1947. The position led him to cooperate with the faculty administration and the directors of other departments, especially for collaborative research projects on Quebec City.[26] He waited only three years before being granted tenure with a specialization in community organization, a subject he taught in addition to courses on crime and delinquency, child welfare, and social service administration. The following year, he accepted a position as professor of social work at McGill University. He then began a prestigious career in senior public administration, first in the federal government as vice-president of the Canada Mortgage and Housing Corporation and then at the provincial level as deputy minister for family and social welfare, a position he held until 1970.

Hayda Denault also joined Father Lévesque's team at the founding of the faculty. This underappreciated woman stood at the heart of social services organizing in Quebec City and taught at the École de service social. However, there is practically no biographical data on her,[27] apart from what Father Lévesque has to say about her in his *Souvenances*:

> She started out as a journalist, and I detected a rather informed social understanding in her articles. One day in May 1939, attending our courses as an auditor, she gave me the impression that she wanted to specialize and join our team afterwards. Leaping on the opportunity, I suggested she focus on social work with an eye to filling the chair mentioned before. She immediately began studies at Columbia University in New York, before continuing them at McGill's Montreal School of Social Work and crowning them with a master's from the École de service social at the University of Montreal. From these different schools, in 1941, she brought to Quebec City the data that constituted the core data for training social workers. Unfortunately, at that time, we were unable to establish the chair in question, and the school even less so. In the meantime, our candidate agreed to become director of the Bureau d'assistance aux familles des combattants. It was during the war. She was also the first social work professional in Quebec City. Luckily, the École de service social was founded in 1943, and Hayda Denault became its

guiding spirit. It was even in her home that the first meeting, preparing for
the founding, took place, and where we developed a temporary program.[28]

Although she might have been the school's guiding spirit, Denault never
held a management position within it or the university structure. She had to
wait until 1948 to become an associate professor, 1956 for full professor –
six years after her colleague Marier was promoted. Yet she had been behind
the founding, in 1943, of the Service familial de Québec, which she directed
until the early 1950s.[29] It was the first professional social welfare agency in
Quebec City and a central force in moving social services from Catholic
authorities (notably the Society of Saint Vincent de Paul) to lay, then public,
powers. The Service familial de Québec was a space in which an original
vision of welfare and assistance was built using, on the one hand, Catholic
and French influences and, on the other, American professional knowledge
gained during Denault's training – in other words, two influences often presented as being opposed and conflicting.[30] Denault then focused on teaching the casework method and on supervising placements. In 1960, five years
before she retired, she became president of the Canadian Association of
Social Workers; in the early 1970s, she sat on the Castonguay-Nepveu Commission; and, finally, she became a member of the Order of Canada in 1975.
Denault remained single throughout her life.

The primary oppositions that would come to structure women's and men's
divergent paths in the social work profession are already evident in the careers
of Marier and Denault. On the men's side, we see general studies in social sciences, where the social relations that will later be used for career progress in
the political and administrative fields are formed. Mens' specialization in social
work is often belated, and their teaching is oriented towards general, theoretical, and methodological issues, towards other social sciences and administration and away from domestic affairs such as families, children, and individual
support. Community organization emerged early as a male specialty. Men's careers then progress rapidly and uninterrupted, from management functions in
the university structure to, in many cases, an early departure from social work
and the assumption of functions in senior public and university administration.

Women, in contrast, specialized more directly in social-work studies,
which meant that they could move from their discipline to the other social
sciences, as did their male colleagues. They specialized in the specific methods of social work (casework and group work), professional practice, and
the management of local social services. They were humble women who left
no traces to posterity and whose intellectual contributions were rendered

invisible because they associated their practice with dedication, talent and self-effacement, as did peace activist Julia Grace Wales, the subject of Chapter 4 in this volume. Thus, Denault is depicted by Father Lévesque as having "a professional competence at once *discreet* and *lively* inserted into the *humanism* of a rich general culture, assisted by an *always attentive and available dedication*."[31]

The Second Cohort: Transient Men and Specialized Women, 1950–60

The career paths of the second cohort of professors, hired at the École de service social between 1950 and 1960, confirm the division of labour between the sexes seen in the first cohort. The decade continued to be marked by a great deal of disciplinary interpenetration in the Faculté des sciences sociales, despite a clear process of specialization. Thus, as early as the 1951–52 school year, courses associated with social action and social hygiene (the closest to social work) disappeared from the common curriculum of the Départements de sociologie, d'économique, et de relations industrielles, while the program at the École de service social gained independence, offered fewer and fewer courses specializing in sociology, and changed the economics courses from compulsory to optional.[32]

The role of male professors in maintaining strong ties between social work and the other social sciences became clear in the 1950s. Women, in contrast, became the primary actors in the process of professionalization and disciplinary specialization as they strengthened ties between the school and the local practice setting, engaged in practical instruction of the two primary methods (social-group work and casework), and organized placements and established new lay-operated social services in Quebec City.

When Poulin left as director of the school in 1957, the position was not given to Hayda Denault or Simone Paré, even though the latter had also been an instructor since 1947, associate professor since 1950, and full professor since 1956. Instead, Jean-Marie Martin, a former economics professor and then dean of the faculty, held the position until it was given, the following year, to Guy Rocher, a young sociologist and PhD graduate from Harvard University who had taught previously in the Département de sociologie. As director, Rocher brought social work and sociology closer together and put a particular emphasis on research.[33] He also championed the need to broaden "the formula followed thus far [by the journal *Service social*, which should publish] not only studies prepared by social workers, but projects by sociologists and other representatives of the disciplines underlying social work."[34] Rocher left the position two years later, however, when he agreed to be director of the Département de sociologie et d'anthropologie at the University of Montreal. At that time, he was also appointed to the Royal Commission of Inquiry on Education in the Province of Quebec. Upon leaving the École de service social, he expressed the wish that a professor be hired to oversee the new research orientation he had championed as director. To that end, he recommended that "a sociologist, for example Mr. Marc Laplante, currently assistant in the faculty's Centre de recherches, eventually be given a position in the École de service social, after acquiring instruction in this discipline."[35] Hierarchical disciplinary outlooks and networks were formed at the school when individuals were promoted because they had profiles (usually male profiles) similar to those valorized by the administrators.

In 1960, Simone Paré became the first French Canadian woman to be awarded a doctorate in social work, from Columbia University, and was named director of the school, where she stayed until 1967. Over the next thirty years, she was the cornerstone of the journal *Service social*, which allowed her to draw on her specialization in social-group work, which she had acquired during years of intense volunteer work with the Girl Guides.[36] Although she took on multiple administrative duties, much more so than Denault, Paré also taught and organized professional training at the École de service social until the end of her career. As her professional correspondence shows, the social and intellectual networks in which she invested the most time were tied directly to social work as a profession and discipline. In light of these findings, it can be argued that women preferentially form local professional networks while men form political and intellectual networks located more on the national (Quebec-Canada) level.

Much like Denault, Paré also played an important role in the early years of the Conseil central des Oeuvres de Québec, founded in 1945 to coordinate social-assistance financing.[37] Although she conducted extensive empirical research, it was local in nature and not adopted or integrated by her colleagues into the body of Quebec sociological work.[38] That Paré has been forgotten today can also be linked to her modesty. This very Catholic woman often refused praise and deferred to other, male, voices, which she characterized as "more competent and more authoritative" than her own.[39] When asked to produce a text in honour of her colleague, sociologist Jean-Charles Falardeau, for example, she chose to remain in the territory of personal anecdotes, as she often did in her writings.

Prior to 1960, two other women were hired as professors. Georgette Dorval Guay had an even more mysterious career path than Hayda Denault. She earned a doctorate in philosophy in 1940, taught medical social service at the school starting in 1950 (the same year as her husband), and became an associate professor in 1956. That she was the first married female professor at the school does not seem to have enhanced her profile at the school. Indeed, references to her are strangely absent from the annual reports and archives of the École de service social, despite her many years of service and despite the fact that she was named a member of the Order of Canada in 1976 in recognition of her university career and, especially, for establishing "socio-medical services in the province's hospitals."[40] Mathilde du Ranquet, a French social worker who came to hone her skills at Laval, was hired in 1959 as the professor responsible for supervising placements and teaching social casework. She left the university several years later, however, to care for her ill mother in France.[41] These pioneers left behind major social achievements (both in the field of teaching and in organizing new social services in Quebec City in the 1940s and 1950s) but very few traces or records in university archives or memoirs.[42]

This cohort of professors also included three men who left the school relatively quickly to take up other, more prestigious, positions. Guy Rocher (not surprisingly, given that his training in sociology and his intellectual interests were not grounded in social work) left in 1960 to become director of the Département de sociologie et d'anthropologie at the University of Montreal. Edgar Guay, husband of Georgette Guay and less educated than she (he received a master's of social work from Laval in 1948), was hired one year before his wife and quickly, in 1957, found a seat on the Conseil de l'École. In 1954, after becoming involved in government, he accepted the chairmanship of the Comité interdépartemental sur l'enfance, established by Paul Sauvé.[43] He left his university duties permanently in 1959 to become assistant deputy minister with the Ministry of Social Welfare in Quebec City, then deputy minister for forests in the 1970s.

Claude Morin's career path exhibited many similarities to Guay's. He received a master's degree in economics from Laval in 1954. With the promise of obtaining a professorial position in the École de service social, he then left for New York, where he earned a master's in social work and studied theories of public policy. When he returned in 1956, he became a professor at the school and taught economics and community organization. He, too, quickly moved into government, sitting on the Study Committee on Public Assistance in 1961. Two years later, he left the university, at the request of Jean Lesage, to become, in turn, economic adviser to the Executive Council of the Government of Quebec and deputy minister for federal-provincial affairs and intergovernmental affairs. In his autobiography, Morin describes the steps and networks that led him to the political field and the secondary nature of social work in his preoccupations and interests. Although he affirms that everything in university teaching "pleased [him] and fulfilled [his] childhood hopes," he mentions neither his colleagues at the École de service social, men or women, nor the issues facing the profession at the time.[44] Morin details how his political education started early, in 1939, when his father granted him the privilege, as eldest son, of listening at his side, in silence, to the radio on election night.

From the moment he entered the Faculté des sciences sociales, Morin's attention turned towards public service and the game of politics, much like his male colleagues, rather than towards social services in Quebec City, the focus of his female ones. When Maurice Lamontagne went into politics in 1957, Morin gave him a hand up, along with other former students and colleagues. The following year, an old professor recommended Morin to Maurice Sauvé, who was then an adviser to Jean Lesage, to sit on a Liberal Party working group. This was only the first step towards much more active involvement in politics, especially during the next election campaign and after the Liberals took power in 1960. "Shifting into gear" led Morin to take on more and more responsibility in the senior civil service, where he found many former male colleagues from the faculty.[45] In the sole empirical study performed by Morin while he was a professor, completed in 1958 for the Conseil central des oeuvres in Portneuf County, he thanks only his male colleagues, especially those from the Département de sociologie.[46] In his autobiography, he recounts the bad memories he associates with this research, particularly the difficult and conflictual experience of managing relationships with people involved in social work in a non-university setting, a duty usually performed by the women of the École de service social.

When Rocher and Guay left the École de service social in 1960, new professors urgently needed to be hired. The school hired two candidates: Michel Trottier, a psychologist who had already been teaching for several years at the school,[47] and Christiane Dussault, an unmarried social worker specializing in social-group work and responsible for practical instruction. In short, women's trajectories, still marked by singlehood in the 1950s, were characterized by involvement in local, specialized professional networks with an eye to organizing new social services on the eve of the Quiet Revolution and specialized education and the supervision of placements. Conversely, men hired as professors simply passed through the École de service social and the discipline in general. During their studies, they built networks in the other social sciences and focused their specializations on public policy and the national and governmental organization of work and social assistance. Social work was only one segment of career paths that, by the end of their careers, was a segment that they rarely recalled following long careers during which they received multiple forms of official recognition.[48]

The Third Cohort: Disciplinary Specialization and the Research-Practice Opposition, 1960–72

Starting in the 1960s, the pace at which new professors entered the École de service social picked up in response to a growing demand for professional social workers in various public institutions. The Boucher Report, submitted in 1963, enshrined a new interventionist conception of the state in social services, and this conception was reaffirmed with the final submission of the Castonguay-Nepveu Report in 1972.[49] Between these two dates, the government ordered numerous studies and passed legislation on health insurance, welfare, rent control, and public health that gave the state primary responsibility for supporting the disadvantaged.[50] The state relied on new professionals in the socio-health sector, including social workers, to carry out the reforms and new programs. From 1960 to 1972, an average of two professors per year joined the faculty at the École de service social.

It is impossible to describe the trajectories of these twenty new professors in the same detail as those of their predecessors, but primary areas of transformation can be outlined. First, the era witnessed the professionalization of professors of both sexes. With the exception of Michel Trottier, who was trained in psychology, the new professors had social work training. Generally hired after they attained master's degrees, some of them pursued doctoral studies or professional follow-up instruction in addition to their professorial duties.[51] Although nearly all the professors in this cohort remained in the social work field throughout their professional lives, orientations and timeframes continued to be differentiated by sex. Several women left their positions quickly in the 1960s: Christiane Dussault in 1966, for no explicit reason; Françoise Turgeon in 1965, to marry; and Madeleine Valois in 1967, to return to social work practice. Suzanne Blais-Grenier, Pauline Baril, and Claudette Boivin did not remain for long and left few traces in the institutional archives and annual reports. Of the professors hired in this era, only Georgette Béliveau-St-Arnaud and Céline Bédard remained on faculty at the end of the 1970s and until retirement. Like the women in previous cohorts, they largely continued to specialize in medical or psychiatric social work, in specialized methods (casework or social group work), and in the supervision and practical application of these methods.

Their male colleagues continued research and work tied more closely to other social sciences. In this cohort, their work was clearly rooted in the discipline, but their study of community organization privileged the community and institutions over the individual (the privileged unit of medical and psychological intervention, social casework, and even social group work, which were mostly the purview of women). Their focus on large units of observation placed men in more narrow relation with the male colleagues of the other social sciences.[52] The most strongly masculinized sectors, especially community organization, took up more and more space not only in the teaching program but also in the practice of social work in Quebec City as men became invested in professional organization.[53] Apart from Pierre Laplante (who was appointed director of the Conseil des Oeuvres de Montréal in 1965), René Boisvert, Jean-Charles Guindon, and Gérard Poirier (who left the school after several years of teaching), the professors hired in the late 1960s and early 1970s – Martin Poulin, René Auclair, Laval Doucet, and Gérald Doré – spent their entire careers at Laval University.

The differentiation between male and female professors at the École de service social was articulated not only horizontally but also vertically, in the form of a greater presence of men in administrative positions and in funded research. In 1967, when Paré left as director of the school, Nicolas Zay replaced her. A new hire in 1966, Zay had taught for several years in the École de service social at the University of Montreal. The archives do not explain the precise motivations behind this hire, but it is thoroughly possible that Zay's reputation and doctoral degree made his candidacy more appealing than those of other, less educated, colleagues, especially in the context of student complaints about the poor quality of scientific training and insufficient preparation for research. From the students' point of view, social work professors were less rigorous than social science professors, and their teaching was not sufficiently tailored to the requirements of social work research and professional practice.[54]

In the 1960s, funded research, encouraged more and more by university administrators, was primarily conducted by the men in the school. Women mostly performed research for local or private organizations, often on a small scale, with very little financing or peer evaluation from outside the university. Blais-Grenier collaborated on a research project on child socialization issues under the aegis of the Canadian Conference on Children, Paré conducted research on Beauport, and Baril and Bélanger produced studies on housing policies in Quebec City and on placement assessment instruments for agencies.[55] Zay, conversely, was heavily involved in the university and ministerial bodies in charge of financing research (the Conseil consultatif des octrois de recherche and the Comité de sélection des bourses in the Department of National Health and Welfare) and in 1971 became the first professor from the school to receive public funding to conduct a longitudinal study on the aging process.[56] The following year, André Beaudoin received funding from the Department of Social Affairs to study poverty in and the structural features of Quebec communities.[57] By 1962, research development was perceived as "a vital necessity for the school," but the school's failure to compete successfully with other schools for funded research became a recurring preoccupation, especially after 1973.[58]

Conclusion

The career paths of the professors at the École de service social between 1943 and 1972 reveal a division between intellectual and professional social work that positioned women, on one hand, in some of the most practical and relationship-oriented specializations (placement supervision and intervention methods, for example), specialities that went hand-in-hand with local networks and the front-line fieldwork from which many women professors had come or to which they returned. On the other hand, the men specialized on research, general theoretical questions, and other social sciences, specializations that went hand-in-hand with national social science networks in government and university institutions. Few of the men worked as social workers in the field, especially prior to 1960, and their departures from the school were often the result of their being offered social advancement in administrative apparatuses. Women, in contrast, left to marry, have children, return to social work practice, or retire. This gender structure broadly follows those discovered by Sara Z. Burke and Shirley Tillotson, historians of English Canada, but it also has features specific to the Quebec context, its Catholic culture, and the particularities of the Quiet Revolution. Through their research projects, teaching, and intervention, women at the École de service social contributed to the transformation of social relationships based on sex, especially by empirically documenting the social realities affecting women more than men, which raised awareness of gender issues, an essential condition to the emergence of new forms of feminism in the late 1960s.

The sex-based division of labour at the Laval University's École de service social was transformed in the 1960s as social workers and university professors were professionalized. While women in the 1950s and early 1960s represented disciplinary continuity compared to their male colleagues (who only passed through the school), this trend reversed between 1965 and 1972, despite Paré's position as director. The men hired in this period universally remained in their positions until retirement, and during their tenure, they gradually climbing the ladder of institutional recognition. Conversely, the women in this cohort often left the school after only a few years of service. For now, it is impossible to know the exact influence of marriage, child-bearing, and household duties on their career paths, not to mention institutional discrimination, which is nearly invisible in the official archives. To determine this would require finding these women and conducting individual interviews or finding their personal documents (correspondence or journals) to enlarge our understanding of their self-representations, the representations, or identities, that resulted from the differential socialization of girls and boys, which impelled the former to foster humility and to engage in concrete, relationship-based work and care and the latter to develop authority and intellectual confidence and to engage in theoretical and administrative work. As chapters by Gail Campbell and Heidi McDonald in this volume point out, these materials would also allow historians to document the professional networks formed by men and women, networks that helped increase social status for the former while impeding it for the latter. It was thanks to these networks, these provisions, and their greater availability to men that men were more often and more quickly appointed to positions of authority, whether within the university or in public administration, from where they imposed their definition of priorities and their outlook on legitimate issues and, over time, came to be considered the sole architects of the Quiet Revolution. Their female colleagues, in contrast, were quietly forgotten.

NOTES

1 Danielle Juteau and Nicole Laurin, "La sécularisation et l'étatisation du secteur hospitalier au Québec de 1960 à 1966," in *Jean Lesage et l'éveil d'une nation: Les débuts de la Révolution tranquille* (Quebec City: Presses de l'Université du Québec, 1989), 155–67.
2 Only a few pioneering studies focus on social services in the city, notably Johanne Daigle and Dale Gilbert, "Un modèle d'économie sociale mixte: La dynamique des services sociaux à l'enfance dans la ville de Québec, 1850–1950," *Recherches Sociographiques* 20, 1 (2008): 37–72. There is still no study on the history of the social work discipline and profession in Quebec City. For Montreal, see especially, "Amélie Bourbeau, la réorganisation de l'assistance chez les catholiques montréalais: La Fédération des oeuvres de charité canadiennes-françaises et la Federation of Catholic Charities, 1930–1972" (PhD diss., Université du Québec à Montréal, 2009) and Lionel-Henri Groulx, *Le travail social, analyse et évolution, débats et enjeux* (Laval: Éditions Agence d'Arc, 1993).

3 Nancy Christie, *Engendering the State: Family, Work, and Welfare in Canada* (Toronto: University of Toronto Press, 2000); Sara Z. Burke, *Seeking the Highest Good: Social Service and Gender at the University of Toronto, 1888–1937* (Toronto: University of Toronto Press, 1996); and Shirley Tillotson, *Contributing Citizens: Modern Charitable Fundraising and the Makings of the Welfare State* (Vancouver: UBC Press, 2008).

4 This identification, reached through the titles of courses offered by men and women, as well as titles of capstone projects filed with the École de service social at the University of Montreal, does not help us understand the social processes through which these preferences were constructed, and it remains far too close to the surface of the phenomenon. See also Denyse Baillargeon, Amélie Bourbeau, and Gilles Rondeau, "Motivation et formation des travailleurs sociaux francophones: Quelques parcours pionniers (1942–1961)," *Intervention* 125 (December 2006): 169–79.

5 Causer, Pfefferkorn, and Woehl, *Métiers, identités professionnelles et genre* (Paris: L'Harmattan, 2007), and Claude Dubar and Pierre Tripier, *Sociologie des professions* (Paris: Armand Collin, 2008).

6 Claude Dubar, "Trajectoires sociales et formes identitaires: Clarifications conceptuelles et méthodologiques," *Sociétés Contemporaines* 29 (1998): 72–85.

7 Sixteen of the fifty recipients of the Government of Quebec's Artisan de la Révolution tranquille medal in 2010 were graduates of or teachers in the Faculté des sciences sociales at Laval University. Of those fifty recipients, only two political women – Thérèse Forget-Casgrain and Claire Kirkland-Casgrain – were honoured. See http://www.revolutiontranquille.gouv.qc.ca/index.php?id=116.

8 The Faculté des sciences sociales at Laval University has been the subject of numerous research projects and analyses, including Jean-Philippe Warren's *L'engagement sociologique: La tradition sociologique du Québec francophone (1886–1955)* (Montreal: Boréal, 2003). Strangely, these studies never address the history or sociology of the École de service social, except at its founding.

9 Françoise Blum, "Regards sur les mutations du travail social au XXe siècle," *Le Mouvement Social* 199, 2 (2002): 83–94; Christine Rater-Garcette, *La professionnalisation du travail social: Action sociale, syndicalisme, formation (1880–1920)* (Paris: L'Harmattan, 1996); Causer, Pfefferkorn, and Woehl, *Métiers, identités professionnelles et genre*.

10 Warren, *L'engagement sociologique*, 299–352. Frédéric Parent and Paul Sabourin, eds., "Les sciences sociales au Québec: L'héritage leplaysien," special issue, *Les Études Sociales* 151 (2010). This dualism is also characteristic of Leplaysian social science in France, which nonetheless remained institutionalized in non-university spaces, a fact that helps explain the position of social work outside the university in that country. Bernard Kalaora and Antoine Savoye, *Les inventeurs oubliés: Le lay et ses continuateurs aux origines des sciences sociales* (Paris: Champ Vallon, 1989).

11 Georges-Henri Lévesque, "Sciences sociales et service social," *Service Social* 1, 1 (1951): 3–6.

12 Mary-Jo Deegan, *Jane Addams and the Men of the Chicago School, 1892–1918* (New Brunswick/Oxford: Transaction Books, 1988).

13 Burke, *Seeking the Highest Good*; see also, on the United States and English Canada, Katherine A. Kendall, *Council on Social Work Education: Its Antecedents and First Twenty Years* (Alexandria, VA: Council on Social Work Education, 2002); Ronald A.

Feldman and Sheila B. Kamerman, eds., *The Columbia University School of Social Work: A Centennial Celebration* (New York: Columbia University Press, 2001); and Tillotson, *Contributing Citizens.*

14 Marlene Shore, *The Science of Social Redemption: McGill, the Chicago School, and the Origins of Social Research in Canada* (Toronto: Toronto University Press, 1987), and Christie, *Engendering the State.*

15 Groulx, *Le travail social.*

16 Bourbeau, *La réorganisation*, 181, uses the expression "absence de la 'première génération' masculine" (absence of the male "first" generation).

17 Annual Report of the École de service social of Laval University, 1958–59, Laval University Archives, Fonds U683.

18 According to student records, female and male graduation rates at the École de service social between 1943 and 1972 were comparable to the ratio of students of each sex.

19 Michael Gauvreau, *Les origines catholiques de la révolution tranquille* (Montreal: Fides, 2008).

20 Jean-Charles Falardeau, Guy Rocher, and Fernand Dumont, in *Recherches Socio-graphiques* 15, 2–3 (1974): 219–27, 243–48, 255–61.

21 Letter signed "the dean," "Projet relatif à un changement de status du département de service social de la Faculté des sciences sociales," 1944, Fonds de l'École de service social, Laval University Archives, U683.

22 Marie-Paule Malouin, *Le mouvement familial au Québec: Les débuts, 1937–1965* (Montreal: Boréal, 1998). The family movement in Quebec was a network of associations and groups that defended and promoted the Catholic family.

23 The teaching load of each professor was identified by going through the calendars of the Laval University École de service social from 1943 to 1972.

24 The empirical research used for sociological analyses would seem to have been conducted by social work students, but the analysis is signed only by professors Poulin, Marier, and Falardeau.

25 Jean Hamelin, *Les Franciscains au Canada, 1890–1990* (Sillery: Septentrion, 1990), 325.

26 Especially surveys of various parts of the city in 1947–48 and a study on housing in 1944.

27 The archives of Laval University have kept practically no traces of Hayda Denault, who submitted the papers of her father, Amédée Denault, a reasonably well-known journalist and author, but not her own.

28 Georges-Henri Lévesque, *Souvenances 1* (Ottawa: Éditions la Presse, 1983), 54–55. The original French quote is as follows:

> Elle avait été journaliste d'abord [et] j'avais décelé dans ses articles un sens social assez averti. Un jour de mai 1939, assistant à nos cours comme auditrice libre, elle me laisse entendre qu'elle aimerait se spécialiser et se joindre à notre équipe par après. Sautant sur l'occasion, je lui suggère de s'orienter vers le service social en vue d'occuper la chaire déjà mentionnée. Elle entreprend aussitôt des études à l'Université Columbia de New York, pour ensuite les poursuivre à la Montreal School of Social Work de McGill et les couronner par une maîtrise à l'École de service social de l'Université de Montréal. De ces dif-

férentes écoles elle apporte à Québec, en 1941, les données qui constituent les données fondamentales de la formation des travailleurs sociaux. Malheureusement, à ce moment, nous ne sommes pas en mesure d'établir la chaire en question, encore moins l'École. En attendant, notre candidate accepte la direction du Bureau d'assistance aux familles des combattants. C'était la guerre. Elle est aussi la première professionnelle du service social à Québec. Par bonheur, l'École de service social est fondée en 1943, et Hayda Denault en devient l'âme dirigeante. C'est même chez elle qu'eut lieu la première réunion préparatoire à cette fondation et où l'on procéda à l'élaboration d'un programme temporaire.

All quotations translated by Matthew Kayahara.

29 Hayda Denault, "Rapport du Service Familial de Québec pour l'année 1949–50," *Service Social* 1, 3 (1951): 129–33.

30 See the chapter by Karen Balcom in this collection.

31 Lévesque, *Souvenances 1*, 55 (emphasis mine): "Une compétence professionnelle à la fois *discrète* et *entraînante*, insérée dans l'*humanisme* d'une riche culture générale, secondée par un *dévouement toujours attentif et disponible*."

32 Calendars of Laval University, 1943–59.

33 Minutes of the Conseil de l'École de service social of Laval University, 28 October 1958, Fonds de l'École de service social, Laval University Archives, U683.

34 Minutes of the Conseil de l'École de service social of Laval University, 10 November 1958, Fonds de l'École de service social, Laval University Archives, U683.

35 Minutes of the Conseil de l'École de service social of Laval University, 29 August 1960, Fonds de l'École de service social, Laval University Archives, U683.

36 Fonds Simone Paré, Laval University Archives, P335.

37 Hayda Denault, "Les services sociaux à Québec" (master's thesis, University of Montreal, 1945), and Simone Paré, "L'école de service social de l'Université Laval," in *Cinquante ans de sciences sociales à l'Université Laval: L'histoire de la Faculté des sciences sociales (1938–1988)*, ed. Albert Faucher (Quebec City: Faculté des sciences sociales de l'Université Laval, 1988), 219–49.

38 Notably her doctoral work. See Simone Paré, *La participation sociale à Beauport, province de Québec, en 1957–58* (Quebec City: École de service social de l'Université Laval, 1960).

39 "Témoignages," *Recherches Sociographiques* 23, 1–2 (1982): 11–44.

40 Website of the Governor General of Canada, http://www.gg.ca/honour.aspx?id=690&t=12.

41 Annual Report of the École de service social of Laval University, 1964–65, Fonds de l'École de service social, Laval University Archives, U683.

42 Especially hospital social work, the Conseil central des oeuvres, the Centre social Saint-Vallier, the Service social familial, Sauvegarde de l'enfance, and Centre psycho-social. Only the Service de réadaptation sociale was founded and run right from the start by men, Gonzalve Poulin and Gérard Lortie. This was a service aimed at offenders, an area of intervention heavily occupied by men.

43 Jean-Louis Roy, *La marche des Québécois: Le temps des ruptures (1945–1960)* (Montreal: Éditions Leméac, 1976).

44 Morin, *Les choses comme elles étaient,* 107. This same silence can be seen in the accounts by Guy Rocher, Jean-Charles Falardeau, and Fernand Dumont. See, especially, the interviews by Guy Rocher, with François Rocher, *Guy Rocher: Entretiens* (Montreal: Boréal, 2010) and Fernand Dumont's autobiography, *Récit d'une émigration* (Montreal: Boréal, 1997).

45 This quote borrows from the title of the chapter in Morin's autobiography where these events are recounted. See Morin, *Les choses comme elles étaient,* 113 and 132.

46 Claude Morin, *Enquête sociale sur le comté de Portneuf* (Quebec City: Conseil Central des Oeuvres du diocèse de Québec, 1958).

47 Simone Paré wanted the school to hire a man to attract and retain male students, as she says in a letter to rector Vachon in 1960: Fonds de l'École de service social de l'Université Laval, Fond U683. However, we should note her sensitivity to recruiting young women into the university when she wrote to Alphonse-Marie Parent, vice-rector and secretary general, on 25 April 1951, suggesting visits to Quebec City's women's colleges to recruit students to the faculty. Fonds Simone Paré, P335, Laval University Archives.

48 See, especially, Morin, *Les choses comme elles étaient,* and Guy Rocher's interviews with François Rocher, *Guy Rocher.*

49 See Bourbeau, *La réorganisation,* 293–97, on the differences between the Boucher Report and the Castonguay-Nepveu Report.

50 In Quebec, la Loi de l'assurance-hospitalisation passed in 1961, the Loi sur le régime des rentes in 1965, the Loi des allocations familiales in 1967, the Loi générale d'assistance sociale in 1969, the Loi de l'assurance-maladie in 1970, the Loi sur les service de santé et les services sociaux in 1971, and the Loi sur la santé publique in 1972, to name just a few.

51 Including Suzanne Blais, Jacques Laplante, and Jean-Charles Guindon.

52 According to Simone Paré, social group work has a "dual purpose: it seeks to develop, by means of group living, the personality of each individual; it seeks to adapt this personality to the group for better social performance of the individual." Simone Paré, *Service social de groupe et guidisme* (Quebec City: École de service social, Laval University, 1945), 1–2.

53 Robert Mayer, *Évolution des pratiques en service social* (Boucherville: Gaëtan Morin éditeur, 2002); Marie-Andrée Couillard, Jean-Louis Gendron, and Hector Ouellet, *Histoire et développement du mouvement centraide de Québec* (Sainte-Foy: Faculté des sciences sociales, 1995). Moreover, in 1966, when male students briefly outnumbered female ones, the student association requested that community organization take up more space in the social work study program. See, especially, Association des Étudiants en Service social de l'Université Laval, "Mémoire sur la formation professionnelle donnée à l'École de service social de l'Université Laval, 1966," Fonds de l'École de service social, Laval University Archives, U683

54 See Association des Étudiants en Service social de l'Université Laval, "Mémoire des étudiants de troisième année, 1958–1959, 1962, 1964–1965, Mémoire sur la formation professionnelle donnée à l'École de service social de l'Université Laval," 1966, Fonds de l'École de service social, Laval University Archives, U683. The exact composition of this student association is not known, for the memos always bore a

collective signature. This association does not appear to have played a role comparable to that of the corresponding student association at the University of Toronto. See Burke, *Seeking the Highest Good.*

55 Annual Reports, 1963–64, 1970–71, Fonds de l'École de service social, Laval University Archives, U683.

56 Annual Reports, 1970–71, 1971–72, Fonds de l'École de service social, Laval University Archives, U683.

57 Annual Report, 1972–73, Fonds de l'École de service social, Laval University Archives, U683.

58 Annual Report, 1973–74, Fonds de l'École de service social, Laval University Archives, U683.

Teaching June Cleaver, Being Hazel Chong
An Oral History of Gender, Race, and National "Character"

KRISTINA R. LLEWELLYN

When I first contacted Hazel Chong by phone as a potential participant for my research on gendered experiences of postwar teaching, she asked whether she was the first woman of Chinese origin to teach in a Canadian public school. I did not know the answer. Starting as a home economics teacher in the rural community of Armstrong, British Columbia, in 1949, she was certainly among the first Canadian women of Chinese origin to enter a profession. Hazel concluded our first interview in her Vancouver suburban home in 2005 by once again stating her interest in knowing whether she had indeed been the first. This was not my pressing research question. After Hazel read my work, she kindly responded with a handwritten note in which she expressed pleasure with her given pseudonym. I felt a sense of missed opportunity as a feminist historian in the field of education for not pursuing Hazel's repeated inquiry into her pioneering status. During a trip to Vancouver in 2008, I interviewed Hazel for a second time in her home, at which point she gave me permission to use her given name. My intention at that time was to garner more explicit stories about her racialization and ethnicity.[1] The stories I received, however, were much the same as those of the first interview. As if she had rehearsed, Hazel recounted almost word for word how fate had brought her to home economics teaching and student recognition of her dressing sensibilities. This was not the narrative I had expected from a trailblazing minority educator. She hesitated to name misogynist and racist educational structures and instead expressed pride in her teaching of June

Cleaver–like domesticity. After I pressed her for rebellious tales, she stated at the end of the second interview, "You must think I was a 'yes' woman."[2]

It was not until reviewing these parting words in the transcript that I recognized that I had treated her life story as a form of constrained consciousness regarding oppression. As a leftist, white, woman scholar, I was intent on tracing the manifestations of Anglo-Canadian racism as it was imposed on the Chinese female identity. Within this Foucauldian gaze, Wing Chung Ng argues, Chinese "initiatives and conscious motivations" are absent.[3] I returned to my interview transcripts to hear Hazel's oral history anew. Why did Hazel actively seek to be remembered as a pioneer in teaching yet recount a narrative of accommodation to Anglo-Celtic, patriarchal ideals of postwar citizenship? What does it mean that Hazel was aware of racism in her childhood and career but presented herself as an autonomous individual unshackled by discrimination? Such contradictions, or what Kathleen Weiler terms bad fits, highlight the very point at which the oral history subject negotiates her concept of self.[4]

Hazel's choice of presentation is significant. First, Hazel's depiction of an assimilable character reflects her status as a local-born Chinese, or *tusheng* woman.[5] This generation, who became adults after the Second World War, welcomed opportunities for social and economic integration that had once been inaccessible.[6] Second, Hazel's story of domestic skillfulness speaks to her active participation in Canadian nationhood. Experts considered dress and food preparation, central elements of home economics, the bedrock of pro-consumerist, nuclear family ideals in the anti-communist age.[7] Third, Hazel's construction of her professional enculturation highlights everyday negotiations of the political landscape. Postwar officials made promises of egalitarianism in Canada's liberal democracy. Rather than freedom from discrimination, these promises afforded new public space for the performance of right citizenship. Hazel's pioneering spirit is evident, then, not in her rebellious tales, but in her perceived ability to grasp the opportunities of the period and shape the culture of post-Second World War Canada. This oral history of Hazel Chong does not determine if she was indeed the first woman of Chinese origin to teach in a Canadian public school. It does reflect the new postwar territory Hazel negotiated, changing racial politics and conceptions of domesticity to assert Canada's "egalitarian" national character.

Oral History as a Feminist Encounter

Feminists have long embraced oral history for its potential to restore women's voices to the historical record.[8] Community and public history projects have been particularly important in recording and publishing the stories of Canadian women minorities. These projects include *Jin Guo: Voices of Chinese Canadian Women* by the Women's Book Committee of the Chinese Canadian National Council and the National Film Board production *Under the Willow Tree: Pioneer Chinese Women in Canada*.[9] Oral history serves critical goals as a feminist encounter: to validate the political meaning of women's experiences, to reject androcentric notions of objectivity, and to create resources about women's experiences with oppression.[10]

These goals are not unproblematic. Oral historians wrestle with the power inequalities inherent in the interviewer-interviewee relationship, from the question-answer format to the interpretive process. Oral historians struggle with how to redistribute power over meaning making, with developing what Michael Frisch calls a shared authority between interviewer and interviewee.[11] Such strategies include treating the interview as a conversation, asking subjects to review transcripts, and collaborating in publications.[12] My interviews with Hazel were researcher-centred, based on a predefined interpretive framework, and without formative consultation. According to Kathryn Anderson and Dana Jack, such an approach means that "I am already appropriating what she says to an existing schema, and therefore I am no longer really listening to *her*."[13]

In addressing sensitivities to research inequalities, however, Karen Olsen and Linda Shopes argue that academics may overestimate their importance in the interview process. They write: "If we define the terms of inquiry by asking the questions, they [interviewees] also define it by answering the questions as they wish."[14] In the act of oral history telling, whether remaining silent on a subject or rehearsing answers before the interview, participants perform stories for their own purposes.[15] Hazel had her own agenda for our interviews. She set out archival documents (at times insisting I read them on the record), chose particular metaphors, and repeated stories to control the composition of her life story.

My feminist approach to oral history respects Hazel's ability to define her own history but acknowledges my explicit role as researcher in the history constructed.[16] It is in an effort to listen deeply when re-reading Hazel's interview transcripts that I share intellectual authority with her.[17] Given that the language we use to conceptualize the self is not unitary, I do not look for coherence, which may obscure meaning. Instead, I pay attention to Hazel's discursive strategies, or the "controlling metaphors, notions, categories and norms which develop and delimit the subjects' conceptions and expressions of personal, work and social relations."[18] As Mikhail Bakhtin argues, notions that separate the private self from the social self are myth.[19] Subjectivities, and the language choices used to construct them, are grounded by material worlds, past and present. I approach Hazel's oral narratives, therefore, with simultaneous interpretations, namely, a reading for structure or the experience and working of the material world, and a reading for culture, or the ways memories of events are organized through language.[20] Through my readings, Hazel's narrative of her teaching self provides a messy and, at times, contradictory image of her negotiated position at the boundaries between the white, male domain and the Chinese, female domain. It also speaks to the tension-ridden and malleable characteristics of the often taken-for-granted conceptions of democracy and egalitarianism in our history.

Outsiders within Postwar Liberal Democracy

Hazel Chong, a second-generation Chinese Canadian, was one of the first women to be accepted into the education profession. It is difficult to ascertain from school records if she was the first, because immigrant families often anglicized their names and because women changed names when they married. We do know that federal and provincial restrictions before the Second World War limited the Chinese female population and their economic activity. The head taxes of the late nineteenth and early twentieth centuries were intended to stop women's immigration and the permanent settlement of families. In 1921, females only accounted for 2,424 individuals (half of whom lived in British Columbia) out of a total Chinese population of 39,587.[21] The Chinese Immigration Act of 1923, also known as the Exclusion Act, made it practically impossible for Chinese to enter Canada. Disenfranchised by the province until 1947, Chinese Canadians could not hold political office or enter the medical and legal professions.[22]

Employment opportunities and entrepreneurial activities were proscribed by the social construction of "the Chinese" as criminally and sexually dangerous.[23] Provincial white women's labour laws, on the books from the 1910s to the late 1960s, prohibited Chinese men from hiring white women. Legislators and reformers were concerned about the purity of white women – the "guardians of the race" – who were exposed to the reported plural marriage, concubinage, and drug addiction of Chinese men.[24] Colonial panics regarding the character of Chinese women also stopped them from being accepted into teaching and nursing, professions open to white women.[25] Before the war, Chinese Canadian women who taught were confined to the segregated schools that opened in the 1920s. Historian Timothy Stanley argues that advocates of segregation constructed Chinese students as disease carriers, caused by poor household sanitary conditions, and thus a threat to white children.[26] School officials believed "that a Chinese woman would naturally be better adapted to teaching boys and girls of her own race than a white teacher."[27] Segregated schools existed until after the Second World War.

The key to altering discriminatory restrictions was a paradigm shift in human rights after the Second World War.[28] The war was a battle of competing ideologies – Western democracy and liberation against fascism. Canadians sought to avoid totalitarianism in the wake of the Holocaust and ensure participatory citizenship at a time of growing civil rights and decolonization movements. There was international support for the expression of human rights, not attached to nation-states, expressed through the United Nations Charter in 1945 and, in 1948, with the Universal Declaration of Human Rights, drafted by Canadian John Humphrey. Democratic measures gained renewed prominence on the political scene, promising to deliver the fundamental freedoms of what is often memorialized as a golden era. According to the liberal ideology of the day, Canadian democracy seemingly offered patriotic individuals an equal part in state citizenship.[29] In this image, the postwar federal government ensured some public entitlements, including renewed social security initiatives, such as health insurance, unemployment insurance, and workmen's compensation.[30] Specific promises to women were made by officials, such as fair remuneration and the elimination of the marriage bar among civic employees, including teachers.[31]

Open discrimination that specifically targeted a minority population, which the Exclusion Act accomplished uniquely, ran counter to Canada's claim on egalitarian principles. Civil rights agitation and the acknowledgment of patriotic services by Chinese men on the battlefield and Chinese women on the home front made it increasingly disgraceful for the government to limit rights according to race and gender.[32] The assimilable character of the Chinese began to appear in government and news reports, which stressed that they were "virtuous, heroic, dignified, and patient – in contrast to the Japanese, who were considered proud and arrogant."[33] These civilizing characteristics would only be possible, proponents argued, if women and children were allowed entry into the country, because then Chinese would build a normal family life in Canada.[34] Expanded suffrage for Chinese Canadians, the repeal of the Exclusion Act, and the removal of a marriage bar for women would open up the professions by the late 1940s. Teaching would become a possible career for a virtuous Chinese woman.

Much of Chinese Canadian history stops with the postwar triumph over repressive legislation. Canadian historians have begun, however, to explore the inequities of liberal democracy in the postwar period. They have demonstrated that the popularization of liberal democratic rhetoric emerged as a national internal defence against the uncertainties of the age.[35] These uncertainties included the threat of the atomic bomb, a rise in immigration, and disruption to the nuclear family, particularly from higher rates of women's paid labour. Fear of these changes formed a basis for the Cold War mentality of the era, by which social authorities forwarded an agenda that acquiesced to reform in so far as it contained dissension and radicalism.[36] The primary model of internal defence was to champion national togetherness under the liberal pluralist banner of a fully democratic, egalitarian nation.[37] Commonality and stability were defined according to a desired hegemonic norm: English, middle-class, white, Protestant, and heterosexual citizenship.

Prime Minister King, when discussing the extension of rights to Chinese Canadians in 1947, made it clear that the appearance of egalitarianism had to be achieved without "the fundamental alteration to the present character of the Canadian population."[38] Those outside of the British character of the nation continued to be represented as a contaminating influence. Vancouver Chinatown residents who rejected suburban life, while exotic individuals, were deemed unhealthy.[39] Single women and men who rejected marriage were deemed emotionally maladjusted.[40] A new hegemonic citizenship discourse emerged; British male exclusivity was replaced with racial and gender adaptability. Himani Bannerji refers to this as the lie of liberal democracy:

> [I]f we problematize the notion of "Canada" through the introjections of the idea of belonging, we are left with the paradox of both belonging and non-belonging simultaneously. As a population, we non-whites and women (in particular, non-white women) are living in a specific territory. We are part of its economy, subject to its laws, and members of its civil society. Yet we are not part of its self-definition as "Canada" because we are not "Canadians" (read white and male).[41]

Like Bannerji's experience of Canadian multiculturalism, Hazel's narrative provides historical understanding of a woman who lived as an "outsider within" liberal democracy.[42]

A form of postwar freedom came for Hazel through accommodation to normative citizenship. Before cultural pluralism was a mantra for the country and before mainstream social life was accessible, local-born Chinese would have struggled to be enthusiastic about cultural retention.[43] With the expansion of opportunities, Wing Chung Ng explains, Canadian-born Chinese "generally looked beyond the ethnic boundary for economic and symbolic resources to nurture their sense of identity and autonomy."[44] This generation would act as cultural brokers for Chinese integration of Western organizations and behavioural norms. Hazel constructed her story through this generational lens. She was careful throughout the interview to refer to herself as *Canadian of Chinese origin* and not today's common vernacular – *Chinese Canadian*. She spoke of embodying and teaching the edicts of Western cooking and respectable dress for homemakers – the characteristics of iconic postwar television mother June Cleaver. She described growing up with friends who were ashamed of their heritage and targeted as enemies, "I fell into that syndrome – hide what you really are." Describing her postwar identity, Hazel stated: "My look was Caucasian, you know, like a banana – I was yellow on the outside and white on the inside."[45] *Banana* was a term used by post-1947 immigrants from South China as an accusation of deculturation by local born.[46] Hazel seemed cognizant of such accusations of identity deficiency. As Antonio Gramsci's concept of hegemony illuminates, Hazel performed postwar citizenship, which might have legitimated the ruling order by which she was marginalized; doing so, however, enabled her to extract, to some advantage, the identity of the good citizen and good teacher.[47]

Performing Right Citizenship

As a girl, Hazel could not imagine teaching as a career. In 1941, when she was twelve years old, the Women's Missionary Society reported: "only the occasional girl is fortunate enough to be able to train as a nurse or a teacher, partly because of the expense, and partly because public opinion is not yet educated to the place of accepting the Orientals in the professional world."[48] In addition to racist attitudes towards Chinese Canadians, college education was expensive, and her family struggled to put her through school. Hazel's father and maternal grandfather were among those who had emigrated from Canton China to mine gold and build the national railway. Like many bachelor men who came to Canada for work, they did not return home. Using old family birth certificates and photos culled from her basement, Hazel reconstructed her family history. In 1901, Hazel's parents met and married in Yale, British Columbia. They moved in 1912 to Vernon's Chinatown, in the interior region, to farm. Her mother, born in Yale, was one of only a few first-generation Chinese Canadian women. Her family, also from the Canton region, had been merchants. She gave birth to thirteen children; Hazel, the youngest, was born in 1929. Hazel's memories of her childhood were primarily defined by her mother's unpaid labour: making "utilitarian dresses" for the girls and boys, creating costumes for Chinese to exhibit their civic pride in parades, and hanging fish and salted bok choy to stretch the food budget. These memories might have been prominent for Hazel because creating fashions and preparing practical meals would become her life's work as a teacher. Her description of her mother's fine domestic skills and, later, her own aptitude, may also have been used to counter historical accusations by white society of unsanitary conditions in Chinese households. By 1945, her widowed mother had to support the family, a common experience for Chinese women who married older men from the first wave of migration. Contrary to prescriptive literature that insisted that children should go to school instead of work, many children from working-class ethnic families continued to play an important role in the family economy in postwar Canada. Hazel's mother had "a little market garden, and I grew up having to deliver vegetables to all the local stores before I went to school in the morning."[49]

Hazel expressed pride in the Chinese community of Vernon as she showed me photos of Chinese-run businesses and the Chinese Masonic Hall. Despite a strong ethnic community, she remembered "racial problems." Hazel described the Chinese population as "ghettoized" and related that her siblings had stayed away from their nonsegregated school because they were called "Chinky-Chinky Chinaman." Her parents hoped to protect their children from racism by making sure they were tutored in English and did not learn Cantonese after Grade 3. They also gave each child an Anglo-Saxon name that mirrored those of the Dixon family, who owned a local orchard. Hazel praised this decision, "It was good thinking on their part because we would have had a birth certificate with a Chinese name." Hazel's childhood memories reflect the stigma of poverty and of being Chinese: "I was an unhappy Oriental. I would sit and think, maybe if I wasn't Chinese, and I'd listen to music, and some days I was a black blues singer. I wanted just one day in my life to be white, just to see what their diet was and what their lifestyle was." "Emancipation" came, Hazel insists, when she learned the skills of home economics at school, beginning in Grade 8. Unlike her mother's utilitarian domesticity, at school she learned how to sew a blouse that was "silky, feminine and her own." Surveying the family photos, Hazel recalled: "I thought for the longest time maybe I was a little boy because I wore my brothers' older clothes." Her white, young home economics teacher provided the feminine ideal that she wanted to emulate: "she was from a well-established family, with a degree; she wore a string of pearls, a cashmere sweater, and matching hand-bag." In terms that invoke racial and Christian uplift, Hazel recalled this teacher taking a particular interest in instilling a desire in her for the "finer things." As "someone she could mould ... she showed me how to dye things, to make bright coloured clothing a little more conservative." Hazel won all of the home economics cups in the school, and the teacher eventually recommended her for her first teaching job.

As the youngest child, Hazel could take advantage of expanded educational opportunities for Chinese Canadians, but family support was as important as postwar reforms. It was Hazel's older brother and sister who insisted she attend university after graduating from high school. Hazel enrolled in 1947 at the University of British Columbia's School of Home Economics. She had the financial support of her siblings, who had not completed school. Before the late 1930s, only 11 Chinese students had graduated from the university, but 230 had enrolled officially by the late 1950s.[50] By the time Hazel started university, "college-educated Chinese-Canadian women in Vancouver could obtain a job in an office rather than a fruit and vegetable store."[51] Hazel still understood, however, that her degree offered limited careers options: "you became either a home economics teacher or a dietician, so I went into teaching." Hazel actually credits fate with stopping her from accepting lower-paying jobs at a bank and department store in her early working years. She described fate as a mysterious man "in a felt brown hat with a brief case" from the Nanaimo board who "found out that I was a qualified home ec teacher" and came knocking on her door. Hazel reasoned: "So what does that tell you? Maybe that was my calling in life." More than fate, home economics, particularly a passion for clothing design, allowed Hazel to have a good-paying job that was also respectable for a woman. Hazel joined other female professionals, including dieticians, nurses, and social workers, to produce middle-class, Canadian standards for wholesome family living.[52] As is evident in Catherine Charron's discussion of paid domestic workers and Hélène Charron's description of women in the School of Social Work at Laval in this volume, women in the helping professions, while undervalued, made critical contributions to the national landscape. The Canadian homemaker was at the centre of Cold War efforts by experts to "demonstrate abundance, capitalist superiority, democratic modernity, and 'kitchen consumerism.'"[53]

The nuclear family model would, however, exist in tension with the need for working women in the postwar years. Hazel was encouraged to enter teaching to fill a national shortage in the rapidly expanding school system. F. Henry Johnson, the British Columbia Department of Education's coordinator for teacher education, told local newspapers that the province would be short 750 secondary school teachers by 1956.[54] The Department of Education resorted to issuing letters of permission, temporary certificates requiring only one year of training after Grade 13 and crash summer courses.[55] The department also put out advertisements encouraging married teachers to return to work.[56] Lured by the salary, and "granted an elementary temporary teaching certificate," Hazel interrupted her degree in 1949 to take a one-year contract as a teacher in the rural area of Armstrong.

Hazel became angry when she recalled the deplorable conditions of her first teaching placement (and told me that I would not have lasted a week): "[T]he home economics lab was in the basement. There was a dripping vapour pipe, no refrigerator, no washing machine, and two wood stoves for my food work. I had to teach eight different classes ... I don't think I slept more than four hours a night." Women were regularly placed in isolated, rundown, and small-budget schools run by male principals because urban secondary schools, which had their first choice of teachers, preferred to hire men.[57] Charles Ovans, the general secretary for the British Columbia Teachers Federation (BCTF), admitted that "[g]iven the choice in anything above primary grades, a school will take a man to a woman."[58] In secondary schools, men and women teachers were also divided. Men were considered suited to the intellectually rigorous math and science needs of the space-race era. Women were confined mostly to English, physical education, and home economics, subjects that officials deemed a public service because of their nurturing propensity.

Hazel asserted that, as a Canadian woman teacher of Chinese origin, she was a "third-class citizen." Upon graduation from university, she was instructed by the head the home economics department to state her "Chinese origin" on all applications, because, unlike her Anglo-Saxon name, her maiden surname, Joe, sounded "Native West Coast Indian, and that would prevent me from getting a job." She laughed uncomfortably when she observed astutely, "They were left out more than we were, I guess." She explained with agitation that she did not apply to Vancouver schools for years because she knew she would not be granted a position: "first of all, I am 'Oriental,' and they would only take the top ten [graduates]." Hazel's decision to use *Canadian of Chinese origin* to describe her ethnicity at most points in the interviews may well have been informed by these events.

Hazel returned to finish her degree in 1952, but, unable to afford full-time tuition fees, she attended three years of summer courses in Victoria to obtain her teaching certificate. After three contract positions, two in the rural areas of Lumby and Vernon and one in Nanaimo, Hazel applied to the Vancouver Board of Education. She obtained a permanent position in home economics at John Oliver Secondary School in 1956. She taught at Sir Charles Tupper and Eric Hamber Secondary Schools from 1963 until 1974 and returned to John Oliver until her retirement in the early 1980s. Hazel acknowledged that to get a job in Vancouver she had to be a perfectionist and prove herself "110 percent, so there was no room for criticism." She also relied on personal connections and recommendations from previous teachers and administrators, which, as Cecilia Reynolds's work on women educators has shown, was the most viable route to better employment.[59] But it was her domestic fitness and moral deportment as a Chinese woman that Hazel quietly credits with her obtaining a job in the city and eventual promotion to the head of Home Economics.

Hazel's reasoning is in keeping with the primary aim of the expanded secondary school in the postwar period; a gateway for democratic citizenship, it was at the forefront of establishing the character of the people and the nation. New curriculum initiatives addressed public concerns that youth, faced with wartime atrocities and transgressions of traditional values, were rejecting proper citizenship. As Mary Louise Adams argues, public expressions of fear escalated over a supposed rise in juvenile delinquency, which was attributed to inferior wartime mothering, an increasingly consumer-oriented culture, and exposure to communist sentiments.[60] School psychologists' aptitude tests for student employability, elective Bible study courses to affirm Christian values, history texts that illustrated that British Columbia had been born out of white man's progress, and an experimental "Effective Living" course that aimed to develop "stable heterosexual patterns, habits of loyalty and acceptance of conventions" all served disciplining and sorting functions.[61] Home Economics played a particularly important function, preparing wives and mothers for their "primary responsibility for feeding and nurturing healthy families, managing modern, efficient, and well-equipped households, and raising well-adjusted children."[62]

But officials agreed that teachers, perhaps more than curriculums, played the central role of ensuring liberating citizenship through lessons in conformity. Newsletters for teachers' federations across the country made the patriotic duty of the teacher clear: "[S]chool is a miniature nation, where the young citizens are forming habits, acquiring attitudes toward the world they live in ... The teachers – it is almost too awful a responsibility to put down

in black and white – are the statesmen in those miniature nations."[63] Sidney
Katz echoed the belief of many when he wrote in a 1953 *Maclean's Magazine* article that "moral behaviour can't be taught as a subject like reading ...
the greatest influence for good is what the teacher is and how he acts."[64]
Although commentators often used the male pronoun, women shouldered
the primary responsibility for the character development of students. Madeleine Arnot and Jo-Anne Dillabough argue that within Western democratic
thought, women serve to uphold the state as virtuous, reproductive beings.[65]
Women are the keepers, cultivators, and symbols of democracy.[66] *The B.C.
Teacher*, the BCTF's newsletter, published moral imperatives. In a 1946 issue, the editors reprinted a report by Toronto principals that referred in
detail to housewife-like duties as critical, silent influences on the character
of students. In this description, each teacher produces a learning environment by "dressing modestly and tastefully; keeping her desk and window-
sills neat ... and arranging displays of work in an artistic manner."[67]

Hazel knew that her performance of right citizenship inside and outside
the classroom was under surveillance by administrators and students. Her
teaching identity was confirmed through what Judith Butler refers to as
the "stylized repetition of acts."[68] Butler argues that gendered, and I would
add racialized, identities are bodily interpretations of already existing de-
rivatives that are "put on, invariably, under constraint, daily and incessantly,
with anxiety and pleasure."[69] Hazel explained: "What I wore was more important than what I said ... better than any lesson I could plan. Like, if I wore
something, where a student said, 'Miss Chong, did you make that?' That was
an inspiration." Hazel "devised a little system" of dress while teaching at John
Oliver that she used until she retired. With one of her handwritten monthly
dress calendars from 1974 in hand, she explained:

> I would dress in navy blue one week, and next week it might be cranberry ...
> Every week there was a different colour, and the object of the game was to
> teach kids how to colour coordinate and to accessorize. You only need three
> things, but you mix and match them differently. I would bring a bunch of
> necklaces to expand their wardrobe. So that said more about me than what
> I could tell them in handouts.

Her efforts to look the part were rewarded. On Hazel's 1955 evaluation,
when she was teaching in Vernon, Bertha Rogers, the provincial director of
home economics, noted: "Miss Joe sets a good example for her students in
grooming and appearance."[70]

Hazel was aware of the broader postwar social purpose of her teaching subject: "it was basically a course for living ... The focus was on getting the family unit back again following the war and to be self-sustaining." Whether providing lessons in canning, budgeting, or sewing, Hazel understood her job as critical to the reaffirmation of the nuclear family – a national symbol for a strong consumer economy, cohesive and peaceful relations, and a defence against communism.[71] Lessons in appearance were most prominent in Hazel's memories of teaching. Hazel, for example, instructed female students about how to present themselves in job searches, asserting that, "in the '50s, appropriate dress was really important ... your appearance is your first key to your whole personality." She continued: "The grade twelves would bring something we would wear on a first job interview, and we would critique one another. Should it be downplayed, or do you need to inject a bit of old personality in? Or we talked about different kinds of jobs." Although preparation for employment was "basic," Hazel asserted that it "allows you to get into the world – an entry level job."

Hazel told stories of students who had recently thanked her for teaching them to sew. She also celebrated former students who became home economics teachers, five of whom were "Oriental." Rather than interpret her lessons in appropriate female dress as limiting for students, Hazel believed she had opened up new opportunities for her female students. Her association of comportment with opportunity was based on her own experience learning to make clothes in childhood, which, she argued, emancipated her from the stigma of the Chinese lifestyle. Yet she also looked back on the subject of home economics with second-wave feminist insight, remarking sarcastically: "[O]ur job was to teach people how to be homemakers ... all encompassing. She was the little accessory to her husband that helped him to fame and fortune because she had these skills." Catherine Gidney's chapter in this volume regarding women on staff at Victoria College likewise describes the transitional character of professional life during the period. Women embraced their right to a public career, but opportunities were limited by their commitment to the ideals of motherhood and being respectable role models for female students.

Hazel upheld the gender order for democratic citizenship. At the same time, she undermined that order by her very presence as a professional in the public world. Because the marriage bar was removed in 1944, Hazel did not need to defend her right to work after marrying George Chow in 1958.[72] Her narrative is nevertheless dominated by her desire to justify her employment after she had two sons in the early 1960s. Hazel told me emphatically that she had had no intention of returning to teach. Each time she left to have a child, though, her colleagues at the Vancouver Board of Education organized a "phone campaign" to convince her to come back to school. Hazel was convinced by her coordinator, who stated, "With your mind, you'd just sit home and vegetate ... You know your children don't have the quantity of time with you, but I am sure they have the quality, because you always take them everywhere." Hazel asserted that she had been reluctant to go back to work because she enjoyed being a mother, but she always found good child care. Hazel maintained her status as a good teacher for female students by ensuring that her own standards of domesticity aligned with postwar expectations.

Hazel was a racialized woman who held a professional career during an era in which policy makers claimed to erase open discrimination but would not directly name sexist or racist structures. Retrospectively, she did consider race her "biggest hurdle [because] they're going to judge a book by its cover." Unlike her colleagues, Hazel could not visibly replicate Anglo-Celtic citizenship.[73] She still had an active role in manufacturing consent for white domesticity. Hazel spoke at length about the Mother's Day teas, annual fashion shows, and school plays that put her specialized knowledge of Canadian clothing and cooking on display for the community. Hazel's discussion of the curriculum fit with postwar liberal rhetoric: "it didn't have any ethnic origin to it." The only accommodation she made for ethnic difference was to provide kosher kitchen utensils for Jewish students in the early 1960s. She remembered teaching at Hamber:

> Someone should have told me that 80 percent of the population was Jewish. I said to them, "None of you put any of the food from the casserole into your face. What's going on here?"
>
> "At home, we have separate dishes for dairy products and for meat."
>
> So, I thought and thought. I bought soup bowls and paper plates, and I said, "Okay, these plates are going to be throw-aways."

Later, she stated firmly, "Using the old worn out saying 'the mosaic of Canada is a fusion of all these different nationalities' – no, there was only one way to do it, and that was the English way." Hazel denied the existence of international food nights and ethnic crafts shows, events that historian Franca Iacovetta claims helped gatekeepers promote the cultural diversity of postwar Canada. She might not have associated the multicultural fair with the postwar period given its primary purpose was to assimilate minority women. School boards offered night courses and cooking classes to women immigrants to assist them in adopting seemingly healthier Canadian life-style choices.[74] These programs were a way to police the personal lives of working-class immigrant women in the name of Western democratic free-doms.[75]

Hazel's narrative of teaching speaks to her part in the domestic contain-ment of others in postwar democracy. Her memories of her racial and gen-der adaptability also reflect her experience of being contained domestically. She recalled students who rejected her credibility. One of her most painful memories took place in the early 1950s in Lumby:

> I was teaching a lesson on less tender cuts of meat ... All of a sudden, I heard a chair snap, and this girl stood up ... She said, "I'm not gonna take anything from a goddamn Chinaman anymore!" She banged out the door. My only salvation was that I did have lots of Kleenex, and I dried my eyes, and the kids knew I was visibly upset. And the bell rang, luckily, for lunch.

Hazel recalled that the English teacher tried to console at lunch by saying, "It really wasn't a slur against you; it was just the most obvious difference." The student returned to Hazel's class a few days later to apologize. In response, Hazel told the young woman, "Unfortunately, I'm still Chinese, and I'll be Chi-nese for the rest of my life ... I can't change my stripes for you." There would be a few other volatile incidents in her career. She recalled when white students and colleagues treated her as "the exotic other" and demanded that she ex-press more authentic Chineseness. She recalled another incident at Lumby: "I was doing something on the board, and there was a 'Hey, you!' And I stopped dead, and she said, 'You know how to use chopsticks?' Hazel responded, 'My name is Miss Joe. As for the other part of your question, yes, I do know how to use chopsticks.'" Hazel also recalled that Chinese students sought her ad-vice on "dating someone Caucasian" because they could not discuss such issues with their parents. Although Hazel sympathized, she knew that the subject was taboo and did not offer any specific advice. As a Chinese Can-adian woman teacher, she was continually under character surveillance from both her peers and students. Consequently, she quietly acknowledged that her normative teacher self was always incomplete. Unable to be white, she was never quite fully acceptable as a housewife or a home economics teacher.

Conclusion

Like gender and race, Hazel's identity was historically situated and nei-ther static nor fixed. Hazel remarked that she became more vocal in her resistance to discrimination at the end of her career: "I really didn't think about my heritage until thirty years later, and now, you see, I have all kinds of Oriental motifs." As I looked around her home, I noticed vases and wall hangings painted with Chinese characters. Hazel's self-consciousness of more modern concepts of liberation was apparent in this statement. Was this a nod towards my push for more rebellious tales or what she thought I wanted to hear? Was this a happy ending to a life story, one filled with the insights of second-wave feminism and official multiculturalism? Perhaps. It would be a mistake for me to interpret her narrative as reflecting a constrained consciousness of the mechanisms of domination. Instead, I attempt here to read Hazel's oral history by synthesizing the micro experiences of sense making and the macro structures of social institutions.[76] Hazel Chong's narrative is an example of the complex responses from an "outsider within" to Canada's liberal agenda. She presents a softer form of subjugated difference that respects the contributions of Chinese Canadians and women to the national tapestry. Hazel understood that her teaching and, ultimately, her performance of normative citizenship were necessary during the era: "I think ... more opportunities opened, but they were very careful in selecting who were admitted."

NOTES

Funding support for this research came from the Social Sciences and Humanities Research Council of Canada. I wish to thank Hazel Chong for sharing her life story. I also extend thanks to Nancy Janovicek and Catherine Carstairs and the other contributors to this collection for their feedback on drafts of this chapter.

1 Kay Anderson uses the term *racialization* to refer to "the process by which attributes such as skin colour, language, birthplace, and cultural practices are given social significance as markers of distinction." Kay Anderson, *Vancouver's Chinatown: Racial Discourse in Canada, 1875–1980* (Montreal/Kingston: McGill-Queen's University Press, 1991), 191.

2 Hazel Chong, interview with author, June 2008, Vancouver, British Columbia. See also my interview with Hazel Chong, September 2005, Vancouver, British Columbia. The first interview is part of my dissertation, "In the Name of Democracy: The Work of Women Teachers in Toronto and Vancouver, 1945–1960" (PhD diss., University of British Columbia, 2006). I acknowledge the Social Sciences and Humanities Research Council of Canada for its financial support.

3 Wing Chung Ng, *The Chinese in Vancouver, 1945–80: The Pursuit of Identity and Power* (Vancouver: UBC Press, 1999), 6. Ng's book focuses on identity construction among various generations and socio-economic groups. Gender, as a form of social organization, is rarely mentioned in the study.

4 Kathleen Weiler, "Remembering and Representing Life Choices: A Critical Perspective on Teachers' Oral History Narratives," *Qualitative Studies in Education* 5, 1 (1992): 43.

5 David T.H. Lee, *A History of Chinese in Canada* (Taipei: Canada Free Press, 1967), as quoted in Ng, *The Chinese in Vancouver,* 40.

6 Ng, *The Chinese in Vancouver,* 41.

7 Franca Iacovetta, *Gatekeepers: Reshaping Immigrant Lives in Cold War Canada* (Toronto: Between the Lines, 2006), 11.

8 Sherna Berger Gluck and Daphne Patai, eds., *Women's Words: The Feminist Practice of Oral History* (New York: Routledge, 1991), and The Personal Narratives Group, eds., *Interpreting Women's Lives: Feminist Theory and Personal Narratives* (Bloomington: Indiana University Press, 1989).

9 National Film Board of Canada (NFB), *Under the Willow Tree: Pioneer Chinese Women in Canada* (1997), and Women's Book Committee, Chinese Canadian National Council, *Jin Guo: Voices of Chinese Canadian Women* (Toronto: Women's Press, 1993). Hazel Chong was interviewed for the NFB film, and she shared the raw footage of the interview with me for this project. See also May Yee, "Chinese Canadian Women: Our Common Struggle," *Canadian Ethnic Studies* 19, 3 (1987): 174–85.

10 Sherna Gluck, "What's So Special about Women?" in *Women's Oral History: The Frontiers Reader,* ed. Susan H. Armitage, Patricia Hart, and Karen Weathermon (Lincoln: University of Nebraska Press, 2002), 5, as quoted in Lynn Abrams, *Oral History Theory* (New York: Routledge, 2010), 71.

11 Michael Frisch, *A Shared Authority: Essays on the Craft and Meaning of Oral and Public History* (New York: State University of New York Press, 1990). See also Steve High, Lisa Ndejuru, and Kristen O'Hare, eds., "Sharing Authority: Community-University Collaboration in Oral History, Digital Storytelling and Engaged Scholarship," special issue, *Journal of Canadian Studies* 43, 1 (2009).

12 Abrams, *Oral History Theory,* 72.

13 Kathryn Anderson and Dana C. Jack, "Learning to Listen: Interview Techniques and Analyses," in *Women's Words: The Feminist Practice of Oral History,* ed. Sherna Berger Gluck and Daphne Patai (New York: Routledge, 1991), 11–26.

14 Karen Olsen and Linda Shopes, "Crossing Boundaries, Building Bridges: Doing Oral History among Working-Class Women and Men," in *Women's Words: The Feminist Practice of Oral History,* ed. Sherna Berger Gluck and Daphne Patai (New York: Routledge, 1991), 196–97, as quoted by Pamela Sugiman in "I Can Hear Lois Now: Corrections to My Story of the Second World War Internment of Japanese Canadians – for the Record," unpublished paper, in possession of author.

15 Abrams, *Oral History Theory,* 136–37.

16 Leslie Bloom, "Stories of One's Own: Nonunitary Subjectivity in Narrative Representation," *Qualitative Inquiry* 2, 2 (1996): 176–88.

17 Anna Sheftel and Stacey Zembrzycki, "Only Human: A Reflection on the Ethical and Methodological Challenges of Working with 'Difficult' Stories," *Oral History Review* 37, 2 (2010): 191–214.

18 Kathleen Casey, *I Answer with My Life: Life Histories of Women Teachers Working for Social Change* (New York: Routledge, 1993), 31.

19 Mikhail Bakhtin, *The Dialogic Imagination* (Austin: University of Texas Press, 1988), as paraphrased by Casey in *I Answer with My Life,* 26.

20 Popular Memory Group, "Popular Memory: Theory, Politics, Method," in *Making Histories*, ed. Richard Johnson, Gregor McLennan, Bill Schwartz, and David Sutton (London: Hutchinson, 1982), 228–34. See also Peter Munro, *Subject to Fiction: Women Teachers' Life History Narratives and the Cultural Politics of Resistance* (Buckingham: Open University Press, 1998).

21 Tamara Adilman, "A Preliminary Sketch of Chinese Women and Work in British Columbia, 1858–1950," in *British Columbia Reconsidered: Essays on Women*, ed. Gillian Creese and Veronica Strong-Boag (Vancouver: Press Gang Publishers, 1992), 326. The Exclusion Act was effective in limiting the Chinese population. In 1941, the Chinese population in Canada was 34,627 (30,713 male and 3,914 female). See Anderson, *Vancouver's Chinatown*, 174.

22 Carol F. Lee, "The Road to Enfranchisement: Chinese and Japanese in British Columbia," *BC Studies* 30 (1976): 44–45. Chinese Canadians in Ontario, unlike those in British Columbia, were enfranchised and permitted to enter professions in law and medicine. Although there is no mention in the secondary literature of the first Chinese woman to graduate from a Normal School, Victoria Cheung graduated from the University of Toronto medical school in 1923. See Dora Nipp, "'But Women Did Come': Working Chinese Women in the Interwar Years," in *Looking into My Sisters Eyes: An Exploration in Women's History*, ed. Jean Burnet (Toronto: Multicultural History Society of Ontario, 1986), 190.

23 John Zucchi, *A History of Ethnic Enclaves in Canada*, CHA Booklet 31 (Ottawa: Canadian Historical Association, 2007), 9. See also Patricia Roy, "British Columbia's Fear of Asians, 1900–1950," *Social History* 13, 25 (1980): 161–72; Harry Con, Ronald J. Con, Graham Johnson, Edgar Wickberg, and William E. Willmot, *From China to Canada: A History of Chinese Communities in Canada* (Toronto: McClelland and Stewart, 1982); and Jin Tan and Patricia E. Roy, *The Chinese in Canada*, CHA Booklet 9 (Ottawa: Canadian Historical Association, 1985).

24 Constance Backhouse, "White Female Help and Chinese-Canadian Employers: Race, Class, Gender, and Law in the Case of Yee Clun, 1924," *Canadian Ethnic Studies* 26, 3 (1994): 34–52.

25 N.L. Ward, *The Oriental Missions in British Columbia* (Aberdeen: Aberdeen University Press, 1925), 69, as quoted in Adilman, "A Preliminary Sketch," 327.

26 Timothy J. Stanley, "Carrying into the Schools What Already Exists in Every Other Institution of Society: Colonialism and the Discourse on Chinese School Segregation in British Columbia during the Early Twentieth Century," *International Journal of Educational Policy, Research and Practice* 1, 4 (2000): 455–58. See also Timothy J. Stanley, *Contesting White Supremacy: School Segregation, Anti-Racism, and the Making of Chinese Canadians* (Vancouver: UBC Press, 2011).

27 "No More Chinese Teachers Here," *Daily Colonist*, 30 August 1922, 5, as quoted by Timothy J. Stanley in "Bringing Anti-Racism into Historical Explanation: The Victoria Chinese Students' Strike of 1922–23 Revisited," *Journal of the Canadian Historical Association* 13 (2002): 150.

28 Stephanie D. Bangarth, "'We Are Not Asking You to Open Wide the Gates for Chinese Immigration': The Committee for the Repeal of the Chinese Immigration Act and Early Human Rights Activism in Canada," *Canadian Historical Review* 84, 3

(2003): 396. See also Carmela Patrias and Ruth A. Frager, "'This Is Our Country, These Are Our Rights': Minorities and the Origins of Ontario's Human Rights Campaign," *Canadian Historical Review* 82, 1 (2001): 1–35, and Ross Lambertson, *Repression and Resistance: Canadian Human Rights Activists, 1930–1960* (Toronto: University of Toronto Press, 2005).

29 Iacovetta, *Gatekeepers*, 11. Such promises extended primarily to current British, heterosexual, and anti-communist subjects. Although there would be mass immigration in the postwar years, newcomers were mostly from Britain and Europe, in keeping with long-standing preference for a "white" Canada. This era is also well known for its political surveillance and persecution of homosexuals and Communist sympathizers.

30 Gail Cuthbert Brandt, Naomi Black, Paula Bourne, and Magda Fahrni, *Canadian Women: A History*, 3rd ed. (Toronto: Nelson Education, 2011), 339–99; Ann Porter, "Women and Income Security in the Postwar Period: The Case of Unemployment Insurance, 1945–1962," *Labour/Le Trvail* 31 (1993): 111–44; Susan Prentice, "Workers, Mothers, Reds: Toronto's Postwar Daycare Fight," *Studies in Political Economy* 30 (1989): 115–44; and Shirley Tillotson, "Human Rights Law as Prism: Women's Organizations, Unions and Ontario's Female Employees Fair Remuneration Act, 1951," *Canadian Historical Review* 72, 4 (1991): 532–57.

31 In 1954, the BCTF adopted a fair remuneration policy, which had been enacted by the newly elected W.A.C. Bennett Social Credit government. See Punham Khosla, Laura King, and Linda Read, *The Unrecognized Majority: A History of Women Teachers in British Columbia* (BCTF: Status of Women Committee in British Columbia, 1979). In 1944, Vancouver women who married after placement were guaranteed "security of tenure." See "Report to Personnel Committee, February 7th 1955, Status of Married Women as Teachers," 1955, City of Vancouver Archives (CVA), Public School Records, Vancouver Personnel and Research Subject Files, Loc. 59-A-1, File 18. Ontario would lift its marriage bar in 1946. See Patricia Anne Staton and Beth Light, *Speak with Their Own Voices: A Documentary History of the Teachers of Ontario and the Women Elementary Public School Teachers in Ontario* (Toronto: Federation of Women Teachers' Associations of Ontario, 1987), 143–44.

32 Bangarth, "We Are Not Asking You," 401; Anderson, *Vancouver's Chinatown*, 171–72. Approximately five hundred Chinese Canadians served in the war. See Peter Li, *The Chinese in Canada* (Toronto: Oxford University Press, 1998), 90–91.

33 Bangarth, "We Are Not Asking You," 401.

34 Ibid., 414.

35 Shirley Tillotson, *The Public at Play: Gender and the Politics of Recreation in Postwar Ontario* (Toronto: University of Toronto Press, 2000), and Mona Gleason, *Normalizing the Ideal: Psychology, Schooling and the Family in Postwar Canada* (Toronto: University of Toronto Press, 1999). See also Doug Owram, *Born at the Right Time: A History of the Baby-Boom Generation* (Toronto: University of Toronto Press, 1996), and Mary Louise Adams, *The Trouble with Normal: Postwar Youth and the Construction of Heterosexuality* (Toronto: University of Toronto Press, 1994).

36 A strategy of containment within the postwar period of the United States is discussed by Elaine Tyler May in *Homeward Bound: American Families in the Cold War Era* (New York: Basic Books, 1988).

37 Tillotson, *The Public at Play,* 4–6.

38 Bangarth, "We Are Not Asking You," 416.

39 Anderson, *Vancouver's Chinatown.*

40 Madiha Didi Khayatt, *Lesbian Teachers: An Invisible Presence* (Albany: State University of New York Press, 1992), 21–26.

41 Himani Bannerji, "Geography Lessons: On Being an Insider/Outsider to the Canadian Nation," in *Gender Relations in Global Perspective: Essential Readings,* ed. Nancy Cook (Toronto: Canadian Scholars' Press, 2007), 282.

42 Patricia Hill Collins refers to this as the perspective of the "outsider within," a double consciousness experienced by oppressed individuals who interact within a dominant group. See Patricia Hill Collins, "Learning from the Outsider Within: The Sociological Significance of Black Feminist Thought," in *Feminist Approaches to Theory and Methodology: An Interdisciplinary Reader,* ed. Sharlene Nagy Hesse-Biber, Christine K. Gilmartin, and Robin Lydenberg (New York: Oxford University Press, 1999), 135–78.

43 Ng, *The Chinese in Vancouver,* 50.

44 Ibid., 52.

45 Hazel used the same metaphor of the banana repeatedly in both interviews.

46 Ng, *The Chinese in Vancouver,* 53.

47 Antonio Gramsci, *Selections from the Prison Notebooks* (New York: International Publishers, 1971). See also Antonio Gramsci, *Selections from Cultural Writings* (London: Lawrence and Wishart, 1979), and Esteve Morera, "Gramsci and Democracy," *Canadian Journal of Political Science* 23 (1990): 5–37. See also Anderson, *Vancouver's Chinatown,* 25–26.

48 Women's Missionary Society annual report, 1941–42, United Church Archives, Vancouver School of Theology, UBC, 115, as cited by Adilman, "A Preliminary Sketch," 330. Although Chinese Canadian women could train as teachers, as this report indicates, teaching positions were most likely restricted to segregated Chinese schools.

49 Mona Gleason, "Race, Class, and Health: School Medical Inspection and the 'Healthy' Children in British Columbia, 1890–1930," in *Children's Health Issues in Historical Perspective,* ed. Cheryl Krasnick Warsh and Veronica Strong-Boag (Waterloo: Wifrid Laurier University Press, 2005), 298–99. Gleason interviewed Mary Jong, a Chinese Canadian woman who similarly described having to work in the family vegetable garden each morning. Jong was still ashamed that her row of classmates never received a star for hygiene because she did not have time to clean up before attending school.

50 Ng, *The Chinese in Vancouver,* 47.

51 Lee, "The Road to Enfranchisment," 51.

52 Iacovetta, *Gatekeepers,* 137–39.

53 Ibid., 139.

54 "Next Year – BC Short of Teachers by 1,700," *Vancouver Sun,* 5 March 1955.

55 Hebert Edgar Smith, "Teacher Training," in *Canadian Education Today: A Symposium,* ed. Joseph Katz (Toronto: McGill-Hill), 168.

56 Smith, "Teacher Training," 168. Sheila L. Cavanagh argues that policies enticing married women into the profession cannot be seen purely as a triumph against gender discrimination. Instead, women of the "marrying variety" or who were married were

hired as symbols of society's heteronormativity. Sheila Cavanagh, "The Heterosexualization of the Ontario Woman Teacher in the Postwar Period," *Canadian Women Studies* 18, 1 (1998): 65–69.

57 Cecilia Reynolds, "Hegemony and Hierarchy: Becoming a Teacher in Toronto, 1930–1980," *Historical Studies in Education* 2, 1 (1990): 106–7.

58 "Board Won't Pay More Pence, Marriage's But Indulgence," *The Province*, 14 February 1957.

59 Reynolds, "Hegemony and Hierarchy," 106–7.

60 Adams, *The Trouble with Normal*, 40–41.

61 Thomas Fleming and David Conway, "Setting Standards in the West: C.B. Conway, Science and School Reform in British Columbia, 1938–1974," *Canadian Journal of Education* 21, 3 (1996): 294–317; James London, "Lay Control in Public Education: The British Columbia School Trustees Association, 1905–1946," in *School Leadership: Essays on the British Columbia Experience, 1872–1995*, ed. Thomas Fleming (Mill Bay: Bendall Books, 2001); and Timothy J. Stanley, "White Supremacy and the Rhetoric of Educational Indoctrination: A Canadian Case Study," in *Children, Teachers, and Schools in the History of British Columbia*, ed. J. Barman, N. Sutherland, and J.D. Wilson (Calgary: Detselig, 1995).

62 Iacovetta, *Gatekeepers*, 139.

63 H.L. Tracy, "In Praise of Teachers," *The Bulletin* (October 1951): 162. Similar commentary is found in *The B.C. Teacher*. See, for example, "The Teacher," *The B.C. Teacher*, February 1953, 197.

64 Sidney Katz, "The Crisis in Education – Part 2," *Maclean's Magazine*, 15 March 1953, 49.

65 Madeleine Arnot and Jo-Anne Dillabough, "Feminist Politics and Democratic Values in Education," *Curriculum Inquiry* 29, 2 (1999): 165.

66 Ibid., 164.

67 "Are You a Weak Teacher?" *The B.C. Teacher*, February 1946, 186.

68 Judith Butler, *Gender Trouble: Feminism and the Subversion of Identity* (New York: Routledge, Chapman and Hall, 1990), as quoted in Kathryn McPherson, "'The Case of the Kissing Nurse': Femininity, Sexuality, and Canadian Nursing, 1900–1970," in *Gendered Pasts: Historical Essays in Femininity and Masculinity in Canada*, ed. Kathryn McPherson, Celia Morgan, and Nancy Forestall (Don Mills, ON: Oxford University Press, 1999), 181.

69 Judith Butler, "Performative Acts and Gender Constitution: An Essay in Phenomenology and Feminist Theory," in *Performing Feminisms: Feminist Critical Theory and Theatre*, ed. Sue-Ellen Case (Baltimore, MD: John Hopkins University Press, 1990), 282.

70 Hazel Chong's personal papers, "Report on Teacher or Principal – Miss Joe (Hazel Audry)," signed by Bertha Rogers, 5 May 1955.

71 Joy Parr, "Introduction," in *A Diversity of Women: Ontario, 1945–1980*, ed. Joy Parr (Toronto: University of Toronto Press, 1995), 5.

72 "Report to Personnel Committee, February 7th 1955, Status of Married Women as Teachers," 1955, CVA, Public School Records, Vancouver Personnel and Research Subject Files, Loc. 59-A-1, File 18.

73 Reynolds, "Hegemony and Hierarchy," 116–17. Reynolds's statistics for Ontario show that in 1941, 82 percent of women teachers were of British origin and that that number had only dropped to 72 percent in 1961.

74 Franca Iacovetta, "Recipes for Democracy? Gender, Family and Making Female Citizens in Cold War Canada," in *Rethinking Canada: The Promise of Women's History*, 4th ed., ed. Veronica Strong-Boag, Adele Perry, and Mona Gleason (Oxford: Oxford University Press, 2002), 301.

75 Ibid., 301–2.

76 Anderson, *Vancouver's Chinatown*, 248.

10

The Ontario Women's History Network
Linking Teachers, Scholars, and History Communities

ROSE FINE-MEYER

During the 1960s and 1970s, feminist activists established women's organizations and lobbied governments and institutions on a wide range of issues, from discriminatory hiring practices to wages for housework. They were also interested in learning more about women's history. Female academics began writing women's history, and there was a popular market for books that trumpeted women's accomplishments. Until feminists started drawing attention to the absence of women in curricula, women were rarely included in nation-building narratives that prioritized the successes of elite and public men. Scholars such as Gerda Lerner noted that "history as a profession has spoken in the voice of exclusion, in which a small elite of trained male intellectuals has interpreted the past in its own image and in its own voice."[1] In Ontario, public-school history texts were usually written by male teachers and department heads, some of whom also sat on the Ministry of Education's committees and wrote the course guidelines. The curriculum included little about women's experiences and focused on major political and economic events such as the Rebellions of 1837–38, Confederation, and Canada's participation in the Second World War. Feminist scholarship throughout the 1980s and 1990s argued that women had played an essential role in nation building and should be included in the curriculum at all levels, from elementary school to university.

Advocating for the history of women on a curricular or professional-development level was complicated because many history teachers worked within school boards and history departments that contained androcentric resource materials and programs. One Toronto teacher remarked, "In Canadian history, women were not represented as a distinct group from men – it was just male-centric – with a strong male bias."[2] Although this hampered the overall influence of new scholarship in women's history, teachers interested in including women in their history courses actively networked outside of their schools for supplementary resources and were in contact with feminists in various communities and through membership in women's organizations. The work of including women in history relied heavily on networks that provided teachers with the support they needed to bring women's voices into the history curriculum.

This chapter examines the activism of the Ontario Women's History Network (OWHN) and its work in developing, supporting, and sharing women's history course materials in schools throughout Ontario. The network's members, mainly feminist academics and history educators, brought teachers and academics together at annual conferences and produced educational resources for both teachers and students to broaden understanding of women's roles and contributions.[3] I draw on archival materials and the oral histories of Toronto teachers and OWHN's executive members to examine the ways in which women's efforts to create an equitable curriculum played out within the Toronto school system.

Background

The second-wave feminist movement had a dramatic impact on the field of history. Feminist historians wrote extensively about women's participation in society through paid and unpaid labour and on women's role in the family and as community builders.[4] Historians, both academic and community-based, believed that writing women's history was an important battlefront in the feminist movement, to paraphrase historian Judith Bennett.[5] By the 1980s, a significant feminist scholarship had emerged to legitimize the field of women's history. Canadian universities created women's studies programs, and history departments added women's history courses to undergraduate survey courses.[6] The number of graduate students working on women's history topics increased. Although there were few female faculty members, and although some male professors expressed resistance to women's history, significant progress had been made. Similar achievements were far more difficult for feminist educators in public schools.[7] Teachers were expected to follow provincially mandated curricula and faced limited opportunities to effect change, except in their own classrooms.

Educational changes that took place in the 1980s stemmed from developments in the late 1960s and early 1970s, developments that had encouraged educators in Ontario to rethink traditional curriculum. During those decades, activist educators, parents, and communities demanded educational reform and a greater voice in school board policies. Magazines and newspapers such as the *Toronto Community School Paper; This Magazine Is All about Schools;* and *NOW Magazine* offered radical new visions of what schooling could be and drew attention to the issues facing working-class and immigrant communities.[8] In response, the Ontario government moved towards a child-centred philosophy of education. The Hall-Dennis Report (1968), followed by a new credit system, had come out strongly in support of student-centred learning, allowing students greater course options.[9] Although this new approach released subject areas from their silos, it also had a disastrous effect on enrolments in history courses in Ontario, as students fled from history to social science courses.[10] In their efforts to draw students back to history, educators expanded their courses to include new scholarship in social and labour history.[11] Social history altered pedagogies and demanded different resources because it placed greater emphasis on groups that had been sidelined or omitted from traditional history textbooks. One Toronto teacher noted that, by the 1980s, "I would say that I approached history as social history. It was about dealing with groups that were marginalized in history and in the texts. I spent time focusing on labour and the family and the poor working class – and women."[12]

At roughly the same time, the report of the Royal Commission on the Status of Women (1970) criticized the omission of women from curricular materials. The report recommended that the provinces and the territories adopt textbooks that portrayed women in diversified roles and occupations.[13] As a result, provincial governments and schools boards responded to gender inequalities by allocating funds for the development of curricular materials. School boards, such as the Toronto Board of Education (the Toronto Board) held conferences in the late 1970s, developed joint projects and publications, and organized events at its offices that addressed "sexist" behaviour in schools and that provided teachers with teaching units to insert into courses. The resource materials developed by the Ontario Ministry of Education and the Toronto Board were optional, however, and therefore had only a limited impact on history departments. The school board emphasized increasing the number of women in administrative positions; in other words, it provided an "easy fix" to demands for change in the school system.[14] Rebecca Coulter argues that governments "often passed weak legislation or developed soft gender equity through education policies, designed to offend no one."[15]

Although school board women's committees, teachers' unions, small publishers, and women's organizations created and supported women-specific history resources throughout the 1980s and 1990s, these resources continued to marginalize women's voices in history courses. Their developers focused on creating separate units in which to "add women," and an equitable curriculum never materialized.

The lack of an equitable history curriculum was discussed in the fall 1989 issue of *History and Social Science Teacher* (a leading professional magazine for secondary school history teachers), the first issue devoted to women and women's studies. Paula Bourne, research associate at the Centre for Women's Studies in Education at the Ontario Institute for Studies in Education (OISE), University of Toronto, and guest editor, complained that even though resource materials for teaching about women existed, little new scholarship was finding its way into secondary school classrooms.[16] A 1989 study conducted by OISE confirmed her concerns. The study surveyed sixty-six textbooks and found that none of them met the criteria of the school board's "sex equity" policies. It revealed that less than 13 percent of the content had *any* reference to women.[17] Integrating women into the curriculum was not a priority for publishers and history teachers, and subject departments were reluctant to change. When former history teacher Peter Flaherty, as part of a curriculum-writing team, asked members of history departments in Toronto to rank a list of units according to whether they would like to see them developed, they ranked the one dealing with the women's movement last.[18] Clearly, school boards' equity policies, which paid little attention to the delivery of curriculum, were ineffective. In reaction, teachers began to look for women's history resources outside the schools.

Interested teachers found a number of organizations interested in supporting women's history, including the Canadian Federation of University Women; the Federation of Women Teachers' Associations of Ontario; Educators for Gender Equity; the Ontario Secondary School Teachers' Federation; the Congress of Black Women of Canada; the Native Women's Association of Canada; and the Canadian Committee on Women's History. These organizations concentrated on networking and fundraising through conferences, publications, special events, and workshops, and they acted as models for other women's organizations. A number of universities provided venues for these events, and teacher education faculties and women's studies departments promoted productive partnerships among women's groups, school board educators, scholars, and teachers. For example, beginning in 1987, York University held annual equity conferences that brought together Toronto educators.[19] The "Equity in the Classroom, Equity in the Curriculum" conferences provided a wealth of resource materials for teachers to use in history and social science classrooms. The conferences were sponsored jointly by five or six school boards in the Toronto area, as well as by the York University Centre for Feminist Research. These events, and others, developed as feminist organizations formed strong advocacy groups to promote educational change.

Independent women's education organizations began to spring up throughout Ontario. For example, Educators for Gender Equity (EDGE), a group of teachers and members of the Status of Women Committee of the Ontario Secondary School Teachers Federation (OSSTF) in London, Ontario, formed in the mid-1990s and sought to "develop and maintain a network to promote curricular policies, programs, resources and practices related to gender equity in elementary and secondary education." The group, like others in the province, was anxious to find ways to alter curricula and provide a platform for collaboration.[20] Other history education organizations included the Ontario Women's History Network (OWHN), the Women's History Network of British Columbia (WHN/BC), the Women and History Association of Manitoba (WHAM), Women in Alberta and Saskatchewan History (WASH), and the Canadian Committee on Women's History (CCWH).[21] Members of these organizations also joined a larger network of local and provincial historical societies and educational communities.[22]

A number of women's organizations provided forums and support for the development and promotion of women's history resources. The WHN/BC, for instance, offered in-service programs and curriculum resources.[23] As active members in women's organizations, feminist scholars and educators sought out new networks each time they moved or experienced a change in their careers. Like other female scholars, historian Alison Prentice was an active member of the CCWH and OWHN. When she moved to Victoria from Toronto, she became active in the WHN/BC. When I corresponded with her, she noted that "both OWHN and WHN/BC were especially concerned with getting more women's stories into history or social studies courses in schools."[24] Feminist scholars recall feminist activism and scholarship as being equally important strategies for change.[25] By pressing for and, one could argue, developing women's history resource materials, feminist educators broadened the traditional historical narratives present in all school history courses.

The Ontario Women's History Network (OWHN)

The Ontario Women's History Network is representative of activism in Toronto during the 1990s. The organization was formed to address the lack of
women's history materials in school curricula and the problems teachers
faced in accessing scholarly materials:

> The goal of the OWHN is to stimulate the study and further the knowl-
> edge of women's history in Ontario. Our twice yearly conferences in cen-
> ters across Ontario provide an opportunity to meet others who share your
> interest in women's history, to learn more about women's history and to
> discover new avenues and information for learning and spreading women's
> history.[26]

Members of OWHN focused on building bridges between various communities. Mainly feminist academics and educators, they were committed to en-
gaging with diverse communities through a dedicated plan that included
twice-yearly conferences and meetings, publishing an annual newsletter and
resource materials (including women's history posters), supporting women's
presses and bookstores, promoting women's and local history, and establishing an effective networking system. This web of like-minded women brought
women's history into Ontario schools. Their accomplishments provide insight into the efforts of activist organizations to influence curriculum change.

Sparked by the work of Alison Prentice and research associates at the
Canadian Women's History Project at OISE's Centre for Women's Studies in
Education, OWHN's first meeting took place in June 1989. Its founders were
influenced by the Women's Studies Research Colloquium, which provided
a venue for scholars to meet regularly to "share papers, discussion and dinner," and the Canadian Committee on Women's History, founded in 1975 to
"promote teaching and research in the field of women's history."[27] At OWHN's
first meeting, academics, educators, archivists, and private scholars gathered
to focus on two proposals: the development of an archival research tool for
Canadian women's history and the formation of an Ontario women's history
society.[28] They planned to develop resource guides to link teachers and other
users to archival sources, but they did not raise enough funds. From its beginning, OWHN fulfilled a unique need among feminist historians in Ontario.
The new organization focused attention on networking and the development
of annual conferences for educators throughout the province.

The first conference, titled "Bridging the Gap: Women's History in the
Classroom," took place at OISE on 22 September 1990 and was funded by

the Federation of Womens Teachers' Associations of Ontario (FWTAO). Workshops carried titles such as "Multiculturalism and Native Studies," "Community Resources," and "Black History."[29] These workshops reflected women's historians' desire to move beyond white women's experiences and capture the diversity of Canada's past, as seen in the work of Sylvia Van Kirk, Jean Burnet, Marilyn Barber, and Veronica Strong-Boag, to name only a few.[30] After this first conference and until well into the new century, OWHN sponsored conferences in centres throughout Ontario, providing an opportunity for educators to share resources, learn about women's history, and brainstorm new ways of incorporating women's history into classrooms. The organization provided free women's history resource materials for teachers, and these resources became one of OWHN's greatest strengths.

The 1991 conference, "Breaking the Stereotypes," which was held at OISE, included Elizabeth Perrott, a University of Toronto sociologist affiliated with the Indigenous Education Network, and Jeanette Corbier Laval, a First Nations counsellor. It reflected OWHN's emphasis on including the histories of Aboriginal, racialized, and immigrant women. The conference included a panel on Aboriginal women in fur trade society and an exhibit about Chinese women in Canada.[31] Because the organization included a wide range of educators and researchers, from a variety of multiracial and multiethnic backgrounds, its members had a rich foundation from which to draw. They invited speakers from diverse backgrounds to highlight the issues of race and ethnicity, and they asked graduate students, independent scholars, and representatives from various communities to present their research material or speak about their personal experiences at each conference. They offered essential opportunities for networking at a time when divisions were surfacing within women's organizations.[32] Founding member Pat Staton recalls that the organization "worked hard" to be inclusive and was sensitive to the fact that teachers, working within diverse classrooms in Toronto, were continually seeking history resource materials that reflected a wide range of women's experiences.[33]

Gail Cuthbert Brandt, historian and founding member of OWHN, remembers that Toronto at that time was "a hotbed of women's issues related to race and ethnicity" and that bringing in diverse voices was critical to the success of the conferences. The organization had a format that partnered panels of "experts" in the field with women active in the community.[34] The 1992 conference, "Telling Our Stories" featured a panel on the history of the Holocaust that included Paula Draper, director of the Holocaust Documentation Project at the Toronto Jewish Congress, and Gerta Steinitz, a Holocaust survivor.[35] Brandt believes the conferences had a number of strengths: scholars could add new perspectives to their work, women found a welcoming space in which to share their life experiences, and teachers found new and diverse resources for their classrooms. Placing conferences within public secondary schools and school boards facilitated participation from teachers and school educators. "Women's History: New Technologies and New Resources," was a one-day conference held in 1997 at Martingrove Collegiate, a school in West End Toronto, and specifically aimed at Toronto secondary school teachers. Among the workshops, Marguerite Alfred and Afua Cooper offered one titled "Black Women and Canadian History," which provided new materials for placing black women's experiences into course studies.[36] Although OWHN also wanted to build relationships with francophone teachers and scholars, the conferences usually took place in Toronto, they had limited funds for translation, and most of the members came from English-speaking parts of Ontario.[37]

Some conferences were well attended because they brought together groups that had previously had little formal association. For instance, according to the *Sudbury Star*, "Women of Steel: Mining Their History," held in 1999 at Laurentian University in Sudbury, helped to integrate the work of academics and women working in the mining industry. The article also reflected on the ways in which the organizers had linked the themes of the conference to the politics and economy of the host institution or city.[38] Over the years, OWHN developed important relationships with feminist scholars at faculties of education by offering support and sharing resources. The "History of Aboriginal Women" conference, held in 2004 in the new Indigenous Studies building at Trent University in Peterborough, was co-sponsored by Trent's School of Education and Professional Learning, the Indigenous Studies Department, and the Kawartha Pine Ridge District School Board and provided opportunities for local educators to network. The women's history poster theme that fall was "Native Women in the Arts."[39] The most successful conferences involved partnerships with a wide range of diverse groups.

Conferences hosted by OWHN attracted an average attendance of sixty to one hundred people, and provided teachers with an opportunity to participate in discussions with scholars. Peggy Hooke, a teacher with the Toronto Board and a member of OWHN, noted, "The conferences were motivating, and exposed me to experts in their field. They provided me with an awareness of larger issues and concepts that I could integrate into my teaching."[40] A conference held at Seneca Falls, New York, in 2002, focused on women and the history of national historic sites in both Canada and the United States, while one at Queen's University, in 2003, focused on women and health care.[41] Teachers received copies of keynote speeches; handouts, including biographies, at panel discussions and workshops; and articles and full bibliographies of materials related to the conferences' themes. Jan Haskings-Winner, a Toronto teacher and OWHN member, noted that she used these resource materials "for student research projects and recommended OWHN materials to school board libraries."[42] Conferences provided opportunities to forge links between professional women's organizations and educators. For example, the 1999 meeting created links with the Ontario Law Society. The poster theme that year was "Canadian Women and the Law," which featured women lawyers and judges. OWHN played a central role in linking various feminist communities.

When Status of Women Canada proclaimed October Women's History Month in 1992, OWHN took advantage by holding its conference on Parliament Hill and inviting prominent female politicians such as Monique Bégin, the former minister of health; Audrey McLaughlin, leader of the federal NDP; and Mary Collins, minister for the status of women and national defence.[43] The bilingual resource material included biographical sketches of prominent women in politics.

Members of OWHN also co-sponsored the annual publication of a Canadian women's history poster. Printed on parchment coloured paper, the inaugural poster listed the names and accomplishments of dozens of Canadian women and came with a teacher's guide. Pat Staton, founder of the publishing company, Green Dragon Press, a small independent press in Toronto, produced equity materials that focused on Canadian women. Staton recalled how the poster came to be: "At a presentation that I was giving for a school board [in 1990], a man at the back of the room interrupted, stating 'I don't see why we should put women in the curriculum, because they didn't do anything.'" Staton went back to OISE, where she also worked as a research associate with the Centre for Women's Studies, and put a paper box under her desk. "Every time I noted a woman's historic accomplishment, I wrote it down and put it in the box."[44]

Posters in later years were funded by the Toronto Education Equity Studies Centre, the Elementary Teachers Federation of Ontario (ETFO), and OWHN. The posters often reflected the theme of the annual conferences – "Women in Science and Technology" (1997), "Women in Sports" (1998), and "Celebrating Immigrant Women" (2002) – and illustrated the broad experiences of women. Thousands were placed in schools and school boards across the province. These posters visually represented the diversity of women's experiences and celebrated the achievements of women from many racial, ethnic, and social backgrounds; from different areas of the country; and from various historical periods. Teachers had students incorporate materials from the posters into their projects and perform further research.

The Ontario Women's History Network operated on a modest budget. Membership fees were only twenty dollars, and there were never more than two hundred members. Early efforts to acquire funding from the Ministry of Education were not successful, and OWHN never developed an endowment fund.[45] The FWTAO, and later ETFO, provided financial support for publications, posters, and events, but constantly changing educational agendas prevented it from making long-term commitments.[46] Members and workshop leaders often donated the resources provided at conferences, a practice that reflected a common reality for many not-for-profit, volunteer-based women's organizations. Conference fees were kept at a minimum, and support was provided for students, retired members, and those with financial need. Conference delegates also received a number of free resources from conference co-sponsors and local history societies, as well as from others such as Parks Canada and the Museum of Civilization. Independent publishers (such as Second Story Press, Green Dragon, and Sumach Press) and bookstores (such as A Different Booklist and the Women's Bookstore) set up tables at each conference and provided books at reduced prices. Green Dragon provided free Canadian women's history posters for all delegates.

In keeping with the organization's focus on teachers, OWHN conferences were often co-sponsored by faculties of education and were held on campuses such as at OISE, Western, Trent, Laurentian, the University of Ottawa, and York University. All conferences held at OISE or York University in Toronto included teacher candidates and were supported by faculty members. In 1994, OWHN also partnered with the Royal Military College (RMC) and the History Department and Faculty of Education at Queen's University to focus on women in Canada's military past. Partnering with faculties of education allowed the organization to reach out to beginning teachers at a time when they were most receptive to using new resource materials. OWHN invited teacher candidates and history graduate students to attend conferences at reduced costs, elicited their input in conference planning and workshop leadership, provided opportunities for networking, and featured their scholarship in panels.[47]

The conferences introduced delegates to new scholarship in the field. The 1995 conference, "Counting Women In: New Ways of Thinking about Women and Work," for instance, explored the history of women's paid and unpaid work and included speakers such as Bonnie Fox, Meg Luxton, Bettina Bradbury, Valerie Korinek, and Joan Sangster.[48] The conferences reached out to teachers of all subject areas, stimulating discussion and research and support for professional development. One teacher who attended the conference in Ottawa to take part in the unveiling of the "Famous Five" statue recalled that she "used anecdotes and knowledge garnered from this experience often in my history classes."[49] The conferences bridged the gap between academic scholarship and teacher practice. According to historian Gail Cuthbert Brandt, it is difficult to document the larger impact of the conferences, but they did have an impact on a personal level: they exposed people to new scholarship and facilitated the development of networks. "We were not like a service club, where you can point to a specific community project, but rather the conferences provided an impact on more of an intellectual and social level."[50] Members felt that networking produced valuable associations and the opportunity to share resources. Although OWHN did not conduct studies on the impact of conference materials in classrooms, its members indicated that they developed friendships and networks and appreciated the opportunity to collaborate with like-minded colleagues.[51] Sharon Cook pointed out that "OWHN ensured a public program that encouraged the teaching of women's history, the respect that it deserved, and the resources needed to carry it forward."[52]

The Ontario Women's History Network depended on support from OISE in the 1980s and from the Equity Studies Department at the Toronto District School Board, which was headed by Myra Novogrodsky, in the 1990s. Both venues provided space, secretaries, and financial support. Funding cuts in the late 1990s, however, challenged the organization's survival. It had become dependent on these venues and on key individuals who chaired the committees for conferences and served on the executive. But sustaining the commitment was difficult, as most members had busy lives and were members of numerous professional and volunteer committees and organizations. Early on, the organization had discussed the possibility of creating local chapters throughout the province, which might have provided a foundation for growth. However, regional chapters would have added another level of complexity for the executive.[53] The level of commitment necessary to orchestrate biannual conferences and meetings was already formidable and certainly one of the reasons the organization ultimately eliminated one of the meetings.

By 2000, the organization no longer had a permanent home. Conferences drew smaller numbers, membership decreased, and the organization lost its former cohesion and direction. One of the problems was the lack of a website maintained by OWHN. The organization relied instead on phone calls and twice-a-year mailings to members, which limited the executive's ability to expand and remain current. The other challenge was convincing young scholars and teachers to join. As universities and schools began to include more women's history content, younger women felt less of a need to seek out new materials. Attracting new members has been a challenge for many organizations formed during the height of the second-wave women's movement. The Ontario Women's History Network was also influenced by broader changes affecting society and women in the late 1990s. Ideas about feminism were changing, putting pressure on established women's organizations to find ways to remain relevant and active. The urgent need for new resources and networks, so immediate in the 1980s, no longer drove women's organizations.

A change in focus in Ontario education has also challenged some of the advances in gender equity.[54] An antifeminist backlash in the 1990s and the rise of neoliberalism had an impact, as did curriculum policy changes. In 1993, Bob Rae's government introduced the common curriculum, which was outcome-based and included provincial assessment of students at various grade levels.[55] In 1995, Mike Harris's Conservative government implemented stronger curriculum controls as part of the "Common Sense Revolution," which focused on balancing budgets and increasing standardized testing.[56] These political changes instituted new educational priorities in Ontario, which had an impact on the structure of history curricula in the schools. Feminist organizations found it difficult to create new strategies in the wake of such educational paradigm shifts.[57]

Finally, the drive that had united the founding members lessened as scholars, publishers, and teachers began recognizing women in their writing, teaching, and publications. As well, understandings about the importance of inclusivity in course studies became more widespread. Today's textbooks and history resource materials now feature women, and teachers today have a greater sense of the importance of including a diversity of voices in their history courses.

Despite these advances, members of OWHN recognized the need to update their organization, and they regrouped in 2007. Under the guidance of its chair, Gail Cuthbert Brandt, the History Department at the University of Waterloo became the organization's new home. A website was set up within a year.[58] The organization moved to hosting only one annual meeting, which was combined with the women's history conference and which alternated between Toronto and another Ontario city. The 2009 conference in Ottawa, "The Persons Case and Canadian Women's Political Activism," was co-sponsored by the Women's Legal Education and Action Fund (LEAF), Ottawa, demonstrating OWHN's ability to continue to partner with other women's organizations. Having hosted or produced thirty-five conferences, seventeen posters, and numerous practical educational resources, not to mention lobbying the Ministry of Education on the importance of mandatory history courses, the organization could proudly declare it had provided a wide range of tools and resources to incorporate women's narratives into the history and social sciences curricula.

Conclusion

The Ontario Women's History Network continues to stimulate the study and further the knowledge of women's history in Ontario. Its 2012 conference, which took place at Fort York, Toronto, addressed the theme "Women and the War of 1812" and included a wide range of scholars, academics, graphic artists, teachers, and graduate students. Nearly one hundred delegates networked and shared stories, resource materials, and posters. In many ways, little had changed from the early 1990s, when the conferences offered opportunities to learn about new scholarship in Canadian women's history.

Even so, despite the substantial efforts of second-wave feminists, feminist scholars, and women's organizations such as OWHN, public school history continues to marginalize women's history in course materials and course studies. This oversight may reflect a failure on the part of the Ontario Ministry of Education to develop a clear and unified approach – replete with means, methods, and materials – for the integration of women's history resources into the curriculum. Instead, teachers in Ontario continue to be responsible for sorting through a range of materials to deliver a balanced history curriculum.

The work of women's organizations such as OWHN demonstrates the potential of grassroots activism for making institutional change. The networks they helped create led to women's history resources in classrooms. The teachers I interviewed indicated that the conferences provided a vital common space in which to network and share scholarship in the field of women's history. One teacher noted, "The sharing of knowledge and learning from the women who were experts in their fields contributed significantly to my classroom lectures and lessons."[59]

The biggest challenges that remain for the organization are recruiting new members and developing creative and varied ways to network with educators. Teachers in Ontario, and across the country, are turning first to the Internet rather than community networks for information. The Ontario Women's History Network must embrace the digital age and transform their web of networks into an online web. As more teachers use the Internet to network and obtain resources for their classrooms, OWHN could position itself as a much-needed provider of digitally based content and promote women's history research online. As teachers in Ontario continue to grapple with a curriculum that is slow to fully incorporate gender equity, organizations such as OWHN can and will play a critical role in providing accessible and inclusive scholarship as well as resources to history educators.

NOTES

1 Gerda Lerner, *Living with History/Making Social Change* (Chapel Hill: University of North Carolina Press, 2009), 36.
2 Teacher C, interview by author, Toronto, 11 January 2010.
3 This essay is part of a larger research study that explores the ways in which women's movement activism influenced teachers to include women in course studies in Toronto's secondary schools from 1968 to 1993.
4 See, for example, Janice Acton, Penny Goldsmith, and Bonnie Shepard, eds., *Women at Work: Ontario 1850–1930* (Toronto: CWEP, 1974); Linda Kealey, ed., *A Not Unreasonable Claim: Women and Reform in Canada, 1880s–1920s* (Toronto: Women's Press, 1979); and Meg Luxton, *More Than a Labour of Love: Three Generations of Women's Work in the Home* (Toronto: Canadian Women's Press, 1980). On women as a valid historical subject, see Veronica Strong-Boag, "Raising Clio's Consciousness: Women's History and Archives in Canada," *Archivaria* 6 (Summer 1978): 70–82; Alison Prentice, Paula Bourne, Gail Cuthbert Brandt, Beth Light, Wendy Mitchinson, and Naomi Black, *Canadian Women: A History* (Toronto: Harcourt Brace Jovanovich, 1988); Joan Wallach Scott "Women's History," in *New Perspectives on Historical Writing*, ed. Peter Burke (London: Polity Press, 1991), 42–66.
5 Judith M. Bennett, *History Matters: Patriarchy and the Challenge of Feminism* (Philadelphia: University of Pennsylvania Press, 2006), 1.
6 Historians Natalie Zemon Davis and Jill Conway developed the first women's history course at the University of Toronto in 1971 (Davis, interview with author, Toronto, February 2010). A number of universities introduced women's history courses in the 1970s. For the United States, see Judith P. Zinner, *History and Feminism: A Glass Half Full* (New York: Twayne Publishers, 1993); for Canada, see Wendy Robbins, Meg Luxton, Margrit Eichler, and Francine Descarries, eds., *Minds of Their Own: Inventing Feminist Scholarship and Women's Studies in Canada and Quebec, 1966–76* (Waterloo: Wilfred Laurier University Press, 2008).
7 A study of textbooks in 1970 examined themes of national importance to Canadians. Women were absent. See Marcel Trudel, *Canadian History Textbooks: A Comparative Study* (Ottawa: Queen's Printer for Canada, 1970). A 1989 OISE study found only

small changes. See Beth Light, Pat Staton, and Paula Bourne, "Sex Equity Content in History Textbooks," *History and Social Science Teacher* 25, 1 (1989): 18–20.

8   See *This Magazine Is All about Schools* (1966–) and *Community Schools* (1971–74). Private collection of Myra Novogrodsky, Toronto.

9   Provincial Committee on Aims and Objectives of Education in the Schools of Ontario, *Living and Learning Report* (Toronto: Newton Publishing, 1968).

10 Ontario Department of Education, "Recommendation and Information for Secondary Schools," Circular HS1 1972/73. Principals were advised to work with staff and parents to classify courses under four broad areas: communications, social and environmental studies, pure and applied sciences, and the arts.

11 Paul Axelrod, "Historical Writing and Canadian Education," *History of Education Quarterly* 36, 1 (1996): 19–38. The study of women was placed within social or labour history topics such as suffrage and factory work.

12 Teacher K, interview with author, Toronto, 30 November 2009.

13 The Government of Canada's Royal Commission on the Status of Women was established on 16 February 1967. The report was published in 1970. Section 69 recommended that the provinces and the territories adopt textbooks that portray women and men in diversified roles and occupations.

14 Toronto Board Archives, Affirmative Action Files, 1985; and Lise Julien, *Women's Issues in Education in Canada: A Survey of Policies and Practices at the Elementary and Secondary Levels* (Ottawa: Government of Canada, 1987). The Toronto Board offered principal training in the evenings and expanded entrance requirements.

15 Rebecca Priegert Coulter, "Gender Equity and Schooling: Linking Research and Policy," *Canadian Journal of Education* 21, 4 (1996): 433–52.

16 *History and Social Science Teacher* 25, 1 (Fall 1989): 6. Christopher Moore, email interview with author, 7 June 2012. Moore, editor, notes the journal (published from 1974 to 1990) began with Ontario History and Social Sciences Teachers and was then taken over by Grolier publishers. He adds, "A group of educators acted as an advisory board. The journal's intended audience was secondary school teachers, although it had readers and contributors from across the country."

17 Beth Light, Pat Staton, and Paula Bourne, researchers at the Centre for Women's Studies in Education at OISE, reviewed textbooks listed on the provincially approved list, Circular 14, as part of the Canadian Women's History Project (CWHP). They received a grant from the Ministry of Education for the study. The report, titled *Sex Equity Content in History Textbooks*, was written in 1987 and published in the *History and Social Science Teacher* 25, 1 (1989): 18–21. A number of research studies took place throughout the 1970s. See Elaine Batcher, Demaris Brackstone, Alison Winter, and Vicki Wright (co-ordinator) ... *And Then There Were None*, a report commissioned by the Status of Women Committee and the Federation of Women Teachers' Associations of Ontario (Toronto, September 1975); Canadian Teachers' Federation, *Challenge '76: Sexism in Schools* (Ottawa: Canadian Teachers' Federation, 1976); and Elaine Batcher, Alison Winter, and Vicki Wright, *The More Things Change – The More They Stay the Same* (Toronto: Federation of Women Teachers' Associations of Ontario, 1987).

18 *History and Social Science Teacher* 25, 1 (1989): 18–21.

19 Myra Novogrodsky, Toronto, private collection of equity conference brochures. Novogrodsky, a retired Toronto Board teacher, was also a member of OWHN and chair of the Women and Labour Studies and Equity Department and an instructor in the Faculty of Education at York University.

20 Rebecca Coulter, "Educators for Gender Equity: Organizing for Change," *Canadian Woman Studies/Cahiers de la Femme* 17, 4 (1998): 103–5; OWHN archive files, marked "Correspondence," document from EDGE explaining its mandate and activities, no date.

21 See the Women's History Network of BC (http://www.whnbc.blogspot.ca/), whose members parallel those of OWHN. The website notes that "the WHN/BC was originally inspired by the 1994 conference, 'BC and Beyond: Gender Histories,' held in Victoria, B.C." The network holds annual conferences.

22 OWHN archive files, correspondence, letters from EDGE. OWHN was affiliated with the Ontario Historical Society (OHS) and Educators for Gender Equity (EDGE). OWHN archival boxes are stored at the Archives of Ontario.

23 Examples include the FWTAO, the ETFO, and the Ontario Women's Directorate.

24 Alison Prentice, email interview with author, 5 March 2010. See also Wendy Robbins, Meg Luxton, Margrit Eichler, and Francine Descarries, eds., *Minds of Their Own* (Waterloo: Wilfrid Laurier University Press, 2008).

25 Judith P. Zinsser, *History and Feminism: A Glass Half Full* (New York: Twayne Publishers, 1993), 42. Zinsser quotes Joan Kelly, who recalls scholars collaborating to explore new approaches to the study of history during the 1970s.

26 OWHN archive files, binders, OWHN conference materials, membership directory, OWHN newsletter, January 1999.

27 This quote is from Gail Cuthbert Brandt, University of Waterloo. Brandt is a founding member of OWHN and was chair from 2007 to 2010. See the Canadian Committee on Women's History website, http://www.chashcacommittees-comitesa.ca/ccwh-cchf/en/index.html.

28 OWHN archive files, minutes, 23 September 1989. Participants present at the first meeting were as follows: Paula Bourne, Gail Cuthbert Brandt, Ruth Brouwer, Barbara Craig, Bernadine Dodge, Karen Dubinsky, Jane Errington, Rosemary Evans, Nancy Forestell, Pauline Greenhill, Julie Guard, Marie Hammond, Linda Hecht, Marguerite Hudson, Margaret Kellow, Jeanne L'Esperance, Beth Light, Lynne Marks, Lucille Marr, Jean Matthews, Kathryn McPherson, Wyn Millar, Beverly Mulkwich, Jan Noel, Diana Pedersen, Johanne Pelletier, Alison Prentice, Colin Read, Cecilia Reynolds, Jane Scherer, Johanna Selles-Roney, Christabelle Sethna, Pat Staton, Terry Thompson, Cheryl Warsh, Garron Wells, and Shirley Wigmore.

29 OWHN archives files, "Founding Conference," 3 February 1990. The conference's keynote speaker was Wendy Mitchinson, and it included workshops, walking tours, and community research projects.

30 Sylvia Van Kirk, *"Many Tender Ties": Women in Fur-Trade Society, 1670–1870* (Winnipeg: Watson and Dwyer, 1980); Jean Burnet, ed., *Looking into My Sister's Eyes: An Exploration of Women's History* (Toronto: Multicultural History Society of Ontario, 1986); Linda Kealey, ed., *A Not Unreasonable Claim: Women and Reform in Canada, 1880s–1920s* (Toronto: Women's Press, 1979); and Veronica Strong-Boag, *The New*

Day Recalled: Lives of Girls and Women in English Canada, 1919–1939 (Toronto: Copp Clark Pitman, 1988).

31 OWHN archives files, Folder 4, 21 February 1991; The conference was titled "Breaking the Stereotypes: Women in Society, Past and Present," OISE, University of Toronto, 2 February 1991.

32 There was growing acknowledgment by the 1990s of the intertwined nature of matrices of oppression (gender, race, class, and ethnicity). See, for example, Vanaja Dhruvarajan, "A Lifetime of Struggles to Belong," in Wendy Robbins, Meg Luxton, Margrit Eichler, and Francine Descarries, eds., *Minds of Our Own* (Waterloo: Wilfrid Laurier University Press, 2008), 148–55. Dhruvarajan argues against the "one world" perspective of studying women.

33 Pat Staton, interview with author, Toronto, 8 June 2012.

34 Gail Cuthbert Brandt, interview with author, Bright, Ontario, 13 March 2010.

35 OWHN archives files, Folder 4, "Breaking the Stereotypes: Women in Society, Past and Present," 21 February 1991; Folder 5, "Women Making a Difference" and "The Walk: OISE and the Native Canadian Centre of Toronto," 21 September 1991; Folder 6, "Telling Our Own Stories: Three Women's Lives," 1 February 1992.

36 OWHN archive files, Folder 16, "Women's History: New Technologies and New Resources," 5 April 1997.

37 One exception was the 1992 OWHN conference, which was held in partnership with the federal government in Ottawa. The federal funding meant that the program, resource materials, and poster were fully bilingual. OWHN archives files, Folder 7, "Women and the Political Process," 3 October 1992.

38 OWHN archive files, Folder 21, "Women of Steel: Mining Their History," 13 October 1999.

39 OWHN archive files, Folder 31, "Repositioning Native Women in Canada," 22 October 2004.

40 Peggy Hooke, interview with author, Toronto, 3 January 2011. Hooke notes, "I didn't go [to OWHN conferences] specifically for the resources but more for the issues that were discussed, bringing them back to the school as a teacher and department head, and I was convinced of the importance of the OWHN agenda."

41 OWHN archive files, Folder 29, "Body and Soul: Women and Healthcare in an Historical Perspective," 17 and 18 October 2003. The conference was at Queen's University and co-sponsored by the Department of History, Queen's University, the Royal Military College, and the Museum of Healthcare, Kingston. Folder 27, "Seneca Falls, New York," 20–22 September 2002.

42 Jan Haskings-Winner, instructional leader, TDSB, interview with author, Toronto, May 2012.

43 OWHN archive files, letter from the minister responsible for the Status of Women, 7 May 1993. In this letter, Minister Mary Collins states, "the aim of the women's history month each October is to foster an appreciation for the past and present contributions of women in Canada and to recognize their achievement as a vital part of our heritage."

44 Pat Staton, interview with author, Toronto, March 2009.

45 Pat Staton, interview with author, Toronto, 9 June 2010.

46 Support for women's organizations is visible in the FWTAO's newsletters, affirmative action reports, and publications. The ETFO also funded the work of women's organizations through kits, posters, and handbooks.

47 The OWHN files reveal that many Canadian women's history scholars participated in its conferences when they were graduate students.

48 OWHN archive files, Folder 12, "Counting Women In: New Ways of Thinking about Women and Work," 1 April 1995.

49 S.K. Gibson, interview with author, Toronto, 12 May 2012.

50 Gail Cuthbert Brandt, interview with author, Bright, Ontario, 13 March 2010.

51 Wendy Robbins, Meg Luxton, Margrit Eichler, and Francine Descarries, eds., *Minds of Our Own: Inventing Feminist Scholarship and Women's Studies in Canada and Quebec, 1966–1976* (Waterloo: Wilfrid Laurier University Press, 2008), 34.

52 Sharon Anne Cook, email interview with author, 21 December 2009.

53 Gail Cuthbert Brandt, email interview with author, 27 December 2010.

54 For a discussion of changes to Ontario's curriculum, see R.D. Gidney, *From Hope to Harris: The Reshaping of Ontario's Schools* (Toronto: University of Toronto Press, 1999); for a discussion of changes to humanities education, see P. Axelrod, *Values in Conflict: The University, the Marketplace, and the Trials of Liberal Education* (Montreal/Kingston: McGill-Queen's University Press, 2002); and for an international discussion of history education, see Tony Taylor and Robert Guyver, eds., *History Wars and the Classroom: Global Perspectives* (Charlotte, NC: Information Age Publishing, 2012).

55 The Education Quality and Accountability Office is an arm's-length Crown agency of the Ontario government. See Stephen Anderson and Sonia Ben Jaafar, *Policy Trends in Ontario, 1990–2003*, OISE working papers, Toronto, September 2003.

56 See Gidney, *From Hope to Harris;* Clara Morgan, "A Retrospective Look at Educational Reforms in Ontario," *Our Schools, Our Selves* 15, 2 (2006): 127–41; and L. Angus, "Teaching within and against the Circle of Privilege," *Journal of Education Policy* 27, 2 (2012): 231–51.

57 See Gidney, *From Hope to Harris,* and Tim McCaskell, *Race to Equity: Disrupting Educational Inequality* (Toronto: Between the Lines, 2005). In 2009, the University of Guelph closed its women's studies program.

58 OWHN archive files, Folder "AGM 2008"; the conference took place 2 and 3 May 2008 at the University of Waterloo.

59 S.K. Gibson, interview with author, 12 May 2012.

Fighting the "Corset of Victorian Prejudice"
Women's Activism in Canadian Engineering during the Pioneering Decades (1970s–80s)

RUBY HEAP

In 1975, the Engineering Institute of Canada's *Engineering Journal* marked International Women's Year by publishing a special feature titled "Women in Engineering." Colleen Isherwood noted, "engineering may still be considered by some as a 'male profession,' but women engineers are definitely entering the public eye ... For the first time in Canadian history girls are being told 'You could become a geologist, a physicist, a mathematician, a surgeon, a biologist, or even a professional engineer.'"[1] There were other encouraging signs: women were studying engineering in increasing numbers; female students were leading undergraduate student councils; and the Ordre des Ingénieurs du Québec had recently appointed its first women president.

Elsie Gregory MacGill, commonly identified as Canada's first woman engineer, was not as enthusiastic. At seventy years of age, MacGill had been a successful engineer for more than four decades. She was also a third-generation feminist: her grandmother was a suffragist, and her mother, Helen MacGill, was a promoter of women's rights and the first female judge in British Columbia.[2] In 1967, MacGill served as a member of the Royal Commission on the Status of Women.[3] Engineers, admitted MacGill, were a "relatively fortunate, educated, small middle-class group" who seldom lived through "deprivation and real hardship." Even so, "management misconceptions and hang-ups" had squeezed women engineers into a "corset of Victorian prejudice," a constraint that she herself had experienced during her career. Their professional future was at the mercy of "the male power clique that makes its decisions at the all-male engineers table in the company dining room, or in the washroom." MacGill believed that to improve the situation, more women needed to enter into engineering faculties, discriminatory hiring and promotion practices had to be eliminated, and the engineering community needed to be convinced that women could succeed in the profession.[4]

This chapter brings to light the growing activism of professional women engineers and examines their uneasy relationship with the second-wave women's movement in Canada. American feminist historians have shown how, in the context of the resurging feminist movement of the late 1960s and early 1970s, women in science and engineering began to voice their discontent about their second-class status and to fight for equal rights. According to Margaret Rossiter, their greater consciousness and their accelerated move towards collective action contributed to the creation of a "women's movement in science and engineering" in the United States.[5] In the 1980s and 1990s, the encounter between women's studies and science and technological studies created the vibrant fields of feminist science studies and gender and technology studies, which have unmasked the gendered nature of science and technology and investigated the linkages between feminism and science and engineering.[6] Nothing comparable has happened in Canada. Women scientists and engineers have remained largely outside the lens of feminist historians, including researchers interested in the entry of women in the so-called masculine professions.[7] Similarly, scholarly studies and firsthand accounts of the second-wave movement have tended to overlook the activism of women scientists and engineers, as well as the potential impact of feminism on these fields.[8]

The history of female engineers has much to tell us about the diversity and complexity of feminism and its impact on male-dominated professions. This chapter explains how Canadian women engineers in the 1970s and 1980s began to develop a sense of identity and to voice their concerns about the obstacles that were preventing their full participation in the profession. Drawing on social movement studies, I identify the leading advocates, describe their motivations, and examine the ways they moved towards organization and collective action.[9] Women engineers were nervous about being labelled feminists because they did not want to draw attention to gender differences between themselves and their male colleagues. Moreover, they did not share the widespread feminist views on the negative impact of technology on women's lives.

The Road to Activism: Identifying the "Problem" of Women in Engineering

When Elsie MacGill was appointed to the Royal Commission on the Status of Women she stood out as the only commissioner with a strong feminist track record.[10] In 1966, MacGill was instrumental in the creation of the Committee for the Equality of Women, which lobbied for the creation of the royal commission. After the commission's report was tabled in 1970, she took part in the creation of the National Action Committee on the Status of Women (NAC), an umbrella organization established in 1972 to ensure the implementation of the recommendations. During the 1970s and early 1980s, NAC and other feminist groups campaigned for gender equality in the job market and the eradication of wage discrimination. Lobbying for measures that gave women access to occupations traditionally held by men was one way to achieve these goals. Their efforts led to the adoption of pay and employment equity laws and policies by the federal government and by several of its provincial counterparts. In 1982, feminists mobilized to lobby for the entrenchment of the principles of gender equality and employment equity in the Canadian Charter of Rights and Freedoms.[11]

These feminist victories were important to the growth of women's activism in engineering, but earlier investigations of women's employment also influenced their goals and strategies. In 1954, the federal government had established the Women's Labour Bureau to bring attention to the "problems of women workers."[12] Under the leadership of its first director, Marion Royce, it grew increasingly concerned with women's rights and their equality in the workplace.[13] In 1957, the bureau found that only 6 percent of people employed in professions associated with the natural sciences (biologists, chemists, geologists, mathematicians, and physicists) were women and that three-quarters of them were in biology and chemistry. The number of women in engineering was too negligible to record. The data showed that women in the sciences were largely confined to a few spheres of activity, including research work, laboratory services and, to a lesser degree, teaching.[14] Subsequent studies revealed that there were significant wage gaps between male and female scientists and engineers and very few women in management.[15] In 1964, Royce noted that girls with a "mechanical attitude" and a bent for mathematics and science were often steered towards other fields of study and work that seemed "less demanding" or were regarded as "more suited to women." In her view, to "exclude gifted women with scientific interests from such exciting and creative fields is to bring grave loss, not only to them but to the nation, and even the world."[16]

During the 1970s and early 1980s, the federal government and many of the provinces adopted initiatives to generate enthusiasm and support for the entry and retention of girls in nontraditional fields. They targeted schools because they believed that education was the source of the problem of the underrepresentation of women in science and engineering. The 1975 International Women's Year's "Why Not?" campaign drew the attention of schoolteachers and students to the few women in nontraditional occupations. In 1983, the National Film Board profiled successful Canadian women engineers in the documentary *I Want to Be an Engineer*, which became a major promotional and educational tool for advocates of women in engineering.[17]

In 1981, the Science Council of Canada, a body established in 1966 to advise the federal government on science and technology policy, organized a national workshop to discuss the low participation of girls in high school math and science. The majority of participants were women, mainly academics, educators, and civil servants from all levels of government. One important attendee, Dormer Ellis, was a leading advocate for women in engineering. Ellis had graduated with a degree in engineering physics from the University of Toronto in 1948. After working in industry and teaching, she obtained a doctorate in education and became a faculty member at the Ontario Institute for Studies in Education in the 1960s.[18] In her comments, published in the conference report titled *Who Turns the Wheel?*, Ellis underlined the importance of parental encouragement and the need for female role models. Rose Sheinin, a biology professor at the University of Toronto, delivered the keynote address, in which she decried that young women still believed that achievement in the world of science was incompatible with their prescribed feminine roles as wives and mothers.[19] Workshop participants pointed out that Canada lagged behind countries such as England and the United States. All these discussions prompted the council to publish a statement of concern the following year. The statement called attention to the serious social, political, and economic consequences of the low number of female students in science, mathematics, and technology.[20]

The Changing Profile of Women Engineers

These measures, combined with the growing influence of the women's movement and the removal of the more blatant legal and administrative barriers to women's access to employment opportunities, began to have an impact: the proportion of bachelor's degrees granted to women in engineering and the applied fields increased from 3 percent in 1975 to 13 percent in 1989. The number of women obtaining graduate degrees remained small, but the number of women earning a master's degree rose from 37 to 196, and the number of women earning doctoral degrees increased from 9 to 19 in the same time period.[21] The influx of women into engineering schools had an important impact on the composition of the profession: before the 1970s, the majority of female engineers in Canada had studied engineering before immigrating to Canada, mainly from Eastern Europe.[22] In the early 1980s, Dormer Ellis undertook a nationwide survey of over a thousand registered professional women engineers: by then, 67 percent of the nine hundred women who completed the questionnaire had been educated in Canada. Because of their recent entry into the profession, most respondents were still young: the median estimated age of the Canadian-educated cohort was thirty. More than 86 percent were married, two-thirds of them to engineers, and almost half had children. Three-quarters of the respondents reported that having a family had not interrupted their careers and that they had been continuously employed since becoming engineers. Over 90 percent of the respondents claimed that they enjoyed an egalitarian marriage, which meant that their husbands supported their career and shared family responsibilities. About a third reported that they had full-time domestic help at home when there was an infant, while others relied on relatives or part-time employees.[23]

In comparison to the women in the domestic services sector that Catherine Charron discusses in her contribution to this volume, women engineers were a "favoured group."[24] On the other hand, Ellis's survey shed light on the challenging and fast-paced lifestyles being led by the generation who had entered engineering during the 1970s. Many of her young respondents combined marriage and motherhood with the pursuit of full-time careers in a male-dominated workplace. Their comments on sharing domestic responsibilities with their spouses, relatives, or paid help show us how they managed, but none of the respondents mentioned accommodations or supports provided by their employers. In short, these women were expected to succeed "in a man's world," according to its established rules, which confined marriage and motherhood to the private domain.

There were, however, indications that women engineers were starting to question some of the practices and policies developed by the homogenous male engineering population. According to Dormer Ellis, the impressive response rate to her survey was a clear sign that women engineers felt the need "to record details about themselves and to share their experiences in an occupation that is so non-traditional for women."[25] In fact, several respondents expressed interest in joining or participating in separate women's associations.[26]

Building the Institutional Foundations of Women's Activism in Engineering

Unlike the United Kingdom and the United States, Canada had no established associations for women engineers. Some British-born women were members of the Women's Engineering Society (WES), established in 1919. The WES also welcomed Canadian-born engineers such as Dormer Ellis. So did the American Society of Women Engineers (SWE), founded in 1950, whose Canadian members included Ellis and MacGill. The scarcity of women engineers in Canada certainly made organizing difficult in the 1950s and 1960s. According to Dormer Ellis, another contributing factor was the resistance or disinterest of immigrant practitioners from Eastern European countries, where women already made up a substantial proportion of the profession and where separate women's associations did not exist at the time.[27] It could also be, as Margaret Rossiter suggests with respect to the American profession, that these foreign-born women were reluctant to appear critical of the country that had welcomed them and of Canadian institutions that had allowed them to succeed in the engineering profession.[28]

During the 1970s and 1980s, women engineers in Canada began to organize under a new generation of leaders who were young and who usually combined a successful professional life with marriage and motherhood. Many also held graduate degrees. Montreal-born Claudette MacKay-Lassonde, a top-level manager at Hydro-Ontario, was one of the most influential leaders. In 1977, at the age of twenty-nine, she founded Women in Science and Engineering/Femmes en Science et en Ingénierie (WISE). Bringing together women scientists and engineers was a logical move because of the small number of engineering practitioners at the time. WISE aimed to provide mutual support for women and to provide role models and mentorship to aspiring scientists and engineers. The association's bilingual name reflected Lassonde's resolve to appeal to her colleagues from both linguistic groups.[29] By the mid-1980s, WISE had attracted more than four hundred university students, academics, and practitioners and had established chapters in Ontario, Quebec, Newfoundland, and New Brunswick. Members organized career guidance sessions in high schools, talks with undergraduate female students in faculties of engineering, tours of industries, and discussion groups on topics of concern to women in the profession.[30]

The organization's expansion was propelled by another landmark initiative spearheaded by Claudette MacKay-Lassonde – the Canadian Convention of Women Engineers. The first conference was held in May 1981. Participants came from every province and included professional engineers, recent graduates from engineering schools, and engineering students. The meeting received national media attention. The *Toronto Star* reported that day care, stress on the job, and male animosity were the main concerns expressed by the delegates, who were "giving each other moral support in their battle to earn a larger share of the male-dominated profession."[31] Lassonde spoke passionately about the need for women engineers to join organizations that offered mutual support, invoking the frustration she suffered herself while breaking into the field: "Unless you've lived it, you wouldn't know how hard it is," she confessed and then explained how "every time a woman reaches a level that hasn't been broken by others, she faces resistance, and men will be mean."[32] The convention ended with a formal recommendation to make WISE a national organization. Armed with the slogan "Challenge Knows No Gender," the association's mission remained, first and foremost, to bring more women into engineering.[33]

As the press aptly put it, Claudette MacKay-Lassonde was a "powerhouse at uniting women engineers."[34] Her successful efforts to break their isolation marked the beginning of an important wave of organization that helped establish the institutional foundation for collaboration and networking among women engineers. They established a myriad of advocacy committees, support networks, and women's caucuses in universities and professional associations across the country. In April 1981, women scientists and graduate students in Toronto established the first Canadian chapter of the US-based Association for Women in Science (CAWIS).[35] That same year in Vancouver, Mary Vickers, Hilda Lei Ching, Abby Schwarz, Mary Jo Duncan, and Margaret Benston organized the Society for Canadian Women in Science and Technology (SCWIST) to promote equal opportunities for women in these fields. In 1983, the "undaunted five" hosted the first National Conference for Women in Science, Technology and Engineering, which was attended by four hundred participants, including speakers from the United States and the United Kingdom.[36] The desire for a national network of mutual support led to the formation of the Canadian Conference of Women in Science, Engineering and Technology, an organization that sought the advancement of women in these areas mainly through the coordination of conferences hosted by local chapters of WISE and CAWIS. In 1992, delegates from WISE, CAWIS, SCWIST, and five other advocacy groups joined forces in the Canadian Coalition of Women in Engineering, Science, Trades and Technology (CCWESTT). With the creation of CCWESTT, activists could now rely on a central organization that would function as a lobby group with the government, industry, and the media.[37]

The movement's considerable growth in little over a decade is testimony to the skills and high profile of its leadership during these formative years. Leaders such as Micheline Bouchard, a rising executive at Hydro-Québec, and Claudette MacKay-Lassonde had, by this time, achieved considerable professional success and were elected, respectively, president of the Ordre des Ingénieurs du Québec and the Professional Engineers of Ontario, the two largest and most influential professional engineering regulatory bodies in the country. Their lobbying efforts had a major impact on the profession: the Canadian Council of Professional Engineers (CCPE), which acted as the national voice of the provincial engineering bodies, and the National Council of Deans of Engineering and Applied Sciences each joined their efforts to bring women engineers together and to attract more women to the profession.[38]

Links with the Women's Movement

As a leading representative of the new generation of engineering activists, MacKay-Lassonde would later credit the women's movement for creating "an awareness of women's ability to achieve," which helped increase the number of women in engineering and technology and allowed them to advance in the field.[39] Their emphasis on removing barriers to equality was consistent with the goals of liberal feminism as well as the government's agenda for promoting women's equality, which prioritized promoting women's participation in the paid workforce even though it did not accept feminist arguments about the need to provide services, such as day care, that enabled women to do so.

A fundamental goal of this group of activists was changing the assumption that science and engineering were male professions. Female engineers were eager to prove that engineering was compatible with femininity and motherhood. During the 1981 convention of women engineers, Lassonde insisted that the persistent "hard-hat image" of the profession had to be dispelled, along with the "nonsensical myth" that engineering was a "very masculine and very demanding job."[40] On the other hand, many women engineers believed that they had to behave "like one of the boys" to succeed in the profession and were therefore reluctant to be identified as "woman engineers."[41] Promoting the achievements of successful female engineers such as Claudette MacKay Lassonde, Micheline Bouchard, and Danielle Zaikoff, the first woman president of the Canadian Council of Professional Engineers, was one way to reconcile these tensions. For Ellis, these activists were, indeed, "role models *par excellence*" because they successfully combined their careers with two symbols of femininity: marriage and motherhood.[42] Indeed, Zaikoff and her colleagues accepted the super-woman image; "The more things you have to do, the more you can do!" declared Zaikoff in 1975.[43] But female engineers were becoming increasingly concerned with managing the stress that came from trying to balance professional lives with home life. Ursula Franklin, a University of Toronto engineering professor, explained to the *Globe and Mail* that one of the key goals of the newly formed CAWIS was to challenge the notion that women needed to act as "superwomen" to succeed.[44] In this, engineers shared a great deal with the women's movement, which was critical of the fact that women's new roles in the paid workforce did not diminish their duties at home.[45]

The burst of organizational growth triggered by the creation of WISE in the late 1970s coincided with the energized activism of the Canadian women's movement. Like grassroots feminist groups, newly formed women engineer associations benefitted from the financial support of the Secretary of State's Women's Program.[46] Since one of its goals was to break traditional female job ghettos, NAC also kept abreast of the growing activism of women scientists and engineers, notably through CAWIS, which became one of its institutional members.[47]

Despite their shared goal of equality in the workforce, most advocates of women in engineering were not inclined to identify themselves as feminists. One strategic reason for maintaining a distance from feminism was to secure the support of the men in their profession, most of whom continued to identify with the masculine culture that permeated faculties of engineering and the engineering workplace. Moreover, activists had to consider the views of the rank-and-file members they hoped to recruit in their new organizations; indeed, one of the startling findings of Ellis's survey was the number of uninvited comments from women who were afraid to be labelled as feminists. Interestingly, they tended to equate feminism with drawing attention to one's sex. "Why rock the boat by making a big deal about being female?" asked one of them.[48] Such views need to be interpreted in the light of responses to the question concerning gender-based discrimination in the workplace, as more than half of the respondents claimed that they had not experienced any kind of discrimination. The more serious cases that were reported had occurred several years prior to the survey, while there were no recent instances of institutional discrimination. Ellis interpreted these responses as the positive result of various antidiscrimination and antisexism laws and regulations adopted during the 1970s.[49] The young generation of women engineers who responded to Ellis's survey thus seemed to share an optimistic view that laws and regulations had eliminated gender discrimination in their workplace. On the other hand, the strong organizational drive of the 1980s suggests that more and more women engineers realized that these interventions were not enough to combat bias and prejudice against women.

The feminist critiques of technology that emerged in the 1980s were bound to create a rift between NAC and the women engineers' organizations. Inspired by feminist theory that emphasized the differences between men and women, feminist scholars argued that science itself was not gender neutral and that technology was an instrument of patriarchal domination. Feminine values such as empathy, cooperation, subjectivity, and caring had been disregarded in the design of many technologies. They also pointed to the exclusion of women from engineering and the profession's control by white, middle-class men.[50] At the same time, influenced by Carol Gilligan's claim that women speak with a different voice, social theorists began to suggest that women might "think" and "do" engineering differently because of their distinctive "feminine" values and priorities. In their view, gender equality could only be achieved by envisaging a "feminist engineering" that would deeply transform the content, culture, and practices of the profession.[51] Historian Pamela Mack has demonstrated that women engineers in the United States were unreceptive to the critiques of technology and engineering developed by feminist scholars. Mack contends that female engineers were reluctant to accept that there were "essential differences" between themselves and their male colleagues, even though the increasing number of women in the profession was due to laws and incentives adopted to promote equal opportunities for women.[52] In Canada, NAC was the driving force in the emergence of feminist critiques of technology. NAC was involved in the national debate over the potentially adverse effects of office automation on the health and jobs of women engaged in clerical and secretarial work. In 1982, negative views of modern technology received widespread press coverage as a result of a conference on women and the impact of technology, organized by NAC and other feminist organizations, with the support of the federal government.[53]

Ursula Franklin and Margaret Lowe Benston were among the most prominent Canadian feminist critics of technology. A member of the Canadian Voice of Women, Franklin viewed the achievement of women's equality as a precondition to the achievement of a peaceful and just society.[54] But this view was also firmly grounded in her experience as a woman academic working in a domain monopolized by men and masculine values. Franklin decried the continuing male dominance of the field; girls, she insisted, would be unable to succeed until the sexism and the chilly climate that impregnated engineering schools and workplaces were eradicated.[55] In 1985, she published a groundbreaking feminist analysis of the technological order; firmly grounded in difference feminism, she argued that the input of women and the inclusion of feminist approaches would foster technologies that put more emphasis on moral values and less on economic interests.[56] Another seminal contribution was made by one of Franklin's close colleagues, Margaret Benston, professor in women's studies and computer science at Simon Fraser University. Before her untimely death in 1991, Benston produced a sophisticated feminist critique of science and technology largely informed by her influential theoretical contributions to Marxist feminism.[57]

Since Franklin and Benston belonged to a small group of academic women scientists and engineers linked to the emerging interdisciplinary field of women's studies, the wider community of women engineers probably knew little of their work. Even so, there is evidence that suggests that feminist critiques of the natural and physical sciences were convincing some female university students to dismiss science and engineering as "antiwoman" and "antifeminist."[58] The full impact of the tensions that ensued between academic feminists and women scientists and engineers remains to be explored in the Canadian context.

Fulfilling the "Manpower" Needs of the Canadian State

The ambiguous links between the women's movement and women engineers also stemmed from the relationship between advocates of women in engineering and the federal government. The political context was quite favourable to the growth of the women's movement in science and engineering. In theory, at least, the Liberal government was receptive to the idea that women should have equal employment opportunities and equal rights.[59] During the 1970s, the federal government was very concerned about the impact of rapid technological change and the skill level of the Canadian workforce. Government officials identified the underutilization of women's skills and abilities as a major obstacle to efficiency in the labour market. In 1980, Lloyd Axworthy, then minister of employment and immigration as well as the minister responsible for the status of women, declared that educating and training women would solve Canada's skilled-labour shortage.[60] He promised to strengthen the government's affirmative action programs and to introduce more effective training programs to encourage women to pursue nontraditional occupations, especially in the science and technology sectors.

Axworthy's pledge represented a strong endorsement of professional women in science and engineering and of those who advocated on their behalf.

Another key development that drew attention to the cause of female engineers was the development of a national science and technology policy in Canada. In the early 1980s, the Ministry of State for Science and Technology predicted a serious shortage of university-trained scientists and engineers. At its 1983 "Canada Tomorrow" conference, delegates discussed the threat new technologies posed to women in traditional female white- and blue-collar jobs. But contrary to feminist critiques of science, there was also strong support for the view that technology had the potential to offer higher status and more lucrative employment to women trained in science and engineering.[61]

In 1987, the federal Conservative government announced a new National Science and Technology Policy. It called for the implementation of a national system of innovation that would rely heavily on the use of science and technology research and the training and retraining of highly qualified "manpower."[62] Even though it did not adopt gender-neutral language, the state-industry-university partnership promoted by the Conservatives created several support programs designed to attract more young women to science and engineering. The Natural Sciences and Engineering Research Council (NSERC) sponsored some of the most important programs. Since the 1970s, NSERC had feared critical shortages of scientific expertise because of aging and retiring university faculty. As a result, it began to give special undergraduate research awards to young women, and it created Women Faculty Awards to encourage universities to appoint outstanding women with doctorates to faculty positions in science and engineering.[63]

In 1987, Lassonde became the first female vice president of the board of NSERC; she also became a member of the newly created National Advisory Board on Science and Technology, an organization chaired by the prime minister, Brian Mulroney.[64] Lassonde's presence within these influential federal agencies, as well as her new position at Northern Telecom, a multinational telecommunications equipment manufacturer, was bound to give more national prominence to the women in engineering movement. Indeed, she was closely associated with NSERC's most groundbreaking initiative at the time: the establishment, in May 1989, of the national NSERC/Northern Telecom Chair for Women in Science and Engineering at the University of New Brunswick. This university-based chair, the first of its kind in the world, was devoted to the recruitment and promotion of women in these fields. The women in engineering movement was thus able to take advantage of the federal government's growing concern with technological innovation and the creation of a skilled labour force. At the same time, the relationship between NAC and the state had severely deteriorated, especially after the election of the Conservative Party and NAC's prominent role in widespread opposition to specific government policies, especially free trade and the Meech Lake Accord (which is discussed in Anthony Hampton's chapter in this volume). These developments did little to increase collaboration between the women's movement and women in engineering advocates who, for their part, were called upon by the state to help raise Canada's science and technology profile in an increasingly competitive world.

Conclusion: The Montreal Massacre and the End of an Era

The pioneering era of women's activism in Canadian engineering ended abruptly on 6 December 1989 with the brutal murder of fourteen young women, twelve of them students, at Montréal's École Polytechnique. This tragedy drew attention to the barriers that women in science and engineering faced and led to a renewed and more self-reflective concern for the status of women among members of the profession. There were immediate and emotional responses from Claudette MacKay-Lassonde and Micheline Bouchard, who were both Polytechnique alumnae.[65] A few years after the tragedy, Ursula Franklin recalled, "it became possible to speak publicly about the chilly climate, about bias, about sexism, misogyny and patriarchy."[66] Indeed, leaders of the profession in the private and public sectors were confronted with increasing calls to transform the masculine environment that continued to deter women from enrolling in engineering programs in universities and pursuing careers in the field. In response, governments, industry, universities, and professional associations conducted studies to reveal the barriers preventing the full participation of women in the profession, and many initiatives were adopted to recruit and retain them. A new generation of women advocates played a leadership role in these various efforts, starting with Monique Frize, who, at the time of the Montreal Massacre, had just taken on her new role as the NSERC/Northern Telecom chair.

Similar to the friendship and professional networks examined by Catherine Gidney and Karen Balcom in this volume, the solid foundations established by Lassonde, Bouchard, and other pioneer activists proved invaluable to Frize and her colleagues as they undertook their own advocacy work in the 1990s. This largely unknown manifestation of women's activism should, in fact, be fully integrated into the history of the second-wave women's movement in Canada. It confirms the movement's diversity and dynamic character; as pointed out by Margaret Rossiter, one of its great successes was to raise the consciousness of various groups of women, including women engineers, a small group of professional women who were said to perform a "man's job." From this perspective, this chapter sheds additional light on the ways contemporary feminism has fostered change through an examination of its impact on the approaches and analyses of various professions.

In the case of engineering, the impact of feminism on women in the profession varied according to different contexts and circumstances. For advocates in the 1970s and 1980s, low numbers, lack of recognition, access to jobs, equity in the workplace, and strong gender stereotyping about men's and women's roles in society were the key issues for women engineers. Even more fundamentally, they were anxious to demonstrate that women could do engineering as well as men. The basic principles of liberal feminism thus suited their concerns at the time, although increasing attention was paid to the difficulty of reconciling professional and family responsibilities. The relationship between feminism and women engineers was also marked by ambiguity and tension. Despite the growing influence of feminist organizations in the 1980s, engineers generally tended not to acknowledge feminism's influence, and many adopted an antifeminist stance. The development of feminist critiques of technology was bound to create rifts. Finally, the federal government was mobilizing women engineers in the implementation of its Science and Technology Policy at a time when it was expressing open hostility towards the women's movement. I hope this study convinces women's historians of the need to examine more closely the personal and professional paths followed by Canadian women in science and engineering, since these investigations can help us to better understand the complexity of feminism in this country.

NOTES

I would like to acknowledge the support of SSHRC, which funded the research for this chapter. Many thanks to my research assistants – Amy Gill, Tanya Daley, Mike Thompson, Caroline d'Amours, and Anne Millar – and to my research associates, Crystal Sissons and Anabel Paulos. I am most grateful to Catherine Carstairs and Nancy Janovicek for their editorial skills, patience, and continuing support.

1 Colleen Isherwood, "Women in Engineering," *Engineering Journal* (November-December 1975): 6, 8.
2 Crystal Sissons, "Engineer and Feminist: Elsie Gregory MacGill and the Royal Commission on the Status of Women (1967–1970)," *Scientia Canadensis* 29, 2 (2006): 75–97.

3   Monique Bégin, "The Royal Commission on the Status of Women in Canada: Twenty Years Later," in *Challenging Times: The Women's Movement in Canada and the United States*, ed. Constance Backhouse and David H. Flaherty (Montreal/Kingston: McGill-Queen's University Press), 28.

4   Elsie Gregory McGill, "Women Engineers Meet a 'Corset of Victorian Prejudice,'" *Engineering Journal* (November-December 1975): 12.

5   Margaret W. Rossiter, *Women Scientists in America before Affirmative Action, 1940–1972* (Baltimore: John Hopkins University Press, 1995), 361. See also Amy Bix, "Feminism Where Men Predominate: The History of Women's Science and Engineering Education at MIT," *Women's Studies Quarterly* 28, 1–2 (2000): 24–45, and Pamela E. Mack, "What Difference Has Feminism Made to Engineering in the Twentieth Century?" in *Feminism in Twentieth-Century Science, Technology, and Medicine*, ed. Angela N.H. Creager, Elizabeth Lunbeck, and Londa Schienbinger (Chicago: University of Chicago Press, 2001), 149–68.

6   On the development of these new interdisciplinary fields in the United States, see Evelyn Hammonds and Banu Subramaniam, "A Conversation on Feminist Science Studies," *Signs: Journal of Women and Culture in Society* 28, 3 (2003): 923–44, and Angela N.H. Creager, Elizabeth Lunbeck, and Londa Schienbinger, "Introduction," in *Feminism in Twentieth-Century Science, Technology, and Medicine*, eds. Angela N.H. Creager, Elizabeth Lunbeck, and Londa Schienbinger (Chicago: University of Chicago Press, 2001), 1–19. See also Sergio Sismondo, *An Introduction to Science and Technology Studies*, 2nd ed. (Malden, MA: Wiley-Blackwell, 2010), 72–80.

7   Ruby Heap, "Writing Them into History: Canadian Women in Science and Engineering since the 1980's," in *Out of the Ivory Tower: Feminist Research for Social Change*, ed. Andrea Martinez and Meryn Stuart (Toronto: Schumach Press, 2003), 49–67, and Ruby Heap, "Women and Gender in Canadian Science, Engineering and Medicine," *Scientia Canadensis* 29, 2 (2006): 3–15. The Canadian historical scholarship on the entry and status of women in other male professions is more abundant. Monographs include R.D Gidney and W.P.J. Millar, *Professional Gentlemen: The Professions in Nineteenth-Century Ontario* (Toronto: Ontario Historical Studies/University of Toronto Press, 1994); Mary Kinnear, *In Subordination: Professional Women, 1870–1970* (Montreal/Kingston: McGill-Queen's University Press, 1995); Tracey L. Adams, *A Dentist and a Gentlemen: Gender and the Rise of Dentistry in Ontario* (Toronto: University of Toronto Press, 2000); Annemarie Adams and Peta Tancred, *"Designing Women": Gender and the Architectural Profession* (Toronto: University of Toronto Press, 2000); and Jean Brockman, *Gender in the Legal Profession: Fitting or Breaking the Mould* (Vancouver: UBC Press, 2001). The essential reference for Canadian women in science remains Marianne G. Ainley, ed., *Despite the Odds: Essays on Canadian Women in Science* (Montreal: Véhicule Press, 1990). For an overview and discussion of the literature, see Ruby Heap, Wyn Millar, and Elizabeth Smyth, eds., *Learning to Practise: Professional Education in Historical and Contemporary Perspective* (Toronto: University of Toronto Press, 2005), and Elizabeth Smyth, Sandra Acker, Paula Bourne, and Alison Prentice, eds., *Challenging Professions: Historical and Contemporary Perspectives* (Toronto: University of Toronto Press, 1999).

8

8   Judy Rebick admits that she left out several stories that defined second-wave feminism in Canada, such as "women's access to and rise in the professions" and the "significant changes" that feminists brought to the field of science. See *Ten Thousand Roses* (Toronto: Penguin Canada, 2005), xiii.
9   Dominique Clément, *Canada's Rights Revolution: Social Movements and Social Change, 1937–82* (Vancouver: UBC Press, 2008), 56–60.
10 Bégin, "The Royal Commission," 28.
11 On the NAC, see Jill Vickers, Pauline Rankin, and Christine Appelle, *Politics as If Women Mattered: A Political Analysis of the National Action Committee on the Status of Women* (Toronto: University of Toronto Press, 1993); on Canadian feminism and the Charter of Rights and Freedoms, see Lise Goteil, *Feminism, Equality Rights and the Charter of Rights and Freedoms*, Feminist Perspectives Féministes No. 16 (Ottawa: Canadian Research Institute for the Advancement of Women, 1990).
12 See Women's Bureau, *Women at Work in Canada* (Ottawa: Department of Labour, 1957), n.p.
13 Joan Sangster, *Transforming Labour: Women and Work in Post-War Canada* (Toronto: University of Toronto Press, 2010), 236–37.
14 Women's Bureau, *Women at Work in Canada*, 28. The bureau does not provide more information on these spheres of work. However, women scientists during this period tended to perform functions considered women's work; they worked as research associates and lab assistants and taught science in high schools and women's colleges. A good overview is found in Suzanne Le-May Sheffield, *Women and Science: Social Impact and Interaction* (New Brunswick: Rutgers University Press, 2006), 157–82.
15 See, for example, Women's Bureau, *Fields of Work for Women: Physical Sciences, Earth Sciences, Mathematics* (Ottawa: Department of Labour, 1964); Women's Bureau, *Report of a Round-Table Conference on the Implications of Traditional Divisions between Men's Work and Women's Work in Our Society, held March 12, 1964* (Ottawa: Department of Labour, 1964); Women's Bureau, *Women in the Labour Force: 1970 Facts and Figures* (Ottawa: Department of Labour, 1971).
16 Women's Bureau, *Fields of Work for Women*, n.p.
17 Dormer Ellis, "Educating a Growing Minority – Canadian Women Engineers," *Interchange* 17, 4 (1986): 55.
18 Dormer Ellis, "Times Have Changed" (address presented at the Business and Professional Women's Club Canada convention, 9 June 2010, Horseshoe Valley, Ontario), http://www.bpwtoronto.com/hp_15.html. Her strong commitment to the cause of women engineers led to several awards, including the Woman of Distinction Award from the YWCA of Metropolitan Toronto (1983) and the Elsie Gregory McGill Award from PBW Canada (1988). Ellis was also the first woman to be made a fellow of the Engineering Institute of Canada (1987) and the only Canadian among the pioneers honoured by the International Congress of Women Engineers and Scientists in 2002.
19 Science Council of Canada, *Who Turns the Wheel?* (Ottawa: Science Council of Canada, 1981), 11.

20 Science Council of Canada, "The Science Education of Women in Canada: A Statement of Concern," Ottawa, January 1982.
21 University and College Affairs Branch, *Women in Science and Engineering*, vol. 1, *Universities* (Ottawa: Industry, Science and Technology Canada, 1991), 9, 13, 39, 41.
22 Dormer Ellis, *These Women Are Engineers: Summary Report of a Questionnaire Survey for the 2nd Convention of Women Engineers of Canada* (Ottawa: Canadian Council of Professional Engineers, 1983), 2. Ellis refers to a 1971 survey that identified only 101 women engineers in Canada, the majority of whom had been trained outside of the country.
23 Ibid., 57–58.
24 McGill, "Women Engineers Meet a 'Corset of Victorian Prejudice,'" 12.
25 Ellis, "Educating a Growing Minority," 58.
26 Ellis, *These Women Are Engineers*, 39.
27 Ibid., 38.
28 Rossiter, *Women Scientists in America*, 381.
29 No separate francophone women's association was created during this period. L'Association de la francophonie à propos des femmes en science, technologies, ingénierie et mathématiques (AFFESTIM), based in Quebec, was formed in 2003.
30 WISE Ottawa, "WISE's History," WISE website (accessed on 25 October 2005).
31 "Women Engineers Build on Moral Support," *Toronto Star*, 5 May 1981, 1.
32 Ibid.
33 Ibid.; "Women Engineers Form Association," *Globe and Mail*, 5 May 1981, 22; Dormer Ellis, "Professional Engineering, an Excellent Career Choice for a Woman," *Engineering Digest* 32 (November 1986): 8.
34 "Women Engineers Build on Moral Support," 1.
35 "New Group for Women Scientists," *Globe and Mail*, 11 April 1981, 4.
36 SCWIST, "Our History," retrieved from http://www.scwist.ca/main/about/about-us; Hilda Lei Ching, "Concluding Remarks," *Proceedings of the First National Conference for Women in Science, Engineering and Technology, May 20–22 1983* (Vancouver: SCWIST, n.d.), 162.
37 On the creation of CCWESTT, see http://www.ccwestt.org/. The first president of CCWESTT was Susan Best, one of the directors of the Toronto-based Women Inventors Project (WIP) and one of the new organization's founding members.
38 Ellis, *These Women Are Engineers*, iii; "What Is NCDEAS?" *ED*, 29 (September 1983): 6.
39 Christine Lang, "The Evolution of Women in Engineering: Participation and Acceptance," *Engineering Digest* (September-October 1997): 31.
40 "Women Engineers Build on Moral Support," *Toronto Star*, 5 May 1981, 1.
41 Monique Frize reflects on this dilemma, which she faced herself as a young woman engineer in the 1960s. See Frize, *The Bold and the Brave: A History of Women in Science and Engineering* (Ottawa: University of Ottawa Press, 2009), 246.
42 Ellis, "Educating a Growing Minority," 55.
43 Isherwood, "Women in Engineering," 9.
44 "New Group for Women Scientists," *Globe and Mail*, 11 April 1981.

45 Annis May Timpson, *Driven Apart: Women's Employment Equality and Child Care in Canadian Public Policy* (Vancouver: UBC Press, 2001).

46 As indicated by funding reports of the Women's Program, located in the NAC Fonds at the Canadian Women's Movement Archives, University of Ottawa Archives and Special Collections (CWMA).

47 NAC's interest in the activism of women scientists and engineers is evident in several press clippings and memos in the NAC Fonds. For a list of NAC members in the 1980s, see Vickers et al., *Politics as If Women Mattered*, 313.

48 Ellis, *These Women Are Engineers*, 41.

49 Ibid., 59, 53.

50 A good overview of liberal feminism and difference feminism with respect to gender and technology and engineering can be found in Judy Wajcman, *TechnoFeminism* (Cambridge: Polity, 2004), 10–31.

51 Mack, "What Difference Has Feminism Made," 151–54; see also Londa Schienbinger, *Has Feminism Changed Science?* (Cambridge, MA: Harvard University Press, 1999), 4–5.

52 Mack, "What Difference Has Feminism Made," 155–61.

53 Jacqueline Pelletier, ed., *"The Future Is Now": Women and the Impact of Microtechnology* (Ottawa: Women and Technology Committee, 1983).

54 Ursula Franklin, *The Ursula Franklin Reader* (Toronto: Between the Lines, 2006), 9.

55 Ibid., 11–15.

56 Ursula Franklin, *Will Women Change Technology or Will Technology Change Women?* (Ottawa: Canadian Research Institute for the Advancement of Women, 1985).

57 Ellen Balka, " Margaret Lowe Benston, 1937–1991," *Labour/Le Travail* 28 (Fall 1991): 11–13. In 1993, the feminist journal *Canadian Women's Studies* published a special issue devoted to her legacy as a feminist scholar and activist.

58 This was reported in a survey of university female students conducted in Toronto by Georgina Feldberg in the late 1980s. See Rachelle Sender Beauchamp and Georgina Feldberg, *Girls and Women in Medicine, Math, Science, Engineering and Technology* (Toronto: Ontario Advisory Council on Women's Issues, 1991), 41–43.

59 See Timpson, *Driven Apart*, chaps. 3–6.

60 Minister of Employment and Immigration, 7 July 1981, University of Ottawa Archives, NAC Fonds, Box 846.

61 See *Canada Tomorrow Conference, November 6–9, 1983: Proceedings* (Ottawa: Ministry of State, Science and Technology, 1984).

62 Daniel Brassard, "Science and Technology: The New Federal Policy," Library of Parliament, Background Paper 414E, Ottawa, April 1996.

63 Frize, *The Bold and the Brave*, 182–83.

64 See http://archives.concordia.ca/timeline/histories/lassonde.

65 Claudette Mackay-Lassonde immediately mobilized the community of engineers across Canada, calling for measures to incite girls to enter the profession. In 1990, with the support of the Canadian Council of Professional Engineers and of the Association des étudiants de Polytechnique, she spearheaded the creation of the Canadian Engineering Memorial Foundation, which awards scholarships to outstanding female engineering students at the undergraduate and graduate levels. For her part, Micheline Bouchard urged Quebec women engineers, the Ordre des Ingénieurs du

Québec, and the Association des étudiants de Polytechnique to attend the funeral and to wear the wife scarf, symbol of the fight to end violence against women. See Micheline Bouchard, "Rien n'est jamais acquis," in *Polytechnique, 6 décembre,* ed. Louise Malette and Marie Chalouh (Montreal: Éditions du remue-ménage, 1990), 170–71.

66 Franklin, "Looking Forward, Looking Back," *The Ursula Franklin Reader,* 345.

12

Ad Hoc Activism
Feminist Citizens Respond to the Meech Lake Accord in New Brunswick

ANTHONY S.C. HAMPTON

From 1987 through 1990, a group of determined citizens in New Brunswick worked against the ratification of the Meech Lake Accord by their provincial government. The New Brunswick Ad Hoc Committee on the Constitution (NBAHCC) formed the hub of a wheel of anti-Meech Lake activism throughout the province. Informally led by four "ring leaders" in Fredericton, the committee took action by organizing letter-writing campaigns, distributing information, and holding a major conference. Members drew on their experience and personal connections to raise awareness and pressure the government. Many were feminists who had worked on equality-seeking campaigns addressing a broad range of issues. The NBAHCC had a unique role among groups opposed to Meech Lake. It informed citizen's groups around New Brunswick about the impact that the accord would have on their lives and connected these local groups to one another as well as to the national campaign. It also played a crucial role in convincing the provincial legislature to delay the accord, which ultimately led to the accord's unravelling.

Using the records of the NBAHCC and the oral histories of key organizers and government officials, I examine two under-researched historiographical areas: the response of citizens, in particular New Brunswickers, to the accord, and the history of second-wave feminism in New Brunswick.[1] This chapter draws three broad conclusions. First, there was a profound difference in constitutional understanding between citizens and those in the government who formed the constitutional elite.[2] Second, the distinctive structure and actions of the NBAHCC, as well as its philosophical outlook, was a product of second-wave feminism. Third, the actions of the NBAHCC and other citizens' groups played an important role in the collapse of the accord, an event that continues to have a profound effect on constitution making and the political culture of Canada.

The Constitution Amendment, 1987, more commonly known as the Meech Lake Accord, was an effort to persuade the province of Quebec to sign on to the 1981 constitutional agreement, which had patriated the constitution and added the Charter of Rights and Freedoms, with what Prime Minister Brian Mulroney termed "honour and enthusiasm."[3] The patriation settlement of 1981–82 enshrined a liberal conception of individual rights and freedoms, a vision of Canada championed by Prime Minister Pierre Elliott Trudeau, into Canada's most important law.[4] This view was one that appealed to the core members of the NBAHCC,[5] and helps explain why the group was at odds with the communitarian thrust of the Meech Lake Accord, designed to "protect and promote" the culture of francophone Québécois.[6] Many opponents of the accord, particularly feminists, argued that it would created a dangerous hierarchy of rights within the Constitution.

Informal and secretive negotiations on the accord were held throughout 1986. Canadians who opposed the accord objected to this secretive process. The discussions were based on five minimum conditions outlined by the Quebec government: recognition of Quebec as a "distinct society," the entrenchment of the province's expanded role in immigration, a formal limit on federal spending power, the recognition of a Quebec constitutional veto, and Quebec's participation in the nomination of Supreme Court judges.

The first ministers met at Wilson House on the shores of Meech Lake at the invitation of Brian Mulroney on 30 April 1987. The biggest initial stumbling block was the determination of virtually every premier to adhere to the principle of equality of the provinces, as entrenched in the amending formula adopted with the 1981 compromise. Mulroney had a solution: anything he offered to Quebec, he offered to every other province. The only exception was Quebec's call for formal recognition that it was not "une province comme les autres" – a condition that Mulroney addressed with the distinct society clause. With the federal government willing to offer so much, the provinces soon fell into general agreement.

The political consensus reached at Meech Lake was finalized at what was expected to be a brief follow-up meeting on 3 June 1987 at the Langevin

Block of Parliament Hill. The Langevin meeting turned into an all-night bargaining session, during which Mulroney worked feverishly to persuade Manitoba's premier, Howard Pawley, and Ontario's premier, David Peterson, to overcome their reservations. As the only New Democrat at the table, Pawley feared that limitations on federal spending would make future shared-cost social programs difficult – a concern shared by feminists, including members of the NBAHCC, during the ratification debate.[7] Peterson, as the leader of Canada's most multicultural province, worried about the effect the distinct society clause would have on those Canadians whose origins were not British or French.[8] At five o'clock in the morning, the horizon brightening over Quebec, the first ministers emerged, having agreed to a legal text to match their political consensus. When the Quebec National Assembly ratified the accord on 23 June 1987 and the clock started ticking on the accord's three-year ratification window for the remaining provinces, politicians and the press concluded it would be smooth sailing for the proponents of Canada's latest constitutional amendment.[9]

Before the Langevin text had even been negotiated, Pierre Elliott Trudeau fired the first major salvo against it. His criticism was a major catalyst in moving the NBAHCC to act. Published simultaneously in *La Presse* and the *Toronto Star* on 27 May 1987, the former prime minister's essay was a scathing attack on the Meech Lake Accord. Trudeau sought to explain his vision of the 1981 constitutional settlement, defend what he saw as an attack on the powers of the federal government, and impugn the motives of the first ministers, particularly Brian Mulroney, whom he labelled "a weakling," "wimp," and "sly fox."[10] As much as Trudeau's intervention rattled the premiers at the Langevin meeting, it was not his essay's effect on the constitutional elite that had the greatest importance: it was the way in which those who admired Trudeau politically were roused by his words to oppose the accord.

The four New Brunswickers who were at the core of the Fredericton chapter of the NBAHCC brought a history of involvement in political issues with them to their fight against the Meech Lake Accord. C. Anne Crocker, the law librarian at the University of New Brunswick, had a long history of engagement in local feminist causes. Crocker noted that her involvement in feminist causes led her to question the accord, "I had been involved for a long time with the feminist movement – equality-seeking activities – and it appeared to me that after the success of the Charter of Rights and Freedoms that this Meech Lake Accord had the potential ... to throw a significant spanner into those works."[11] Raised bilingually in Moncton, she described herself politically as "a Trudeau Liberal." Gayle MacDonald, originally from Cape

Breton and also bilingual, was a PhD candidate in sociology at the University of New Brunswick. She was also active in feminist causes, including founding the New Brunswick chapter of the Women's Legal Education and Action Fund (LEAF).[12] Max Wolfe moved to Jemseg, New Brunswick, from Alberta in 1981. Wolfe had been heavily involved in politics since his student days in his native Glasgow. After immigrating to Canada, he ran for the New Democratic Party, but he was also a fan of Trudeau.[13] The fourth core member of the committee, Elaine Wright, was a long-standing and active member of the Liberal Party at both the federal and provincial levels.[14] MacDonald recalled how useful Wright's connections were: "Elaine could get a message to the premier in a day. She'd done tons of political campaigns. And she knew him personally."[15] Although many other people joined the group, it was these four individuals who formed a stable core, delegating work and building bridges with other organizations. The group was informal, and membership lists were not kept, so it is difficult to know exactly who was active in the group at any given time. The group followed the ad hoc committee model, borrowed from various campaigns launched by second-wave feminists.

Although the ad hoc committee was a ubiquitous part of second-wave feminism in Canada, there has been little structural analysis of it as a model of organization. Ad hoc committees began to spring up to lobby the government in the early 1960s.[16] The groups who used the model tended to share nonhierarchical organizational features such as fluid membership without fees, executives, bylaws, incorporation, or offices. Although there were usually several dedicated individuals at the core of ad hoc committees, these individuals did not have formal titles. Other members drifted in and out of the group, depending on interest and their ability to contribute, but they also served as bridges to other organizations. Anne Crocker explained that ad hoc committees "would just spring up like mushrooms."[17] Even the umbrella organization for women's groups in Canada, the National Advisory Council on the Status of Women (NAC), grew out of a 1972 conference in Toronto arranged by the National Ad Hoc Committee on the Status of Women.[18] Ad hoc committees either dispersed once their goals were accomplished or, in the case of NAC, took on a more formal structure.

Following the publication of the *Report of the Royal Commission on the Status of Women,* in 1970, women in New Brunswick began organizing to lobby for the implementation of its recommendations. The Fredericton Ad Hoc Committee on Women's Issues worked for the establishment of the New Brunswick Advisory Council on the Status of Women, which was created in 1975. When its first members were finally named in 1977, after a great deal of lobbying, Crocker became vice chairwoman.[19] During this same period, organizations serving women's needs proliferated in the province, including transition houses for women victimized by domestic violence in Moncton, Saint John, and Fredericton and a rape crisis centre that opened in Fredericton in 1975.[20] The Fredericton ad hoc group re-formed in 1977 to support Tobique women, who were then occupying the band office on the Tobique Reserve.[21] For feminists in the Fredericton area, as elsewhere, the ad hoc model proved to be a successful way to organize around specific issues.

The most noted ad hoc organization emerged as part of the "taking of twenty-eight" episode during the patriation of the Constitution. *Twenty-eight* refers to section 28 of the Charter of Rights and Freedoms, which guarantees equality of the sexes, notwithstanding anything else in the Charter. An event that has attained a highly symbolic status in feminist Canadian history, the taking of twenty-eight was precipitated in January 1981 by a decision by the minister responsible for the status of women, Lloyd Axworthy, to cancel a conference on women and the Constitution that had been organized by the Canadian Advisory Council on the Status of Women.[22] In response, a group of women in Ottawa and Toronto who were determined to go ahead with the conference independent of Status of Women Canada and the advisory council formed the Ad Hoc Committee of Canadian Women on the Constitution. Drawing on their various networks, the women organized a national conference attended by over 1,300 women.[23] Although sex equality had achieved some protection under section 15 of the proposed Charter, the greatest impact of the conference was a call for an additional clause that could not be limited by anything else.[24] This earlier action influenced the political strategies of the NBAHCC.

Once the attendees left Ottawa, they also mobilized to press the government for the inclusion of section 28 in the Charter. This network proved its strength again following the final first ministers' bargaining session in November 1981. At the time, Prime Minister Trudeau announced that section 28 would be subject to the notwithstanding clause (section 33).[25] Although the federal government quickly reversed its position, the lobbying network established by the Ad Hoc Committee of Canadian Women on the Constitution quickly sprang into action, forcing the provincial governments that had agreed to the terms to change their position. Following a tsunami of telegrams, letters, and telephone calls from women, the reversal was secured in fewer than ten days.[26]

The taking of twenty-eight was only one side of the torrent of public input the federal government allowed into the constitutional process, largely through the Special Joint Committee of the House of Commons and Senate on the Constitution of Canada, which heard suggestions and criticisms of the proposed Charter.[27] Political scientist Alan Cairns argues that the process and the Charter itself changed the way many Canadians viewed their Constitution. The consultations gave many a sense of ownership over the Charter "by defining [Canadians] as bearers of rights, as well as by according specific constitutional recognition to women, aboriginals, official-language minority populations, ethnic groups ... and to those social categories explicitly listed in the equality rights [section 15] of the Charter."[28] This process stood at odds with the traditional method of constitutional negotiation: executive federalism. As with the negotiation of the Meech Lake Accord, executive federalism consists of the eleven first ministers negotiating exclusively with one another, sometimes with the aid of senior officials. Despite the participation of citizens in the Charter process, it was through this process that the remainder of the patriation of the Constitution was ultimately negotiated.

Although Canadians were included in discussions about the Charter, giving many of the groups that achieved recognition a sense of ownership over the document, they were not included in the negotiation of the amending formula and changes to the functioning of Canadian federalism. Cairns argues that this led to a bifurcation in constitutional consciousness in Canada, with the governing elite on one side and citizens on the other. He argues that "the constitutional compromise of 1982 is, accordingly, unstable, as government domination of the amending process is considered illegitimate by many Canadians."[29] Donald Dennison, New Brunswick's assistant deputy minister and, later, deputy minister of intergovernmental affairs during the constitutional negotiations, reflects this division in his own thinking: "I don't think ... that 1981 was any magic period of public involvement."[30] This statement stands in stark contrast to accounts of the taking of twenty-eight.[31] Although those who participated in the negotiation of the Meech Lake Accord saw executive federalism as a legitimate form of constitutional reform, many citizens took offence, not just to the proposed changes in the accord but also to the process. As Gayle MacDonald noted in 1989 during the committee's appearance before a group of MLAs studying the accord, "*The* significant flaw is the lack of consultation with people ... The process and the lack of input ... we find insulting to Canadians."[32] The accord, presented as a fait accompli after negotiation through executive federalism, angered those Charter Canadians included in the 1981–82 settlement.

Although their activist pedigree suggests the ad hocers would have launched a spirited campaign against the accord regardless of where they lived, their place in New Brunswick catapulted them into a position of great importance in the citizen-level fight against the accord. The shift came on 13 October 1987, when an election swept Richard B. Hatfield's Progressive Conservatives out of office and Frank McKenna's Liberals into every seat in the provincial legislature. Apart from a long string of scandals and the general disdain for a government that had enjoyed seventeen years in power, another factor in McKenna's stunning victory was his opposition to the Meech Lake Accord. Jane Barry, a former Liberal MLA and co-chair of the New Brunswick legislative committee that examined the accord, recalled that the accord had come up frequently during the election.[33] McKenna's stance appealed to Trudeau Liberals, concerned francophone New Brunswickers, and francophobic anglophone voters. To the consternation of many proponents of the accord, Hatfield had failed to ratify the accord before calling the election.[34] McKenna, appearing before the federal committee that briefly examined the accord in the summer of 1987, explained his concerns about several aspects of Meech Lake, particularly its potential to weaken the rights of francophone Canadians outside Quebec.[35] Given the consensus reached by all the other provincial governments, his election offered a glimmer of hope to those across the country who opposed the accord.[36]

Among the hopeful, and determined, were members of the recently formed NBAHCC. Although the very nature of ad hoc committees makes their precise origins hard to identify, in the case of the NBAHCC, the idea of forming a group took shape over the summer of 1987 – likely during conversations between Crocker, MacDonald, and Wright. As Crocker recalled, the ad hoc structure seemed the natural route to take: "We weren't interested in spending a whole lot of time thinking up a fancy name ... and we weren't really an organized group. We were women who knew each other ... and if something came up that one of us or half a dozen of us felt needed to be addressed, then we would just fire up the telephone."[37] The committee did not have a long-term strategy or specific goals but instead identified two tasks: recruiting and consciousness raising.[38] MacDonald recalled, "When we started out, we didn't really think about where we were headed, any more than ... we thought this thing [had] to be stopped and people [had] to be educated. But it was a juggernaut."[39]

The first public meeting of the group took place the evening of 28 September 1987 in the St. John Room of the Beaverbrook Hotel in Fredericton. MacDonald recalled that "hundreds showed up at the main ballroom, and the media was all over the place."[40] Similar to the way the Ad Hoc Committee of Canadian Women on the Constitution built a powerful lobbying force from the attendees at their Ottawa conference in 1981, the NBAHCC used the contact list from their Fredericton meeting, which included seventy-five people in the capital region alone. Throughout late 1987, chapters sprang up in Moncton, Saint John, and Shippagan and organized information meetings in these cities.[41] The committee's strength did not arise out of local chapters but from the porous nature of the organization. This fluidity allowed committee members to easily share information with other organizations to which they belonged. The NBAHCC also had more formal relations with other groups – for example, Crocker addressed the Gagetown Rotary in October 1988. The invitation had come because Max Wolfe was active in the local community in the area. Along with Wright's political connections to the Liberal Party and Crocker's and MacDonald's connections to women's organizations and the academic community in Fredericton, the group's core members were well poised to build a network of individuals and groups with anti-Meech Lake sentiments.

Outside the province, other ad hoc committees worked against the accord. Second to the NBAHCC, the revived Ad Hoc Committee of Canadian Women on the Constitution, based in Toronto, was the most active. The two groups were independent of each other, but they formed part of a national network of ad hoc committees with roots in almost every province. Until the election of Clyde Wells as premier of Newfoundland in April 1989, Frank McKenna was the only premier to have publicly demanded changes to the accord. New Brunswick was, therefore, the first important battleground for opponents of Meech Lake. MacDonald recalled how the other ad hoc groups gave the NBAHCC a lot of attention: "They said, 'If it's going to be stopped, it could be in New Brunswick' ... So there was a little bit of – I wouldn't call it pressure – it felt more like support."[42] The ad hoc committees did work in concert, holding a press conference in Ottawa and courting media attention.[43] The NBAHCC and the Ad Hoc Committee of Canadian Women on the Constitution were the focus of a Canadian Broadcasting Corporation (CBC) radio documentary about feminist opposition to the accord.[44] Despite these important connections, the NBAHCC always operated independently, not as a chapter of its central Canadian allies.

The CBC radio broadcast occurred on the day of the NBAHCC's most intensive exercise in consciousness raising. On 17 April 1988, the fifth anniversary of royal assent of the Constitution Act, 1982, the group held a major conference in Moncton called "We Can Afford a Better Accord."[45] The conference allowed the group to educate New Brunswickers and expand their network for future efforts, such as letter-writing campaigns. The event also drew a new individual into the group who would quickly become one of its core members: Max Wolfe.

Wolfe had had little exposure to the women's movement before he became involved with the NBAHCC, and he was quickly impressed by the committee's organization and dedication: "[I saw the] Ad Hoc Committee [in action, and] I thought, my God, these guys are bright, they're capable, they're competent, they're effective ... It was a surprise, in all sexist honesty."[46] It is worth noting that Wolfe's reasons for opposing the accord were unlike those of the other core members of the group. While Crocker and MacDonald were motivated by feminist concerns, Wolfe's activism was rooted in his conception of federalism and his place on the left side of the political spectrum.[47] Wolfe's attitude towards the women's movement was transformed through his participation in the NBAHCC. "I never had much time for the women's movement, to be perfectly honest ... The Meech Lake experience made me realize why the women's movement can be very powerful and very effective. I think I gained a lot of respect ... as a result."[48] In addition to building the group's profile provincially, this event also brought together Meech Lake opponents from across the country.

Confronted with the need to fundraise and attract speakers, committee members once again turned to the ad hoc model. The overlap between and importance of personal and professional relationships are now becoming clear to historians, as is evident in this volume in Karen Balcom's chapter on the personal and professional friendship of Charlotte Whitton and Katherine Lenroot, Lorna McLean's chapter on the peace activism of Julia Grace Wales, and Catherine Gidney's chapter on first-wave feminists at Victoria College. One can also see similar organizational strategies on the part of feminists in Rose Fine-Meyer's chapter on the Ontario Women's History Network.

Although the group did not manage to land the highest-profile critic of the accord, Trudeau did encourage Donald Johnston to speak. Johnston had defied Liberal leader John Turner and quit the federal shadow cabinet, and eventually the Liberal caucus, over his opposition to the accord.[49] Former Manitoba Liberal Party leader and CanWest founder Izzy Asper also spoke and donated $200 to the committee.[50] Drawing on its Liberal Party connections, the NBAHCC also convinced the New Brunswick government to send Aldéa Landry, the intergovernmental affairs minister, and Ellen King, deputy director of the New Brunswick Women's Directorate.[51] Gayle MacDonald's ties to LEAF were especially helpful in fundraising and attracting speakers: "I went in and gave this rousing speech to the board of directors ... trying to get money, and they were all pitching over hundred dollar bills ... I just gave this passionate speech about Canada and how we were holding our own in New Brunswick and [how] they needed to help us do this."⁵² Marilou McPhedran, who was active in the Ad Hoc Committee of Canadian Women on the Constitution during the patriation and Meech Lake rounds and who was then working as a lawyer for LEAF, led a panel discussion on equality rights, provincial powers, and free trade with MacDonald. Although LEAF contributed $680, the largest single donation came from Nancy Jackman (now Senator Nancy Ruth), who contributed $2,000. The ad hoc structure of the NBAHCC allowed its members to use their connections to other organizations and individuals to raise money.⁵³

The conference in Moncton was favourably covered in the press and enlarged the circle of contacts for the NBAHCC. New Brunswick newspapers devoted the most column inches to the addresses given by Johnston and Asper, who argued that the Meech Lake Accord represented a threat to Canada's constitutional order.⁵⁴ Representatives from organizations seeking to develop their own position on the accord – such as the New Brunswick Aboriginal Peoples Council, the New Brunswick Federation of Labour, the National Association of Immigrant Women, and the New Brunswick Advisory Council on the Status of Women – came away from the conference aware of the many concerns being raised.⁵⁵ The conference made the NBAHCC into an unofficial anti-Meech Lake blanket group for the province. In Crocker's words, it became "a very loose umbrella organization for a number of other interests that were out there in the community."⁵⁶

In addition to connecting with other organizations developing anti-Meech Lake positions, the NBAHCC also helped build a national network of anti-Meech Lake organizations. This was particularly true of Elaine Wright, who, through her political affiliations, was in contact with many Liberals opposed to the accord. Stephen E. Patterson, then a historian at the University of New Brunswick in Fredericton, recalled how Wright and her sister, who worked for a Liberal senator in Ottawa, had put him in contact with other anti-Meech Lake figures such as fellow historian Michael D. Behiels and Deborah Coyne, who would become constitutional adviser to Newfoundland's premier, Clyde Wells, during the Meech Lake period. Patterson, Behiels, Coyne, and others belonged to the Canadian Coalition on the Constitution, a national network of individuals dedicated to thwarting the accord's ratification. "Elaine would always be the point person here in New Brunswick. [She] was a wonderful organizer, of things and of people," recalled Patterson.⁵⁷ The NBAHCC was not only a hub of Meech

Lake opposition in New Brunswick; it was also an important part of a national network of opponents to the accord.

Although rallying and connecting those concerned about the accord were major goals, the committee also developed its own position on the accord and lobbied the government directly. Following the conference, the NBAHCC pressured the McKenna government to follow through on its promise to hold committee hearings.[58] MacDonald recalled that the committee encouraged McKenna in his opposition to the accord but that she had doubts from the beginning.[59] To make matters worse, although the committee was struck in May 1988, it was not until January 1989 that the first members of the public made their submissions to the Select Committee of the New Brunswick Legislative Assembly on the 1987 Constitutional Accord. Given that New Brunswick continued to be the province in which the accord's opponents were most hopeful of derailing its ratification or significantly altering the terms of agreement, the New Brunswick hearings carried special weight.

New Brunswick's hearings also took on special meaning in light of the hearings process at the federal level and in several provinces. A Special Joint Committee of the Senate and the House of Commons on the 1987 Constitutional Accord met over the summer of 1987. Senator Lowell Murray, then minister of state for federal-provincial relations, angered many when he declared that the Meech Lake agreement was "a seamless web" that could be modified only if "egregious errors in drafting" were discovered.[60] Committee hearings in Prince Edward Island and Ontario left many who opposed the accord similarly frustrated. Although Manitoba would later hold hearings that gave more credence to the critics of Meech Lake, its hearings were limited to Manitoba residents, whereas the New Brunswick hearings were open to all Canadians.

For the core members of the NBAHCC, the hearings were an opportunity to publicly lay out all the arguments they had been formulating since the summer of 1987. As with many tasks the committee tackled, writing the brief was a collective process. Crocker recalled, "The brief was pretty important to us ... It was Gayle and I who did most of the work on that, at my kitchen table, mostly on a Sunday afternoon. I did a rough draft, and then Gayle did some more, and then we sort of put it together."[61] The presentation dealt with nine issues that touched on every aspect of the accord. True to Crocker's self-identification as a Trudeau Liberal, the committee focused on the accord's potential to weaken individual rights and shift power from the federal to provincial governments. The ad hocers' belief in a strong central government stemmed from their sense that it was important to national unity, that a strong welfare state could offer social programs important to women, and that equalization would lead to the equality of the provinces. In other words, in the view of the NBAHCC, changes to the constitutional status quo, by extension, threatened their larger equality-seeking agenda, especially causes near and dear to the women's movement.[62] Concurrent debates about the effect of the Free Trade Agreement likewise focused on the trade treaty's potential to weaken federal power. The debates also highlighted the lack of consultation with the Canadian people, both in the development of the accord and its call to enlarge the use of first ministers' meetings and executive federalism as a means of constitutional negotiation. As Crocker summarized during her appearance with MacDonald before the select committee, "I don't think Canadians are going to sit still and let it happen."[63] In addition to the many representatives of organizations with whom the NBAHCC had shared information, Max Wolfe also presented his own brief. It focused on what he described as the combined threat of Meech Lake and the recently negotiated Free Trade Agreement with the United States – a shift of power from Ottawa to the provinces – which he described as "a provincial power grab."[64] The NBAHCC offered one of the best-prepared and broadest presentations. Co-chair Edmond Blanchard remarked, "It is quite obvious you did your homework."[65] In total, fifty-six groups and forty individuals appeared before the select committee, which received briefs from thirty-eight groups and thirty-six individuals. There was roughly equal representation of anglophone and francophone groups, and approximately 97 percent of the submissions opposed the accord's ratification without amendment or additional protection for francophone Canadians outside Quebec.[66] Two issues of particular interest to New Brunswick were not covered by the NBAHCC's brief or presentation: the question of fisheries jurisdiction and the possible entrenchment of Bill 88, formally the Act Recognizing the Equality of the Two Official Linguistic Communities in New Brunswick. Although she was careful to point out that the group (unlike some Meech Lake opponents) did not have an anti-francophone bias, MacDonald suggested that francophone New Brunswickers and fishers were well represented and spoke out for themselves: "[T]he Acadians were very organized on their own ... It was certainly not because we wanted to alienate francophone [New Brunswickers]."[67] Crocker reiterated this, adding that the group intentionally focused on what it saw as national issues, as opposed to provincial ones, indicating the national importance they attached to the hearings.[68]

After their presentation, members of the NBAHCC regarded the hearings favourably. The overwhelming majority of presentations cautioned the government against ratifying the accord. If McKenna needed proof of popular opposition to the accord when talking with other premiers, he need only have pointed to the select committee hearings for evidence. MacDonald recalled how positively she felt the NBAHCC was received, "What we found was that people on the committee were very, very interested in hearing from people ... As I remember, I really did feel like we were being listened to."[69] For the committee members, their efforts appeared to be paying off.

Over the course of 1989, the NBAHCC's relationship with the provincial government and McKenna became strained. Throughout the ratification period, despite his own early pronouncements against the accord, McKenna had only been clear on one point: he would not be rushed into a final decision. MacDonald articulated the growing frustration the committee members felt with McKenna through 1989: "He was infuriating because he would just waffle. He wouldn't come down on one side [or] the other."[70] As New Brunswickers were fond of saying at the time, the one issue on which McKenna took a clear stand as premier of New Brunswick was the Meech Lake Accord, and he managed to take that stand on both sides of the issue.[71]

In June 1989, the committee launched a mass-mailing campaign and followed it up with a light-hearted publicity stunt designed to keep up pressure on McKenna. Willi Evans Wolfe, who worked with the NBAHCC and presented a brief before the select committee on behalf of the Jemseg Women's Institute, recalled that the group had felt pressured by McKenna's growing distance. "He was beginning to sound like he was about to go along with [Meech Lake], and we said, 'Let's just do something that draws attention to it.'"[72] The committee printed postcards that declared "Flamingos All Agree: Beach Meech." The postcards were addressed to McKenna's office at the Legislative Assembly building in Fredericton, and hundreds arrived at his office from every corner of the province.[73] In addition to the letters and postcards, early on the morning of 30 June, the NBAHCC placed fifty plastic flamingos on the front lawn of McKenna's house in Fredericton. Forty-nine of the birds wore red ties, as sported by the premier, and one wore a blue tie, representing the Progressive Conservative premier of Manitoba, Gary Filmon, who had begun to vacillate on whether to ratify the accord. Activists made two signs: one read "Beach Meech" and the other "Thanks, Frank." The stunt was timed so photographs of the birds would appear in the paper on Canada Day.[74] The public enjoyed the humorous stunt, but the committee's relationship with the government continued to deteriorate.[75]

The select committee released its report on 24 October 1989, and its findings fell far short of the NBAHCC's expectations. The report criticized the accord's negotiation process but did not find that it undermined its legitimacy. The select committee recommended expanding the distinct society clause to require Parliament to both preserve and promote English- and French-speaking communities and insulate the sex-equality provisions in section 28 of the Charter, alongside multicultural and Aboriginal rights, from any effects of the distinct society clause. The select committee also called for an affirmation of the principle of equalization among the provinces in light of the provision in Meech Lake allowing provinces to opt out of national shared-cost programs.

The NBAHCC felt that the select committee had not gone far enough on some points and had totally failed to address others. On the question of shared-cost programs, for example, the committee expressed the concern of many feminist groups that an opt-out clause would make social initiatives of benefit to women impossible, such as a national day care scheme.[76] Although the select committee had suggested reinforcing the principle of equalization and ameliorating provincial differences, as found in the Constitution Act, 1982, the NBAHCC and many others felt the opt-out clause was a necessary deletion. Most importantly for the ad hocers, the select committee had failed to deal with what they felt was the accord's fundamental problem: it would shift power away from Ottawa and have a destabilizing effect on Confederation. If the federal government were weakened in this way, they feared the end of the federal government as a tool for progressive change.

The NBAHCC was quick to condemn the report in the press. In a newspaper interview, Crocker characterized it as "namby-pamby," concluding that "the people who took the time and effort to make representations have every right to feel betrayed by this report."[77] Despite early optimism, Max Wolfe felt they had been duped by McKenna: "I think we knew that they had their mind made up ... I think, in that sense, the hearings were pretty much a sham."[78] Those who had hoped that the select committee's report would signal the New Brunswick government's intention to sink the accord were disappointed.

During the remaining eight months in the ratification window, events began to overtake the NBAHCC. Most importantly, New Brunswick ceased to be the province most likely to derail the accord. In Manitoba, the election of a new minority government and the loss of a federal government contract rendered the accord's status uncertain.[79] Newfoundlanders elected

Clyde Wells in April 1989, and his government rescinded the province's ratification of the Meech Lake Accord on 6 April 1990.[80] Meanwhile, the New Brunswick government began to pursue a parallel accord, which, according to McKenna, would add to, but not subtract from, Meech Lake and entrench New Brunswick's bilingual status to protect the province's francophone population. As a result, the ad hocers were forced to refocus their efforts outside the province.

Although the NBAHCC prepared a second brief, it was not able to present it to the Charest Committee, the next major round of hearings on the Meech Lake Accord. Drafted primarily by Crocker, Wright, and MacDonald, the brief focused largely on what the group saw as McKenna's betrayal of the province's interests: "We reject ... the implication that New Brunswickers in the majority wholly support the specific recommendation included in Mr. McKenna's resolution. They do not. We do not."[81] When the Charest Committee's report was released on 17 May 1990, roughly five weeks before the ratification deadline, it received a chilly reception. Quebec remained disinclined to accept any further compromises beyond its basic bargaining position on the accord, and Wells remained intransigent. Worse still for Mulroney, Lucien Bouchard quit the federal cabinet over the report, taking much of the nationalist Quebec support for the federal Tories with him.

The final attempt to save the accord came with a marathon seven-day first' ministers' meeting, during which the provinces tried to reach a compromise. With around-the-clock coverage on the CBC and Mulroney's famous comment that, at this juncture, he had chosen to "roll the dice" through high-pressure negotiations, this was constitution making at its most dramatic.[82] The premiers came up with an agreement by the end of the week that was ultimately defeated. Clyde Wells agreed to it, pending a free vote by the House of Assembly. In Manitoba, the issue was more complicated. The minority Conservative government, acting in concert with the opposition Liberals and New Democrats, had agreed to expedite a hearing process that would take weeks to conclude. To do this, the unanimous consent of all MLAs was required. Elijah Harper, a Cree and New Democratic Party MLA, steadfastly refused to yield on the procedural question. Unhappy with the lack of attention the first ministers had given to Aboriginal issues, Harper seized the opportunity to sink the accord.[83] Without action in Manitoba, Wells elected not to hold the vote; he feared the accord would be rejected and damage relations with Quebec further. In New Brunswick, however, McKenna forged ahead with ratification.

In Fredericton, immediately following the announcement of the first ministers' new accord, Anne Crocker recorded a commentary for CBC Radio. Attacking McKenna, she proclaimed: "For those who had been effectively denied representation in other than the most patriarchal sense, the native peoples, women, multicultural minorities, and the disabled, it was a bitter harvest indeed ... Mr. McKenna's principles, such as they were, demanded that he defend the views and interests of New Brunswickers, and the interests of Canada as a whole, more vigorously than he did."[84] Despite the bitter words, the "feeling of embarrassment and taste of ashes" to which Crocker referred in her editorial did not last long.

A flurry of last-minute machinations by the federal government could not save the accord. At noon on Friday, 22 June 1990, the Manitoba Legislature adjourned for the weekend without having moved beyond its procedural quagmire; Elijah Harper, with the support of Aboriginal groups, was resolute. At eight o'clock that evening, the Newfoundland House of Assembly followed suit, and the Meech Lake Accord, with one day left on the ratification calendar, gave up the ghost. In Ottawa, the federal government was in full-scale damage-control mode, and in Quebec, the political discourse turned angrily to talk of a second sovereignty referendum.

Reaction to the death of the accord among the core members of the NBAHCC was quite different. Crocker recalled elation: "Yippee! It didn't matter that we hadn't done it here. But we had contributed to the overall rejection of Meech ... we took a bit of credit for that, because it was New Brunswick, initially ... that started raising hell."[85] Crocker's remarks reveal the importance of the NBAHCC in the Meech Lake saga – it delayed the ratification in New Brunswick for almost three years. By pressuring the McKenna government to follow through with its promise of public hearings and by connecting with other organizations and supplying them with information through its conference in Moncton, the NBAHCC delayed the accord until elections in Manitoba and Newfoundland made those provinces more significant players in the movement to oppose the Meech Lake Accord. In this sense, although the McKenna government's endorsement of the constitutional amendment signalled the loss of the battle over Meech Lake in New Brunswick, the citizens' groups that rallied against it ultimately won the war. MacDonald argued that popular opposition to Meech Lake was rooted in a rejection of executive federalism: "I always believed that the people of Canada wouldn't let it happen ... And the politicians just couldn't see how the country couldn't accept something on the whole that was dealt in secret ... It was an old strategy that had worked for many years, but Mulroney pulled it one too late."[86]

The NBAHCC was only part of a larger national citizens' response to the Meech Lake Accord, but it was important for several reasons. As the only organization in New Brunswick dedicated solely to the accord's defeat or radical transformation, the committee was a major factor in the fight to keep the New Brunswick government from ratifying the accord. With its demands for inclusive constitution making and condemnation of the Meech Lake process, the NBAHCC revealed a bifurcation in understanding between government and citizens over what acceptable negotiations of constitutional renewal should look like. The referendum on the Charlottetown Accord in 1992 was an attempt to address this schism. Although the NBAHCC was often critical of the McKenna government, the interaction between it and the New Brunswick Liberal Party and provincial government demonstrates that constitution making in the Meech period can be best understood as a dialogue between citizens and governments. Focusing on this dialogue offers an alternative approach to constitutional history, one in which the focus is not entirely on governing elites – as is traditionally the case – nor on citizens alone. The NBAHCC's structure and actions also demonstrate the influence of feminist activism in New Brunswick and Canadian constitutional history, revealing, as historian Gail Cuthbert Brandt advocates, the links between women's history and political history.[87]

To truly reveal political activism as feminist history, just how explicit do the links between action and ideology need to be? Were the ad hocers motivated by feminism or by Trudeau liberalism? Perhaps their activism was an outgrowth of the "militantism of the 1960s and 1970s?"[88] In interviews, all of the women involved in the campaign pointed to feminism as a motivating factor in their opposition to the Meech Lake Accord. Moreover, I think it is a mistake to try to attach labels such as feminism or liberalism to motivations. As the oral history of the NBAHCC demonstrates, political actions, coalitions, and allegiances flow from a variety of sources. The same reservations apply to trying to attach labels to the form their actions took. Were ad hoc committees feminist in origin or, rather, simply a form of organization favoured by feminists? The answer does not matter. Women took ownership of this form of activism and tailored it to fit their political goals from the 1960s to the 1990s. These political ends were part of a long tradition of feminist activism in New Brunswick.

Finally, the NBAHCC's resistance to the Meech Lake Accord suggests the power citizens can have over their governments, even when presented with a fait accompli. As Crocker noted when reflecting on the experience, "If you feel strongly about something and are prepared to use the political process, you can have an impact on your community ... You can get like-minded people together and make a presentation to government ... All you have to do is want it enough ... I don't feel powerless as a citizen. And if something is important enough, then I know that I can do something about it."[89]

NOTES

1   I interviewed five anti-Meech Lake activists, two former officials with the New Brunswick government, and one former MLA.

2   The constitutional elite to which I refer is the narrow band of individuals who form the focus of study in traditional constitutional history: first ministers, attorneys general and ministers of justice, intergovernmental affairs ministers, and senior bureaucrats from related ministries and departments. This argument draws on the work of political scientist Alan C. Cairns, who noted the bifurcation in constitutional understanding following the 1981 patriation. See Alan C. Cairns, "Citizens (Outsiders) and Governments (Insiders) in Constitution-Making: The Case of Meech Lake," in *Disruptions: Constitutional Struggles, from the Charter to Meech Lake*, ed. Alan Cairns and Douglas E. Williams (Toronto: McClelland and Stewart, 1991), 66–107.

3   Mulroney made the remark in a speech he gave in Sept-Îsles, Quebec, on 6 August 1984. See Andrew Cohen, *A Deal Undone* (Vancouver: Douglas and McIntyre, 1990), 67–68.

4   Trudeau had long articulated his constitutional vision for Canada. See *The Constitution and the People of Canada* (Ottawa: Queen's Printer, 1969), which he published as minister of justice.

5   C. Anne Crocker, interview with author, 22 March 2007; Gayle MacDonald, interview with author, 11 June 2007; and Max Wolfe, interview with author, 5 April 2007.

6   Robert C. Vipond, *Liberty and Community: Canadian Federalism and the Failure of the Constitution* (Albany, NY: SUNY Press, 1991).

7   As with other women's groups that objected to the accord, the NBAHCC cited the impossibility of a national day care program as an example. NBAHCC, "A Brief Opposing the Meech Lake Accord," 6–7, University of New Brunswick Archives (UNBA), UA RG 355, New Brunswick Ad Hoc Committee on the Constitution fonds, folder 1, series 2.

8   Patrick J. Monahan, *Meech Lake: The Inside Story* (Toronto: University of Toronto Press, 1991), 125.

9   This date was heavy with symbolism; 23 June was not only the date that Robert Bourassa formally rejected the Victoria Charter in 1971 but also the eve of St. John the Baptist Day, Quebec's National Holiday.

10   "Say Goodbye to the Dream of One Canada," *Toronto Star*, 17 May 1987, quoted in Donald Johnston, ed., *Pierre Trudeau Speaks Out on Meech Lake* (Toronto: Stoddart/General Paperbacks, 1990), 22.

11   C. Anne Crocker, interview with author, 22 March 2007. At the time the NBAHCC was active, Crocker was president of the Muriel McQueen Fergusson Foundation,

which works to put a stop to domestic violence. She was also involved in the establishment of Transition House in Fredericton.

12 MacDonald identified herself politically as supporting the New Democratic Party and, occasionally, the Liberals.

13 Max Wolfe listed three reasons for his initial opposition to the accord: "Point 1 ... the whole Meech Lake process looked like a gutting of the federal Parliament and a weakening of Canada ... Point 2, the process ... [Point 3, to] a significant extent ... an overall animus to Brian Mulroney." Max Wolfe, interview with author, 5 April 2007.

14 Unfortunately, Elaine Wright has passed away in the intervening years.

15 Gayle MacDonald, interview with author, 11 June 2007.

16 See Judy Rebick, *Ten Thousand Roses: The Making of a Feminist Revolution* (Toronto: Penguin Canada, 2006).

17 C. Anne Crocker, interview with author, 22 March 2007.

18 Rebick, *Ten Thousand Roses*, 26–27.

19 C. Anne Crocker, interview with author, 22 March 2007.

20 Nancy Janovicek, "'If It Saves One Life, All the Effort Is ... Worthwhile': Crossroads for Women/Carrefour pour femmes, Moncton, 1979–1987," *Acadiensis* 35, 2 (2006): 27–28; Elspeth Tulloch, *We the Undersigned: A History of New Brunswick Women, 1784–1984* (Fredericton: New Brunswick Advisory Council on the Status of Women, 1985), 18.

21 Janet Silman, ed., *Enough Is Enough: Aboriginal Women Speak Out* (Toronto: Women's Press, 1987). At the time, a woman's right to band housing was based on marriage to a male band member who had status, and even then, only at the pleasure of her husband.

22 Penny Kome, *The Taking of Twenty-Eight: Women Challenge the Constitution* (Toronto: Women's Press, 1983), 27, 39.

23 Ibid., 57.

24 For example, section 15 is subject to section 1, the reasonable limits clause.

25 The change was made at the insistence of the Government of Saskatchewan. Section 35, which deals with the recognition of Aboriginal rights, was also altered.

26 Kome, *The Taking of Twenty-Eight*, 87. Roy Romanow, John Whyte, and Howard Leeson, *Canada ... Notwithstanding: The Making of the Constitution, 1976–1982* (Toronto: Carswell/Methuen, 1984), 213–14. Quebec was not a signatory to the accord that secured repatriation.

27 The committee heard from 90 groups, 5 individuals, and 6 governments over 56 days and 270 hours of televised hearings, in addition to briefs or petitions-to-appear from 914 individuals and 294 groups, including multicultural groups, women's organizations, Aboriginal groups, disabled Canadians, and many more. Robert Shepard and Michael Valpy, *The National Deal: The Fight for a Canadian Constitution* (Toronto: Fleet Books, 1982), 137.

28 Cairns, "Citizens (Outsiders) and Governments (Insiders)," 149.

29 Ibid., 109.

30 Donald Dennison, interview with author, 11 July 2007. Dennison was assistant deputy minister of intergovernmental affairs under Barry Toole and his successor, Francis McGuire. He was then McKenna's deputy minister during the Meech years.

31 See Kome, *The Taking of Twenty-Eight*, 23.

32 Gayle MacDonald, presentation to the Select Committee, video recording, 15 February 1989, Public Archives of New Brunswick (PANB), MC 1750, Cassette 043.

33 Jane Barry, interview with author, 5 June 2007.

34 Donald Dennison was able to shed some light on Hatfield's reasons for waiting to ratify the accord. The premier had Dennison check his position on the Fulton-Favreau amending formula to see whether, as an opposition MLA, he had called for public hearings on constitutional amendments. Hatfield had indeed called for hearings, and with the legislature already prorogued for the summer, Dennison believes his desire to hold hearings on Meech Lake kept him from re-calling the legislature for a ratification vote. The decision by Hatfield not to ratify before the election of the McKenna government opened a major window of opportunity for opponents of the accord in New Brunswick. Donald Dennison, interview with author, 11 July 2007.

35 Frank McKenna, "Presentation to the Special Joint Committee on the Constitution," 25 August 1987, UNBA, UA RG 355, New Brunswick Ad Hoc Committee on the Constitution fonds, folder 5, series 2.

36 Evidence of this can be seen in the immense volume of letters that poured into Liberal headquarters and, after he had assumed power, the Premier's Office. See PANB, Frank McKenna Operational Records, RS 738, box 0–88–2, file 2112–1, for examples of letters and tabulations of anti-Meech letters to McKenna.

37 C. Anne Crocker, interview with author, 22 March 2007.

38 *Consciousness raising,* a phrase popular in the women's movement during the 1960s and 1970s, was how Crocker described the activities of the group.

39 Gayle MacDonald, interview with author, 11 June 2007.

40 Ibid.

41 Conference Documents, UNBA, New Brunswick Ad Hoc Committee on the Constitution fonds, UA RG 355, folder 5, series 1.

42 Gayle MacDonald, interview with author, 11 June 2007.

43 For an example of the working relationship between the two groups, see C. Anne Crocker and Marilou McPhedran, fax correspondence, September 1987, UNBA, New Brunswick Ad Hoc Committee on the Constitution fonds, UA RG 355, folder 1, series 1.

44 Linden McIntyre and Carol Jerome, "Women and Meech," *Constitutional Discord: Meech Lake,* CBC Digital Archives, 2006, http://www.cbc.ca/archives/.

45 "Accord Lays Groundwork for Confederation Breakup," *Fredericton Daily Gleaner,* 19 April 1988, 1, 3, and Ad Hoc Committee of Women on the Constitution press release, UNBA, New Brunswick Ad Hoc Committee on the Constitution fonds, UA RG 355, folder 3, series 3.

46 Max Wolfe, interview with author, 5 April 2007.

47 Ibid.

48 Ibid.

49 "Johnston Resigns from Shadow Cabinet Citing Freedom to Speak Out over Meech," *Fredericton Daily Gleaner,* 9 May 1987. Johnston quit the Liberal caucus on 19 January 1988.

50 Izzy Asper to Elaine Wright, 18 July 1988, UNBA, New Brunswick Ad Hoc Committee on the Constitution fonds, UA RG 355, folder 5, series 1.
51 Conference documents, UNBA, New Brunswick Ad Hoc Committee on the Constitution fonds, UA RG 355, folder 7, series 1.
52 Gayle MacDonald, interview with author, 11 June 2007.
53 Conference documents, UNBA, New Brunswick Ad Hoc Committee on the Constitution fonds, UA RG 355, folder 7, series 1.
54 See "Asper Says 'Secret Deal' Could Hurt Francophone Rights outside Quebec," *Telegraph-Journal*, 18 April 1988, 4; Laurie Armstrong, "Interest Groups Say Meech Lake Signed in 'Reckless Haste,'" *Telegraph-Journal*, 18 April 1988, 1; Heather Dunsmuir, "Accord Lays Groundwork for Confederation Breakup," *Fredericton Daily Gleaner*, 19 April 1988, 1, 3; "Johnston Says There Will Be No Second Round of Accord Talks," *Telegraph-Journal*, 19 April 1988, 4.
55 Conference documents, UNBA, New Brunswick Ad Hoc Committee on the Constitution fonds, UA RG 355, folder 5, series 1. The New Brunswick Aboriginal People's Council and New Brunswick Labour Council both later made Meech-skeptic presentations before a New Brunswick government committee.
56 C. Anne Crocker, interview with author, 22 March 2007.
57 Stephen E. Patterson, interview with author, 16 July 2007.
58 Jane Barry, interview with author, 5 April 2007.
59 When, exactly, the Liberal government would get around to holding committee hearings and who would be invited to appear at them (in addition to the public) became questions of much speculation in the provincial press as well. As one columnist quipped, "[I]t would be easier to get Mikhail Gorbachev's home telephone number than it was to pry from the committee members an answer to the simple question of whether former Prime Minister Pierre Trudeau would be invited to state his opposition to the proposed constitutional changes." Don Hoyt, "Accord Committee Should Be Operating in the Open," *Telegraph-Journal*, 18 August 1988, 4.
60 Lowell Murray, "The Constitutional Politics of National Reconciliation," brief to the Special Joint Committee of the House of Commons and Senate on the 1987 Constitutional Accord, in Michael Behiels, ed., *The Meech Lake Primer: Conflicting Views of the 1987 Constitutional Accord* (Ottawa: University of Ottawa Press, 1989), 14, 27. Murray was the first witness to appear before the committee.
61 C. Anne Crocker, interview with author, 22 March 2007.
62 Ibid.
63 C. Anne Crocker, presentation to the select committee, video recording, 15 February 1989, PANB, MC 1750, Cassette 043.
64 Max Wolfe, presentation to the select committee, video recording, 9 February 1989, PANB, MC 1750, Cassette 043.
65 Edmond Blanchard, remarks at the select committee hearings, video recording, 15 February 1989, PANB, MC 1750, Cassette 043.
66 David Terrence Pye, "Interest Group Articulation in Public Policy Formation: A Study of New Brunswick's Meech Lake Hearings, January-February 1989" (master's thesis, University of New Brunswick, 1990), 93–94, and *Select Committee on the*

1987 Constitutional Accord: Final Report on the Constitutional Amendment, 1987 (Fredericton: Supply and Services, 1989), Appendix F.

67 Gayle MacDonald, interview with author, 11 June 2007. Still sensitive to the accusation that all Meech Lake opponents were anti-francophone, all three ad hocers took pains during interviews to highlight their belief in a bilingual Canada.

68 C. Anne Crocker, interview with author, 22 March 2007.

69 Gayle MacDonald, interview with author, 11 June 2007.

70 Ibid.

71 With thanks to Donald Wright.

72 Willi Evans Wolfe, interview with author, 5 April 2007.

73 PANB, Frank McKenna Operational Records, RS 738, Box 0–89–1, 2012–13.

74 See *Saint John Telegraph-Journal,* 1 July 1989.

75 Gayle MacDonald, interview with author, 11 June 1987. The Fredericton police took the woman setting up the birds to breakfast after questioning her about her suspicious activity.

76 NBAHCC, "A Brief Opposing the Meech Lake Accord," 6–7, UNBA, New Brunswick Ad Hoc Committee on the Constitution fonds, UA RG 355, folder 1, series 2.

77 "Group Worried McKenna May Give in to Pressure," *Fredericton Daily Gleaner,* 18 October 1989.

78 Max Wolfe, interview with author, 5 April 2007.

79 The election of Gary Filmon as premier in Manitoba and the loss of a lucrative defence contract by a local firm moved the province to the Meech-skeptic camp.

80 Monahan, *Meech Lake,* 171. Deborah Coyne, *Roll of the Dice: Working with Clyde Wells during the Meech Lake Negotiations* (Toronto: James Lorimer, 1992), 77.

81 "Brief of the New Brunswick Ad Hoc Committee on the Constitution to the House of Commons Special Committee on the Proposed Companion Resolution to the Meech Lake Accord," UNBA, New Brunswick Ad Hoc Committee on the Constitution fonds, UA RG 355, folder 17, series 2.

82 The dice remark appeared in an interview in the *Globe and Mail* published three days after the first ministers' conference ended. Coyne, *Roll of the Dice,* 136–37.

83 Monahan, *Meech Lake,* 234, and Coyne, *Roll of the Dice,* 139.

84 C. Anne Crocker, "Commentary," broadcast by the Canadian Broadcasting Corporation, June 1990, UNBA, New Brunswick Ad Hoc Committee on the Constitution fonds, UA RG 355, folder 17, series 1.

85 C. Anne Crocker, interview with author, 22 March 2007.

86 Gayle MacDonald, interview with author, 11 June 2007.

87 Gail Cuthbert Brandt, "Canadian National Histories: Their Evolving Content," *History Teacher* 30, 2 (1997): 137–44, especially 142–43. See also Gail Cuthbert Brandt, "National Unity and the Politics of Political History," *Journal of the Canadian Historical Association* 3 (1992): 3–11.

88 I thank one of the anonymous reviewers for this insight.

89 C. Anne Crocker, interview with author, 22 March 2007.

13

To Help and to Serve
Women's Career Paths in the Domestic Services Sector in Quebec City, 1960–2009

CATHERINE CHARRON

In Canada, more and more women, especially married women, have entered the job market since the 1960s.[1] This profound socio-economic transformation has gone hand in hand with the development of service jobs, including personal and domestic services.[2] The outsourcing of domestic work is the engine driving the growth of the domestic services sector, the result of both rising demand, primarily from the middle class, and an increased supply of female labour.[3] Domestic service is not a new line of work; in 1891, it accounted for 41 percent of female labour in Canada.[4] Domestic service at the turn of the twentieth century featured the figure of the live-in housekeeper working for her "master."[5] The types of jobs that appeared in the second half of the century, however, broke with tradition and include cleaning lady, babysitter, and personal aide. Updating the idea that domestic work is naturalized female knowledge and conceptions of domestic service as an informal, personalized service relationship, the world of domestic service jobs since the 1960s has both fed on and fed into the phenomenon of the casualization of work, and it is a world in which new faces of an old type of exploitation can be seen.

After painting a general picture of changes in the relationship between women and the job market in the latter half of the twentieth century, I examine the ways in which paid domestic service activities became part of the career and life trajectories of a sample group of working-class women.[6] I analyze these women's circumstances at different points in their personal and professional pathways, as well as the relationships between the various work worlds in which they were involved. Although I base my analysis on twenty interviews, I present two individual journeys in greater detail. I situate the accounts of Ms. Giguère and Ms. Samson, several excerpts from which are interspersed throughout this chapter, not only in the context of larger trends in domestic service but also in the context of their own personal and professional paths.[7] I believe, along with Kristina Llewellyn, Heidi Macdonald, and Gail Campbell, whose work appears in this volume, that a biographical approach can allow us to more intimately grasp the socio-historical dynamics at work in women's lives. Oral interviews, despite their limitations, appear to be the most fruitful, not to say the only, way of accessing areas that are socially invisible because they are embedded in the day-to-day activities of domestic work.[8] In light of the recurrence of paid domestic service work in the lives of these women, I first draw attention to the structuring role of these experiences in their career paths. I then outline several islands in an archipelago that has scarcely been mapped by labour historians and sociologists.[9] This archipelago of domestic women's work emerged in the second half of the twentieth century and came to define the working world of the women who are the subject of this chapter.

The Integration of Women into the Job Market since the 1960s

At its height in the early 1970s, the so-called Fordist model of labour regulation – which combines regular full-time work for a single employer with union rights and a social safety net guaranteed by the state – applied to a significant number of industrial workers and expanded to include workers in other economic sectors.[10] However, simultaneously and paradoxically, less secure forms of work – self-employment and part-time, temporary, and on-call work – also flourished during this period and at an increased rate from the mid-1970s. Women, who had a greater presence in the job market, were especially affected by this supposedly marginal trend, which was structurally related to the feminization of the wage-earning workforce.[11] In Canada, part-time work in the last quarter of the twentieth century was primarily the domain of women in the sales and service sectors. In the mid-1980s, one in four female workers had a part-time job.[12] In the domestic services sector, part-time work was the norm, not the exception. The economic crisis, followed by the political shift to the right in the 1980s, accentuated this trend towards atypical forms of employment and helped erode the social welfare system, which had been established in prior decades.

In 1971, access to federal unemployment insurance benefits for some women, especially after the birth of a child, represented a step towards recognition of women as workers. Perhaps more important, the establishment of a universal social assistance program in Quebec in 1970, shortly after the liberalization of divorce, benefitted many women who headed households. In terms of family policy, however, Quebec's involvement in day care services was belated and tentative until the mid-1990s, when it introduced a network of child care centres.[13] The fact that the state considered day care a problem to be solved by families, in particular women, has been a serious constraint on the ability of women, particularly with children, to exercise their right to work. In 1976, the employment rate among partnered mothers of preschool-age children was 26.3 percent; by 2008, that number had risen to 73.4 percent. Men in the same situation, on the other hand, held jobs at a rate of 88.7 percent in 2008.[14]

In addition to pushing women to the margins of the wage-earning workforce, the traditional division of labour based on sex penetrated and structured the labour market in industrial society. That women tended to concentrate in certain areas of activity – or certain specialties, in the case of professional women – over the twentieth century is discussed in several of the chapters in this volume, notably those by Donica Belisle, Heidi MacDonald, Catherine Gidney, and Hélène Charron. Working-class women in particular have been confined to the most feminized occupational sectors. With less education, they tend to have less access, in general, to salaried work.[15] In 1971, the two main women's occupations were secretary or stenographer and sales clerk. Women also occupied subordinate office jobs, primarily as cashiers, waitresses, nurses, and primary or preschool teachers.[16] This list remained practically unchanged over the decades that followed.[17] Women interviewed for this research worked almost exclusively in jobs categorized as female and unskilled: office work, restaurant work, retail sales, and, of course, personal services, especially non-professional care. Moreover, as historian Joan Sangster has outlined, in the 1960s and 1970s, there were still many obstacles, both material and ideological, to women taking up salaried work, despite their increased participation in the job market.[18] These realities are reflected in the career paths of women, especially those born before 1950, which were marked by discontinuity, as has been shown by Céline Le Bourdais and Hélène Desrosiers.[19]

I studied the employment paths of women born in the 1940s and 1950s.[20] Most of these women moved to Quebec City from rural communities for family or professional reasons. In a time of increasingly democratized education, several of them pursued post-secondary studies. They entered the job market during a period of strong economic growth and at a time when the public service was recruiting a significant number of new employees. They bore witness to the implementation of the Fordist system of labour regulations in the industrial sector, as well as to the expanding service sector. Their accounts reveal the mechanisms of labour market segmentation as well as how social class and sex shaped men's and women's relationship to work – in short, their accounts reflect the establishment of a new regime of inequalities tailored to the socio-economic realities of postwar Quebec. Oral interviews place these women at the centre of the story.[21]

Two Routes to Domestic Service Work

Ms. Giguère was born in 1949 in a rural community. The daughter of farmers and the eldest of a family of seven children, she left school before completing high school to work for several years as a live-in servant. She married at age nineteen and moved several times because of her husband's studies. She finished high school and found a job as a babysitter. She babysat for a year and a half and then worked as a cleaning lady for several clients for a number of years. In the 1980s, she worked summers for the government. During that time, she had two children and completed a college program. She divorced in the late 1980s. Over the next ten years, she held a series of temporary, short-term jobs: she worked in a small food-preparation factory and as a decorating entrepreneur, babysitter, and cleaning lady. During a period of unemployment, she enrolled in a night course to become a qualified orderly. After earning her diploma, she worked in several private institutions, and then, in 2002, she achieved her dream of opening a retirement home in the area where she had been born. Before establishing her client base, she served lunches to schoolchildren and started a catering service. She sold her retirement home in 2009 but continues to work there full-time, performing the same duties for the new owner.

Ms. Samson was born in 1951 in a rural community to a civil-servant father and stay-at-home mother. She was the youngest in a family of two children. In 1971, she left home for Quebec City, where she began her university studies in the humanities and social sciences. During her studies, she married and gave birth to her first child. After graduation, she worked for a community organization for one year. Pregnant again, she left the workforce for several months, before finding a new job with the federal government. Because of an accident and marital problems, she left the workforce again. She had a third child. In the early 1980s, she started caring for children in her home and became actively involved in social and extracurricular activities. She, along with a friend, opened a lunch and day care service for school children in the basement of a church. Her final return to the workforce came in the early 1990s when she was hired as a cook in a care home run by an acquaintance. She then moved from one cleaning job to another: first in a hotel and later for a large housecleaning franchise, where she stayed for several years. When a co-worker mentioned a domestic help services cooperative, she decided to offer her services. At the time of the interview, she had been working there for eight years.

How Domestic Work Structures the Lives of Women

Paid domestic service activities punctuated the lives of the majority of women I interviewed. When they are situated within a biographical framework, recurrent paid domestic service activities become intelligible, and the individual cartographies of domestic service jobs can tell us as much about the relationship of women to the job market in the latter half of the twentieth century as they can about their place in the family. The women I interviewed, like all of the women studied in this volume, navigated many constraints and opportunities.

Early Introduction to Domestic Service

As Pam Taylor has shown in the case of interwar Great Britain, historically, the socialization of working-class girls was strongly oriented towards the acquisition of domestic skills that could be learned at home and then applied to their jobs as servants.[22] In Quebec, working as a servant was a typical first job for young rural women in the first half of the twentieth century.[23] In the rest of Canada, in contrast, immigrants filled domestic service jobs in this period.[24] In Quebec City, where the immigrant population never exceeded 3 percent in the second half of the twentieth century, the domestic service labour pool was made up primarily of working-class women native to the region or surrounding areas.[25] In the 1960s, when domestic servant jobs are supposed to have disappeared, and when an image of women as queens of the household reigned as the dominant family icon, the practice of live-in domestic service continued to exist alongside the free family work expected of young girls, as the experience of Ms. Giguère illustrates:

I dropped out. I worked in private homes ... There were three kids ... I slept there, too. It was five days a week. I left Friday night and came back Sunday night ... [On weekends] I went back to my parents. I helped my parents ... After that ... when I started going out with Jean, they [Jean's family] had sugar parties. She [her mother-in-law] had a sugar bush, and they hosted dinners ... So I helped out the mother-in-law in a big way, too ... We made ... pea soup ... in milk cans. Y'know ... just so you understand how we made pea soup. And the beans, and the pies, ah! It was crazy, everything we [made].[26]

At a time when job opportunities were burgeoning for women in urban settings, Ms. Samson was able to attain a more "modern" job when she left school in the early 1970s, much like a significant number of educated women who, at that time, entered the lower ranks of the public service. Nonetheless, domestic service continued to be an integral part of the primary socialization of girls, not only in the home, where they contributed greatly to housework, but also through babysitting, which was typically their first experience of paid work. Minding the children of a neighbour or older sister, often for a small amount of money but also for free, almost always involved support and maintenance tasks and meal preparation. Thus, at the beginning of the 1960s, these female workers were gradually being trained for domestic work as cleaning ladies, personal aides, and babysitters.

Periods of Disruption: The Problem of Re-entry into Paid Work
Domestic service jobs generally emerged as an option in women's lives during periods of transition related to divorce, job loss, or relocation. Economic necessity pushed these women to work in the domestic services field, an accessible, flexible sector. Women who had the benefit of a network of acquaintances turned to it to survive when they faced a closed formal job market. Ms. Samson explained why she took the initiative of caring for children in her home: "So there I was with three kids. Out of the job market. We were right in the middle of government cutbacks, so there was no way to go back [into the public service]. Forget it! ... So that was that. We got by."

Many women who looked for a job after several years at home were anxious about the qualifications they might need to re-enter the workforce. Nine of the women interviewed had left the labour market for several years to raise their children. Of the thirteen mothers in the sample, only two had an uninterrupted career path, and two others drew on social assistance benefits for several years when their children were young. Being single was the requirement for entry into paid employment for women in early decades (see the chapter by Heidi MacDonald in this collection), and it is clear that marriage and especially motherhood continued to strongly influence the career paths of the women in the generation that followed. The women of this generation, however, had to deal with a sharp increase in relationship breakdowns, a phenomenon that changed the relationship of women to work. After divorce was legalized in Quebec in 1968, a significant number of women found themselves at the head of single-parent families.[27] Of the women interviewed, half went through a divorce in the 1970s, 1980s, or 1990s. The informality of domestic service work was a first step towards returning to paid work for many women in this situation.

Beyond individual strategies, several other factors influenced women's decision to work in the domestic services sector, among them pressure from their social circle, employment policies that marginalized women, limited access to unemployment benefits, and family responsibilities. Several of the women interviewed participated in various job re-entry programs at the provincial level (through social assistance) or federal level (through unemployment insurance), but these programs generally had little effect on their career progression. Although their interest in improving their chances on the job market is obvious (sixteen participants out of twenty went back to school as adults or attempted to), only a minority of these women were successful in the long term, especially in terms of professional stability.

Jobs in the domestic services sector often represented the only opportunities available for aging women workers whose professional options were dwindling. On the one hand, some of the women who had previously held jobs in sales or service had trouble, past a certain age, finding work. On the other hand, others were tired of difficult working conditions in these sectors and chose to finish out their professional lives as cleaning ladies or personal aides. While some women were clearly vexed by this turn in their professional lives, those who had worked with the elderly were more likely to find personal gratification and accepted their career paths with equanimity.

A Sideline to Improve Their Lot in Life

In the career paths studied, taking up cleaning jobs, and domestic service jobs in general, was often part of a process of achieving financial independence. Ms. Samson wanted a degree of economic independence from her spouse when she was at home full-time. Ms. Giguère took up domestic service in response to insufficient income in strongly feminized and unstable sectors of the economy. To keep her head above water, she often had to hold several jobs at the same time: "[I] never held any jobs that offered a fantastic salary ... That's why, when they put me on unemployment ... I racked my brains, because at eight bucks an hour, you can't really put money aside ... If I'd just worked the one job I had ... I wouldn't have been able... to pay for my home." Hired temporarily in a shop during the busy season or on an on-call or involuntary part-time basis, the women in the sample experienced precarious working conditions for the bulk of their professional lives. Those who had an intermittent relationship with the job market experienced even greater insecurity when they re-entered it. Most of them never earned more than minimum wage.

Transformations in the welfare program greatly affected the fate of the most vulnerable women.[28] The poverty trap restricted these women's access to the formal job market.[29] In these conditions, the underground economy became the only way for many of them to meet their needs and the needs of their families. Women have been over-represented in the informal economy, especially in casual domestic jobs.[30] Survival was the primary reason that the women interviewed chose informal jobs, although some of them emphasized free will when they explained their choices. As Isabelle Puech notes, working in the informal job market can be experienced as a "source of freedom," regardless of the fact that these situations always stem from limited access to the formal market.[31] The outsourcing of domestic service work has been central to the casualization and informalization of women's jobs for several decades. Women's stories help to explain this misunderstood, underground world.

The Archipelago of Women's Work

In her article on urban child caregivers, Liane Mozère points out that all unskilled jobs in which women mobilize "naturally female skills" are structured in a "system of equivalence and interchangeability of duties."[33] A cleaning job leads to a babysitting job, and any combination is possible in the domestic services field. Housekeeping, child care, and home care are the gateways to this archipelago of paid activities that take place in private homes and are strongly associated with women's unpaid domestic work. Opportunities in the domestic services field rise and fall during a woman's life cycle, depending on whether the economic climate is more or less favourable to employing women. On a structural scale, social and demographic changes (especially the aging of the population) at the close of the twentieth century, in addition to state responses to these transformations, contributed significantly to a reconfiguration of the domestic services sector. For example, several of the women interviewed had worked with elderly

clients at different points along their career paths, but more than half of
them were devoted to this type of work full-time in the 1990s and 2000s.

"Personal Aide" and "Cleaning Lady": Two Different Occupations?
Over the course of their lives, many of the women interviewed moved
between jobs as cleaning ladies, personal aides, babysitters, and compan-
ions. Those who worked for elderly clients emphasized caregiving in their
accounts: the relationship dimension of the work and their emotional
investment in this vulnerable clientele dominated their discourse.
Household work – although central to the job description of those non-
professionalized women who worked as personal aides – was nearly absent from their job descriptions. Work with elderly people, which often
happened late in their careers, represented both a professional refuge and
a vector of work-based valorization that had been absent in their previous
experiences.

   Nevertheless, these women's individual trajectories illustrate the concrete interweaving of care and domestic service within the biographical
and occupational frameworks,[34] notably in their earliest work experiences
with young children, either as babysitters or live-in servants. At the end
of their careers, many women found themselves working with elderly
people in a professional world that falls simultaneously under the rubrics
of "care" and "domestic service." Housework represented the shameful
side of the job of these women who worked as personal aides. In their
accounts, they spoke negatively about being the "cleaning lady."[35] In general, since care and housework have always coexisted in the work experiences of these women, negative perceptions of housework often give
rise to contradictory expressions of their relationship to housekeeping.
Ms. Sampson explained,

> It's hard. I often ended up crying over it. And then ... something happened
> last summer. It was my birthday. The whole group of us were together, un-
> der a tent, and it was raining buckets ... And then ... one of my boys started
> to talk, that he had just gone to a *méchoui* at one of our ... one of our uni-
> versity classmates and that everyone had asked about me. *[She pauses.]*
> And then I started crying. Crying ... and I said ... "Hey, I hope you watched
> what ..." He said, "Hey!" I said, "Hey ... I can't take it anymore ... Everything
> I do ... I have a bachelor's ... Those guys are established, the whole bit ...
> Me, I've got a bachelor's, and all I do is housecleaning." And they all stood
> up ... the whole group of them! They said, "Hey, Mom! Do you have any idea

how many old men and old women would be in the hospital if it weren't for you?" That really cheered me up! Just talking about it, I've got tears in my eyes. *[Laughs]*

For those who had not worked with vulnerable seniors and who were "cleaning ladies," the extreme social devaluation associated with the personal service sector put a serious strain on the possibility of valorization through work. Being financially independent, defining themselves as independent workers, or choosing their clients determined whether they were satisfied with their work.

From Private Contract to Employer: The Universe of Deskilled Labour
As with housework, care jobs have developed in accordance with different degrees of institutionalization since the 1960s. The majority of women interviewed entered paid domestic work by minding children or helping a family member. Several women continued to carry out these paid but informal domestic activities intermittently throughout their lives while simultaneously holding jobs in other sectors or more institutionalized jobs in the domestic services field. Generally, child care arrangements were by private contract.[36] These experiences often went unmentioned in interviews because the women themselves rarely thought about these activities in professional terms.

In the communities, domestic work is distributed through women's circles and often combines mutual assistance and paid work. These women's accounts highlight the importance of female networks, something that the chapters by Karen Balcom, Rose Fine-Meyer, and Gail Campbell in this volume also testify to in different historical contexts. Ms. Giguère explained:

That's it. My neighbour, she had a little boy ... He must have been about three years old ... [She was] pregnant with another, and ... she had a day care ... She came looking for me one night, and she said to me ... "I have to close my day care. It's crazy. I'll lose my baby otherwise. The doctor doesn't want me to continue." She said, "Can you help me out?" So ... yeah ... She minded five or six of them. There were three babies, in cribs ... [At my house] it wasn't a problem, because I could put the cribs in my room, and ... y'know, I didn't have a spouse, so it worked out *[laughs]*. There weren't as many constraints ... And the day care's parents, they knew me because I was just next door, and I pretty much knew all of them ... So, I did that for ... oh, almost a year ... Then, after that, she took over her day care again ... She kept it for I don't know how long ... Then she went to school in Shawinigan, and after that she ... Her husband ... he taught CÉGEP in Ste-Foy ... So I, in the morning, I went over to their place to watch their little girl ... I did the housework, and anyway ...

These kinds of arrangements were integrated into women's daily domestic routines. Child minding, for example, proved to be a type of paid work that was particularly well suited to the situation of women who had left the job market to take care of their children full-time, as the case of Ms. Samson clearly shows: "So, as for having children in the house, well ... I started watching other children. So ... then my daughter was born in the middle of all that."

Services to seniors were more likely to appear in institutionalized forms in these women's career paths, especially since the 1990s, when the social economy sector expanded significantly in Quebec.[37] In the career trajectories of the women interviewed, accessing more formal forms of work did not in and of itself lead to professional advancement. The testimonials showed that often, when the number of intermediaries rose, the pace of work and its dehumanization rose as well:

Y'know, they were [private residences], where you enter the room and you have ten minutes to wash the person. Then ... after that, to feed them, too, you have the same amount of time. Then ... that's it. And there wasn't enough grey area to change their underwear. You go right to the next room, and ... I had trouble with that. Someone's thirsty – you give him a glass of water. "But don't give him two, now, or he'll ..." Y'know. I said to myself at a certain point, if he's thirsty ... Y'know. I tried to see my father, my mother in those people. (Ms. Giguère)

At [company X], there's not a lot to say about it, because we had the keys. *The clients were never there* ... So, y'know ... you go in. You put down your vacuum, you do your work, you close the door, and you leave. Period. Y'know. That's it ... You never had any human contact ... It was empty. It was empty. The only thing you had was to turn on the radio when you went in, or the TV, or whatever ... But it was completely empty. (Ms. Samson)

It does appear, however, that the presence of an employer could depersonalize a job, allowing the workers to more easily identify the ways in which they were exploited. Conversely, the informal nature of work by private contract, although it was clearly a source of job satisfaction for these women, muddled the professional relationship, which they experienced ambiguously.[38] Nonetheless, the degree to which the work relationship was institutionalized seems to have had little effect on the women's qualification as workers. Ms. Samson described being hired in a social economy business in the early 2000s:

> I didn't even get any training. They decided that ... I was capable right from the start. Uh ... I don't know how they do it. I have no idea ... I don't have much trouble approaching people and all ... so ... I don't know ... maybe that's what counted ... Then there's the fact that I already had lots of habits in terms of the Scouts, and young kids and their parents, and all that ... I don't know. Maybe that's what did ... what worked for me ... I don't know if they have a checklist.

More than any other type of employment, domestic work forces us to consider, along with Xavier Devetter, Florence Jany-Catrice, and Thierry Ribault, that "qualification is a real social construct in which relationships of power, especially relationships of gender, come into play."[39] In fact, most of the skills the women made use of in these jobs (whether care-oriented or not) were acquired informally during their early socialization and throughout their lives as women. The familial framework of domestic service jobs – the fact of working in private homes – reinforced the naturalization of the skills traditionally assigned to women. There is nothing obvious about the wage relationship in this space of intimacy and specificity, which is difficult to reconcile with classic theories of professionalization.[40]

The difficulty of outlining with precision the career paths of these women stems from the entangled nature of the different occupations, their shifting employment statuses, and the different time periods during which these activities occurred in their lives. Professional pathways in the domestic services field were marked by the mobilization of so-called female skills, which were deployed in a way that was versatile and flexible at every stage and in keeping with the domestic work carried out by women for free within their families.[41] These women's accounts resist analysis in terms of professional versus non-professional activities; they encourage us to represent their trajectories as "bundle(s) of pathways."[42]

Conclusion

Domestic service jobs, as they manifested in the careers of women in the closing decades of the twentieth century, point to a paradox: they are simultaneously a path towards empowerment and a professional impasse. These activities were, and continue to be, an accessible gateway to the job market for a certain number of marginalized women. The accessibility of the domestic service sector, combined with the historical deskilling of the work performed in it, has kept wages low, and relationships within the sector have been contaminated by the housekeeping model and the "domestic logic of the gift."[43] Moreover, since the existence of low-skilled service jobs can be directly linked to socio-economic inequality (which makes these services "low cost"), it is clear that this sector has played a role in perpetuating women's poverty.[44]

Although several of the women interviewed were pushed towards the "domestic services path," others made do. For example, some of those who finished their professional lives working with seniors found their jobs fulfilled their need for social connection and meaning, and they derived personal and professional valorization from them. Jobs in the domestic services sector, however, did not constitute a gateway to a broader labour market for the women of the baby boom generation. On the contrary, since the 1960s, working in the domestic service sector has often meant being confined there, and this is especially true for women with additional social handicaps such as limited education, single parenthood, and social isolation. For these women, these jobs were often a one-way ticket to the archipelago of domestic women's work. In their accounts, these women clearly express the complexity of the choices and the weight of the constraints that marked their histories, but they also reveal the striking range of ordinary and extraordinary strategies that they employed at every stage of their lives.

NOTES

1 In Canada, the labour force participation rate of married women rose from 9.6 percent to 61.4 percent between 1951 and 1995. See Diane-Gabrielle Tremblay, "Les femmes sur le marché du travail au Québec et au Canada," *Travail, Genre et Société*, 8 (November 2002): 194.

2 It is difficult to determine the precise number of jobs in the domestic services sector, primarily because the majority of these jobs are not reported. Moreover, the official classification model for industries and professions makes it difficult to isolate services in individual homes and even more difficult to determine specific changes in these activities over several decades.

3 Susan Thistle, *From Marriage to the Market: The Transformation of Women's Lives and Work* (Berkeley: University of California Press, 2006), 100–12.

4 Collectif Clio, *L'histoire des femmes au Québec depuis quatre siècles* (Montreal: Quinze, 1992 [1982]), 215.

5 Magda Fahrni, "'Ruffled' Mistresses and 'Discontented' Maids: Respectability and the Case of Domestic Service, 1880–1914," *Labour/Le Travail*, 39 (1997): 69–97.

6 The analysis is based on twenty semi-structured interviews, each lasting approximately two hours, that were conducted between October 2009 and November 2010. The subjects met two criteria: they were born before 1960, and they had held a domestic service job in the Quebec City area at some point in their lives. Study participants were asked, first, to describe their entire career path and, second, to describe their experiences in the domestic services field in greater detail.

7 Names have been changed for anonymity.

8 Denyse Baillargeon, "Histoire orale et histoire des femmes: Itinéraires et points de rencontre," *Recherches Féministes* 6, 1 (1993): 53–68. Oral history has given rise to many methodological and theoretical discussions since the 1970s, especially among feminists. The most recent discussions include the following: Joan Sangster, "Telling Our Stories: Feminist Debates and the Use of Oral History," in *Rethinking Canada: The Promise of Women's History*, 4th ed., ed. Veronica Strong-Boag, Mona Gleason, and Adele Perry (Toronto: Oxford University Press, 2002), 220–34; Patricia Baker, "Hearing and Writing Women's Voices," *Resources for Feminist Research* 26, 1–2 (1998): 220–34; and Lynn Abrams, *Oral History Theory* (London: Routledge, 2010).

9 I owe this metaphor to Liane Mozère, who uses it in an article on visiting homemakers' child care workers: "'Maman sérieuse cherche enfants à garder...': Petits métiers urbains au féminin," *Les Annales de la Recherche Urbaine* 88 (2000): 83–89.

10 Louis Côté, *L'état démocratique: Fondements et défis* (Quebec City: Presses de l'Université du Québec, 2008).

11 Judy Fudge and Leah F. Vosko, "Gender Paradoxes and the Rise of Contingent Work: Towards a Transformative Political Economy of the Labour Market," in *Changing Canada: Political Economy as Transformation*, ed. Wallace Clement and Leah F. Vosko (Montreal/Kingston: McGill-Queen's University Press, 2003), 194.

12 Marianne Kempeneers, *Le travail au féminin: Analyse démographique de la disontinuité professionnelle des femmes au Canada* (Montreal: PUM, 1992), 33.

13 Jane Jenson, "Les réformes des services de garde pour jeunes enfants en France et au Québec: Une analyse historico-institutionnaliste," *Politique et Sociétés* 17, 1–2 (1998): 183–216.

14 Institut de la statistique du Québec, http://www.stat.gouv.qc.ca.

15 Francine Descarries-Bélanger, *L'école rose ... et les cols roses: La reproduction de la division sociale des sexes* (Montreal: Albert Saint-Martin/CEQ, 1980), 93.

16 Ibid., 48.

17 Tremblay, "Les femmes sur le marché du travail," 199–200.

18 Joan Sangster, *Transforming Labour: Women and Work in Postwar Canada* (Toronto: University of Toronto Press, 2010).

19 Céline Le Bourdais and Hélène Desrosiers, "Les femmes et l'emploi: Une analyse de la discontinuité des trajectoires féminines," *Recherches Féministes* 3, 1 (1990): 119–34.

20 I also met with ten women born prior to 1940 for a second phase of this research. This article focuses on the findings of the first phase only.

21 Abrams, *Oral History Theory*.
22 Pam Taylor, "Daughters and Mothers – Maids and Mistresses: Domestic Service between the Wars," in *Working-Class Culture: Studies in History and Theory*, ed. John Clarke, Chas Critcher, and Richard Johnson (London: Hutchinson/Centre for Contemporary Cultural Studies, University of Birmingham, 1979), 121–39.
23 Denyse Baillargeon, *Ménagères au temps de la crise* (Montreal: Éditions du remue-ménage, 1991), and Denise Lemieux and Lucie Mercier, *Les femmes au tournant du siècle, 1880–1940* (Quebec City: Institut québécois de recherche sur la culture, 1989).
24 Marilyn Barber, *Immigrant Domestic Servants in Canada* (Ottawa: Canadian Historical Association, 1991). After the Second World War, specific federal programs for foreign recruitment were created to meet urban demand for live-in servants, including in Quebec. In Canada, working conditions and the legal status of foreign domestic service workers have only worsened in the second half of the twentieth century, the result of targeted immigration policies by a state determined to secure a low-cost – and indeed captive – workforce for the most well-off Canadian families. See Patricia Daenzer, *Regulating Class Privilege: Immigrant Servants in Canada, 1940s–1990s* (Toronto: Canadian Scholars' Press, 1993), and Abigail B. Bakan and Daiva Stasiulis, eds., *Not One of the Family: Foreign Domestic Workers in Canada* (Toronto: University of Toronto Press, 1997).
25 Marc Vallières, Yvon Desloges, Fernand Harvey, Andrée Héroux, Réginald Auger, and Sophie-Laurence Lamontagne, *Histoire de Québec et de sa région*, vol. 3, *1940–2008* (Quebec City: PUL/INRS, 2008), 1904. However, no study addresses the situation of foreign or immigrant domestic workers in Quebec City; it is likely that they are over-represented among live-in caregivers. It is important to note that the sample included no women of immigrant origins. Three women originally from eastern Europe answered the call for participants. Two interviews were conducted, but the interviews could not be used because it turned out that these women's paid domestic service work experiences had not taken place in Quebec City.
26 The interviews were transcribed in full so as to reproduce the oral performance as faithfully as possible. However, several minor modifications have been made (elimination of repetition, verbal tics, and so on). The objective, as Lynn Abrams explains, is to find a balance between the authenticity of the transcription and the need to do justice to the remarks to convey their meaning (Abrams, *Oral History Theory*).
27 Renée B. Dandurand, "Peut-on encore définir la famille?" in *La société québécoise après 30 ans de changements*, ed. Fernand Dumont (Quebec City: IQRC, 1990).
28 Sylvie Morel, *Modèle du workfare ou modèle de l'insertion? La transformation de l'assistance sociale au Canada et au Québec* (Ottawa: Condition féminine Canada, 2002).
29 Rosie Cox, *The Servant Problem: Domestic Employment in a Global Economy* (London: I.B. Tauris and Co., 2006), 48.
30 Madeleine Leonard, *Invisible Work, Invisible Workers: The Informal Economy in Europe and the US* (New York: St. Martin's Press, 1998), 130.
31 Isabelle Puech, "Les usages féminins du travail non déclaré: Entre contraintes et stratégies" (paper presented at "Économie informelle, travail au noir: Enjeux

économiques et sociaux," Université de Marne-la-Vallée, 2007), http://www.cee-recherche.fr/colloque_TEPP/eco_informelle/pdf/puech.pdf.

33 Mozère, "Maman sérieuse," 87.

34 For a discussion of the distinction between care and service, see Diemut Elisabet Bubeck, *Care, Gender, and Justice* (Oxford: Oxford University Press, 1995), 183–84.

35 Elsa Galerand, in cooperation with Christine Corbeil and Francine Descarries, *Répit-ressource de l'est de Montréal: Monographie d'une entreprise d'économie sociale en aide domestique* (Montreal: LAREPPS/UQAM, 2004), 88. Dussuet makes a similar observation in France. See Annie Dussuet, *Travaux de femmes: Enquêtes sur les services à domicile* (Paris: L'Harmattan, 2005), 112.

36 Outside the public system of child care centres created in the 1990s, child care has historically been, and continues to be, largely undertaken by non-professional women.

37 In the field of home care services to seniors, domestic-help social-economy businesses are major intermediaries in Quebec between elderly clientele and workers. However, since the beginning of the 2000s, we have seen significant growth in the role of private agencies in the home care field. See Hélène David, Esther Cloutier, and Sara Latour, *Le recours aux agences privées d'aide à domicile et de soins infirmiers par les services de soutien à domicile des CLSC* (Montreal: IRSST, 2003).

38 Annie Dussuet and Sarah Lecomte, "Formes d'emploi féminin dans les services à domicile" (paper presented at Huitièmes journées de sociologie du travail, "Marchés du travail et différenciations sociales: Approches comparatives," Aix-en-Provence, June 2001), 6.

39 Xavier Devetter, Florence Jany-Catrice, and Thierry Ribault, *Les services à la personne* (Paris: La Découverte, 2009), 81.

40 Dussuet and Lecomte, "Formes d'emploi féminin," 3–4, and Karine Vasselin, "Faire le ménage: De la condition domestique à la revendication d'une professionnalité," in *La révolution des métiers,* ed. Françoise Piotet (Paris: PUF, 2002), 77–98.

41 Elsa Galerand and Danielle Kergoat, "Le potentiel subversif du rapport des femmes au travail," *Nouvelles Questions Féministes* 27, 2 (2008): 67–82.

42 Françoise Battagliola, Isabelle Bertaux-Wiame, Michèle Ferrand, and Françoise Imbert, *Dire sa vie entre travail et famille: La construction sociale des trajectoires* (Paris: Centre de sociologie urbaine, 1991), 3.

43 Dussuet, *Travaux de femmes.*

44 Ruth Milkman, Ellen Reese, and Benita Roth, "The Macrosociology of Paid Domestic Labor," *Work and Occupations* 25, 4 (1998): 483–510; Jean Gadrey, *Socio-économie des services* (Paris: La Découverte, 2003); and Sandrine Rousseau and Xavier Devetter, "L'incitation à la création d'emplois de femmes de ménage est-elle socialement juste?" *Revue de Philosophie Économique* 12, 2 (2005): 73–96.

Contributors

Karen Balcom is an associate professor of history and gender studies and feminist research at McMaster University. She is the author of *The Traffic in Babies: Cross-Border Adoption* and *Baby-Selling between the United States and Canada, 1930–1972* (2011). She has ongoing research interests in the history of transnational adoption and in the life and work of Charlotte Whitton.

Donica Belisle is an assistant professor of women's and gender studies at Athabasca University. She is the author of the book *Retail Nation: Department Stores and the Making of Modern Canada* (UBC Press, 2011), which won the Pierre Savard Award in Canadian Studies. She has authored several articles in consumer history and is currently writing a book about Canadian women's consumer politics before the Second World War.

Gail G. Campbell was professor of history at the University of New Brunswick, Fredericton, from 1989 to 2012. A historical demographer, quantifier, and social-political historian who has published extensively on the participation of men and women in the political process, she is engaged in a long-term project to explore the political culture of New Brunswick in the pre-Confederation period. She is also currently preparing a manuscript on the diaries of more than two dozen New Brunswick women.

Catherine Carstairs teaches history at the University of Guelph. She is the author of *Jailed for Possession: Illegal Drug Use, Regulation and Power in Canada, 1920–1961.* She has also published on the history of health food, doping in sport, and water fluoridation. She is currently working on two book-length projects: a history of dentistry and dental health, and a collaborative project on the history of the Health League of Canada.

Catherine Charron is a PhD candidate in history at Laval University (Quebec). Her doctoral dissertation is a study of women's career and biographical paths in the domestic sector, in Quebec City during the second half of the twentieth century. She has taught at Laval University and at Université du Québec à Rimouski.

Hélène Charron holds a PhD in sociology from the Université de Montréal and the École des hautes études en sciences sociales in Paris. From 2009 to 2011, she was a postdoctoral fellow at Université Laval, in the Centre inter-universitaire en études québécoises. She is now associate researcher and lecturer in feminist studies at Université Laval.

Nancy Janovicek teaches history at the University of Calgary. She is the author of *No Place to Go: Local Histories of the Battered Women's Shelter Movement.* She is currently writing a book about the back-to-the-land movement in the West Kootenays.

Kristina R. Llewellyn is an assistant professor in the Department of Social Development Studies at Renison University College, University of Waterloo, and an associate member of the Department of Sociology and Legal Studies at the University of Waterloo. Her areas of teaching and research include the history of education, sociology of education, gender and education, child/ youth studies, qualitative methods, and social policy. She is the author of *Democracy's Angels: The Work of Women Teachers* (McGill-Queen's University Press, 2012).

Rose Fine-Meyer holds a PhD in the history of education from the University of Toronto. She teaches in the Department of Curriculum, Teaching and Learning at the Ontario Institute for Studies in Education, University of Toronto. Her areas of research include the history of curricula development, equitable history curriculum, gender and history, place-based learning, and activism and teaching. She has published in the areas of history education and equity education and has developed interdisciplinary course materials.

She is the founder of HerstoriesCafe (herstoriescafe.com), a locally developed women's history talk series that has been instrumental in linking diverse education communities.

Catherine Gidney is an adjunct professor in the Department of History at St. Thomas University. She is currently working on a history of commercialism in Canadian schools.

Anthony S.C. Hampton studied Canadian constitutional history at Mount Allison University and then at the University of New Brunswick, where he completed the research for this project. He has since started and subsequently abandoned doctoral studies at the University of Guelph and is now pursuing a career in law enforcement in the Toronto area.

Ruby Heap received a PhD from the Université de Montréal and is professor of history at the University of Ottawa, where she also holds the position of associate vice-president, research. She has published extensively on the history of public education and professional women in Canada and Quebec and is currently researching the history of women engineers in Canada. She is the recipient of the Professional Engineers of Ontario's President Award for the promotion of the profession.

Heidi MacDonald is an associate professor of history at the University of Lethbridge. Her two main research interests are youth during the Great Depression and women religious in Canada. She is currently writing a book on women religious in Atlantic Canada since Vatican II.

Lorna R. McLean is an associate professor in the Faculty of Education, University of Ottawa. She is a co-editor of the award-winning book *Framing Our Past: Canadian Women's History in the Twentieth Century*. Her research interests include the history of education, gender, youth, peace and global citizenship education, social studies, pedagogy, and curriculum.

Adele Perry teaches history at the University of Manitoba. She is co-editor of *Rethinking Canada: the Promise of Women's History* (2002, 2006, and 2010) and the author of *On the Edge of Empire: Gender, Race, and the Making of British Columbia, 1849–1871* (2001) and a forthcoming book on the Douglas-Connolly family and the nineteenth-century imperial world.

Index

Note: illustrations are indicated in bold.

Morrison, Lucy, 9, 42, 48, 49, 50, 52, 54
Morton, Suzanne, 60
motherhood: and career trajectories,
    222, 225, 264–65; ideas about, 97,
    106–7; rhetoric of, 98, 109
Mozère, Liane, 266, 272n9
Mulroney, Brian, 229, 238, 239, 251,
    252, 258n82
Murray, Lowell, 247, 257n60

National Action Committee on the
    Status of Women (NAC), 220, 226,
    230, 240; and women engineers'
    organizations, 227, 235n47
National Association of Women
    Deans, 101
National Council of Deans of Engineer-
    ing and Applied Sciences, 225
National Science and Technology
    Policy, 229, 231
nationhood, nuclear family and, 179,
    183, 186–87, 188–89, 190, 197n56
Native Women's Association of Canada,
    203
Natural Sciences and Engineering
    Research Council (NSERC), 229
networks: of ad hoc committees, 244;
    athletic associations, 103–4; cross-
    cultural, 83; extended families as,
    45, 46, 48; fur trade, 27–28; global,
    for social justice, 80, 83 (*see also
    specific organizations*); hierarchy of,
    166; history teachers', 201; male,
    168, 172; Methodist, 100; neigh-
    bourhood, 45–46; professional,
    80–81, 82, 99–103, 223, 224; pro-
    fessional and personal, 66–67, 69,
    72, 83, 103; social, 49–50, 67; trans-
    national, 12–13, 47, 59, 102;
    women's, 60, 172, 203–4, 268–69
    (*see also specific women's organiza-
    tions*). *See also specific educators'
    organizations*
New Brunswick Ad Hoc Committee on
    the Constitution (NBAHCC):
    achievements, 250, 251, 252–53;

concerns about Meech Lake
    Accord, 237–38, 239; conferences,
    244–45, 246; feminist activism and,
    241, 253; founding goals, 243–44;
    strategies, 247–49, 258n75
Newton, Edna, 118, 121, 126–28, 129,
    130, 131, 133n30, 133n33, 133n40
Ng, Wing Chung, 179, 184
Nipay, Miyo, 27, 30
North American Alliance. *See* collabor-
    ation, CWC and USCB
Novogrodsky, Myra, 210, 215n19
nuns, 10, 119, 162

O'Donnell, Lorraine, 139
Olsen, Karen, 180
Ontario, educational priorities, 200–3,
    205, 211, 214n10
Ontario Institute for Studies in Educa-
    tion (OISE), 203, 210; Centre for
    Women's Studies in Education, 205
Ontario Secondary School Teachers'
    Federation (OSSTF), 203, 204
Ontario Women's History Network
    (OWHN), 204; achievements, 210,
    212; challenges, 210–11, 212–13;
    conferences, 205–9, 209–10,
    211–12, 215n28, 216n31, 216n37,
    216nn40–41, 217n47; financial
    issues, 209, 216n37; founding
    members, 215nn27–28; goal, 205;
    reorganization, 211–12; and
    women's history, 201
Ontario Women's History Network/Le
    réseau d'histoire des femmes, 12
oral history, 272n6, 272n8, 273n26; as
    feminist encounter, 179–81; of
    NBAHCC, 237–38; and negotiating
    the self, 179, 180–81
Ordre des Ingénieurs du Québec, 225,
    235n65

Palmieri, Patricia, 108
Paré, Simone, 165, 166, 170, 176n47,
    176n52
Parr, Joy, 5

70–71 (*see also* collaboration, CWC
and USCB)
Willison, Gladys, 118, 121, 124–25,
129–30, 131, 132n23, 133n29
Wilson, Woodrow, 77, 78
Wolfe, Max, 240, 244, 245, 248, 250,
255n13
Wolfe, Willi Evans, 249
womanhood: shaping, 105; visions of,
104–7, 107–8, 110–11
women: Aboriginal, 25, 27–30, 241,
255n21 (*see also* Douglas, Amelia
Connolly); and athletics, 113n21,
115n41; Chinese Canadian, 181; and
curriculum reform, 12; exploitation
of, 259; in fur trade society, 25,
27–30; international peace activism of, 77–78, 78–79 (*see also*
International Congress of Women;
Wales, Julia Grace; Women's International League for Peace and
Freedom); and marriage rate,
118–19; middle-class, 9–10, 49,
56n30, 67, 79; middle-class elite,
100; as policy actors, 59–60 (*see
also* specific policy-influencing
women); professional, 9–10, 13–14,
220–21, 221–22, 229; relationship
to work, 259, 260–62, 264–65;
secondary status of, 78, 143–44;
and social services, 11, 59–60;
socialization of, 96, 105–6, 136,
139, 140–41, 263–64; technologies
and, 219, 227–28; wage-earning,
154–55 (*see also* department
stores); working-class, 10, 119,
261–62
Women and History Association of
Manitoba (WHAM), 204
Women in Alberta and Saskatchewan
History (WASH), 204
Women in Science and Engineering/
Femmes en Science et en Ingénierie
(WISE), 223, 224; and women's
movement, 226

women's activism. *See* activism
Women's Book Committee of the
Chinese Canadian National
Council, 180
Women's Bureau, 233n14
women's education: Methodists and,
98–99, 104–5 (*See also* Victoria
College)
Women's Engineering Society
(WES), 223
women's history. *See* feminist history
Women's History Month, 208, 216n43
Women's History Network of British
Columbia (WHN/BC), 204, 215n21
Women's International League for
Peace and Freedom, 83, 84, 86–87
Women's Labour Bureau, 220
Women's Legal Education and Action
Fund (LEAF), 212, 240, 245–46
women's movement: activism of,
11–12; politics of, 11–12; and
women engineers, 225–28. *See
also* feminism
women's movement in science and
engineering, 219, 228, 229–30
women's organizations: in New Brunswick, 241. *See also specific women's
organizations*
Women's Peace Party. *See* Women's
International League for Peace and
Freedom
women's studies, 5, 201; and science
and technology, 219; and women
engineers, 228
Women's Studies Research Colloquium,
205
women's work: in agriculture, 43–44,
48; archipelago of, 266–67;
casualization of, 260, 265–66; class
and, 9; in department stores,
138–39 (*see also* department
stores, periodicals); in domestic
service, 10, 259, 267–68, 270,
274nn36–37; ethnicity and, 8–9;
and family economy, 56n30, 57n50,

Printed and bound in Canada by Friesens

Set in Futura Condensed and Warnock by Apex Covantage

Copy editor: Lesley Erickson

Proofreader and indexer: Dianne Tiefensee